Career Counseling of College Students

Career Counseling of College Students

An Empirical

Guide to

Strategies

That Work

Edited by

Darrell Anthony Luzzo

American Psychological Association
Washington, DC

Published by
American Psychological Association
750 First Street, NE
Washington, DC 20002

Copies may be ordered from
APA Order Department
P.O. Box 92984
Washington, DC 20090-2984

In the U.K., Europe, Africa, and the Middle East, copies may be ordered from
American Psychological Association
3 Henrietta Street
Covent Garden, London
WC2E 8LU England

Typeset in Century Schoolbook by EPS Inc., Easton, MD

Printer: United Book Press, Baltimore, MD
Cover Designer: Naylor Design, Washington, DC
Technical/Production Editors: Allison L. Risko and Eleanor Inskip

The opinions and statements published are the responsibility of the authors, and such opinions and statements do not necessarily represent the policies of the APA.

Library of Congress Cataloging-in-Publication Data
Career counseling of college students : an empirical guide to strategies that work / editor, Darrell Anthony Luzzo.
        p. cm.
    ISBN 1-55798-708-4 (casebound : alk. paper)
        1. Counseling in higher education—United States. 2. Vocational guidance—United States. 3. College students—United States. I. Luzzo, Darrell Anthony.

    LB2343 .C3273 2000
    378.1′9425′0973—dc21   00-044751

British Library Cataloguing-in-Publication Data
A CIP record is available from the British Library.

Printed in the United States of America
First Edition

This book is dedicated to Charles C. Healy, mentor and friend, who taught me the art and science of translating career theory and research into practice.

—Darrell Anthony Luzzo, Editor

Contents

Contributors

Andrew D. Carson, InterestDiscovery.com, Wheaton, IL

Edward Anthony Colozzi, Career Development and Counseling Services, Winchester, MA

Linda Chrystal Colozzi, Career Development and Counseling Services, Winchester, MA

René V. Dawis, The Ball Foundation, Glen Ellyn, IL

Susan B. DeVaney, Early Childhood Development Center, Texas A&M University, Corpus Christi

Ruth E. Fassinger, Counseling & Personnel Services, University of Maryland, College Park

Thomas J. Halasz, University Career Center, Virginia Commonwealth University, Richmond

Paul J. Hartung, Behavioral Sciences Department, NEOUCOM, Rootstown, OH

William E. Hitchings, Coordinator of Postsecondary Disability Services, St. Ambrose University, Davenport, IA

Aaron W. Hughey, Department of Educational Leadership, Western Kentucky University, Bowling Green

Greg Iaccarino, Student Services Specialist, Department of Bacteriology, University of Wisconsin, Madison

C. Bryan Kempton, University of Maryland, College Park

Rodney L. Lowman, Organizational Psychology Programs, California School of Professional Psychology, San Diego

Darrell Anthony Luzzo, Career Development Services, Mt. Hood Community College, Gresham, OR

Edward A. Martinelli, Jr., Counseling & Counseling Psychology, Auburn University, Auburn University, AL

Kathleen Mitchell, City College of San Francisco, CA

Spencer G. Niles, University of Virginia, Charlottesville

Karen M. O'Brien, Department of Psychology, University of Maryland, College Park

Mark S. Pope, Division of Counseling, University of Missouri–St. Louis

Jeffrey P. Prince, Counseling and Psychological Services, University of Health Services, University of California at Berkeley

Paul Retish, Office of International Education, College of Education, University of Iowa, Iowa City

Donna Palladino Schultheiss, Department of Counseling, Administration, Supervision, and Adult Learning, Cleveland State University, OH

Sarah M. Toman, College of Education, Cleveland State University, OH

Susan C. Whiston, Department of Counseling and Educational Psychology, Indiana University, Bloomington

Preface

A couple of years ago I received a call from a colleague. She was serving as the associate director of career planning and placement at a small college in the Midwest. Apparently, she had been trying to find out whether there were any books that provided an overview of "what we know" about the career development of college students. She had called in hopes that I might be able to help her locate such a source.

It seemed like a reasonable request. After all, I had recently published several articles on the career development of college students, and I was in the middle of a research project evaluating the efficacy of various career interventions among college students. After two weeks of endless searching, I called my colleague with the bad news. I was able to find books that discussed career counseling across the life span. I was able to find individual articles and an occasional book chapter on specific aspects of college student career counseling. But I was not able to find a *single* source that provided a comprehensive overview of college students' career development. At that moment, I decided to do what I could to fill the void.

As I selected the authors to write the chapters of this book, I made sure that each author was well aware of my goal: to develop a book that discussed the important links between career development theory, research, and practice and that focused exclusively on the career decision-making needs of college students.

Throughout the writing process, each author received explicit instructions to ensure that the career counseling strategies and techniques presented in the book are theoretically based and empirically validated. I also encouraged authors to provide readers with a comprehensive review of relevant vocational psychology research and its application to college students' career development. As a result of these efforts, readers can be confident that the pages that follow contain a wealth of useful information that can be effectively applied when providing career counseling services to diverse college student populations.

Whether you are a new graduate student seeking a master's degree in a student affairs preparation program or a doctoral student working on your degree in counselor education or counseling psychology; whether you are an entry-level career counselor at a small, liberal arts college or a seasoned academic advisor at a large, public institution; or whether you are a career services administrator, college or university dean, or private practitioner, one thing is for certain: This book is for you.

I recently received an e-mail message from a colleague. He asked whether I knew of any book that offered a comprehensive overview of the career development of college students—a book that linked career development theory, research, and practice and that focused exclusively on college student populations. It sure was nice, this time around, to say yes!

On behalf of each of the 24 authors who have contributed to this book, I thank you for your commitment to providing quality career counseling services, and I sincerely hope that you will benefit from this book.

Acknowledgments

The quality of an edited volume is inextricably linked to the time and effort that reviewers are able and willing to invest in their review of initial drafts of chapters. In that regard, we wish to salute the college and university career counselors, vocational psychologists, and private practitioners who volunteered their service and provided contributing authors with helpful suggestions for revising their chapters.

Karen Parrish Baker (Marshall University)
Chandlee Bryan (Colby-Sawyer College)
Karen Busocker (Temple University)
James Chang (Oregon State University)
Judy Chartrand (Consulting Psychologists Press, Inc.)
Sadie Chase (The Colorado College)
Nicholas T. Christian (Queens College of Charlotte)
Y. Barry Chung (Georgia State University)
Jill Z. Cornwell (Francis Marion University)
Tracey Cross-Baker (St. Lawrence University)
Ray Davis (University of South Carolina)
David R. DeLorenzo (Georgia Perimeter College)
Andrea B. Dine (University of Cincinnati)
Amy K. Flynn (Massachusetts Bay Community College)
Nancy Gerzon (Amherst, New Hampshire)
Stacy Cooper Glick (Vassar College)
Frankie Harris (University of Southern Mississippi)
Jody Hestand (Southeast Missouri State University)
Carla Dalton Jackson (Emory University)
Lynett James (University of Texas at Austin)
Garry Klein (ACT, Inc.)
Stefan R. Koppi (American University)
Jana L. Lehman (Indiana University East)
Janet E. Lyons (Temple University)
Michael R. Maples (University of Iowa)
Robin Meyer (University of Puget Sound)
Michael Mobley (University of Missouri)
Marirose Moran (University of Maryland)
Ellen Manning Nagy (Bowling Green State University)
Jennifer Niggemeier (University of Michigan)
Kevin J. Nutter (University of Minnesota)
Samuel H. Osipow (Ohio State University)
Paula D. Quenoy (Rice University)
Linda Quinn (University of Dayton)
Bill Satterlee (Career Solutions, Inc.)
Richard S. Sharf (University of Delaware)

Julia B. Sherlock (Central Michigan University)
Mona Singhvi (Carnegie Mellon University)
Amy Stalzer (Georgia Perimeter College)
Linda Mezydlo Subich (University of Akron)
Valerie J. Sutton (University of Maryland)
Lisa A. Tarsi (Albright College)
Edgar J. Townsend (University of Delaware)
Donna Vinton (University of Northern Iowa)
Sandra Vonniessen-Applebee (Quinnipiac College)
Jan Wencel (Curry College)
Sheri Ziccardi (Providence College)

We also wish to express sincere gratitude to our colleagues who reviewed an earlier draft of the entire book manuscript. Both Dennis Nord (University of California, Santa Barbara) and Shirley Barnes (Auburn University) provided insightful recommendations that motivated the authors to improve the quality of their chapters. As a result, we are confident that *Career Counseling of College Students: An Empirical Guide to Strategies That Work* provides readers with a comprehensive set of empirically validated and theoretically based career counseling strategies to use when working with diverse college student populations.

Finally, we wish to thank the members of the APA Books staff who have played an integral role in helping us to complete this project. Without their enthusiasm and dedication to this book, we would not have been able to transform the dream of this edited volume into reality.

Introduction

Darrell Anthony Luzzo

Over the past 10 years, I have had the opportunity to work with thousands of students in a variety of college and university settings. Some of the students with whom I have worked have been of traditional age, seeking a four-year degree at a regional state university. Others have been older adult students returning to a community college after a 20- or 30-year absence from school. I have worked with recent immigrants to the United States, first-generation college students, and students from the lowest socioeconomic backgrounds in settings that include community colleges; small, private colleges; regional and state universities; and large, public institutions. I have counseled students who are not quite sure whether college is an appropriate avenue for their career development, and I have worked with students enrolled in doctoral programs at some of the finest universities in the country. With these varied experiences has come one truth: Providing career counseling services to college students—students of all ages and backgrounds—is both challenging and rewarding.

I have experienced firsthand many of the problems career counselors encounter in college and university settings. I continually question the validity of the methods and techniques that I use when working with clients and struggle to know whether the strategies that work with some clients are necessarily the best strategies to use with others. I often wonder whether recent theoretical developments or empirically validated approaches to career counseling are relevant to my clients and continually try to figure out how to translate theories of career development and findings from empirical research into meaningful practices with diverse college student clientele.

Throughout my professional career, it has always seemed reasonable to me that a resource should be available to help career counselors find solutions to the many challenges that arise when providing career counseling services to college students. And that is exactly why I made a commitment to develop this book.

The purpose of *Career Counseling of College Students: An Empirical Guide to Strategies That Work* is to provide readers with a comprehensive review of vocational theories and empirical literature in an effort to show the links among career development theory, research, and practice as applied to college student populations. The book focuses on practical strategies that career counselors who work with college students can integrate into their work with clients. In fact, this book provides a comprehensive discussion of more than 200 practical strategies to use when providing career counseling services to college students; to that end, it is my hope that the reader will reap many benefits from reading the chapters that follow.

Organization of the Book

This book is organized into four parts: Theoretical Bases and Models for Career Development, Methods and Techniques, Special Populations and Issues, and Professional Issues and Future Directions.

Part I. Theoretical Bases and Models for Career Development

Part I includes four chapters that provide an overview of several traditional and contemporary theories related to the career development of college students. In chapter 1, "Established Career Theories," Paul J. Hartung and Spencer G. Niles discuss John Holland's (1997) theory of vocational personalities and work environments and Donald Super's (Super, Savickas, & Super, 1996) life span–life space approach. The two theories are discussed in relation to ways in which counselors who work with college students can use the theories to guide career counseling practices.

In chapter 2, "Emerging Career Theories," Spencer G. Niles and Paul J. Hartung discuss several recently developed career theories and their application to college student career development. The contemporary theories presented in the chapter include Krumboltz's (Mitchell & Krumboltz, 1996) learning theory of career counseling; Lent, Brown, and Hackett's (1996) social cognitive career theory; Sampson, Peterson, Lenz, and Reardon's (1992) cognitive information processing approach; and Brown's (1995, 1996) values-based model of career choice. The chapter concludes with a discussion of the application of postmodern career development approaches to college students' career decision making.

In chapter 3, "Emotional–Social Issues in the Provision of Career Counseling," Donna Palladino Schultheiss presents an integrated view of college students' career development as she discusses the interconnected nature of career development and late-adolescent emotional and social functioning. The chapter includes a rich blend of theory and research, illustrating that an understanding of career development tasks within the broader context of developmental psychology can help inform career counseling practice.

In chapter 4, "College Students' Callings and Careers: An Integrated Values-Oriented Perspective," Edward Anthony and Linda Chrystal Colozzi—on the basis of more than 14 years of career counseling experience in private practice—share their insights regarding the role that spirituality (i.e., meaning and purpose) plays in the career decision-making process. Case study excerpts from actual clients provide readers with a past–present perspective that illustrates what happens to college students after graduation. The case studies are especially effective in showing how career counseling might have affected clients' career decisions if they had participated in career counseling during their college years.

Part II. Methods and Techniques

Part II consists of five chapters that present an overview of career counseling strategies commonly used with college students. Chapter 5, "Determining the Appropriateness of Career Choice Assessment," by Andrew D. Carson and René V. Dawis, is designed to answer the question "When is career assessment appropriate for college students?" The chapter presents Linda Gottfredson's (1986) taxonomic framework for assessing career choice problems as an especially useful tool for determining the appropriateness of various career assessments in college student career development.

In chapter 6, "Integrating Assessment Data Into Career Counseling," Rodney L. Lowman and Andrew D. Carson discuss general principles of test selection and the importance of assessment in career counseling. The chapter discusses ways in which to make career assessment data more useful when working with college students and presents assessment models—including Lowman's Career Assessment Matrix—that can help students clarify career choices. The chapter concludes with information to help counselors design a system of career assessment intervention for large groups of college students.

In chapter 7, "Individual Career Counseling," Susan C. Whiston summarizes the results of numerous research studies conducted over the past 50 years. She finds that the research supports the claim that individual career counseling continues to be the most effective method of providing career services to college students.

In chapter 8, "Career Planning Workshops and Courses," Thomas J. Halasz and C. Bryan Kempton switch the focus to small-group and large-group career counseling methods. The chapter offers a comprehensive evaluation of the theory, research, and practice supporting the use of career courses and workshops among college students. In addition, the authors identify trends in service delivery and discuss ideas for the integration of theory-based and empirically sound group career interventions into student
affairs.

In chapter 9, "Computer-Assisted Career Guidance Systems," Greg Iaccarino discusses the pros and cons of using computer-assisted career guidance systems (CACGSs) with college students. The chapter includes a brief history of the development of CACGSs and a discussion of practices associated with the use of those systems and the Internet among college students. The chapter concludes with a review of some of the popular CACGSs on college and university campuses and a discussion of the benefits and challenges associated with the use of technology in career counseling.

Part III. Special Populations and Issues

Part III includes six chapters addressing the unique career development needs of specific college student populations. In chapter 10, "Career Development of Returning-Adult and Graduate Students," Darrell Anthony Luzzo focuses on the decision-making needs of students enrolled in graduate studies and those who return to school after spending several years away from educational environments. The chapter describes the characteristics that differentiate traditional- and nontraditional-aged students, the specific career decision-making needs of graduate students and of returning-adult students, and practical career counseling strategies based on previous research with these populations.

Chapter 11, "Career Decision Making and Student–Athletes," by Edward A. Martinelli, Jr., includes a description of student–athletes and their shared experiences as well as a discussion of National Collegiate Athletic Association regulations that directly affect the career decision making of student–athletes. The chapter concludes with a discussion of career counseling strategies and model programs for counselors to consider when working with this population.

In chapter 12, "Career Development Needs of Students With Learning Disabilities," William E. Hitchings and Paul Retish acknowledge the recent increase in the number of students with learning disabilities on college and university campuses and summarize a multiyear, multicampus research program that addresses the career development of this group of students. The authors present six factors that counselors may want to consider when providing career counseling services to students with disabilities. The chapter concludes with a series of strategy recommendations that have been successfully implemented at several colleges and universities nationwide to meet the needs of this expanding student population.

Chapter 13, "Career Development of Ethnic Minority Students," by Susan B. DeVaney and Aaron W. Hughey, begins by discussing some of the recent advances in applying career development theory to ethnically diverse populations. After reminding readers that many questions regarding the career development of ethnic minority college students remain unanswered, the authors present a detailed discussion of empirically validated differences in the career development of African American, Asian American, Latino, and Native American students. The chapter concludes by presenting several strategies to consider when providing career counseling services to ethnically diverse students.

In chapter 14, "Career Counseling With College Women: A Scientist–Practitioner–Advocate Model of Intervention," counseling psychologists Ruth E. Fassinger and Karen M. O'Brien translate the rich theoretical and empirically based literature on women's career development into recommendations for effectively addressing the career-related needs of college women. The chapter addresses the unique issues facing college women in selecting careers and implementing their choices. The authors conclude by offering a series of recommendations to consider when addressing the career decision-making issues of college women, including the use of individual counseling strategies and encouraging changes within the broader context of institutional and social policy.

Chapter 15, "Responsible Career Counseling With Lesbian and Gay Students," by Mark S. Pope, Jeffrey P. Prince, and Kathleen Mitchell, draws from the general literature relevant to the career concerns of lesbians and gay men and proposes strategies that practitioners can use to more effectively meet the career exploration and planning needs of these students. The chapter includes material on the historical context of gay and lesbian issues on campus, assessing counselor and student attitudes, creating affirmative work environments, fostering a positive career identity, and improving campus climate.

Part IV. Professional Issues and Future Directions

Part IV includes two chapters. Chapter 16, "Toward the Development of Systematic Career Guidance," by Edward Anthony Colozzi, presents a "blueprint in formation" for a theory-based, systematic career guidance approach for use in college and university settings. The chapter includes a discussion of the theory behind systematic career guidance programs as well as a discussion of the National Occupational Information Coordinating Committee guidelines (1989) that support a systematic approach. It also offers suggestions for establishing and justifying a systematic career guidance program. The author presents information to assist career service providers in their efforts to implement the model and discusses strategies to justify the provision of career counseling services to college and university administrators.

Chapter 17, "Identification of a Career Development Research and Practice Agenda for the 21st Century," by Sarah M. Toman, summarizes the results of a comprehensive review of nearly 700 journal articles published between 1996 and 1998 that pertain to the career development of college students. The focus of the review is to provide career development researchers and practitioners with an indication of the types of career counseling research and practice issues that are expected to serve as the basis for future developments in the field.

Meeting the Career Development Needs of Diverse College Student Populations

Today's college students are more diverse (e.g., in age, cultural background, and race) than ever before. In the years ahead, this diversity will continue to increase on college and university campuses nationwide. With these changes comes a responsibility among higher education professionals to evaluate the services that are provided in response to these changing demographics.

Readers of this book should keep in mind the role that they can play to ensure that the college students they serve receive the most responsive and effective career counseling services available. As counselors consider the interaction among career development theory, research, and practice with diverse student populations, they will undoubtedly increase their arsenal of career counseling strategies and techniques. As they do, they will become much more effective in their work—work that truly makes a difference in the lives of the students they serve.

References

Brown, D. (1995). A values-based model for facilitating career transitions. *Career Development Quarterly, 44,* 4–11.

Brown, D. (1996). Brown's values-based, holistic model of career and life-role choices and satisfaction. In D. Brown, L. Brooks, & Assoc. (Eds.), *Career choice and development: Applying contemporary theories to practice* (3rd ed., pp. 337–372). San Francisco, CA: Jossey-Bass.

Gottfredson, L. S. (1986). Special groups and the beneficial use of vocational interest inventories. In W. B. Walsh & S. H. Osipow (Eds.), *Advances in vocational psychology: Volume I, The assessment of interests* (pp. 127–198). Hillsdale, NJ: Lawrence Erlbaum.

Holland, J. L. (1997). *Making vocational choices* (3rd ed.). Odessa, FL: Psychological Assessment Resources.

Lent, R. W., Brown, S. D., & Hackett, G. (1996). Career development from a social cognitive perspective. In D. Brown, L. Brooks, & Assoc. (Eds.), *Career choice and development: Applying contemporary theories to practice* (3rd ed., pp. 373–422). San Francisco, CA: Jossey-Bass.

Mitchell, L. K., & Krumboltz, J. D. (1996). Krumboltz's learning theory of career choice counseling. In D. Brown, L. Brooks, & Assoc. (Eds.), *Career choice and development: Applying contemporary theories to practice* (3rd ed., pp. 233–280). San Francisco, CA: Jossey-Bass.

National Occupational Information Coordinating Committee. (1989). *National career development guidelines.* Washington, DC: Author.

Sampson, J. P., Jr., Peterson, G. W., Lenz, J. G., & Reardon, R. C. (1992). A cognitive approach to career services: Translating concepts into practice. *Career Development Quarterly, 41,* 67–74.

Super, D. E., Savickas, M. L., & Super, C. M. (1996). The life-span, life-space approach to careers. In D. Brown, L. Brooks, & Assoc. (Eds.), *Career choice and development: Applying contemporary theories to practice* (3rd ed., pp. 121–178). San Francisco, CA: Jossey-Bass.

Part I

Theoretical Bases and Models for Career Development

1 _____

Established Career Theories

Paul J. Hartung and Spencer G. Niles

Fluctuating economic conditions, increasingly sophisticated technology and information systems, and the changing nature of work and the work force at the dawn of the 21st century prompt more and more people to enter colleges and universities. Whether young adults first entering college, middle-aged adults making career changes, or older adults renewing their lives and careers, a wide range of people seek to advance themselves by obtaining college degrees. As counselors, how do we help college students make effective choices, adjust to those choices, and develop the roles of school and work in their lives? These questions rest at the heart of the college counselor's work.

To help college counselors optimally attend to the career development needs of diverse student groups, this chapter reviews two preeminent theories of career choice and development. The theories, which we selected because they have the most direct applications to college student career development, are (a) the theory of vocational personalities and work environments originated and developed by John Holland (1973, 1997) and (b) the life span–life space approach introduced and advanced by Donald Super and his colleagues (Super, 1957; Super, Savickas, & Super, 1996; Super, Starishevsky, Matlin, & Jordaan, 1963). The theories are considered established because of their relative longevity, prominence, vast empirical support, and proven usefulness for conceptualizing and promoting individual career development and vocational behavior (Brown & Brooks, 1996). Both Holland's and Super's theories remain innovative because they continue to be elaborated on and considered in terms of their relevance for use with diverse groups and in diverse settings (see, for example, Fouad, Harmon, & Borgen, 1997; Hartung et al., 1998). The next chapter considers more recently articulated, or emerging, theories that counselors can use to conceptualize and promote college students' career development.

We begin this chapter with a two-part rationale for using both established and emerging career choice and development theories in counseling college students. The first part asserts that counselors on college campuses provide a variety of career services. The second part asserts that theories provide useful frameworks for guiding delivery of career services in college settings. We then describe a scheme for categorizing career theories generally and follow it with overviews of Holland's person–environment fit theory and Super's developmental approach to careers. The theories are considered in terms of how counselors in colleges and universities can use them to guide their work with students.

College Counselors Provide a Variety of Career Services

Every day, thousands of students on college campuses across the country seek answers to their career problems. Students arrive at the college career center, placement office, or counseling center or turn to career counselors in private practice, the Internet, or their own informal networks of family and friends for help. Counselors in colleges and universities perform vital services by providing students with professional help in resolving their career problems. How any given student's problem is defined, as well as the counseling services that the student receives, depends on the issues involved. A *career problem* may be defined as "a crystallized gap between 'what is' and 'what ought to be'" in one's academic or work life (Cochran, 1994, p. 208). Counselors attempt to bridge this gap by offering a variety of career services (Savickas, 1996), including career therapy, career counseling, career education, vocational guidance, occupational placement, and position coaching. Each service deals with a specific domain of career problems and involves helping students answer central questions related to their educational or vocational pursuits.

Career therapy assists students in developing a clear identity, modifying distorted motives, restructuring personality, and addressing the question of how work can help them grow as a person. *Career counseling* helps students self-reflect, restructure beliefs, mature and deepen their personalities, and answer the question "Who am I?" Students benefit from *career education* that helps them develop constructive attitudes toward and skills for career planning and exploration as well as learn how to shape their academic pursuits and careers. *Vocational guidance* assists undecided students with clarifying their options and making choices that match their personalities. Students need *occupational placement* assistance to secure positions in their chosen fields and learn how to obtain a job. Finally, *position coaching* involves mentoring students to help them learn adaptive job-coping skills and address the question of how they can improve on the job. Career theories, including those of Holland and Super, provide counselors with guidelines for delivering services in the various domains.

Theories Guide Delivery of Career Services

Conventional wisdom holds that there is nothing so practical as a good theory. Theories of career choice and development offer counselors a variety of practical ways in which to understand and promote career development in college students, who so often search for meaning in their academic, career, and other life pursuits. Counselors in colleges and universities can use career choice and development theories as guides for both comprehending students' career problems and constructing strategies to effectively deal with those problems. Without theories to guide their work, college counselors would certainly find their jobs much more difficult to perform effectively and efficiently.

A significant body of theoretical literature aims to describe, predict, and explain individual career development and vocational behavior. Proponents and authors of 10 established and emerging theories of career choice and development have articulated their perspectives in an edited volume that provides an excellent resource for readers who want a primary reference on career theory and its application to counseling practice (Brown & Brooks, 1996). Two additional noteworthy textbooks review and articulate the basic components and constructs of existing career theories and offer useful secondary sources on the subject (Osipow & Fitzgerald, 1996; Sharf, 1997). The textbook by Sharf includes case examples that demonstrate how aspects of the theories can be applied to career counseling practice. Other textbooks aim to identify how the theories might overlap or converge on various themes and concepts (Savickas & Lent, 1994) and articulate specific theories of career counseling (Savickas & Walsh, 1996).

College counselors see the application of career theories most readily, perhaps, in the variety of career assessment instruments (e.g., aptitude tests, interest inventories, and values scales) and vocational guidance materials (e.g., SIGI and DISCOVER computer-assisted career-guidance programs) used in career centers on college campuses throughout the United States. Career assessments and materials typically derive from aspects of major theories of career choice and development—most notably, the work of John Holland and Donald Super.

Textbooks on the subject (e.g., Brown & Brooks, 1996; Osipow & Fitzgerald, 1996) demonstrate that theories of career choice and development have grown in number since Frank Parsons articulated the first model for vocational guidance more than 90 years ago. Parsons, founder of the matching model for vocational guidance, proposed that career choice involves three requisite elements—knowledge of self, knowledge of the world of work, and true reasoning to rationally connect the two sources of knowledge (Parsons, 1909). Parsons's matching model continues to provide the guiding wisdom of trait-and-factor career counseling and person–environment fit career theory (Swanson, 1996). It also has been absorbed or integrated into other career theories, including those of Holland and Super.

Different Theories Emphasize Different Issues

Established and emerging career choice and development theories encompass four fundamental approaches to career theory and counseling practice. These approaches represent differential, dynamic (or personality-based), developmental, and reinforcement-based psychological models (Osipow, 1990).

Counselors who use a *differential approach* focus on matching such student traits as values, interests, aptitudes, and skills to educational or occupational factors that fit those traits. This matching is typically accomplished through career guidance activities such as objective assessment and information seeking. The theory of vocational personalities and work environments (Holland, 1985, 1997), the theory of work adjustment (Dawis & Lofquist, 1984), and person–environment correspondence counseling (Lofquist & Dawis, 1991) exemplify the differential approach to careers.

Counselors who take a *dynamic, or personality-focused, approach* help students develop awareness and understanding of their personality dynamics and styles relative to the world of work. This approach involves conceptualizing career choices and development as a function of early parent–child relationships, childhood memories, family dynamics, and the personal meaning of work and careers. Examples of this approach include Roe's personality development theory (Roe, 1956; Roe & Lunneborg, 1990) and Bordin's psychodynamic model of career choice and satisfaction (Bordin, 1990).

The *developmental approach* to career counseling with college students involves examining and promoting individual progress through various career and life stages. It also focuses on increasing students' career development attitudes and knowledge and their satisfaction with their life roles (e.g., student, worker, citizen, and family member). The life span–life space theory of careers (Super, 1990; Super et al., 1996) and the theory of circumscription and compromise (Gottfredson, 1996) exemplify the developmental approach to career choice and development theory.

Finally, *reinforcement-based approaches* to career development help students examine how social learning and reinforcement patterns shape what they believe about themselves and the world of work. This approach helps students understand and manage the way in which their observations about themselves and the world influence their career aspirations, attitudes, beliefs, choices, and satisfactions. The social learning theory of career decision making (Mitchell & Krumboltz, 1996) and social–cognitive career theory (Lent, Brown, & Hackett, 1996) represent the reinforcement-based approach to careers.

As noted above, Holland's (1997) theory of vocational personalities and work environments represents a decidedly differential, or person–environment fit, approach. In contrast, the theoretical approach advanced by Super et al. (1996), although comprehensive, reflects a developmental perspective on career choice and development. Chapter 2 describes these two theories, and Chapter 3 describes examples of reinforcement-based and personality-focused theories.

Birds of a Feather Flock Together: Holland's Theory of Careers

Working as a vocational counselor in educational, military, and clinical settings provided the impetus for John Holland to develop his theory of careers (Holland, 1985, 1997). His practical experiences emerge clearly in the theory's emphasis on applying abstract concepts to counseling practice. To operationally define and make concepts in his theory practically useful, Holland developed interest inventories, such as the Vocational Preference Inventory (VPI) and Self-Directed Search (SDS). The VPI actually guided much of Holland's theory-building efforts. Later, Holland's model was incorporated into the Strong Interest Inventory (SII), which is one of the most widely used interest inventories available. According to Holland (1985), "the primary concern of the theory is to explain vocational behavior and suggest some practical ideas to help young, middle-aged, and older people select jobs, change jobs, and attain vocational satisfaction" (p. 1). Holland's own language clearly indicates the purpose of the theory: to assist people with making satisfying career choices. Thus, counselors primarily use the theory in providing vocational guidance services to students, helping them match their personality styles to suitable occupations. It ranks as the most widely applied and empirically supported theory of career choice and development (Spokane, 1996).

A Structural–Interactive Model

Holland (1985) described his approach to career choice as "structural–interactive" (p. 11) because it organizes information about people and occupations and assumes that vocational and social behavior result from the interaction of people and environments. Consistent with the differential tradition in vocational psychology, the theory proposes that people seek work environments that fit their personalities. The old maxim that "opposites attract" is discounted in Holland's theory, which instead advances the notion that people seek out environments supportive of their particular personality style. In essence, we feel most satisfied when we work, associate, and live with people who most resemble ourselves. On the college campus, then, the key for the counselor is to work with students to help them understand their primary, secondary, and tertiary adaptive personality styles. The three styles make up a Holland code that counselors try to match to a corresponding environment both on campus and in the world of work. Matching one's type to a corresponding environment allows the person to feel supported and to thrive. Counselors accomplish this task by using interest inventories such as the SDS, VPI, or SII, which incorporate Holland's model and yield a Holland code.

Several primary and secondary assumptions are central to Holland's theory. Those primary and secondary assumptions are considered in the next sections.

Primary Assumptions of Holland's Theory

Holland's theory contains four basic assumptions about people and work environments (Holland, 1997). First, people can be categorized as one of six personality types: realistic, investigative, artistic, social, enterprising, or conventional (RIASEC). Each RIASEC personality type has distinguishing characteristics.

Realistic people are "doers" who prefer activities in which they can manipulate objects, tools, machines, and animals. People of this type value practicality, tradition, and common sense. Realistic types usually avoid social situations and prefer mechanical, technical, and tangible activities. They like the outdoors and physical activity, including athletics. They prefer to work with things, rather than people, ideas, or data, and are perceived as asocial, conforming, hardheaded, natural, practical, and self-effacing. Realistic types prefer college majors such as physical education, engineering, or technology, and they adapt to situations using a primarily physical style

Investigative types are "analyzers" who prefer activities in which they can systematically explore and develop knowledge of the world; they value independence, curiosity, and learning. Investigative people avoid activities that involve persuading or interacting with others and prefer observational, symbolic, systematic, and creative investigation of physical, biological, and cultural phenomena. They prefer to work primarily alone and with data and ideas, rather than people or things. Investigative types are perceived as analytical, cautious, critical, pessimistic, rational, unassuming, and unpopular. They prefer college majors such as chemistry, biology, or sociology. The investigative person adapts to situations using a primarily cognitive style.

Artistic types are "creators" who prefer activities that allow them to innovate and create art forms or products. This type of person values beauty, originality, independence, and imagination. Artistic people avoid clearly defined, highly structured, methodical, and routine activities and prefer ambiguous, unstructured, and imaginative pursuits. Like realistic and investigative types, artistic types prefer working independently and with physical matter. They are perceived as expressive, impulsive, independent, and nonconforming. Artistic types prefer college majors such as music, art, English, drama, or theater and adapt to the world using a primarily emotional style.

Social types are "discussers"; they prefer activities that involve informing, training, developing, or interacting and talking with other people. People of this type value cooperation, generosity, and service to other people. Social people avoid activities involving tools, implements, mechanical, or technological devices and prefer interpersonal and educational endeavors. They enjoy working with people, rather than with things or data, and are perceived as cooperative, patient, kind, generous, helpful, sociable, warm, and understanding. Social types prefer college majors such as education, social work, or nursing. The social person adapts to the world using a primarily interpersonal style.

Enterprising types are "persuaders" who prefer activities in which they can manipulate people to attain organizational, personal, and economic gains. This type of person values risk taking, status, and competition. Enterprising people avoid scientific and observational activities and prefer business-oriented, economic activities in which they can lead other people. They prefer to work with people rather than data or things insofar as they can manipulate them to meet or advance their own or the organization's needs. They are perceived as acquisitive, adventurous, self-confident, optimistic, extroverted, and domineering. Enterprising types prefer college majors such as business administration, marketing, or law. The enterprising type adapts to the world using a primarily influencing style.

Conventional types are "sustainers" in that they like to keep the status quo and follow tradition. Conventional types prefer activities in which they can manipulate data, keep records, or operate business machines to achieve organizational goals. People of this type value accuracy, stability, and efficiency. Conventional people avoid ambiguous, unstructured, impractical situations and prefer well-defined, routine, and methodical activities. They prefer to work with data or things and for other people and are perceived as careful, conforming, efficient, and persistent. Conventional types prefer college majors such as finance, accounting, or economics, and they adapt to situations using a primarily moral style.

The second primary assumption of Holland's theory posits that environments can be similarly categorized as one of six types: realistic, investigative, artistic, social, enterprising, or conventional (RIASEC). Each environment is dominated by a particular type of people and has physical characteristics that support, encourage, and reflect that type. Table 1.1 categorizes several academic departments on college campuses according to their predominant RIASEC type. For example, a department of business administration typically would be dominated by enterprising faculty, staff, and students and it would support the flourishing of this type in its appearance, facilities, teaching style, and academic programs. By teaching students the basic elements of the RIASEC model, counselors can help students make educational choices in terms of the degree to which a student's personality fits with the environmental style of various academic departments. Selecting a satisfying major would eventually translate into a suitable fit in the larger world of work.

The third assumption of the theory proposes that people seek environments that allow them to use their skills and abilities, express their attitudes and values, and take on problems and roles that fit them. This reflects the underlying assumption that "birds of a feather flock together." Types like to be with people who most resemble them.

Table 1.1. RIASEC Types and Environments on a University Campus

RIASEC Category	Sample Departments
Realistic	Physical education, mechanical engineering
Investigative	Physics, biology, geology, chemistry, history
Artistic	Art, music, journalism, English, theater, dance
Social	Social work, nursing, counseling, education
Enterprising	Business administration, law, management, marketing
Conventional	Accounting, criminal justice, economics, library science

The theory's fourth assumption is that the interaction between personality and environment determines individual behavior. Environments, if they resemble a person's personality type, will reinforce and satisfy the person, thereby leading to stable and predictable behavior patterns. The person thus will find success and satisfaction in the job and, in turn, contribute successfully to the work environment. If individual personality and patterns of the work environment do not match significantly, then job changes and dissatisfaction will result. People influence and change the nature of jobs and work environments, and vice versa.

Secondary Assumptions of Holland's Theory

Holland's theory of careers also contains several secondary assumptions, which pertain to relationships between and among types and environments. To articulate those relationships, Holland arranged the six types and environments around a hexagon; Figure 1.1 is Holland's hexagon.

The principle of *consistency* assumes that the shorter the distance on the hexagon between any two types or environments, the more similar are those types or environments. The social and enterprising types are next to each other on the hexagon; therefore, those two types share many more characteristics than would, say, a social and a realistic type (which are opposite each other on the hexagon). A college student with a Holland code of RIA enjoys, values, and has skills and preferences for activities that are

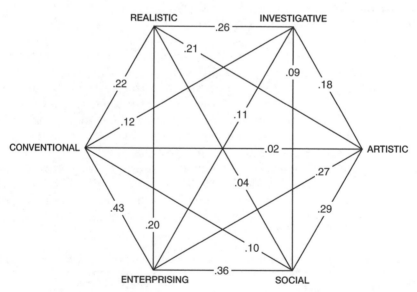

Figure 1.1. The Self-Directed Search and Other Holland-Based Materials. From the *Self-Directed Search Technical Manual* (p. 4), by J. L. Holland, B. A. Fritzsche, and A. B. Powell, 1994, Odessa, FL. Reproduced by special permission of the Publisher, from the Self-Directed Search Technical Manual by John L. Holland, PhD, B. A. Fritzsche, and A. B. Powell. Copyright © 1985, 1987, 1994 by Psychological Assessment Resources, Inc. Further reproduction is prohibited without permission of PAR, Inc.

similar in nature. The realistic, investigative, and artistic types, for example, all prefer to work with things or ideas rather than people. A student with a code of RIA has a much more consistent personality style than does a student with a code of RAE. In practice, people with more consistency in their codes will find a greater number of occupations that fit their skills, interests, and values than will people with less consistent codes. Higher levels of consistency also suggest more predictable behavior and potentially less difficulty in making educational and vocational choices. The college student with an artistic and conventional style will likely have more difficulty striking a balance between his competing needs for independence and fitting in, for ambiguity and structure, and for self-expression and self-control.

Consistency deals with coherence of the traits within a person's style, whereas *congruence* deals with complementarity between a person and his or her environment. The idea of congruence refers to the interaction between a type and an environment. High congruence, or fit, means that a great degree of compatibility exists between a type and an environment. A college student with a Holland code of IRE and majoring in biomedical engineering would exemplify high congruence—she has a great degree of compatibility between her personality type and her academic environment. If her major is elementary education, however, she may feel dissatisfied because her major typically supports much more social and artistic people and involves more social and artistic activities. The congruence, or relatedness, between her style and the environment of elementary education is low. This low congruence would predict less stability and satisfaction.

Differentiation refers to the degree to which a person or environment is well defined. If a person closely resembles only an artistic type and shows little resemblance to any other type, his or her personality is said to be highly differentiated. Similarly, if an environment is dominated by only artistic people, then that environment retains a high degree of differentiation. Differentiation can be operationally defined in terms of scores on interest inventories such as the VPI by subtracting a person's lowest RIASEC scale score from the highest scale score. The greater the difference between the two scores, the higher the magnitude of differentiation. Similarly, counselors can examine interest inventory profiles of scores that use RIASEC types, such as the SII, for peaks and valleys to determine the degree of differentiation in a student's three-letter Holland code.

Identity denotes the degree to which a type or environment possesses clarity and stability in its style. People who have a clear and stable picture of their goals, interests, abilities, and talents related to making occupational choices have a clear identity. Environments with clear goals, tasks, and rewards that remain stable over time similarly have a high degree of identity. For college students, a high level of vocational identity contributes to effective and confident decision making (Holland, Johnston, & Asama, 1993). Counselors can easily assess students' vocational identity using the 18-item Vocational Identity Scale (VIS) of My Vocational Situation (Holland, Daiger, & Power, 1980). Each VIS item consists of a statement that respondents answer either true or false. Each true response receives a score of 0; each false response receives a score of 1. Summing the number of false responses yields a VIS score ranging from 0 to 18. Higher scores indicate greater levels of vocational identity. The VIS is widely used on college campuses for effectively screening students for referral to appropriate career services, in freshmen orientation programs to identify students in greatest need of career services, and as a treatment tool in counseling (Haviland & Mahaffy, 1985; Holland et al., 1993).

Implementing a Self-Concept: Super's Theory of Careers

Having reviewed the basic elements of Holland's (1997) theory and some of its practical implications, we now turn to examining Super's (Super et al., 1996) developmental approach to career choice and development. His life span—life space approach to careers views career choice and development as a fluid process that evolves throughout the life course of a person. Career development involves a lifelong series of decisions and redecisions as well as continual adjustment and adaptation to those decisions. Super (1990) described this approach as segmental, or a creative synthesis of "developmental, differential, social and phenomenological psychology . . . held together by self-concept or personal-construct theory" (p. 194). The life span—life space perspective characterizes career choice and development as an attempt to implement one's self-concept in educational and occupational decisions. Extrapolating from a key proposition of the theory, college students feel more satisfied when they are able to successfully implement their self-concepts in their academic and career pursuits. Self-concept represents one of three key dimensions, or segments, of Super's developmental theory. The other two principal dimensions of the theory include the constructs of life span and life space.

Career development involves movement through a series of career stages that constitute the life span. The *life span* consists of the chronology of life from birth to death as lived in the five distinct stages of career growth, exploration, establishment, maintenance, and disengagement. Each stage presents specific developmental tasks and issues to resolve. Development through the five stages and tasks over time constitutes the "maxicycle" of career development. Because people often revisit developmental stages and tasks through which they have passed earlier in their lives, career development also may involve various "minicycles" of development. For example, a person established in a position in the field of accounting at midlife may consider a career transition to a different occupational field. In so doing, she explores new career options and thus revisits the developmental stage of career exploration and its associated tasks of crystallizing, specifying, and implementing an occupational preference. People thus cycle through various stages of development in a linear progression, and they often revisit career stages in various ways throughout their lives.

Life space refers to the particular roles that a person plays at any given point in the life span. Developmental career theory recognizes that although the work role certainly figures prominently in people's lives, it is not the only role that counselors should consider when working with college students or others. From a developmental perspective on careers, the work role is best perceived in terms of its salience or importance relative to roles played in other theaters, such as school, leisure, the community, and family. Certainly for college students, the roles of student and worker take center stage in the minds of career counselors. However, the importance any given student places on those roles should be considered in terms of the salience of family, community, and leisure roles. The next sections delineate the basic elements of the life span and the life space.

Career Stages Traverse the Life Span

Each of the five career stages contains substages that constitute developmental tasks that the person must complete. Arbona (1995) suggested elaborating the life-span dimension of the theory to include formation of cultural identity as a developmental task. The elements of the life span include approximate chronological ages and characteristic developmental tasks and issues that people face in each stage (Super et al., 1996).

Growth. From ages 4 to 14, children learn about and develop their self-concepts by identifying with significant others. Early in this stage, playful curiosity and fantasy predominate as the child explores her world spontaneously. Later, the child develops specific interests and capacities relative to the world of work. During this period of career growth, children (and adults recycling through the growth stage) must deal with four major career development tasks. Those tasks include cultivating a concern for and an orientation toward the future, establishing control over and direction in their lives, developing a sense of conviction and purpose in school and work, and attaining appropriate work-related attitudes and competencies.

Career growth means forming an initial and realistic self-concept, or mental picture, of one's strengths, limitations, interests, values, abilities, talents, and so on. In childhood, much of this emerging self-concept derives from spontaneous, playful activity. Career growth also involves acquiring an orientation to the future and the ability to "look ahead" (Savickas, 1997; Super et al., 1996). A crucial part of developing a future orientation involves envisioning oneself in a variety of different roles and understanding the personal salience, or importance, of those roles.

Exploration. Following an initial period of growth in their career development, adolescents and young adults from ages 15 to 24 move to a period of career exploration. This stage typifies the developmental progress of traditional-aged college students as well as college students in later life looking for new career options or exploring careers for the first time. In this stage, involvement in the work role increases as people attempt to implement their emerging self-concepts in part-time employment and related occupational endeavors. Three tasks form the basis of the exploration stage: *crystallizing* a career preference, *specifying* an occupational choice, and *implementing* that choice. Crystallizing involves developing a clear and stable self-concept and vocational identity that reflect the person's preferred occupational field and educational and ability level. Exploring this preferred area of the world of work in breadth leads to educational and vocational choices that reflect the occupational self-concept and vocational identity (Super et al., 1996). Once specified, an occupational choice eventually is implemented and realized through preparing for and obtaining a position in the specified occupation.

Career exploration means that adolescents begin to learn more about opportunities in the world of work, implement (i.e., try out) their developing self-concepts, and explore occupations in a variety of areas as they "look around" (Savickas, 1997). During the exploration stage, people develop career maturity by becoming oriented to and making plans for career development, being curious about and willing to explore the world of work, and knowledgeable about career decision-making principles and the occupational world. These aspects of exploration reflect Super's (1974) structural model of adolescent career maturity. Super used the term *career maturity* to mean readiness to make educational and vocational decisions and to characterize adolescent career development. To capture the greater variability in degree of career development among adults, Super and Knasel (1981) coined the term *career adaptability*, which denotes adults' readiness to cope with changing work and work conditions. A recent elaboration of life span—life space theory suggests replacing career maturity with career adaptability because the latter construct better describes career development across all stages of the life span as "a continual need to respond to new circumstances and novel situations, rather than to master a predictable and linear continuum of developmental tasks" (Savickas, 1997, p. 254).

Exploration stage career concerns for initial career explorers include, for example, difficulty in clarifying one's values, skills, and interests and connecting those attributes to occupational roles. Part-time work outside the home; talking with family, relatives, and teachers about occupations; and similar investigative activities intensify during the exploration stage, because explorers broadly survey the world of work to identify what it has to offer. These activities help clarify knowledge of both oneself and available opportunities in the environment.

Establishment. The childhood and adolescent years generally find people developing self-concepts (growth) and tentatively implementing them (exploration) to settle on suitable occupations. Following the first two stages, adults between ages 25 and 44 typically strive to achieve permanence in their chosen fields of work. This period of stabilizing the self-concept and developing a secure place in the work world is the establishment stage of career development.

Three developmental tasks, comprising separate substages, emerge during the establishment stage. The first task, or substage, that adults confront involves *stabilizing* in a job or position (see Super, 1983, p. 7 for definitions). This means settling into a new position and making it secure through competent performance and successful adaptation to the work culture. With increasing job stability, comfort, and fulfillment comes the second task of *consolidating* the position. Workers consolidate their positions by (a) demonstrating responsible and productive work behaviors and attitudes (e.g., completing assignments on time, working with involvement and zeal), (b) sustaining sound interpersonal relations (i.e., getting along with coworkers and supervisors), and (c) adjusting to existing and changing demands of the work environment. With a position now stabilized and consolidated, a third task, or substage, of *advancing* emerges for those who desire and have opportunities to move to higher level positions. People who seek advancement benefit from identifying realistic goals and career paths and developing strategies that will allow achievement of those goals. Successful establishment ultimately translates into stable self-concepts, career patterns, and locations in the world of work.

Maintenance. After establishing themselves in their positions, adults between ages 45 and 65 typically confront a choice: "Should I stay in my current position or reestablish in a new one?" In making this choice, adults may invest much time pondering whether they want to do their present work until they retire and disengage from the work role. Those who choose to leave their positions often transition to new positions or occupational fields by recycling through exploration and establishment. Those who stay in their established positions try to preserve and enhance their niches in the world of work by continually adjusting to their vocational situations. The concern of such people with preserving and enhancing a position during middle adulthood signals the career stage of maintenance.

For adults at midlife, maintaining a place created in the work world requires *holding* an achieved position. People hold a position by continually adapting to its changing demands, sustaining interest in it, and performing proficiently. Career maintenance also involves *updating* and *innovating* tasks. To update, workers expand their knowledge and skills to refine their job competencies. Workers innovate by developing new and creative ways of completing tasks or contributing to their fields. Innovating may enable people who lack opportunity for further vertical career mobility to cope with career plateaus or circumvent midcareer changes resulting from job dissatisfaction or boredom (Tan & Salomone, 1994). Successful maintainers keep their positions, gain fresh knowledge and skills, and continually invent unique ways of fulfilling their self-concepts.

Although not articulated by Super, other researchers (Murphy & Burck, 1976) have proposed a *renewal* stage, in which adults between ages 35 and 45 reevaluate their self-concepts and either readjust or reestablish their careers. Research supports defining a renewal task or stage as "a transitional period between the establishment and maintenance stages" characterized by "questioning future direction and goals . . . [and] encountered primarily by younger maintainers" (Williams & Savickas, 1990, p.

173). Williams and Savickas contend that maintenance-stage tasks may well reflect an adaptive process rather than maturational "age-related social expectations encountered in a reasonably predictable series" (p. 174). Thus, adapting to change (e.g., in life role salience, employment conditions, or status) seems to represent a more global coping process encompassing each maintenance task of holding, updating, and innovating. These aspects of renewal lend support to replacing the construct of career maturity in the theory with career adaptability.

Disengagement. Adults nearing age 60 begin to *decelerate* their workloads and productivity levels. Work activities gradually decrease as issues of retirement and postoccupational life surface with greater intensity. People may ask themselves during this period of disengagement, "What will retirement mean for me?" or "How will I adjust?" The older adult frequently must cope with retirement planning tasks of organizing finances, scheduling daily activities, and establishing a new lifestyle. Adults in their late 60s who have disengaged from the work role often face retirement living tasks such as settling on a place to live, pursuing meaningful leisure activities, and shifting energies to home and family or other life domains.

Roles Encompass the Life Space

People occupy and impart different degrees of significance to various life roles as they cycle or recycle through each career stage (Super, 1990). Understanding this idea prompts counselors also to consider the importance students place on study, work, community, home and family, and leisure roles both now and at later stages of the life span. The Salience Inventory (SI; Super & Nevill, 1985a) gives counselors a useful tool for determining the importance or significance of the various life roles. Results of the SI can be used in conjunction with knowledge of career stages to conceptualize adult career development issues more fully, particularly as they emerge within a client's unique cultural context.

The life span—life space approach to careers recognizes that many roles constitute a life career (Jepsen, 1990; Nevill & Super, 1986; Piel-Cook, 1994; Super et al., 1996). Taking this perspective on work and career helps counselors assist students with comprehending the relative importance of work (i.e., paid employment) and nonwork roles in their lives; this task is a particularly important objective of counseling practice and research, because it involves issues of culture and context (Richardson, 1996; Vondracek, Lerner, & Schulenberg, 1986).

Developmental counselors define the relative importance people ascribe to various life roles as role salience. Super (1990) articulated the construct of role salience for counselors by (a) identifying nine life roles, (b) postulating that roles vary in their importance over the life span, and (c) developing a measure (Nevill & Super, 1986) of the extent to which people participate in, commit to, and expect to realize values in life roles played out in five theaters: school, work, home and family, community, and leisure. The three measured components of role salience (i.e., participation, commitment, and value expectations) aim to assess the behavioral and affective nature of the construct.

Much research has focused on examining gender differences in role salience. Research reviews reveal that women participate more in home roles, whereas men participate more in paid work roles (Niles & Goodnough, 1996; Piel-Cook, 1994). Women and men in college differ little in their levels of commitment to and value expectations for traditional roles, however (Nevill & Super, 1988). Such findings prompted Piel-Cook to conclude that sex role typing leads women and men to differ in their role participation, despite having no apparent difference in their role commitments and values. A recent study (Matzeder & Krieshok, 1995) followed up on Nevill and Super's research by testing the hypothesis that women with high self-efficacy for traditionally male-dominated occupations would report higher work role and lower home role salience. Results of the study failed to support this hypothesis. Like Nevill and Super, however, Matzeder and Krieshok found that women expect to participate more in home-related activities than do men. Overall, the research on gender differences in role salience indicates that prevailing sociocultural norms, in the United States at least, lead women and men to participate in life roles in rather prescribed ways (Piel-Cook, 1993), especially in the areas of work and family. Women's and men's levels of personal comfort with and commitment to work and family roles, however, may be incongruent with their levels of participation in those roles.

Another line of research has examined cross-cultural differences in role salience. Much of this research derives from Super's multinational Work Importance Study. A review of this research concluded that the three dimensions of role salience that the SI measures (i.e., participation, commitment, and value expectations) show similar patterns of inter-relationships in diverse samples from different countries (Niles & Goodnough, 1996).

Developmental Career Counseling and Assessment With College Students

From the theory, Super (1983) developed a practical scheme for counseling, known as Career-Development Assessment and Counseling (C-DAC). Derived from the theory's key elements (i.e., the career stages and work importance), the C-DAC model blends core components of differential, developmental, and personal construct theories into one comprehensive career assessment and counseling system. Counselors can use this model as a practical guide in developmental career assessment and counseling with college students.

Implementing the C-DAC model. Counselors implement the C-DAC model through a four-step process. Although designed for individual counseling, this process also can be adapted for use in group counseling or other counseling center programs. Step 1, *preview*, begins the process with an initial interview to identify the students' presenting concerns. The counselor also reviews any available data from the students' records and develops a preliminary counseling plan. Central to this first step is counselors' determination, through dialogue and formal assessment, of the importance of work to students relative to life roles in other theaters (e.g., study, home and family, community, and leisure). Ascertaining students' levels of work role salience indicates to the counselor whether further career assessment and counseling for each student will be meaningful (high-career salience) or not (low-career salience). Students high in career salience show readiness to maximally benefit from further career assessment, whereas students low in career salience may need help either (a) orienting to the world of work before further assessment or (b) exploring and preparing for other life roles.

In Step 2, *depth view*, the counselor administers instruments to measure students' career stages and concerns (e.g., the Adult Career Concerns Inventory [ACCI]) and level of career choice readiness (e.g., the Career Development Inventory [CDI] or VIS). Step 2 formally assesses the student's readiness for career decision-making activities, such as identifying and exploring occupational interests and work values. When students reach Step 3, *data assessment*, they work with the counselor to objectify their interests (interest inventories), abilities (aptitude tests), and values (values scales). They then move to step four, *counseling*, which involves subjective self-assessments that identify life themes and patterns (Super et al., 1996).

Instruments. The C-DAC model gives counselors flexibility in using various measures in a comprehensive career assessment battery. Four measures, however, compose a core C-DAC battery for college students, including (a) the 170-item SI to measure role salience; (b) the 120-item CDI (Super, Thompson, Lindeman, Jordaan, & Myers, 1981), for traditional-aged college students or initial career explorers to assess career development attitudes and knowledge, or the 61-item ACCI (Super, Thompson, Lindeman, Myers, & Jordaan, 1988), for non-traditional-aged college students to assess career stage concerns; (c) the 106-item Values Scale (Super & Nevill, 1985b), to measure students' intrinsic and extrinsic values; and (d) the SII (Harmon, Hansen, Borgen, & Hammer, 1994) to measure occupational interests. Further descriptions and examples of using the C-DAC model can be found in Niles and Usher (1993), Hartung et al. (1998) and Hartung (1998). Osborne, Brown, Niles, and Miner (1997) provide a complete description and demonstration of the C-DAC approach.

Summary

Career choice and development theories provide counselors with useful frameworks for offering a variety of career services to college students. The theories reflect differential, developmental, dynamic or personality-focused, and reinforcement-based models of career choice and development. Holland's theory of vocational personalities and work environments and Super's theory of life career development are comprehensive and widely applicable approaches for understanding and fostering educational and career choice, adjustment, and satisfaction of college students.

References

Arbona, C. L. (1995). Career intervention strategies and assessment issues for African Americans. In F. T. L. Leong (Ed.), *Career development and vocational behavior of racial and ethnic minorities* (pp. 37–66). Mahwah, NJ: Erlbaum.

Bordin, E. S. (1990). Psychodynamic model of career choice and satisfaction. In D. Brown, L. Brooks, & Assoc. (Eds.), *Career choice and development* (2nd ed., pp. 94–136). San Francisco: Jossey-Bass.

Brown, D., & Brooks, L. (Eds.). (1996). *Career choice and development: Applying contemporary theories to practice* (3rd ed.). San Francisco: Jossey-Bass.

Cochran, L. (1994). What is a career problem? *Career Development Quarterly, 42,* 204–215.

Dawis, R. V., & Lofquist, L. H. (1984). *A psychological theory of work adjustment.* Minneapolis: University of Minnesota Press.

Fouad, N. A., Harmon, L. W., & Borgen, F. H. (1997). Structure of interests in employed male and female members of U.S. racial-ethnic minority and nonminority groups. *Journal of Counseling Psychology, 44,* 339–345.

Gottfredson, L. S. (1996). Gottfredson's theory of circumscription and compromise. In D. Brown, L. Brooks, & Assoc. (Eds.), *Career choice and development* (3rd ed., pp. 179–232). San Francisco: Jossey-Bass.

Harmon, L. W., Hansen, J.-I. C., Borgen, F. H., & Hammer, A. L. (1994). *Strong Interest Inventory applications and technical guide.* Stanford, CA: Stanford University Press.

Hartung, P. J. (1998). Assessing Ellenore Flood's roles and values to focus her career shopping. *Career Development Quarterly, 46,* 360–366.

Hartung, P. J., Vandiver, B. J., Leong, F. T. L., Pope, M., Niles, S. G., & Farrow, B. (1998). Appraising cultural identity in career-development assessment and counseling. *Career Development Quarterly, 46,* 276–293.

Haviland, M. G., & Mahaffy, J. E. (1985). The use of My Vocational Situation with nontraditional college students. *Journal of College Student Personnel, 26,* 169–170.

Holland, J. L. (1973). *Making vocational choices: A theory of careers.* Englewood Cliffs, NJ: Prentice-Hall.

Holland, J. L. (1985). *Making vocational choices: A theory of vocational personalities and work environments* (2nd ed.). Englewood Cliffs, NJ: Prentice-Hall.

Holland, J. L. (1997). *Making vocational choices* (3rd ed.). Odessa, FL: Psychological Assessment Resources.

Holland, J. L., Daiger, D. C., & Power, P. G. (1980). *My Vocational Situation.* Palo Alto, CA: Consulting Psychologists Press.

Holland, J. L., Johnston, J. A., & Asama, N. F. (1993). The Vocational Identity Scale: A diagnostic and treatment tool. *Journal of Career Assessment, 1,* 1–12.

Jepsen, D. A. (1990). Developmental career counseling. In W. B. Walsh & S. H. Osipow (Eds.), *Career counseling: Contemporary topics in vocational psychology* (pp. 117–157). Hillsdale, NJ: Erlbaum.

Lent, R. W., Brown, S. D., & Hackett, G. (1996). Career development from a social cognitive perspective. In D. Brown, L. Brooks, & Assoc. (Eds.), *Career choice and development* (3rd ed., pp. 373–422). San Francisco: Jossey-Bass.

Lofquist, L. H., & Dawis, R. V. (1991). *Essentials of person-environment correspondence counseling.* Minneapolis: University of Minnesota Press.

Matzeder, M. E., & Krieshok, T. S. (1995). Career self-efficacy and the prediction of work and home role salience. *Journal of Career Assessment, 3,* 331–340.

Mitchell, L. K., & Krumboltz, J. D. (1996). Krumboltz's learning theory of career choice and counseling. In D. Brown, L. Brooks, & Assoc. (Eds.), *Career choice and development* (3rd ed., pp. 233–280). San Francisco: Jossey-Bass.

Murphy, P. P., & Burck, H. D. (1976). Career development of men at mid-life. *Journal of Vocational Behavior, 9,* 337–343.

Nevill, D. D., & Super, D. E. (1986). *The Salience Inventory: Theory, application, and research.* Palo Alto, CA: Consulting Psychologists Press.

Nevill, D. D., & Super, D. E. (1988). Career maturity and commitment to work in university students. *Journal of Vocational Behavior, 32,* 139–151.

Niles, S. G., & Goodnough, G. E. (1996). Life role salience and values: A review of recent research. *Career Development Quarterly, 45,* 65–86.

Niles, S. G., & Usher, C. H. (1993). Applying the career-development assessment and counseling model to the case of Rosie. *Career Development Quarterly, 42,* 61–65.

Osborne, W. L., Brown, S., Niles, S., & Miner, C. U. (1997). *Career development assessment and counseling: Applications of the Donald E. Super C-DAC approach.* Alexandria, VA: American Counseling Association.

Osipow, S. H. (1990). Convergence in theories of career choice and development: Review and prospect. *Journal of Vocational Behavior, 36,* 122–131.

Osipow, S. H., & Fitzgerald, L. F. (1996). *Theories of career development* (4th ed.). Boston: Allyn and Bacon.

Parsons, F. (1909). *Choosing a vocation.* Boston: Houghton-Mifflin.

Piel-Cook, E. (1993). The gendered context of life: Implications for women's and men's career-life plans. *Career Development Quarterly, 41,* 227–237.

Piel-Cook, E. (1994). Role salience and multiple roles: A gender perspective. *Career Development Quarterly, 43,* 85–95.

Richardson, M. S. (1996). From career counseling to counseling/psychotherapy and work, jobs, and career. In M. L. Savickas & W. B. Walsh (Eds.), *Handbook of career counseling theory and practice* (pp. 347–360). Palo Alto, CA: Davies-Black Publishing.

Roe, A. (1956). *The psychology of occupations.* New York: Wiley.

Roe, A., & Lunneborg, P. W. (1990). Personality development and career choice. In D. Brown, L. Brooks, & Assoc. (Eds.), *Career choice and development* (2nd ed., pp. 68–101). San Francisco: Jossey-Bass.

Savickas, M. L. (1996). A framework for linking career theory and practice. In M. L. Savickas & W. B. Walsh (Eds.), *Handbook of career counseling theory and practice* (pp. 191–208). Palo Alto, CA: Davies-Black Publishing.

Savickas, M. L. (1997). Career adaptability: An integrative construct for life-span, life-space theory. *Career Development Quarterly, 45,* 247–259.

Savickas, M. L., & Lent, R. W. (Eds.). (1994). *Convergence in career development theories: Implications for science and practice.* Palo Alto, CA: Davies-Black.

Savickas, M. L., & Walsh, W. B. (Eds.). (1996). *Handbook of career counseling theory and practice.* Palo Alto, CA: Davies-Black.

Sharf, R. S. (1997). *Applying career development theory to counseling* (2nd ed.). Pacific Grove, CA: Brooks/Cole.

Spokane, A. R. (1996). Holland's theory. In D. Brown, L. Brooks, & Assoc. (Eds.), *Career choice and development: Applying contemporary theories to practice* (3rd ed., pp. 33–74). San Francisco: Jossey-Bass.

Super, D. E. (1957). *The psychology of careers.* New York: Harper and Row.

Super, D. E. (Ed.). (1974). *Measuring vocational maturity for counseling and evaluation.* Washington, DC: National Vocational Guidance Association.

Super, D. E. (1983). Assessment in career guidance: Toward truly developmental counseling. *Personnel and Guidance Journal, 61,* 555–562.

Super, D. E. (1990). Career and life development. In D. Brown, L. Brooks, & Assoc. (Eds.), *Career choice and development* (2nd ed., pp. 192–234). San Francisco: Jossey-Bass.

Super, D. E., & Knasel, E. G. (1981). Career development in adulthood: Some theoretical problems. *British Journal of Guidance and Counseling, 9,* 194–201.

Super, D. E., & Nevill, D. D. (1985a). *Salience Inventory.* Palo Alto, CA: Consulting Psychologists Press.

Super, D. E., & Nevill, D. D. (1985b). *Values Scale*. Palo Alto, CA: Consulting Psychologists Press.

Super D. E., Savickas, M. L., & Super, C. M. (1996). The life-span, life-space approach to careers. In D. Brown, L. Brooks, & Assoc. (Eds.), *Career choice and development: Applying contemporary theories to practice* (3rd ed., pp. 121–178). San Francisco: Jossey-Bass.

Super, D. E., Starishevsky, R., Matlin, N., & Jordaan, J. P. (1963). *Career development: A self-concept theory*. New York: College Entrance Examination Board.

Super, D. E., Thompson, A. S., Lindeman, R. H., Jordaan, J. P., & Myers, R. A. (1981). *Career Development Inventory: College form*. Palo Alto, CA: Consulting Psychologists Press.

Super, D. E., Thompson, A. S., Lindeman, R. H., Myers, R. A., & Jordaan, J. P. (1988). *Adult Career Concerns Inventory*. Palo Alto, CA: Consulting Psychologists Press.

Swanson, J. L. (1996). The theory *is* the practice. In M. L. Savickas & W. B. Walsh (Eds.), *Handbook of career counseling theory and practice* (pp. 93–108). Palo Alto, CA: Davies-Black.

Tan, C. S., & Salomone, P. R. (1994). Understanding career plateauing: Implications for counseling. *Career Development Quarterly, 42,* 291–301.

Vondracek, F. W., Lerner, R., & Schulenberg, J. (1986). *Career development: A life-span developmental approach*. Hillsdale, NJ: Erlbaum.

Williams, C. P., & Savickas, M. L. (1990). Developmental tasks of career maintenance. *Journal of Vocational Behavior, 36,* 166–175.

2

areer Theories

Sp   *nd Paul J. Hartung*

Chapter 1 focused on lon   velopment theories applied
to college students. This   veral recent career theories
that also offer useful inte   g college student career development. Specifically, tl   career counseling (Krumboltz, 1996), the social–co   (Lent, Brown, & Hackett,
1996), the cognitive inform   ory (Peterson, Sampson, &
Reardon, 1991), and the val   areer choice (Brown, 1995)
are each excellent example   Finally, we briefly discuss
"postmodern" approaches tc   t interventions (Cochran,
1997; Young, Valach, & Coll

One strength of the emerging theories is that they apply to diverse
college student populations. Moreover, they each have practical utility
and, therefore, are useful in advancing career interventions with college
students. Finally, the theories are built on a solid foundation of research
support. (See the annual reviews, 1995–1999, of the *Career Development
Quarterly* and the *Journal of Vocational Behavior*. Brown and Brooks,
1996 also provide an excellent discussion of the research supporting each
of the theories discussed in this chapter.)

John Krumboltz's Learning Theory of Career Counseling

Although aspects of Krumboltz's theory have existed for a number of years,
more recent extensions of his theory place it in the group of emerging
theories. Specifically, Krumboltz and his colleagues (especially Mitchell
and Jones) developed a learning theory of career counseling comprising
two related parts. The first part focuses on explaining the origins of
career choice and is the *social learning theory of career decision making*
(SLTCDM) (Mitchell & Krumboltz, 1996). The second part focuses on career counseling and is the *learning theory of career counseling* (LTCC)
(Mitchell & Krumboltz, 1996). Because the SLTCDM identifies factors influencing the career decisions people make (and is, therefore, subsumed
the LTCC part of the theory) and because the LTCC explains what career
counselors can do to help people make effective career decisions, Mitchell
and Krumboltz called the entire theory the "learning theory of career counseling."

The learning theory of career counseling is based on the application of Bandura's (1969, 1977, 1986) social learning theory to career decision making. Bandura's theory emphasizes the influence of reinforcement theory, cognitive information processing, and classical behaviorism on human behavior. Social learning theory "assumes that people's personalities and behavioral repertoires can be explained most usefully on the basis of their unique learning experiences while still acknowledging the role played by innate and developmental processes" (Mitchell & Krumboltz, 1996, p. 234). Social learning theory also assumes that "humans are intelligent, problem-solving individuals who strive at all times to understand the reinforcement that surrounds them and who in turn control their environments to suit their own purposes and needs" (Mitchell & Krumboltz, 1984, p. 236). Bandura (1986) described the interaction of environment, self-referent thought, and behavior as the *triadic reciprocal interaction system*.

Krumboltz and his colleagues (1976) drew on these theoretical assumptions in developing the learning theory of career counseling. As noted earlier, SLTCDM describes factors influencing individual career decisions, and LTCC describes what career counselors can do to help college students make more effective career choices.

SLTCDM

SLTCDM identifies four factors that influence career decisions:

1. *Genetic endowments and special abilities.* Genetic endowments are inherited qualities such as sex, race, and physical appearance. Special abilities, such as intelligence, athletic ability, musical, and artistic talents, result from the interaction of genetic factors and exposure to selected environmental events.
2. *Environmental conditions and events.* Factors in this category are generally outside of the person's control and can involve a wide variety of cultural, social, political, and economic forces. For example, government-sponsored financial aid programs can increase the likelihood of a person attending college, and family traditions, such as attending a particular college or selecting a certain college major, can influence which college and major he or she selects.
3. *Instrumental and associative learning experiences.* Instrumental learning experiences involve antecedents, behaviors, and consequences.

   Antecedents include the genetic endowments, special abilities, and environmental conditions and events previously discussed as well as the characteristics of a particular task or problem. Behavioral responses include cognitive and emotional responses as well as overt behavior. Consequences include immediate and delayed effects produced by the behavior as well as "self-talk" about those consequences. (Mitchell & Krumboltz, 1996, p. 238)

Associative learning experiences occur when a neutral stimulus is paired with a positive or negative stimulus or consequence. For example, a college student, undecided about a major, attends a job fair to explore career options and has an extremely positive encounter (positive stimulus) with someone employed in an occupation that the student has never really considered before (neutral stimulus). As a result of this positive encounter, the student decides to explore the occupation of the person the student met at the job fair.

4. *Task approach skills*. Task approach skills include the person's work habits, mental set, emotional responses, cognitive processes, and problem-solving skills. Task approach skills influence outcomes and are themselves outcomes of career decisions.

The four factors influence career decisions in a number of ways. For example, special abilities, environmental conditions, and learning experiences interact to shape a persons' beliefs about themselves and their beliefs about the world (e.g., "hard work always pays off," "all accountants are stuffy," "all social workers value altruism over economic rewards"). The factors generally affect students' career decisions in four ways: (a) through self-observation generalizations, (b) through worldview generalizations, (c) through task approach skills, and (d) through actions.

Self-Observation Generalizations. Overt or covert statements evaluating a person's actual or vicarious performance are self-observation generalizations. Such generalizations also include self-assessments of individual interests and values (Mitchell & Krumboltz, 1996).

Learning experiences lead people to draw conclusions about themselves. People compare their performance to the performance of others and to their own performance expectations. They then draw conclusions about performance capabilities (e.g., a first-year college student does well in an introductory psychology course and decides to enroll in additional psychology courses, because it is something the student is "good at"). Conclusions about interests and values also result from learning experiences (e.g., a first-year college student takes an introductory physics courses, experiences a strong disinterest in the course, and then decides to avoid taking any additional courses in physics). Thus, in SLTCDM interests link learning experiences with specific actions.

Self-observations about values are, in essence, statements about the desirability of specific outcomes, behaviors, or events (Mitchell & Krumboltz, 1996). For example, the statement "it is important that my job provides opportunities for helping people" is a values-related self-observation generalization about desirable outcomes resulting from previous learning experiences.

Worldview Generalizations. Likewise, generalizations about the nature and functioning of the world (e.g., "It is better to try and fail than to not try at all") are formed from learning experiences. The accuracy of worldview generalizations depends on the learning experiences that shape such generalizations. For example, if a student is rewarded for hard work, he or she is likely to believe that "hard work pays off." Students not experiencing such rewards may think that other factors override the influence of hard work (e.g., "It's not what you know, it's who you know").

Task Approach Skills. Mitchell and Krumboltz (1996) defined *task approach skills* as "cognitive and performance abilities and emotional predispositions for coping with the environment, interpreting it in relation to self-observation generalizations, and making covert and overt predictions about future events" (p. 246). As noted earlier, task approach skills both influence career decision making and are outcomes of learning experiences that shape career development. Task approach skills that are critical to career development include decision making, problem solving, goal setting, information gathering, and values clarifying. Thus, when college students attend workshops such as those related to time management, stress management, resume writing, and interviewing, they are learning important task approach skills for fostering career development.

Actions. Learning experiences eventually lead people to take actions related to entering a career. Those actions can include choosing a major, applying for a job, entering a training program, applying to college, changing jobs, or taking other overt steps to progress in one's career. Two crucial "action steps" for college students are choosing a college major (typically in the second year of college) and searching for a job to follow the student's final year of college.

SLTCDM suggests that career decision making is "influenced by complex environmental factors, many of which are beyond the control of any single individual" (Krumboltz et al., 1975, p. 75). Based on social learning theory, Krumboltz (1994, p. 19) noted that people will prefer an occupation if the following three conditions apply:

1. They have succeeded at tasks they believe are like tasks performed by members of that occupation.
2. They have observed a valued model being reinforced for activities like those performed by members of that occupation.
3. A valued friend or relative stressed the occupation's advantages to them, they observed positive words and images being associated with it, or both.

Conversely, Krumboltz (1994) noted, people will avoid an occupation under the following three conditions:

1. They have failed at tasks they believe are similar to tasks performed by people in that occupation.
2. They have observed a valued model being punished or ignored for performing activities like those performed by members of that occupation.

3. A valued friend or relative stressed the occupation's disadvantages to them, they have observed negative words and images being associated with it, or both.

Implicit in these assumptions is the call for career services professionals in higher education to provide important learning experiences to students early in their college experience. For example, programs that expose college students to potential occupational role models (e.g., mentoring programs) and that expose students to various work environments (e.g., externship programs) are ways in which career services professionals can construct learning experiences that enhance students' career development.

LTCC

The strength of the SLTCDM is that it provides a description of factors influencing career decision making and identifies outcomes resulting from those factors. As such, it is a useful theory for understanding career paths retrospectively. The understanding acquired from such a perspective is helpful in making current career decisions and in formulating future career goals. Acquiring such understanding is important when students experience difficulties in their career development. Those difficulties typically are related to (a) the absence of a goal, or career indecision; (b) feelings of concern about high aspirations, or unrealism; or (c) a conflict between equally appropriate alternatives, or multipotentiality (Krumboltz, 1996).

Krumboltz (1996) developed the LTCC to guide counselors in constructing career development interventions to help their clients cope more effectively with these career concerns. Specifically, career services professionals using LTCC can help college students (a) acquire more accurate self-observation generalizations, (b) acquire more accurate worldview generalizations, (c) learn new task approach skills, and (d) take appropriate career-related actions. LTCC assumes that counselors must be prepared to help college students cope with four current career-related trends identified by Mitchell and Krumboltz (1996):

1. *The need for people to expand their capabilities and interests and to not base decisions only on existing characteristics.* To maximize college students' career options, counselors must encourage students to explore new activities, develop new interests, and consider new options based on newly formed interests and capabilities. Obviously, the first two years of college often provide the best opportunities for students to engage in this type of broad-based exploration. Career services professionals can help students systematically identify new opportunities and experiences to explore and then help students process the information they acquire from these activities.

2. *The need for people to prepare for changing work tasks and to not assume that occupations will remain stable.* Because change is constant, career services providers must help college students learn how to engage in skill assessment and how to identify new skills to learn. Students also must be assisted in developing strategies for coping with the stress inherent in an ever-changing world of work. One could argue that stress management workshops should be a regular component of career services programming in higher education.

3. *The need for people to be empowered to take action and to not merely give a diagnosis.* For some college students, implementing a career choice is more challenging than making the choice. Many students need ongoing assistance and support from their career counselors as they attempt to implement and adjust to educational and career choices they have made. Their ongoing needs suggest that career services in higher education should be extended to include follow-up interventions and that career decision-making interventions are not concluded when the student identifies an educational or career choice.

4. *The need for career services professionals to play a major role in dealing with all career problems, not just career selection.* Career-related concerns exist beyond the concern of identifying a career choice. Many college students struggle with burnout, family members' reactions to career choices, and low self-efficacy. Career interventions that are counseling-based often are needed to address such issues.

The four trends also highlight the need for career services professionals in higher education to provide college students with learning experiences to (a) correct faulty assumptions, (b) learn new skills and interests, (c) identify effective strategies for addressing issues emanating from interactions between work and other life role activities and concerns, and (d) learn skills for coping with changing work tasks. Thus, the task of career services professionals in higher education is to promote student learning, and the goal of career counseling is to enhance the students' ability to create satisfying lives for themselves (Krumboltz, 1996).

Applying the Learning Theory of Career Counseling

Krumboltz (1996) divided career development interventions into two categories: (a) developmental and preventive and (b) targeted and remedial. The first category includes career education programs, school-to-work initiatives, job club programs, study materials, and simulations. Such career development interventions facilitate the acquisition of accurate self- and occupational information and the use of this information in the career decision-making process. They emphasize learning through active on-the-job participation (e.g., job shadowing, internships, externships, worksite observation).

Targeted and remedial career development interventions, in contrast, include goal clarification, cognitive restructuring, cognitive rehearsal, narrative analysis, role playing, desensitization, paradoxical intention, and humor (Krumboltz, 1996). The learning theory of career counseling also emphasizes the importance of teaching decision-making skills to college students. Learning how to make career decisions helps students resolve current career concerns and equips them with an important task approach skill for coping with changing work and personal conditions in the future (Krumboltz, 1976).

To help career services professionals identify students' problematic beliefs related to each of the career problem categories (i.e., indecision, unrealism, and multipotentiality), Krumboltz (1988) developed the Career Beliefs Inventory (CBI). The CBI is based on the rationale that career decisions are based on what people believe about themselves and the world of work. "If their beliefs are accurate and constructive, they will act in ways that are likely to help them achieve their goals. If their beliefs are inaccurate and self-defeating, they will act in a way that makes sense to them but may not help them achieve their goals" (Krumboltz, 1994, p. 424). The CBI helps counselors understand clients' career beliefs and assumptions. Thus, the instrument is most useful when administered at the beginning of career counseling. The CBI contains 25 scales organized into the following five categories:

1. my current career situation
2. what seems necessary for my happiness
3. factors that influence my decisions
4. changes I am willing to make
5. effort I am willing to initiate.

The categories are related to mental barriers that block clients from taking action.

Evaluation Criteria

Typically, counselors evaluate the success of career interventions by determining whether clients experience a reduction in career indecision and whether they achieve congruence with their work environments. Krumboltz (1994) recommended that career counselors consider revising these criteria. For example, career counselors using the learning theory of career counseling can view indecision as a desirable quality for motivating students to engage in new learning activities. Hence, Krumboltz recommended reframing "indecision" to "open-mindedness." In addition, Krumboltz suggested that the goal of achieving congruence between people and their work environments is unnecessarily restricting because "birds of a feather" do not always "flock together." Two different people can succeed in the same occupation. Krumboltz also argued that the congruence criterion is less useful today because it is based on stagnant definitions of occupational environments and thus overlooks changes in work environments. "Heterogeneity, not homogeneity, within occupations is now more highly valued" (Krumboltz, 1996, p. 73).

In place of these two traditional outcome criteria, Krumboltz (1994) recommended focusing on measuring changes in such client characteristics as skills, values, beliefs, interests and work habits. Career counselors also can ask themselves whether their career interventions have stimulated their students to engage in new learning activities. Process measures can focus on assessing the degree to which students have made efforts to create more satisfying lives (e.g., have they engaged in career-exploratory or information-seeking behaviors?).

Lent, Brown, and Hackett's Social–Cognitive Career Theory

The social–cognitive career theory (SCCT; Brown & Lent, 1996; Lent et al., 1996) builds on the assumption that cognitive factors play an important role in career development and decision making. SCCT is closely linked to Krumboltz's learning theory of career counseling (Mitchell & Krumboltz, 1996). Lent et al. noted, however, that SCCT differs from Krumboltz's theory in several ways. For example, the SCCT

> is more concerned with the specific cognitive mediators through which learning experiences guide career behavior; with the manner in which variables such as interests, abilities, and values interrelate; and with the specific paths by which person and contextual factors influence career outcomes. It also emphasizes the means by which individuals emphasize personal agency. (Lent et al., 1996, p. 377)

SCCT also draws heavily from Bandura's (1986) social–cognitive theory. Specifically, SCCT incorporates Bandura's *triadic reciprocal model of causality*, which assumes that personal attributes, the environment, and overt behaviors "operate as interlocking mechanisms that affect one another bidirectionally" (Lent et al., 1996, p. 379). Within this triadic reciprocal model, SCCT highlights self-efficacy beliefs, outcome expectations, and personal goals. Thus, SCCT incorporates research applying self-efficacy theory to the career domain (Hackett & Betz, 1981; Lent & Hackett, 1987).

Bandura (1986) defined *self-efficacy beliefs* as "people's judgments of their capabilities to organize and execute courses of action required to attain designated types of performances" (p. 391). Self-efficacy beliefs are dynamic self-beliefs and are domain specific; they provide answers to questions pertaining to whether people can perform specific tasks (e.g., Can I make this presentation? Can I pass the calculus exam?). People's beliefs about their abilities play a central role in the career decision-making process because people move toward occupations requiring capabilities they think they either have or can develop. Likewise, people move away from occupations that require capabilities they think they do not possess or that they cannot develop.

Four sources shape self-efficacy beliefs: (a) personal performance accomplishments, (b) vicarious learning, (c) social persuasion, and (d) physiological states and reactions (Bandura, 1986). The most influential of the sources is the first (personal performance accomplishments). Successful accomplishments result in more positive, or stronger, domain-specific self-efficacy beliefs, and failures lead to more negative, or weaker, domain-specific beliefs.

Outcome expectations are beliefs about the outcomes of performing specific behaviors (e.g., What is likely to happen if I apply for a summer internship with a major accounting firm? What job opportunities am I likely to have if I earn a degree in history?). Outcome expectations include beliefs about "extrinsic reinforcement (receiving tangible rewards for successful performance), self-directed consequences (such as pride in oneself for mastering a challenging task), and outcomes derived from the process of performing a given activity (for instance, absorption in the task itself)" (Lent et al., 1996, p. 381). Outcome expectations influence behavior to a lesser degree than do self-efficacy beliefs (e.g., a student who likes history is not likely to major in the subject if he or she thinks the probability of succeeding in the program of study is low).

Personal goals, which relate to a person's determination to engage in certain activities to produce a particular outcome, also influence career behaviors in important ways (Bandura, 1986). Goals help organize and guide behavior over long periods of time (e.g., a student will persist in a statistics course because it is an important step toward earning a degree in psychology).

The relationship among goals, self-efficacy, and outcome expectations is complex and occurs within the framework of Bandura's (1986) triadic reciprocal model of causality. Lent et al. (1996) provided a detailed description of this relationship. In essence, person inputs (e.g., predisposition, gender, race) interact with contextual factors (e.g., culture, geography, family, gender role socialization) and learning experiences to influence self-efficacy beliefs and outcome expectations. Self-efficacy beliefs and outcome expectations, in turn, shape interests, goals, actions and, eventually, attainments. These attainments, however, also are influenced by contextual factors (e.g., job opportunities, access to training opportunities, financial resources).

Applying SCCT

The SCCT is particularly useful in addressing two areas of career concern that confront college students: (a) performance attainment and (b) persistence at overcoming obstacles. Performance is influenced by ability, self-efficacy, outcome expectations, and goals. Ability affects performance both directly and indirectly by influencing self-efficacy beliefs and outcome expectations. "Higher self-efficacy and anticipated positive outcomes promote higher goals, which help to mobilize and sustain performance behavior" (Lent & Brown, 1996, p. 318). Problems in career development emerge when people prematurely foreclose on occupational options as a result of inaccurate self-efficacy beliefs, outcome expectations, or both, and when they forego further consideration of occupational options because of barriers they perceive as insurmountable.

To examine premature foreclosure on occupational options, Lent and Brown (1996) recommended that counselors encourage students to discuss the options that they have eliminated from further consideration. Specifically, in discussing occupations of low interest, counselors should analyze the experiences and beliefs on which the student's lack of interest is based. Here counselors focus on identifying any inaccuracies in the student's self-efficacy beliefs and occupational information. "The basic processes for facilitating interest exploration are, therefore, fairly straightforward and include assessing discrepancies between self-efficacy and demonstrated skill and between outcome expectations and occupational information" (Brown & Lent, 1996, p. 357).

One approach Brown and Lent (1996) suggest for facilitating interest exploration involves the use of a card-sort exercise. In this exercise, students sort occupations according to (a) those they would choose, (b) those they would not choose, and (c) those about which they are unsure. Students then focus on the latter two categories by identifying occupations they (a) might choose if they had the skills (self-efficacy beliefs), (b) might choose if the occupation offered them things they value (outcome expectations), and (c) definitely would not choose under any circumstances. Occupations in the first two categories (those relating to self-efficacy beliefs and outcome expectations) are then examined for how accurately they reflect skill and outcome perceptions.

To analyze obstacles or barriers to students' career development, Brown and Lent recommended adapting Janis and Mann's (1977) decisional balance-sheet procedure. The adaptation involves asking students to first list their preferred career options and then to identify the negative consequences they imagine will occur in pursuing any specific option. Negative consequences are explored as possible barriers to career choice implementation by (a) asking students to consider the probability of encountering each barrier and (b) developing strategies for preventing or managing the barriers students are most likely to encounter.

College students can be helped to modify their self-efficacy beliefs in several ways. When ability is sufficient but self-efficacy beliefs are low as a result of factors such as racism and sex role stereotyping, clients can be exposed to personally relevant vicarious learning opportunities. For example, an African American woman who has sufficient ability for a career in engineering but who has low self-efficacy beliefs can be introduced to engineers who are African American and female (Hackett & Byars, 1996). To counteract their faulty beliefs, students with sufficient ability but low self-efficacy beliefs can be encouraged to gather ability-related data from friends, professors, and others. Counselors also can work collaboratively with such students to construct successful experiences (e.g., by taking specific academic courses, participating in volunteer experiences) to create positive self-efficacy beliefs. In processing successful experiences, counselors can challenge students when they credit external factors for their successes and disregard internal stable causes (e.g., ability).

Cognitive Information-Processing Approach

The cognitive information-processing (CIP) approach (Sampson, Peterson, Lenz, & Reardon, 1992) includes several dimensions. First, the approach uses a pyramid to describe the important domains of cognition involved in a career choice. The first three domains are those traditionally included in career theories: (a) self-knowledge (values, interests, skills), (b) occupational knowledge (understanding specific occupations and educational/ training opportunities), and (c) decision-making skills (understanding how one typically makes decisions). The fourth domain consists of metacognitions and includes self-talk, self-awareness, and the monitoring and control of cognitions (Sampson et al., 1992). Knowledge of self and of occupations forms the foundation of the pyramid, and decision-making skills and metacognitions build on that foundation.

The second dimension of the CIP approach is a cycle that represents a generic model of information-processing skills related to solving career problems and making career decisions. This cycle involves communication, analysis, synthesis, valuing, and execution skills (CASVE).

The CASVE cycle begins with the realization that a gap exists between a real state and an ideal state (e.g., an existing state of career indecision and a more desired state of career decidedness). Becoming aware of such gaps can occur internally through the existence of ego-dystonic emotional states (e.g., depression, anxiety); the occurrence of behaviors such as excessive tardiness, absenteeism, or drug use; or the existence of somatic symptoms (e.g., headaches, loss of appetite). People also can become aware of such gaps through external demands (e.g., the need to select a curriculum of study in college, the need to make a decision to accept or reject a job offer). Career problems, therefore, involve cognitive, affective, behavioral, and physiological components (Peterson, Sampson, & Reardon, 1996). Interpreting internal and external cues involves communication. Specifically, students must ask themselves two questions: (a) "What am I thinking and feeling about my career choice at this moment?" and (b) "What do I hope to attain as a result of career counseling?" (Peterson et al., 1996, p. 436).

Once it is recognized that a gap or career problem exists, the career counselor must analyze what is required for problem resolution. For example, does the student need more self-information (e.g., values, interests) or information about the situation (e.g., my supervisor's expectations, job requirements)? What must the student do to acquire the information or resources necessary to cope more effectively with the career problem (e.g., take an interest inventory, conduct an occupational information interview, seek counseling to enhance self-understanding)?

Synthesis involves two phases: (a) elaboration and (b) crystallization. During *elaboration*, students seek to identify as many potential solutions to their career problems as possible. (As in brainstorming, the focus is on quantity, rather than quality, of solutions.) During *crystallization*, students identify the solutions that are consistent with their abilities, interests, or values. The outcome of the two phases of synthesis is a manageable list of alternatives that are acceptable to the student.

The *valuing phase* involves examining and prioritizing each of the alternatives generated in light of one's value system, the benefits to be gained, the costs incurred with each alternative, each alternative's impact on significant others and society, and the probability that the alternative will result in a successful outcome (i.e., removing the gap). Once the alternatives have been prioritized, the optimal alternative is identified. The primary question for students engaged in the process of valuing is "Which alternative is the best course of action for me, my significant others, and society?" (Peterson et al., 1996, p. 437).

The *execution phase* involves converting the optimal alternative into action. A plan of action is developed to implement the alternative and achieve its goal (e.g., "I will enroll in psychology courses, study 3 hours per day, and take a course to improve my Graduate Record Examination scores to achieve my goal of gaining entry into a highly selective clinical psychology program."). Thus, the execution phase requires students to identify the steps necessary to operationalize the solution chosen in the valuing phase. The primary question in the execution phase is, "How can I transform my choice into an action plan?" (Peterson et al., 1996, p. 437).

Once the plan has been enacted, students return to the communication phase to determine whether the alternative successfully resolved the career problem. Once again, cognitive, affective, behavioral, and physiological states are assessed in evaluating the success of the alternative (e.g., Does the student feel less anxious? Is the student more content with his or her career situation? Has the student's class attendance improved?). If the evaluation is positive, then the student moves on; if the evaluation is negative, the student repeats the CASVE process with the new information acquired from enacting the first alternative.

A third dimension of the CIP approach is the *executive processing domain*, whose function is to initiate, coordinate, and monitor the storage and retrieval of information (Peterson et al., 1991). This domain involves metacognitive skills (Meichenbaum, 1977) such as self-talk, self-awareness, and self-control. Positive self-talk (e.g., "I am capable of choosing an appropriate college major") is required for effective career problem solving. Negative self-talk (e.g., "I can't make a good decision") leads to career indecisiveness. Self-awareness is needed to monitor and control internal and external influences on career decisions. Effective problem solvers and decision makers are aware of their values, beliefs, biases, and feelings and use this awareness to generate and select solutions. Control and monitoring are essential for deciphering the information needed to resolve a career problem and for knowing when one is ready to move to the next phase in the CASVE cycle. The "control and monitoring of lower-order functions insures [*sic*] that an optimal balance is met between impulsivity and compulsivity" (Peterson et al., 1991, p. 39), thereby providing a "quality control mechanism to ensure a complete, orderly, and timely progression through the CASVE cycle" (Peterson et al., 1996, p. 439).

Applying the CIP Approach

The pyramid model can be used as a framework for providing career development interventions. For example, the self-knowledge domain can be addressed through standardized and nonstandardized assessments. The occupational-knowledge domain can be addressed by engaging in job-shadowing exercises and by reading occupational biographies. The five steps of the CASVE cycle can be used to teach decision-making skills. The executive processing domain provides a framework for exploring and challenging students' dysfunctional metacognitions. Peterson et al. (1991) outlined a seven-step sequence for delivering individual, group, and classroom career development interventions.

A Values-Based, Holistic Model of Career and Life-Role Choices and Satisfaction

Brown (1995, 1996) formulated a model of career development based on the importance of values in career decision making. His values-based model draws on the work of Rokeach (1973), Super (1953, 1957, 1990), and Beck (1987). For example, in defining values Brown used Rokeach's notion that *values* are beliefs containing cognitive, affective, and behavioral dimensions. Additionally, Brown (1996) pointed out that values serve as standards by which people evaluate their own actions and the actions of others. Working 80 hours a week for 50 weeks out of the year to earn a significant salary makes sense to the person who values materialism, but is hard to understand for the person who values spending time with family. Thus, values focus our behavior in specific directions and toward particular goals.

The values-based model of career choice is based on seven propositions as stated by Brown and Crace (1996):

1. Values with high priorities are the most important determinants of choices made, providing that people have more than one alternative available that will satisfy their values.
2. The values included in the values system are acquired from society, and each person develops a small number of values.
3. Culture, sex, and socioeconomic status influence opportunities and social interaction; therefore, considerable variation in the values of subgroups in our society can be expected.
4. Making choices that coincide with values is essential to satisfaction.
5. The result of role interaction is life satisfaction, which differs from the sum of the marital, job, leisure, and other role satisfaction indices taken separately.

6. High-functioning people have well-developed and prioritized values.

7. Success in any role depends on the abilities and the aptitudes required to perform the functions of that role.

For each proposition, Brown and Crace identified research findings supporting their assumptions and noted that their assumptions reflect a synthesis of other theories and their own speculations (in addition to values-related research).

Applying the Values-Based Approach

The application of the values-based approach is based on a number of assumptions with various degrees of research support (Brown, 1996, pp. 357–358). For example, the values-based approach assumes that because life roles interact, those interactions need to be incorporated into the career counseling process; that mood-related problems should be dealt with before career-related concerns; that career counselors need to be able to translate various types of psychological data (e.g., interests) into values-based terms; and that because understanding one's values is key to making effective career decisions, counselors must be skilled at helping clients clarify and understand their values.

Values assessment can be accomplished through qualitative or quantitative methods. Qualitative methods include card sorts, checklists, and guided fantasies (Brown, 1996; Brown & Brooks, 1996). Quantitative methods include the use of inventories such Rokeach's Values Survey (1973), the Values Scale (Super & Nevill, 1985), and the Life Values Inventory (Crace & Brown, 1996).

When students have crystallized and prioritized their values, they then focus on career decision making. When this is not the case, Brown uses Rokeach's (1973) suggestion that values can be clarified and changed by the processes of contemplation and conflict. The former process can be incorporated into career counseling through the use of qualitative exercises (e.g., values-clarification activities, analysis of daydreams, and discussing reasons clients admire specific people) or through the use of more quantitative activities using values inventory assessments (Brown & Crace, 1996).

Conflict involves self-confrontation of various values. This type of conflict can be incorporated into career counseling through the use of guided imagery and role-playing exercises. Through the exercises counselors can introduce scenarios in which conflicts among life roles must be confronted and choices between specific values can be juxtaposed. Brown (1996) also recommended using the "why" technique, which involves continuously challenging students by asking why they are making specific statements, as a means for helping students crystallize and prioritize their values.

Postmodern Approaches

Recently, attention has been given by researchers to career development theories and interventions that depart from the positivistic scientific tradition that has dominated social and behavioral sciences research. The term *postmodern* refers to approaches (e.g., narrative, contextual, constructivist) that emphasize the importance of understanding our careers as they are lived or, to put it another way, our subjective experience of career development. Postmodern approaches emphasize personal agency in the career construction process.

Creating Narratives

The narrative is an example of a postmodern approach that highlights personal agency in career development. Specifically, career counseling from the narrative approach emphasizes understanding and articulating the main character to be lived out in a specific career plot (Cochran, 1997). This type of articulation uses the process of composing a narrative as the primary vehicle for defining the character and plot. Howard (1989) noted that

> people tell themselves stories that infuse certain parts of their lives and actions with great meaning and de-emphasize other aspects. But had any of them chosen to tell himself or herself a somewhat different story, the resulting pattern of more meaningful and less-meaningful aspects of his or her life would have been quite different. (p. 168)

Cochran (1997) identified several ways in which narratives help people make meaning out of their life experiences:

- A narrative provides a temporal organization, integrating a beginning, middle, and end into a whole. Such temporal organization offers the possibility of establishing personal continuity over a lifetime.
- A story is a synthetic structure that configures an indefinite expansion of elements and spheres of elements into a whole. A narrative is a "meaning structure that organizes events and human actions into a whole, thereby attributing significance to individual actions and events according to their effect on the whole" (Polkinghorne, 1988, p. 18).
- The plot of a narrative carries a point. The structure of a narrative communicates a problem to be overcome (beginning), attempts at resolving the problem (middle), and an ending that, if positive, represents a solution to the problem or, if negative, represents a resignation to the problem.

Career counseling from a narrative approach begins with the identification of a *career problem*, defined as a gap between one's current career situation and a desired career future (Cochran, 1985). In the narrative sense, the career problem is the beginning; the middle relates to the way in which one is to move from the beginning to an end (Cochran, 1997). The career counseling process involves a number of "episodes" that are incorporated into counseling, depending on each client's career concerns. Cochran (1997) identified seven episodes of career counseling:

1. elaborating a career problem
2. composing a life history
3. founding a future narrative
4. constructing reality
5. changing a life structure
6. enacting a role
7. crystallizing a decision.

Narrative approaches to career interventions highlight the notion that we are the stories that we live. Career counseling provides clients with opportunities to reconstruct a coherent life story. "Stories of self and career can be used by counselor and client to consolidate present self-knowledge and to help guide forward movement into anticipated futures" (Peavy, 1992, p. 219).

Contextualizing Career Development

Evident in the discussion thus far is the fact that postmodern approaches to career development interventions are sensitive to the immediate (e.g., family, cultural heritage, level of acculturation) and distal (e.g., economics, environmental opportunities) contextual factors that influence individual processes of creating meaning (Blustein, 1994; Vondracek, Lerner, & Schulenberg, 1986; Young et al., 1996). Postmodern approaches that identify ways in which contextual factors can be incorporated into the career counseling process are *contextual career theories*. Young et al. (1996) noted five assumptions pertaining to contextual career theories:

1. Acts are viewed as purposive and as being directed toward specific goals.
2. Acts are embedded in their context.
3. Change has a prominent role in career development.
4. Because events take shape as people engage in practical action with a particular purpose, analysis and interpretation always are practical. Researchers look at action for a particular purpose.
5. Contextualism rejects a theory of truth based on the correspondence between mental representations and objective reality.

In their contextual theory, Young and Collin (1992) viewed career development as an action system that achieves social meaning through an interaction between individual intention and social context. In their view, we construct our careers through action, which can be organized according to hierarchical, sequential, and parallel dimensions (Young et al., 1996). *Hierarchy* relates to the prioritization of career goals into superordinate and subordinate construct categories. *Sequence* pertains to the ordering of actions, which can be *parallel* in that "different actions for different goals can coexist" (Young et al., 1996, p. 484).

Thus, career and action are related constructs through which people make sense of their lives and through which events in people's lives acquire meaning (Young & Valach, 1996). Of special import are goal-directed actions that people take in the process of constructing a career. Such actions can be viewed from three perspectives: (a) manifest behavior (i.e., the explicit career-related behavior), (b) conscious cognition (i.e., thoughts and feelings related to the manifest behavior), and (c) social meaning (i.e., the meaning of the action to self and others). The three perspectives provide a framework both for explaining career development and for explaining career development interventions. Concerning the latter, we can view client–counselor interactions as manifest behaviors. Client–counselor thoughts and feelings represent conscious cognitions concerning the behaviors being manifested, and both clients and counselors are embedded in contexts from which they create social meaning from the career counseling experience.

Career counseling thus represents a project involving joint action between the counselor and client. Career and action emerge as the counselor and client engage in the career counseling process (Young & Valach, 1996). To bring important contextual information into the career counseling process, Young and associates made two additional recommendations. First, they suggested that career development practitioners consider conducting their career counseling in settings in which career action actually occurs (e.g., the workplace). Second, they recommended involving the client's significant others in the career counseling process.

Constructivist Career Counseling

A theme connecting Cochran's narrative approach and the contextual theory of Young and associates is that people are active organizers of their own experiences. People construct meaning through the decisions that they make and the actions that they take. This theme forms the basic assumption undergirding Kelly's (1955) theory of personal constructs. Peavy (1992, p. 215) draws on Kelly's theory in identifying four questions that are important for career counselors to consider in *constructivist career counseling*:

1. How can I form a cooperative alliance with this client? (relationship factor)
2. How can I encourage the self-helpfulness of this client? (agency factor)

3. How can I help this client elaborate and evaluate his or her constructions and meanings germane to this decision? (meaning-making factor)
4. How can I help this client reconstruct and negotiate personally meaningful and socially supportable realities? (negotiation factor)

Herr and Cramer (1996) noted that Peavy's questions connect with Cochran's (1997) view that "agency in career, the willingness to act, to bring something about, to achieve life goals, should be the prime topic in career theory" (p. 191). This view, in turn, is consistent with Kelly's (1955) personal construct theory. Particularly useful here is Kelly's (1955) notion that personal constructs cohere to form a matrix of meaning or a system of hierarchically organized dimensions that can be adjusted to a range of events (Neimeyer, 1992). This assumption led to the development of several intervention techniques aimed at exploring and reconstructing the client's unique matrix of meaning. One such technique is the *laddering technique*, which Neimeyer (1992) described as a strategy for helping clients identify their more important (superordinate) and less important (subordinate) constructs.

A more elaborate technique for identifying personal constructs is the *vocational reptest*. Based on Kelly's (1955) Role Construct Repertory Test, the reptest requires clients to systematically compare and contrast a set of career-related elements (e.g., occupations). By considering several occupations at a time, clients identify ways in which two are similar, but different from the third. Then clients provide ratings for each of the occupations along each of the constructs they identified. Neimeyer (1992) noted that "when completed, the vocational reptest provides a useful window into the unique considerations that each person brings to bear in career decision making, as well as the interrelationship among those considerations" (p. 166).

From the constructivist perspective, career counseling outcomes are considered in terms of their "fruitfulness." Fruitfulness refers to the assumption that counseling should result in a changed outlook or new perspective on some aspect of life (Peavy, 1992). Career development interventions are framed as "experiments" conducted both in session and out of session that are directed toward helping clients think, feel, and act more productively in relation to their career concerns. Peavy noted that experiments can be conducted in the imagination of the client (e.g., guided fantasy), by engaging the client in critical self-reflection (e.g. laddering technique), simulation or vicarious experiences (e.g., role playing or skill learning), and "real world" experiences (e.g., job shadowing, job interviewing).

Conclusion

The emerging career development theories discussed in this chapter reflect the vitality within the field. Moreover, the theories fill numerous gaps in the literature. Strengths inherent in the emerging theories include the fact that (a) the theoretical propositions espoused often apply to diverse college student populations, (b) most emerging theories have clear links with practice, and (c) many of the emerging theories incorporate and extend the theory and research base of preexisting theories (e.g., Bandura, 1986; Kelly, 1955; Rokeach, 1973). Not surprisingly, there is the need for more extensive research testing the theoretical propositions and the practical applications of emerging career theories.

References

Bandura, A. (1969). *Principles of behavior modification*. New York: Holt, Rinehart and Winston.

Bandura, A. (1977). *Social learning theory*. Englewood Cliffs, NJ: Prentice-Hall.

Bandura, A. (1986). *Social foundations of thought and action: A social cognitive theory*. Englewood Cliffs, NJ: Prentice-Hall.

Beck, A. T. (1987). *Beck Depression Inventory*. New York: Guilford.

Blustein, D. L. (1994). "Who am I?" The question of self and identity in career development. In M. L. Savickas & R. W. Lent (Eds.), *Convergence in career development theories: Implications for science and practice* (pp. 139–154). Palo Alto, CA: Consulting Psychologists Press.

Brown, D. (1995). A values-based model for facilitating career transitions. *Career Development Quarterly, 44*, 4–11.

Brown, D. (1996). Brown's values-based, holistic model of career and life-role choices and satisfaction. In D. Brown, L. Brooks, & Assoc. (Eds.), *Career choice and development* (3rd ed., pp. 337–372). San Francisco: Jossey-Bass.

Brown, D., & Brooks, L. (1996). *Career counseling techniques*. Needham Heights, MA: Allyn & Bacon.

Brown, D., & Crace, R. K. (1996). Values in life role choices and outcomes: A conceptual model. *Career Development Quarterly, 44*, 211–223.

Brown, S. D., & Lent, R. W. (1996). A social cognitive framework for career choice counseling. *Career Development Quarterly, 44*, 354–366.

Cochran, L. (1985). *Position and nature of personhood*. Westport, CT: Greenwood.

Cochran, L. (1997). *Career counseling: A narrative approach*. Thousand Oaks: Sage Publications.

Crace, R. K., & Brown, D. (1996). *Life Values Inventory*. Minneapolis, MN: National Computer Systems.

Hackett, G., & Betz, N. E. (1981). A self-efficacy approach to the career development of women. *Journal of Vocational Behavior, 18*, 326–329.

Hackett, G., & Byars, A. M. (1996). Social cognitive theory and the career development of African American women. *Career Development Quarterly, 44*, 322–340.

Herr, E. L., & Cramer, S. H. (1996). *Career guidance and counseling through the lifespan* (5th ed.). New York: HarperCollins.

Howard, G. S. (1989). *A tale of two stories: Excursions into a narrative approach to psychology*. Notre Dame, IN: Academic Publications.

Janis, I. L., & Mann, L. (1977). *A psychological analysis of conflict, choice and commitment*. New York: Free Press.

Kelly, G. A. (1955). *A theory of personality: The psychology of personal constructs*. New York: Norton.

Krumboltz, J. D. (1976). A social learning theory of career choice. *Counseling Psychologist, 6*, 71–80.

Krumboltz, J. D. (1988). *Career Beliefs Inventory*. Palo Alto, CA: Consulting Psychologists Press.

Krumboltz, J. D. (1994). Improving career development theory from a social learning perspective. In M. L. Savickas, & R. W. Lent (Eds.), *Convergence in career development theories* (pp. 9–32). Palo Alto, CA: Consulting Psychologists Press.

Krumboltz, J. D. (1996). *A social learning theory of career counseling.* Stanford, CA: Stanford University Press.

Krumboltz, J. D., Mitchell, A., & Gelatt, H. G. (1976). Applications of social learning theory of career selection. *Focus on Guidance, 8,* 1–16.

Lent, R. W., & Brown, S. D. (1996). Social cognitive approach to career development: An overview. *Career Development Quarterly, 44,* 310–321.

Lent, R. W., Brown, S. D., & Hackett, G. (1996). Career development from a social cognitive perspective. In D. Brown, L. Brooks, & Assoc. (Eds.), *Career choice and development* (3rd ed., pp. 373–416). San Francisco: Jossey-Bass.

Lent, R. W., & Hackett, G. (1987). Career self-efficacy: Empirical status and future directions. *Journal of Vocational Behavior, 30,* 347–382.

Meichenbaum, D. (1977). *Cognitive behavior modification.* Morristown, NJ: General Learning Press.

Mitchell, L. K., & Krumboltz, J. D. (1984). Social learning approach to career decision making: Krumboltz's theory. In D. Brown, L. Brooks, & Assoc. (Eds.), *Career choice and development* (2nd ed., pp. 235—280). San Francisco: Jossey-Bass.

Mitchell, L. K. & Krumboltz, J. D. (1996). Krumboltz's learning theory of career choice counseling. In D. Brown, L. Brooks, & Assoc. (Eds.), *Career choice and development* (3rd ed., pp. 233–276). San Francisco: Jossey-Bass.

Neimeyer, G. J. (1992). Personal constructs and vocational structure: A critique of poor status. In R. A. Neimeyer & G. J. Neimeyer (Eds.), *Advances in personal construct psychology* (pp. 91–120). Greenwich, CT: JAI Press.

Peavy, R. V. (1992). A constructivist model of training for career counselors. *Journal of Career Development, 18,* 215–228.

Peterson, G. W., Sampson, J. P., Jr., & Reardon, R. C. (1991). *Career development and services: A cognitive approach.* Pacific Grove, CA: Brooks/Cole.

Peterson, G. W., Sampson, J. P., Jr., & Reardon, R. C. (1996). A cognitive information processing approach to career problem solving and decision making. In D. Brown, L. Brooks, & Assoc. (Eds.), *Career choice and development* (3rd ed., pp. 423–467). San Francisco: Jossey-Bass.

Polkinghorne, D. E. (1988). *Narrative knowing and the human sciences.* Albany: State University of New York Press.

Rokeach, M. (1973). *The nature of human values.* New York: Free Press.

Sampson, J. P., Jr., Peterson, G. W., Lenz, J. G., & Reardon, R. C. (1992). A cognitive approach to career services: Translating concepts into practice. *Career Development Quarterly, 41,* 67–74.

Super, D. E. (1953). A theory of vocational development. *American Psychologist, 30,* 88–92.

Super, D. E. (1957). *The psychology of careers.* New York: Harper & Row.

Super, D. E. (1990). A life-span, life-space approach to career development. In D. Brown, L. Brooks, & Assoc. (Eds.), *Career choice and development: Applying contemporary theories to practice* (2nd ed., pp. 197–261), San Francisco: Jossey-Bass.

Super, D. E., & Nevill, D. D. (1985). *Values scale.* Palo Alto, CA: Consulting Psychologists Press.

Vondracek, F. W., Lerner, R. M., & Schulenberg, S. E. (1986). *Career development: A life-span developmental approach.* Hillsdale, NJ: Erlbaum.

Young, R. A., & Collin, A. (Eds.) (1992). *Interpreting career: Hermeneutical studies of lives in context.* Westport, CT: Praeger.

Young, R. A., & Valach, L. (1996). Interpretation and action in career counseling. In M. L. Savickas & W. B. Walsh (Eds.), *Handbook of career counseling theory and practice.* Palo Alto, CA: Davies-Black Consulting Psychologist Press.

Young, R.A., Valach, L., & Collin A. (1996). A contextual explanation of career. In D. Brown, L. Brooks, & Assoc. (Eds.), *Career choice and development.* (3rd ed., pp. 477–508). San Francisco: Jossey-Bass.

3

Emotional–Social Issues in the Provision of Career Counseling

Donna Palladino Schultheiss

For more than a decade, there has been a movement to view career counseling and personal counseling as an integrated whole. Theoretical and practical advances have been proposed as a means to incorporate the career and noncareer domains of functioning into therapeutic work. Integration of the client's psychological, emotional, and social concerns with issues within the career domain has been conceived of as a more comprehensive framework for counseling. Given that late adolescents and young adults are immersed in multiple concurrent developmental challenges and transitions, it has been proposed here that an integrated view of personal and career issues is crucial for the career counseling of college students. In fact, this interface has particular relevance for students who are simultaneously striving toward self-definition, purpose, and connectedness. An exploration of the embedded nature of career development tasks within the broader context of late-adolescent development would inform counseling practice with traditional-aged college students. Therefore, a call is made for a more focused research and practice agenda that attends to the interconnected nature of students' developmental, psychological, and social issues within the career development process. Thus, the focus of this chapter is to present an integrated view of career development that incorporates the interconnected nature of career development and late-adolescent emotional and social functioning.

This comprehensive view of counseling across the career and noncareer domains reinforces many of Super's (1951, 1963, 1980) key theoretical ideas underlying his life span developmental theory. For example, Super's (1951) emphasis on the importance of both the rational and affective aspects of the vocational counseling process is reflected in his assertion that when counseling a person on career choice and adjustment, one essentially performs both personal and career counseling. Super's (1963) self-concept theory also is consistent with the importance of self-knowledge in the career development process, with career choice representing an implementation of the self-concept. In fact, Super (1988) advocated for a synthesis of vocational and personal counseling to help the client develop and accept an integrated and satisfying self-concept in the world of work. The developmental life stage model and multiple-role concepts in Super's (1980) life–career rainbow also are supported in the integrated views of counseling.

The centrality of career and personal issues for our clients, together with the historically embedded nature of career development within the field of counseling psychology, has generated a number of important theoretical contributions. For example, Wrenn (1988) discussed the need for career counseling to be less focused on the informational aspects of work and more on the psychological aspects of clients. He contended that it is essential to relate to clients as "dynamic wholes" that are composed of many related dimensions. Kidd (1998) recently echoed this view, pointing out that feelings are rarely elaborated on in theories of career development and advocated for a greater emphasis on the role of emotions in theory and practice. Manuele-Adkins (1992) also argued in favor of increased attention to the affective and psychological issues confronting clients with career problems. Similarly, Hackett (1993) asserted that the most pressing task is to determine how to more effectively integrate career counseling and therapy without losing sight of vocational issues and concerns.

Betz and Corning (1993) viewed career and personal counseling as inseparable and advocated a holistic philosophy of counseling that recognized the "whole person" as a constellation of many roles and activities. Richardson (1996) acknowledged and supported this view of moving toward a more holistic conception of the person. She discussed "false splits" between domains of functioning and argued against the idea that aspects of self-experience can be considered independent of the whole constellation of self. She suggested that we bring the locus of work out of the occupational structure and locate it in people's lives to recognize the wholeness and multiplicity of our roles and functioning.

Although these issues have been discussed in some detail in the literature (e.g., Blustein & Spengler, 1995), few have attempted to articulate a conceptual framework to guide integrative treatment. Furthermore, a comprehensive exploration of these interrelated domains has been lacking. Although attention in the literature to the interface of work and psychological well-being has increased, most of this work has focused almost exclusively on adult work concerns (for a review, see Myers & Cairo, 1992). In fact, career counselors and vocational researchers may have a tendency to assume that the career and personal concerns of adult clients are more intertwined than those of high school and college students (Haverkamp & Moore, 1993; Phillips, Friedlander, Kost, Specterman, & Robbins, 1988). Similarly, it has been implied that adult clients would be more likely than younger clients to benefit from a broad counseling perspective that integrates both domains (Phillips et al., 1988). This separation or split in the literature concerning the work–nonwork interface has been commented on elsewhere (Swanson, 1992).

One factor that may contribute to the lack of integration between career counseling and personal counseling on college campuses is that many college career counselors do not have advanced training in psychotherapy. As a result, many counselors may be reluctant to discuss personal issues with their clients. Even if career counselors are not fully trained in psychotherapy, there is still a need to acknowledge how personal issues influence career exploration and decision making. Thus, even counselors without psychotherapy training can discuss the importance of other life issues with their clients and incorporate those issues into counseling.

The most significant context for the study of these career and noncareer issues is late-adolescent psychosocial development. In particular, identity development, the renegotiation of parental bonds, the initiation of mature interpersonal and intimate relationships, and adjustment to college present the most prominent normative psychosocial developmental tasks and challenges facing students during the college-age years. Each of these processes has crucial implications for one's ability to progress effectively and succeed within the career domain. Thus, a view of career development that encompasses the multifaceted dimensions of identity development, the role of relationships, and college student development and adjustment will be the focal point of this chapter. This chapter begins with a summary of the current literature within these overlapping domains of functioning, explores a new perspective to guide practice, and offers implications for counselor training.

Identity Development

Identity development has been identified as a core therapeutic issue in counseling late-adolescent college students (Hamachek, 1988). According to Erikson (1968), *ego identity formation* refers to a process of personal exploration and the formulation of a coherent set of attitudes, values, and beliefs. Compelling evidence suggests that individual differences in identity formation during the college-age years are related to patterns of personal adjustment (Waterman, 1985) and to vocational behavior (Blustein, Devenis, & Kidney, 1989). Blustein et al. provided empirical support for the relationship between the exploration and commitment processes that characterize one's identity formation and career development tasks. Their findings suggested that occupational commitment is inversely associated with the ego identity status of moratorium (i.e., those individuals who are actively involved in personal exploration, but have yet to commit to the various dimensions of identity). This suggests that individuals who are exploring their identity also tend to be in the planning phase of decision making. Blustein et al.'s findings also indicated that career exploration is positively associated with the exploration and commitment of the moratorium and identity-achieved statuses (i.e., those individuals who have committed to following active personal exploration) and inversely related to the diffusion status (i.e., those individuals who have not engaged in exploration and who have not committed to the dimensions of identity).

Blustein and Phillips (1990) provided data to support the relationship between ego identity status and decision-making styles. They found that those who have achieved a stable identity tend to use rational and systematic decision-making strategies (i.e., strategies that rely on logical or planning processes; Harren, 1979; Johnson, 1978). Those in the foreclosed identity status (i.e., those who have not engaged in exploration but have nonetheless committed to an identity) tend to rely on dependent strategies (i.e., they project responsibility for decisions onto others; Harren, 1979) and not on systematic and internal strategies. The diffusion status was related to intuitive (i.e., spontaneous) and dependent styles and an absence of systematic and internal styles. Hence, the authors concluded that their findings provide initial support for the notion that variations in decision-making strategies may be associated with developmental progress in late adolescence.

Savickas (1985) demonstrated that successful resolution of the identity crisis is associated with higher levels of career maturity and with clearer vocational goals and abilities. Wallace-Broscious, Serafica, and Osipow (1994) investigated the relationship among career maturity, development of self-concept, and identity formation in high school students. Self-concept and identity variables were related in predictable ways to career certainty, career planning, and career indecision. More specifically, self-concept was positively related to career certainty and career planning and negatively related to career indecision. Identity achievement was positively associated with career decidedness and career planning, and the moratorium and diffusion statuses were negatively related to career planning and decision making. Therefore, those who have progressed further in identity formation are likely to be more decided in their career choices and more directed and purposeful in their career planning. Identity status emerged as a stronger predictor of career maturity than self-concept. Neither self-concept nor identity was significantly associated with career exploration.

As apparent in the preceding review, significant empirical support exists for the relationship between identity formation and vocational behavior. Therefore, those college students who are able to formulate a personally meaningful set of attitudes, values, and beliefs also are in a good position to progress effectively within the career domain. Hence, several implications for counseling practice emerge from the findings. There is support to suggest that counselors might benefit their clients by intervening to facilitate the exploration and commitment needed for identity development and career development. For example, values clarification exercises along with personal exploration of attitudes and beliefs could be explored in counseling. In addition, the counseling relationship could provide a safe environment for introspective work and risk taking. Through the therapeutic relationship, clients might feel the comfort and empowerment needed to explore and challenge previously held ideals in order to develop a more personally meaningful set of beliefs. Counselors also might support clients in experimenting with new behaviors in novel environments as a means of discovering new or unfamiliar aspects of their personal identity. This introspective work can benefit clients by equipping them with a more crystallized view of themselves as they proceed in the exploration and decision-making tasks essential to career development. Specifically, clients would come to hold clearer views of their abilities and vocational goals, be more purposeful in their career planning, and hold more certainty with regard to their career choices. Thus, this therapeutic approach would place clients in a better position to make career decisions that best match their self-definitions.

Psychosocial Development

Chickering (1969), who has had a major impact on college student development, also presented a useful framework within which to consider personal and career adjustment. The theory proposed by Chickering (1969) and Chickering and Reisser (1993), which focuses on the psychosocial development of college students, provides a useful theoretical framework for viewing the challenges associated with the career and noncareer domains of functioning. Their major contributions—which have had a major impact on higher education, student affairs, and college counseling—concern the practical applications of the theory to psychoeducational practices designed to promote student development.

Chickering (1969) and Chickering and Reisser (1993) provided an extension and elaboration of Erikson's (1968) work on psychosocial identity development. One of Chickering's main intentions was to propose a more refined developmental framework to facilitate healthy functioning across domains. Such a framework could contribute to the counselor's ability to accurately assess client problems, evaluate the interaction between personal and career domains, and intervene to facilitate growth across the two domains. The theory is notable for its level of specificity and propensity to bridge the gap between late-adolescent developmental theory and practice.

To introduce greater specificity into the identity construct, Chickering (1969) described and later revised (Chickering & Reisser, 1993) seven dimensions of college student psychosocial development:

1. Developing Competence, which includes intellectual, physical or manual, and interpersonal competence
2. Managing Emotions, which involves an increasing awareness and acceptance of a full range of feelings, understanding what causes them, and learning to counteract negative feelings with positive ones
3. Moving Through Autonomy toward Interdependence, a process that refers to the importance of interdependence on the road to emotional and instrumental independence
4. Developing Mature Interpersonal Relationships, which is a shift in relationships toward greater trust, independence, and individuality that occurs with the achievement of greater autonomy and a firmer sense of identity
5. Establishing Identity, which encompasses all of the other dimensions and includes the discovery and confirmation of one's core characteristics

6. Developing Purpose, which involves clarifying vocational plans, persistence toward goals, developing priorities based on personal interests, and making lifestyle choices

7. Developing Integrity, which is the clarification of an internally consistent personal set of beliefs that provide a guide for behavior.

Some evidence (Schultheiss & Blustein, 1994) suggests that progress in psychosocial development is related to healthier adolescent functioning. Career exploration and decision making, two primary career development tasks facing college students, play an integral role in late-adolescent and young-adult psychosocial development. In fact, there is empirical support for a positive relationship between the dimension of Developing Purpose and career planning and exploration (Winston, 1990). This finding suggests that students who developmentally have progressed further in formulating clear and realistic future plans and goals also report having progressed further within the career domain. Progress in the tasks associated with the development of autonomy, purpose, and mature interpersonal relationships also has been related to the degree of active involvement in career exploration and career decision making, academic self-concept (Winston & Polkosnik, 1986), and study habits (Winston, 1990). Moreover, Winston and Polkosnik demonstrated a relationship between developing mature interpersonal relationships and academic locus of control. In other words, students who engage in relationships characterized by greater trust, independence, and individuality also tend to perceive that they have more control over successful academic performance.

These findings lend credence to the interconnected nature of psychosocial and career development tasks for college students. It seems apparent that students who are clear on their purpose in life—and are increasingly able to make conscious choices based on a defined set of values and beliefs—also will be more persistent in reaching all of their goals, including those specific to their career.

Students face numerous challenges and decisions that will influence the life they will lead after completing college. Those who have progressed further in developing purpose are better able to plan and persist despite the inevitable obstacles. Similarly, those who have a defined set of personal goals and values are in a better position to be motivated, actively involved in their career development process, and more confident in their actions. Those who are free from ongoing needs for reassurance, affection, and approval are more able to develop confidence in personal judgment, take more focused action, and solve problems in a more self-directed manner (Chickering & Reisser, 1993).

The development of mature relationships involves a balancing of needs for autonomy and attachment. Through relationships, students learn how to express and manage feelings, how to share on a deeper level, how to resolve differences, and how to make meaningful commitments (Chickering & Reisser, 1993). In fact, for women, the process of identity development involves intimacy and attachment to others. Gilligan (1982) and Josselson (1988) have described how women define themselves through their attachments to others. Hence, relationships have a profound effect on students' lives and their futures.

Clear implications for practice emerge from the demonstrated relationship between psychosocial development and progress within the career domain. For example, counselors could assist clients in more clearly developing their purpose in life—to facilitate career planning and career exploration. More specifically, counselors could assist clients in developing priorities based on their personal interests and support them in persevering toward their goals. Specific to the career realm, interventions aimed at the clarification of vocational plans could be accomplished by providing a safe and supportive environment and assisting clients in developing specific, realistic action plans to achieve identified career goals. Other intervention approaches might focus on helping clients balance autonomy and interdependence in interpersonal relationships. This goal might be accomplished by guiding clients in self-reflection and in the development of insight into the structure and nature of their relationships. Counselors are encouraged to attend more closely to relational factors for women, given evidence that women (more so than men) define themselves through their attachments to others (e.g., Josselson, 1988).

Embedded Identity for Career Theory

Blustein (1994) described how recent advances in the study of identity, family relationship factors, and social and environmental factors in late adolescence provide a basis for the synthesis of a number of essential concepts in career development theory. In essence, Blustein advanced the notion of an embedded identity for career theory that builds on Josselson's (1988) notion of the embedded self and other theoretical contributions that address the relational and contextual components of identity (e.g., Gilligan, 1982; Vondracek, 1992). Specifically, the *embedded identity* is referred to as one's internal experience of self-definition (i.e., self-knowledge about one's beliefs, values, attributes, and so forth), consideration of possible identity options, evaluative and emotional aspects of identity (e.g., self-esteem), and familial and sociocultural factors integrated into one's identity. Thus, the embedded identity incorporates internal and external forces that are thought to influence one's identity.

Building on this work, Blustein and Noumair (1996) further defined the concept of *embeddedness* as a means of enhancing the understanding of self and identity in career development theory in a manner that integrates relational and cultural influences. The purpose of this perspective is to offer researchers and practitioners an explicit means of integrating an important array of contextual factors into intrapersonal experience. Hence, Blustein and Noumair encouraged practitioners to carefully consider the relational and cultural aspects of experience when considering the role of identity in the career development process. They suggested that focusing on an embeddedness perspective may help integrate the role of relationships into the career domain and help bridge the artificial boundaries that exist between career counseling and counseling in the noncareer domain. More specifically, in attending to the context of self-experience, counselors can examine aspects of the client's experience that may have been overlooked using traditional approaches to self-exploration. Blustein and Noumair offered the example that clients presenting with an un-focused identity may reflect a history of inadequate relational support, and they pointed to the usefulness of providing a supportive counseling environment that explores the history and consequences of the client's relational world. They also suggested that this approach might facilitate self-exploration and thus help clients develop the self-knowledge that is crucial to the career development process.

A second application that Blustein and Noumair (1996) offered em-phasizes the importance of the cultural context in forming conceptualiza-tions of clients. For example, clients from non-Western cultures that em-phasize interdependency need to be viewed within that context to avoid viewing their self and identity as dysfunctional or problematic.

Role of Relationships

There is emerging literature on the interconnectedness of career and the quality of relationships in one's life. This work has concentrated on the role of significant attachments, or long-term enduring emotional bonds of substantial intensity (Bowlby, 1982). Hence, this chapter focuses on influ-ential family relationships rather than on friendships.

Bowlby's (1982) work provided a useful theoretical perspective for un-derstanding the function of attachment relationships. According to Bowlby, individuals at any age are better adjusted when they have confidence in the accessibility and responsiveness of a trusted other. A number of the-orists (e.g., Josselson, 1988; Kenny, 1990) have argued that an adaptive level of attachment between late adolescents and their parents may be beneficial for developmental progress and adjustment. Drawing on the work of Bowlby (1982) and Ainsworth (1989), a number of investigators have suggested that parental attachment may facilitate the sort of risk taking and exploration that characterizes the developmental tasks of late adolescence and young adulthood (e.g., Grotevant & Cooper, 1985, 1988; Kenny, 1990). More specifically, evidence indicates that an adaptive level of attachment between late adolescents and their parents may be posi-tively related to career development and vocational functioning (Blustein, Walbridge, Friedlander, & Palladino, 1991; Kenny, 1990).

Research has explored the association between attachment and career planning (Kenny, 1990) and progress in commitment to career choices (Blustein et al., 1991). The results of Blustein et al. suggested that women who experience conflictual independence (i.e., freedom from excessive guilt, anxiety, mistrust, responsibility, inhibition, resentment, and anger in relation to parents; Hoffman, 1984) from—and attachment to—both parents also tend to show greater commitment to their career choices and less of a tendency to foreclose. For men, the relationship with their fathers was somewhat more influential than the relationship with their mothers. Men who experienced relatively greater attitudinal independence (i.e., the development of one's own attitudes, values, and beliefs that may or may not be the same as one's parents; Hoffman, 1984) from their fathers tended to be relatively uncommitted with respect to their career choices. In addition, men with some degree of attachment to their fathers, coupled with conflictual independence from their fathers, tended to be relatively more committed to their career choices.

O'Brien and Fassinger (1993) provided evidence to suggest that adolescent women with a close attachment to their mothers tended to report affirmative values about their career pursuits. Support for the association between attachment and career self-efficacy (i.e., confidence in one's abilities in self-appraisal, goal selection, future planning, problem solving, and knowledge of occupational information), career orientation, and congruence of career choice was demonstrated by O'Brien (1996) in the initial phase of a longitudinal investigation studying high school women. The findings from the longitudinal follow-up study further supported the positive association between attachment to parents and career self-efficacy (O'Brien, Friedman, Lin, & Tipton, 1997).

Ketterson and Blustein (1997) provided evidence to support a significant positive association between attachment to parents and environmental exploration, but not self-exploration. Ryan, Solberg, and Brown (1996) found that for women, attachment to mother and degree of family dysfunction (i.e., overinvolvement, role reversal, conflict) was associated in predictable ways with career search self-efficacy. For men, only attachment to the mother was significantly associated with career search self-efficacy.

Attachment relationships with significant siblings also have been associated with progress in the career development tasks of college students. Schultheiss (1998) provided evidence to suggest that attachment to father, attachment to siblings, and negative interactions with siblings were associated in predictable ways with the tendency to foreclose as well as vocational exploration and commitment. Those findings suggest that those individuals who report stronger attachments to their father and most important sibling—together with few negative interactions with siblings— are less likely to foreclose on a career decision and more likely to experience a greater commitment to their career choices.

Although traditional models of career decision making have focused on the role of reason and independent judgment, Phillips (1997) described a number of ways in which one might redefine notions of adaptive career decision making to include approaches that use relationships with others as a central resource in the decision-making process. Support for this notion is provided by Phillips, Christopher, and Lisi (1998), who used a qualitative analytic approach to provide a view of the role of relationships in career decision making. Using data from interviews with young adults who had recently made significant career decisions in the transition from school to work, the investigators uncovered themes that reflected different ways in which others involve themselves (actions of others), are invoked by the decider (recruitment of others), or are excluded from an individual's deliberations (pushing others away). As Phillips et al. suggested, these themes provide a view of the many ways in which relationships with others are used in the decision-making process.

In a qualitative investigation of the role of attachment relationships in the career development process, Schultheiss (1998) assessed the role of college students' experiences of their relationships on their career exploration and decision-making processes. This investigation provided a more in-depth examination of the facilitative factors associated with precisely how relationships are influential in the career development process. Support, personality characteristics, direct educational or career assistance, role model influences, and confidence in abilities were all identified as important factors in participants' descriptions of how their relationships with their mother, father, and siblings were influential in their career decision making. Several differences emerged across relationships. Participants reported that mothers emphasized education and offered direct assistance with educational tasks, emphasized the financial aspects of career choice, and were responsible for influential childhood experiences. Fathers were reported to be a source of career information and were more frequently supportive by providing freedom to explore, make decisions, and learn from mistakes.

The findings presented here offer support for career counselors to attend to the relational lives of their clients. Although some initial evidence indicates that the association between relationships and progress in career development is more pronounced for women than for men, more research is needed to clarify these gender differences. Thus, although counselors might attend more closely to relational factors for women than for men, the current literature suggests that both men and women would benefit from interventions that have a relational basis. Counselors are encouraged to assess the quality and availability of relational resources in their clients' lives and to assist clients in accessing and using significant others as emotional resources as they approach novel and potentially anxiety-producing challenges within the career domain. Counselors also might intervene to help clients improve conflicted relationships or establish new, healthier alliances to enrich their relational world and potential for support.

College Student Adjustment

As is evident from the preceding review, the college years are replete with personal and developmental challenges, transitions, and adjustments. Late adolescents are intimately involved in self-definition in both the personal and vocational realms as they renegotiate their familiar bonds with parents and establish new ones with friends and intimates. For some students, leaving home to attend college may be the first time that they are faced with a completely novel environment separate from the familiar emotional, social, and instrumental supports of home. Indeed, for many students this can be an exciting time, albeit an uncertain and anxiety-producing one. Hence, all of these issues undoubtedly have a profound impact on the student's emotional and social well-being and on his or her ability to progress effectively in his or her career. Although one might hypothesize that a positive relationship exists between the student's social–emotional functioning and ability to progress within the career realm, research is lacking to support this contention. In fact, empirical research examining the association between college adjustment and progress in career development clearly is needed to guide an integrated practice perspective.

The primary focus in the empirical literature concerning college student adjustment has been on the influence of family dynamics (e.g., Lopez, 1991; Lopez, Campbell, & Watkins, 1989). Attachment theory (Ainsworth, 1989; Bowlby, 1982) has been used to explain the facilitative nature of close and supportive parental relationships. Kenny and Rice (1995) offered an excellent overview of the relevance of the attachment model for understanding how attachments assist with the developmental and adjustment challenges that adolescent college students typically face. They described how attachment theory has been used to help explain how parental closeness can serve as a protective source of security throughout adolescence. In effect, the attachment model stresses the importance of supportive and interdependent relationships during periods of stress and anxiety. Furthermore, theoretical formulations (e.g., Gilligan, 1982; Josselson, 1988) implicate gender differences in the role that attachment relationships play in development. In particular, the centrality of relationships and emotional closeness in women's lives has been highlighted in feminist relational theory (Josselson, 1988).

Much of the empirical work (e.g., Kenny & Donaldson, 1991, 1992) on college student adjustment and attachment relationships has focused on the transition away from home and beginning college. Research has suggested that adolescents who are securely attached to their parents are able to more easily negotiate the process of individuation and adjust to new situations, including the college environment (Grotevant & Cooper, 1985). Thus, the relational context through which adolescents separate from their families might influence the late adolescent's ability to adjust to the emotional and career development demands of college. For example, Kenny and Donaldson (1991) found that for women, close parental attachments within a family structure that supports individuation are likely to be related to higher levels of social competence and fewer psychological symptoms (i.e., fewer of those symptoms most frequently reported by people seeking outpatient counseling and therapy such as depression and anxiety). Their results were insignificant with the male sample, suggesting that attachment relationships are more influential in the adjustment of women than of men.

Rice and Whaley (1994) reported similar findings related to gender, discovering that for women, attachment to both parents was associated with academic, interpersonal, and emotional well-being. For the men in their sample, only attachment to father was significantly associated with adjustment, and only during high-distress periods shortly before the end of the semester. Kenny and Donaldson (1992) offered further support for the relationship between secure parental attachment and adjustment to college for women; they found that women who reported close attachments with their parents, together with conflictual independence and attitudinal dependence, also reported better academic and personal adjustment.

Lapsley, Rice, and Fitzgerald (1990) provided evidence that supports the relationship between attachment and personal and social identity, and adjustment to college, finding that these relationships were stronger for upperclass students than for first-year students. Rice, Fitzgerald, Whaley, and Gibbs (1995) found support for the importance of current and past perceptions of attachment in late-adolescent development and adjustment. Attachment to parents was positively associated with a variety of concurrent indexes of college student adjustment. Furthermore, attachment assessed during the freshman year was positively associated with academic and emotional adjustment in the junior year. Rice, Cunningham, and Young (1997) recently found support for the association among parental attachment, emotional adjustment, and social competence. Their findings suggested that the relationship between parental attachment and emotional adjustment was mediated by social competence. This model fit reasonably well for both White and Black students, regardless of gender.

As presented here, the literature on college student adjustment supports interventions that are sensitive to the influential role of attachment relationships. A similar theme related to gender differences in the association of attachment and career development emerges within the college student adjustment domain. Initial support exists for the theoretical assumptions concerning the importance of relationships in women's development and adjustment.

A Relational Career Counseling Perspective

A relational career counseling perspective is offered as a framework for incorporating the integral relationship between problems in career development and emotional and interpersonal concerns. In essence, the client's relational context is used as the interconnected base across the personal and career domains. Drawing on Blustein's (1994) concept of the embedded identity for career theory, a novel approach of assessing and intervening in the personal and career domains of college student functioning is proposed. This approach uses a relational lens through which to view and intervene in the facilitation of healthy functioning across domains. Given the research supporting the facilitative nature of significant relational networks in identity development (Lopez, 1992), career development (Blustein, Prezioso, & Schultheiss, 1995), and adjustment (Kenny & Rice, 1995), it is important to begin work with student clients by assessing their relational context. One model based on the work of Schultheiss (1998) illustrates this approach with the intention of generating further developments in this area.

Inquiry into the role of significant relationships in career development might begin by having the client identify the relationship that has been most influential in his or her career exploration and decision making. The interview progresses by exploring in depth how this and other significant relationships (e.g., with parents, the most important sibling, and other siblings), have influenced or impacted the client's career exploration and decision-making. Clients are encouraged to discuss the specific influential aspects (including psychological aspects) or qualities of their relationships that are influential. This exploration should include positive or facilitative factors, along with inquiry into important conflictual or challenging relationship dimensions. An examination of past decision-making processes— including any reliance on others for support, advice, or information—also is useful.

Explicit information might be obtained by asking clients to describe a difficult career decision that they have had to make and to recount the role of relationships in that decision. This process would include a discussion of who, if anyone, was a source of support or conflict. Examining difficult career decisions may help clients focus on a specific example and allow them to extrapolate from it. Often, interesting patterns in relational influence emerge with this inquiry. For example, as reported in Schultheiss (1998), some participants revealed that certain relationships (i.e., father, coworker) were more important at critical times (i.e., of importance or distress), whereas other relationships (i.e., mother, most important sibling) were more salient at all other times. One example is a client who heretofore describes her mother as most influential and supportive and her father as playing a more peripheral role. When asked about a difficult career decision, she discloses that she turned to her father for information, advice, support, and guidance, and not her mother. Thus, the precise role of relationships may vary with the degree of importance placed on the career task at hand or the degree of anxiety evoked by the given challenge.

The process of revealing meaningful relational influences helps the counselor assess the relational, emotional, and supportive context within which his or her client is striving toward self-knowledge and choice. Through this process, the positive relational resources are revealed as well as the vulnerable shortcomings in the availability and accessibility of secure figures in one's life. Thus, the counselor's role is to assist the client in identifying, accessing, and using the positive relational resources that have been identified through this collaborative exploration.

For example, consider a college student who comes to career counseling with a history of functional and secure attachments. This client reveals that her older sister has been the most influential in her career exploration and decision making and that she has been an available and accessible source of support and career information. The counselor might assist this client in effectively availing herself of her sister's support and seeking it out in times of stress and when confronted with challenging exploratory and decision-making tasks. Likewise, the counselor might encourage the client to use her sister as a resource for career information and as someone to assist her with researching and accessing career guidance resources. The counselor might also suggest novel ways for this client to use her relationship with her sister as a resource. For example, one might suggest and guide the client in exploring the benefits of using her sister as a role model, a source of confidence in her abilities, or as a source of particular personality strengths or characteristics (Schultheiss, 1998).

When weaknesses emerge within a client's relational network, the counselor might intervene to assist the client in improving his or her relationships, resolving conflicts, or developing alternative sources of relational support. For example, consider a client who reports a close but conflictual relationship with his mother and father and more distant relationships with siblings. The counselor might help identify ways to resolve or improve the conflictual aspects of the client's parental relationships so that one or both of his parents might be potential relational resources. Additionally, the close aspects of his relationship with his parents could be assessed, and the client might be encouraged to draw on those positive resources that are accessible to him. Specifically, the counselor could have the client discuss the ways in which he and his parents are close and explore how this closeness might be accessed despite the conflicts that are evident in the relationship. The counselor also could inquire about the likelihood of this client reuniting with one or more of his siblings in a more close and meaningful relationship.

When few, too weak, or strained relationships exist, the counselor might guide the client in developing alternative sources of relational connection and support and help him or her understand and appreciate the positive functions of personal growth in connection with others. Extended family members, supportive teachers, advisors, or supervisors might be explored as potential sources of connection. In addition, the counseling relationship itself might be used as a source of security and support.

The preceding scenarios exemplify how the counselor can intervene across the career and noncareer domains of functioning by using the relational context as the interconnected base for case conceptualization and treatment. Through this process, the counselor can proceed with a more complete, contextualized view of relational resources and needs that could affect the client's ability to successfully accomplish career tasks. By considering and intervening across domains, the counselor can more effectively improve client functioning and enhance the clients' success in accomplishing their personal and career goals.

Based on our current knowledge of the facilitative nature of relationships, several individual and group interventions from a relational career counseling perspective may be useful. Treatment provided in a group format could use the curative factors of the group (Yalom, 1995). Specifically, cohesion and universality might aid in the development of the group as a relational resource or secure base. The group could be used to evoke a sense of relatedness among its members. Although at times this relatedness is a by-product of career development groups, it is suggested here that it be one focal point of the group. Through the group process, clients come to rely on the group as a reliable and accessible source of security in the face of anxiety evoked by uncertainty generated by the exploration of new domains and commitment to vocational choices. Similarly, group interventions, whether initially focused on the personal or career domain, could facilitate the development of insight into the personal and unique meaning of the integration of emotional and career functioning.

Both counseling groups and psychoeducational groups could be used to this end. College student development programming frequently takes place in group formats to facilitate the dissemination of information. This also might include information about how relationships can be positive resources in career development and planning. Kenny and Rice (1995) suggested that workshops for entering college students and their parents could address anticipated life changes and offer ways of negotiating a new balance between connection and autonomy in these relationships. Groups for continuing students might focus on how to access, maintain, and use one's relational network as one navigates the challenges of college life and confronts decisions important to one's future. For students who have conflicted or no parental or sibling relationships on which to rely, interventions might be directed toward the development of new bases of support (Kenny & Rice, 1995). Counselors also might encourage formal or informal mentoring between students and faculty, as well as the development of supportive peer relationships.

As discussed elsewhere (Betz & Corning, 1993; Blustein & Spengler, 1995), individual counseling interventions might assist the client in incorporating material from the personal and career domains. This type of integration would help develop and enhance a holistic view of functioning. For example, Blustein and Spengler (1995) presented a domain-sensitive approach to counseling that addresses the need to attend to both the career and noncareer domains. This domain-sensitive approach refers to client interventions that include an array of human experiences and are intended to enhance adjustment and development in both the career and noncareer domains. One defining feature of this approach is its emphasis on the context (i.e., settings that influence developmental progress, including family, social, and economic experiences; Blustein & Spengler, 1995). A second defining feature is that the approach fosters integrative treatment interventions because the counselor has the liberty to intervene across domains and to use the relationship between the career and noncareer domains to better understand and help his or her clients. In using this approach to integrative treatment, the counselor must first conceptualize the parallels and distinctions between functioning in the two domains, thereby providing clients with an opportunity to validate their life experiences across domains. Blustein and Spengler (1995) offered the following example to illustrate this concept: If a client desires to shift careers because of interpersonal conflicts at work, and a history of conflict with parents and other authority figures is revealed, the latter conflicts may become the initial focus of treatment.

Another manner in which this approach might be applied in individual counseling is to allow the counselor to serve as the "secure base" for the client to facilitate risk taking and exploration in the face of anxiety and uncertainty (Pistole, 1989). Thus, the client can eventually rely on the counselor to provide a secure relational environment within which he or she might explore new environments and experiment with new behaviors without fear of rejection or abandonment. The security that ensues would enable clients to engage in exploration that would assist in the decision-making process.

The preceding assessment and intervention practices are not intended to replace current counseling methods. Instead, these suggestions are offered to augment and enrich current career counseling practices. This approach calls for refocusing our attention on the personal and relational lives of clients. This relational lens is intended to help illuminate the complex, interconnected nature of clients' career and noncareer domains of functioning.

Training Issues

Career counseling requires skill in both career and personal counseling. Although students are traditionally trained in both areas, the challenge for faculty is to emphasize the need for cross-application of skills and to provide training opportunities for integrated practice. Certainly, it is important to help students to appreciate how the skills that are learned within each area are not mutually exclusive. As such, Brown (1985) suggested that counselor training programs need to increase students' exposure to methods of incorporating sophisticated counseling techniques into their career counseling courses. Perhaps training across domains could be accomplished by encouraging students to develop their own theory of counseling that integrates both personal and career theories. Doing so would encourage the development of an integrated theoretical approach that defines one's work. Case studies with personal and career issues for case conceptualization and treatment planning would provide further opportunity for incorporating the concepts into practice. In practica and internships, students ideally should be exposed to clients with diverse issues across domains of functioning. Eliminating separate internship experiences for career and personal counseling and creating integrated experiences might best facilitate this type of integration. Training then would need to include guidance on how to frame these interrelated issues for clients so that they can comprehend the importance of incorporating personal and career issues as well as understand the utility of attending to both in counseling. Faculty enthusiasm and modeling also are important in increasing student enthusiasm for career counseling (Hackett, 1993). Students need to see from their mentors and supervisors that this type of integration is an important and worthwhile enterprise that is essential for client growth.

Given the time-limited nature of many college counseling interventions, as well as the current managed care environment that has spurred an interest in brief and short-term interventions, new models of counseling incorporating personal and career domains need to be sensitive to time demands. Thus, particular attention should to be given to methods of integration that could be accomplished in a time-efficient manner.

Conclusion

This chapter presents evidence in support of an integrated view of college student career development that incorporates the interconnected nature of career development, identity development, the role of relationships, and college student adjustment. Research attesting to these overlapping areas of functioning clearly supports theoretical contributions calling for an interface in counseling across career and noncareer domains (Betz & Corning, 1993; Blustein & Spengler, 1995; Hackett, 1993). This type of integration appears to be particularly relevant for college students who are simultaneously striving for self-definition, relatedness, competence, and purpose. Thus, a comprehensive framework for counseling that is sensitive to the many interrelated dimensions of clients clearly will enrich our therapeutic work.

A relational career counseling perspective is a novel approach to assessment and intervention across related domains. This approach, which is based on research supporting the facilitative nature of attachment relationships in regard to development and adjustment, uses a relational lens to conceptualize and intervene in the personal, emotional, and career development challenges of college students. The client's relational context is used as the interconnected base across personal and career domains. Methods for assessing and intervening with college students using this relational perspective are offered in the hope that they may guide the practitioner in generating other novel approaches to integrated practice.

Additional research is needed that offers direct support for the relationship between emotional and social functioning and progress in career development. This work might specifically address psychological and interpersonal functioning as factors related to one's ability to successfully accomplish typical career development tasks. Furthermore, training practices that implement an integrated practice agenda need to be refined to provide a more seamless approach to counseling practice.

In summary, much can be gained from taking an integrated view of college student career counseling that incorporates personal and career issues. Theoretical and empirical support for an integrated practice perspective has become increasingly evident in the literature. Scholarly efforts aimed at developing practical frameworks to guide treatment would strengthen our conceptual understanding and improve counseling interventions designed to enhance the holistic functioning of clients.

References

Ainsworth, M. (1989). Attachments beyond infancy. *American Psychologist, 44*, 709–716.

Betz, N. E., & Corning, A. F. (1993). The inseparability of "career" and "personal" counseling. *Career Development Quarterly, 42*, 137–142.

Blustein, D. L. (1994). "Who am I?": The question of self and identity in career development. In M. L. Savickas & R. W. Lent (Eds.), *Convergence in career development theories* (pp. 139–154). Palo Alto, CA: Consulting Psychologists Press.

Blustein, D. L., Devenis, L., & Kidney, B. (1989). Relationship between the identity formation process and career development. *Journal of Counseling Psychology, 36*, 196–202.

Blustein, D. L., & Noumair, D. A. (1996). Self and identity in career development: Implications for theory and practice. *Journal of Counseling and Development, 74*, 433–441.

Blustein, D. L., & Phillips, S. D. (1990). Relation between ego identity statuses and decision-making styles. *Journal of Counseling Psychology, 37*, 160–168.

Blustein, D. L., Prezioso, M. S., & Schultheiss, D. P. (1995). Attachment theory and career development: Current status and future directions. *The Counseling Psychologist, 23*, 416–432.

Blustein, D. L., & Spengler, P. M. (1995). Personal adjustment: Career counseling and psychotherapy. In W. B. Walsh & S. H. Osipow (Eds.), *Handbook of vocational psychology: Theory, research, and practice* (2nd ed., pp. 295–329). Mahwah, New Jersey: Lawrence Erlbaum.

Blustein, D. L., Walbridge, M., Friedlander, M. L., & Palladino, D. (1991). Contributions of psychological separation and parental attachment to the career development process. *Journal of Counseling Psychology, 38*, 39–50.

Bowlby, J. (1982). *Attachment and loss: Volume 1. Attachment* (2nd ed.). New York: Basic Books.

Brown, D. (1985). Career counseling: Before, after, or instead of personal counseling. *Vocational Guidance Quarterly, 33*, 197–201.

Chickering, A. W. (1969). *Education and identity*. San Francisco: Jossey-Bass, Inc.

Chickering, A. W., & Reisser, L. (1993). *Education and identity* (2nd ed.). San Francisco: Jossey-Bass.

Erikson, E. (1968). *Identity, youth and crisis*. New York: W. W. Norton.

Gilligan, C. (1982). *In a different voice*. Cambridge: Harvard University Press.

Grotevant, H. D., & Cooper, C. R. (1985). Patterns of interaction in family relationships and the development of identity and role-taking skill in adolescence. *Child Development, 56*, 415–428.

Grotevant, H. D., & Cooper, C. R. (1988). The role of family experience in career exploration: A lifespan perspective. In P. Baltes, R. H. Lerner, & D. Featherman (Eds.), *Life-span development and behavior* (Vol. 8, pp. 231–258), Hillsdale, NJ: Erlbaum.

Hackett, G. (1993). Career counseling and psychotherapy: False dichotomies and recommended remedies. *Journal of Career Assessment, 1*, 105–117.

Hamachek, D. (1988). Evaluating self-concept and ego development within Erikson's psychosocial framework: A formulation. *Journal of Counseling and Development, 66*, 354–360.

Harren, V. H. (1979). A model of career decision-making for college students. *Journal of Vocational Behavior, 14*, 119–133.

Haverkamp, B. E., & Moore, D. (1993). The career-personal dichotomy: Perceptual reality, practical illusion, and workplace integration. *Career Development Quarterly, 42*, 154–160.

Hoffman, J. (1984). Psychological separation of late adolescents from their parents. *Journal of Counseling Psychology, 31*, 170–178.

Johnson, R. H. (1978). Individual styles of decision making: A theoretical model for counseling. *Personnel and Guidance Journal, 56*, 530–536.

Josselson, R. (1988). The embedded self: I and Thou revisited. In D. Lapsley & F. Power (Eds.), *Self, ego, and identity: Integrative approaches* (pp. 91–106). New York: Springer-Verlag.

Kenny, M. (1990). College seniors' perceptions of parental attachments: The value and stability of family ties. *Journal of College Student Development, 31*, 39–46.

Kenny, M., & Donaldson, G. (1991). Contributions of parental attachment and family structure to the social and psychological functioning of first-year college students. *Journal of Counseling Psychology, 38*, 479–486.

Kenny, M., & Donaldson, G. (1992). The relationship of parental attachment and psychological separation to the adjustment of first-year college women. *Journal of College Student Development, 33*, 431–438.

Kenny, M. E., & Rice, K. G. (1995). Attachment to parents and adjustment in late adolescent college students: Current status, applications, and future considerations. *The Counseling Psychologist, 23*, 433–456.

Ketterson, T. U., & Blustein, D. L. (1997). Attachment relationships and the career exploration process. *Career Development Quarterly, 46*, 167–178.

Kidd, J. M. (1998). Emotion: An absent presence in career theory. *Journal of Vocational Behavior, 52*, 275–288.

Lapsley, D., Rice, K. G., & Fitzgerald, D. (1990). Adolescent attachment, identity, and adjustment to college: Implications for the continuity of adaptation hypothesis. *Journal of Counseling and Development, 68*, 561–565.

Lopez, F. G. (1991). Patterns of family conflict and their relation to college student adjustment. *Journal of Counseling and Development, 69*, 257–260.

Lopez, F. G. (1992). Family dynamics and late adolescent identity development. In S. D. Brown & R. W. Lent (Eds.), *Handbook of counseling psychology* (2nd ed., pp. 251–283). New York: Wiley & Sons.

Lopez, F. G., Campbell, V. L., Watkins, C. E. (1989). Effects of marital conflict and family coalition patterns on college student adjustment. *Journal of College Student Development, 30*, 46–52.

Manuele-Adkins, C. (1992). Career counseling is personal counseling. *Career Development Quarterly, 40*, 313–323.

Myers, R. A., & Cairo, P. C. (1992). Counseling and career adjustment. In S. D. Brown & R. W. Lent (Eds.), *Handbook of counseling psychology* (2nd ed., pp. 549–580). New York: Wiley & Sons, Inc.

O'Brien, K. M. (1996). The influence of psychological separation and parental attachment on the career development of adolescent women. *Journal of Vocational Behavior, 48*, 257–274.

O'Brien, K. M., & Fassinger, R. E. (1993). A causal model of the career orientation and career choice of adolescent women. *Journal of Counseling Psychology, 40*, 456–469.

O'Brien, K. M., Friedman, S. C., Lin, S. G., & Tipton, L. C. (1997, August). Attachment and women's vocational development: A longitudinal analysis. In K. M. O'Brien (Chair), *Role of attachment in psychological and vocational well-being.* Symposium conducted at the annual meeting of the American Psychological Association, Chicago, IL.

Phillips, S. D. (1997). Toward an expanded definition of adaptive decision making. *Career Development Quarterly, 45*, 275–287.

Phillips, S. D., Christopher, E., & Lisi, K. (1998, August). Making career decisions in a relational context. In D. L. Blustein (Chair), *Interface of work and relationships: The nexus of human experience.* Symposium conducted at the annual meeting of the American Psychological Association, San Francisco.

Phillips, S. D., Friedlander, M. L., Kost, P. P., Specterman, R. V., & Robbins, E. S. (1988). Personal versus vocational focus in career counseling: A retrospective outcome study. *Journal of Counseling and Development, 67*, 169–173.

Pistole, M. (1989). Attachment: Implications for counselors. *Journal of Counseling and Development, 68*, 190–193.

Rice, K. G., Cunningham, T. J., & Young M. B. (1997). Attachment to parents, social competence, and emotional well-being: A comparison of Black and White late adolescents. *Journal of Counseling Psychology, 44*, 89–101.

Rice, K. G., Fitzgerald, D., Whaley, T., & Gibbs, C. (1995). Cross-sectional and longitudinal examination of attachment, separation-individuation, and college student adjustment. *Journal of Counseling and Development, 73*, 463–474.

Rice, K. G., & Whaley, T. (1994). A short-term longitudinal study of within-semester stability and change in attachment, separation-individuation, and adjustment to college. *Journal of Counseling and Development, 35*, 324–330.

Richardson, M. S. (1996). From career counseling to counseling/psychotherapy and work, jobs, and career. In M. L. Savickas & W. B. Walsh (Eds.), *Handbook of career counseling theory and practice* (pp. 347–360). Palo Alto: Davies-Black Publishing.

Ryan, N. E., Solberg, V. S., & Brown, S. D. (1996). Family dysfunction, parental attachment, and career search self-efficacy among community college students. *Journal of Counseling Psychology, 43*, 84–89.

Savickas, M. L. (1985). Identity in vocational development. *Journal of Vocational Behavior,* *27,* 329–337.

Schultheiss, D. (1998). Parental and sibling attachment in career development: A cross-cultural comparison. In D. L. Blustein (Chair), *Interface of work and relationships: The nexus of human experience.* Symposium conducted at the annual meeting of the American Psychological Association, San Francisco.

Schultheiss, D. E., & Blustein, D. L. (1994). Contributions of family relationship factors to the identity formation process. *Journal of Counseling and Development, 73,* 159–166.

Super, D. E. (1951). Vocational adjustment: Implementing a self-concept. *Occupations, 30,* 88–92.

Super, D. E. (1963). Self-concepts in vocational development. In D. E. Super (Ed.), *Career development: Self-concept theory* (pp. 1–16). New York: College Entrance Examination Board.

Super, D. E. (1980). A life-span, life-space approach to career development. *Journal of Vocational Behavior, 16,* 282–298.

Super, D. E. (1988). Vocational adjustment: Implementing a self-concept. *Career Development Quarterly, 36,* 351–357.

Swanson, J. L. (1992). Vocational behavior, 1989–1991: Life-span career development and reciprocal interaction of work and nonwork. *Journal of Vocational Behavior, 41,* 101–161.

Vondracek, F. W. (1992). The construct of identity and its use in career theory and research. *Career Development Quarterly, 41,* 130–144.

Wallace-Broscious, A., Serafica, F. C., & Osipow, S. H. (1994). Adolescent career development: Relationships to self-concept and identity status. *Journal of Research on Adolescence, 4,* 127–149.

Waterman, A. S. (1985). Identity in the context of adolescent psychology. In A. S. Waterman (Ed.), *Identity in adolescence: Processes and concepts* (pp. 5–24). San Francisco: Jossey-Bass.

Winston, R. (1990). The Student Developmental Task and Lifestyle Inventory: An approach to measuring students' psychosocial development. *Journal of College Student Development, 31,* 108–120.

Winston, R., & Polkosnik, M. (1986). Student Developmental Task Inventory (2nd ed.): Summary of selected findings. *Journal of College Student Personnel, 27,* 548–559.

Wrenn, C. G. (1988). The person in career counseling. *Career Development Quarterly, 36,* 337–342.

Yalom, I. (1995). *The theory and practice of group psychotherapy* (4th ed.). New York: Harper Collins.

4

College Students' Callings and Careers: An Integrated Values-Oriented Perspective

*Edward Anthony Colozzi
and Linda Chrystal Colozzi*

What are the main career and personal issues facing college students, graduates, and other deciders who reach out for assistance with making career decisions from a private practice setting? How do they feel about their career counseling experiences in college settings? Why do most people not take advantage of career services while enrolled as students in colleges or universities? What contributes to a person's decision to become involved in the career counseling process, while others seem not to be ready? Is there a main life-directive theme (i.e., a calling to a purpose) in the stories of career deciders? How can we, as facilitators of their journeys, best hear it as we help them grow and take responsibility for realizing their inner wisdom?

This chapter seeks to answer some of these questions, based on clinical observations that we have made over the past 14 years in the context of private practice and on preliminary findings from a recent qualitative investigation covering a 21-month period involving 253 people (E. A. Colozzi, in press). Also included is a focus on values clarification as an intervention to assist with career decision making. Much of the initial development and refinement of the values clarification approach (Colozzi, 1978) described herein was based on the first author's work with college and graduate students from 1978 through 1989.

More than three fourths of the people who contact our office and participate in an initial intake and orientation session indicate that spirituality is an expressed need and is important to them in their career decision-making process. This finding indicates that people in transition may have more on their minds than simply earning income; they want their work to provide a sense of meaning and purpose. This chapter examines the role of spirituality, or meaning and purpose, in how clients view their work and discusses the "callings" that many clients seek. It describes theoretically based models to provide a context for appreciating how people cope with making career and life decisions and includes case study excerpts on two clients in their early 30s to provide a past–present perspective. It is hoped that this perspective will provide an understanding of what happens to college students after graduation and how college career counseling might have affected their decisions had they received it during their college years.

Background

Since 1990, we have owned and are partners in a private practice. After a complimentary 1.5- to 2-hour intake and orientation session, clients who decide to continue with the career counseling complete seven to eight counseling sessions covering 12 to 16 hours and participate in a number of activities, including various assessments of interests and values, a self-rating of abilities, and the creation of a carefully crafted "ideal career." They deal with the life space–life span perspective, school–work–family balance issues, and other appropriate career counseling topics. A fairly equal distribution of women and men choose to obtain the counseling. Although most are White and have some exposure to a Judeo-Christian faith tradition, approximately one third represent a wide variety of ethnic and other religious backgrounds, including Hinduism and Buddhism.

Depth-Oriented Values Clarification

One main intervention strategy used in our private practice is a Depth-Oriented Values Extraction (DOVE) clarification process described further ahead in this chapter. Values have been the focus of much discussion as theorists and practitioners strive to comprehend their mercurial, elusive posturing in the decision-making struggles of clients (Brown, 1995; Kinnier, 1995; Raths, Harmin, & Simon, 1966; Rogers, 1964/1977; Rokeach, 1973/1977; Super, 1957; Super, Savickas, & Super, 1996; Super & Sverko, 1995). Simply stated, trying to comprehend values and get a handle on them is similar to the experience of attempting to pick up a piece of mercury with two fingers. Rogers (1964/1977) discovered useful distinctions in his scrutiny of values based on Morris' (1956) research and discussed two conflicting values systems that are referenced further on in this discussion. All people experience career and life transitions, often with some degree of conflict, and it is helpful to examine the role of values in the decision-making processes associated with career and life transitions. This is especially true for college students, who continually face many personal and career-related issues as discussed throughout this book.

Values clarification is an additional useful, timely tool for assisting clients with career and life choices, given the large numbers of adult deciders involved in school-to-work transition concerns (Elmhirst et al., 1994; Gardner, 1999; Hoyt & Lester, 1995; Pascarella & Terenzini, 1991). Brown (1995) offered an important and guiding focus for viewing the role of values in decision making. He challenged counselors to discover how to translate various types of psychological data into values-based terms. The DOVE clarification process described in this chapter attempts to accomplish this.

Expressed and Implied Values

It is important to describe various ways in which values are conceptualized. Some evidence supports the existence of two distinct values systems that operate in the career decision-making process (Colozzi & Haehnlen, 1982). One system can be misleading and cause confusion to a client; the other is a truer and more accurate criterion for making self-actualizing career and life choices. However, both systems constantly contribute to cognitive and affective processes associated with decision making.

The first system, that of expressed values, often serves as the predominant influence over the second system, implied values. *Expressed values* are those which a person says are his or her values and are readily available to a person's awareness when asked what his or her most important work or life values are; they seem to be influenced by external sources (e.g., parents, peers, and life circumstances). Expressed values are most synonymous with Rogers's (1964/1977) discussion of *conceived values*, which accumulate throughout people's lives, especially from early childhood, and become the introjected value patterns by which people live. Rogers believed that most people are influenced by introjected conceived values that are rarely examined or tested and are held as fixed concepts. They also are similar to Fowler's (1981) *assumptive value system*, which is influenced by external sources of authority defined by a group or group membership that can hinder a person's capacity for critical reflection on his or her own identity and outlook.

The second system, that of *implied values*, generally is hidden and unavailable to a person's awareness and usually is brought to conscious operative use through an in-depth analysis and reflection of interests. Analyzing a person's interests can help him or her more fully comprehend the role of values in career and life decision making, because interests are one manifestation of values (Rokeach, 1973/1977). Dewey (1897/1959) believed that a child's interests are the "signs and symptoms of growing power . . . dawning capacities . . . [that] prophesy the stage upon which he [or she] is about to enter" (p. 29). Super et al. (1996) considered the important relationship between values and interests:

> Values provide a sense of a purpose. They serve as stars to steer by in guiding individuals to specific places within life spaces, places that can be the center of meaning, locales for need satisfaction, and venues for the expression of interests. Values are more fundamental than interests because values indicate qualities or goals sought, whereas interests denote activities or objects in which values are sought. (p. 138)

Gradually, through a reflective dialogue, clients can begin to focus on and be more in touch with recurring patterns or themes about what is important to them and what descriptions they are naturally drawn to—their interior insights trickle forth from a well of wisdom deep within their past. Rogers (1964/1977) interpreted this process as the person's present-moment experience of the memory traces of all the relevant learnings from their past that influence the valuing process. This highly subjective period of introspection helps clients concentrate on the self-as-subject to comprehend the personal meaning of their values and how they coalesce into life themes (Super et al., 1996).

The DOVE clarification process usually results in the identification of four or five specific, mutually exclusive implied values or values themes. Implied or hidden values are just that; they often are hidden and usually are not available to guide one's life; they therefore can be overshadowed by external consequences. Because they are stable and grounding (at an unconscious level), they often come into conflict with a person's more conscious expressed values, leaving the person feeling unfocused or unsure about why they are unhappy or unsatisfied. For example, a college sophomore or junior gradually may find his or her major coursework to be less satisfying for no apparent reason and begin to feel that the major no longer fits him or her. Family and friends may add to the feelings of confusion and conflict when they assert, "This is such a good fit for you! You'll be so successful if you just stick with it!" Or a person may feel the need to leave his or her present job, only to hear friends exclaim, "How crazy you are to be thinking of leaving that great job of yours!" Likewise, a graduate may accept a new job with an excellent salary and benefits and somehow know from the first day that it does not fit at all. How do people know that something is not quite right for them? Their implied value system contributes information that conflicts with their expressed values.

Implied values are similar to Rogers's (1964/1977) discussion of *operative values*, which are the behaviors that show preferences for one object or objective over another. He referred to this behavior as an "organismic valuing process" that can deal with complex value problems and further explained how a person weighs, selects, or rejects what he or she is experiencing, depending on whether it tends to actualize the organism or not. Implied values also resemble Fowler's (1981) *tacit system*, described as the principally unexamined system of informing images and values to which people are committed.

Rogers (1964/1977) believed that by introjecting the value judgments of others—taking them on as their own—people lose touch with their organismic valuing process, desert their wisdom, and give up their locus of evaluation and discernment. To gain approval or hold love, people choose to behave according to values set by others. In this way, they develop conceived values, which remain throughout people's lives to confuse, even haunt them. Over time, the person's world becomes filled with confusion, leading to a lack of clarity of beliefs or purpose. Values provide standards against which people judge their own actions and play a central role in the decision-making process because they are the basis of goal setting. Living one's life with confusing standards is difficult, even painful and depressing (Brown, 1995, 1996), and is especially difficult when a person does not know he or she is confusing standards. Often a wide and unrecognized discrepancy exists between the evidence supplied by a person's experience and his or her conceived values (Rogers, 1964/1977). Most people can identify their expressed or conceived values and firmly believe that these are indeed their true values. Rogers explained that a person must hold his or her conceived values in a rigid and unchanging fashion because the alternative would be a collapse of the value system. Hence their values are "right."

To illustrate the events that contribute to the exchange of operative values for the introjected conceived values of others, Rogers (1964/1977) offered this example of a college student's struggles:

> A boy senses, though perhaps not consciously, that he is more loved and prized by his parents when he thinks of being a doctor than when he thinks of being an artist. Gradually he introjects the values attached to being a doctor. He comes to want, above all, to be a doctor. Then in college he is baffled by the fact that he repeatedly fails in chemistry, which is absolutely necessary to becoming a physician, in spite of the fact the guidance counselor assures him he has the ability to pass the course. Only in counseling interviews does he begin to realize how completely he has lost touch with his organismic reactions, how out of touch he is with his own valuing process. (pp. 259–260)

Rogers believed that when people take on the conceptions of others as their own, they lose contact with the potential wisdom of their own functioning and lose confidence in themselves. Value constructs often are sharply at variance with what is going on in a person's experience, resulting in a divorce of people from themselves and accounting for much modern strain and insecurity. Some observers see an important role for values clarification in mental health intervention (Brown, 1995, 1996; Kinnier, 1995; Rogers, 1964/1977; Westgate, 1996).

Relationship of Values With Holland-Type Scores

Our observations of this valuing process have indicated an evident relationship among clients' Holland-type scores and their implied values themes, thus providing a translation of this psychological data into values-based terms, or themes, as suggested by Brown (1996). Values themes can help guide clients; in helping them decide what specific work environments best match who they are, values themes bring about a more "wholesome," a more holistic and complete application of their Holland-type scores. Implied values often relate to a client's deep sense of purpose and calling and can help with the selection of appropriate college and graduate school majors. Given the changing labor market and unpredictable work opportunities facing large proportions of the population, values themes can be used to identify activities in nonwork roles in which clients may more fully express themselves, allowing clients to proactively choose and use work in the context of other role choices (Holland, 1996). Holland acknowledges the shift from career counseling to life counseling and sees using work as an important facet of creating a more satisfying life, hence the focus by Colozzi (1984) on *Creating Careers with Confidence* and using the creation of an ideal career as an effective "storytelling" intervention strategy for adults in transition (Krieshok, Hastings, Ebberwein, Wettersten, & Owen, 1999). Much of the exploration and decision making across Super's (1996) life–career rainbow roles can be based on one's true values, making exploration context-rich (Blustein, 1997).

Most clients are unable to identify any of their top-ranked implied values in their initial list of expressed work values. Their two lists usually are not similar. Yet clients often make decisions about their college majors, career goals, and job changes based on their expressed values, resulting in a values conflict that can precipitate incongruous choices. These inappropriate choices can include occupational fields and specific jobs and can influence relationships, leisure time activities, and other choices made throughout Super's life–career rainbow. Results from using this DOVE clarification process with our clients indicate that they always identify their implied values list as being their true work values when asked to compare it with their expressed work values list. Values themes seem to offer clients a helpful, accurate, and liberating description of who they are, what they are able to offer (to a work environment), and the work environment they seek that will give them purpose and meaning. This increased congruence (of person–position fit) further develops the self toward greater wholeness and engagement in the world, thereby permitting the client to become more like the person that he or she wants to be (Savickas, 1997).

The following case study helps illustrate the difference between expressed and implied values and the career and personal issues that are evident in deciders' lives. (It is not intended to present a step-by-step description of the counseling processes and interventions used.) The case study involves a woman who completed higher education and, as a result of career counseling, returned as a nontraditional student for specific training from which her parents distracted her in earlier years. It offers insights that might be lost with a case example of a currently enrolled or recently graduated traditional college student. The additional life history of this client provides a view of what happened before, during, and after her higher education experience. The excerpts are from a client's written autobiographical homework, comments documented during sessions, telephone conversations, and written reflections. This qualitative perspective can be valuable to practitioners who work with currently enrolled students to better understand how nontraditional students experience the career decision-making process (Luzzo, 1999) and the complex interface of career and personal issues that follow traditional students beyond their college years. This case is typical of many clients across a wide age span.

Case Study: Elizabeth

Elizabeth, age 31, White, and in transition, completed most of the counseling, assessment, and values clarification processes in six sessions over a 3-month period. She is the second oldest of five children raised by a mother who was a full-time homemaker and a father who was a student advisor. Major issues for this client included her desire for creative expression and independence in the context of a controlling home atmosphere, security needs, and a pattern of making choices according to opinions of others.

I had a good childhood, and my older sister and I were always watching out for the three little kids. I did very well in school. I was painfully shy until the fourth or fifth grade. I observed interactions among people, their behavior, even listened on the side to their conversations and how people told their stories. I did this in school and at home, everywhere. Teens were very difficult. I was a bit of a tomboy, and my sisters and mother are as well. Of the girls, I am the most feminine. My interests included art, German, and history. I was in advanced placement courses and excelled in all three. My teachers in these subjects were inspirational, challenged my mind, and dared me to learn.

In high school as well as in college there were "guidance counselors" and "career counselors" who did not provide adequate counseling. They seemed so quick and routine in their dealings with us and how they assembled us as a group and told us, "We need to get two questions answered today. Are you planning to attend college and if so, please write down the major you will be studying." There was little to no interaction on a personal level. No one took the time to notice or discuss my very high Advanced Placement Test scores in art. My guidance counselor was very busy wearing different hats and doing a number of other activities at school. There was no questioning and asking me "why" I was choosing this or that or doing very well in this area (art), no relating to students as individuals, and very little counseling at all. Nobody really took the time to listen. I was just one of the "mill."

I graduated from high school and wanted to pursue art (at a specialized art school) but was not encouraged financially by my parents. Their view of artists was, "a dime a dozen—and you'll never make a living at it!" I always heard about "starving artists" and how they remained at entry-level jobs for 30 or 40 years. They told me they would not provide any financial assistance if I chose art as a major. I informed them I wanted to take a year off and work so I could make the money for art school. They objected to this, and I was persuaded by my parents to start college in the fall. I think they thought that if I did not attend college right away, I may [sic] not ever go to college. I went to a college in northern New England to escape a dominant and controlling atmosphere at home.

I majored in marketing (so I could receive financial assistance from my parents) and minored in studio art. I participated in all the "artsy" things on campus: college radio, piano, and art trips to the city. My summer jobs were in restaurants, and my college job was working as a computer monitor. My activities and hobbies were mostly related to art. I graduated from college and worked as a receptionist, then as a customer service representative in an ad agency with my eyes on the paste-up artist position. They hired another person for the position. A year later I was laid off.

After bouncing here and there, as one tends to do when first out of college, I accepted a job as a temporary development coordinator of a community organization. I was offered a permanent position and refused. I wanted to find something more artsy. As I began looking in 1990, jobs were becoming scarce. I panicked. I accepted a job with a wholesale goods corporation. The money was good and I stayed. I tried a management-related position for 1 year and then transferred to a receiving secretary position. After transferring to my third warehouse, it became ever more apparent that I was dissatisfied with the field of work I was in. I felt there was something missing, but couldn't pinpoint it. I had fallen into management and administrative positions, and I was doing things I was naturally good at. I received feedback from others at work about my administrative and detail skills and how I could relate well to others. This was a conflict for me; doing something I was naturally good at but *not* something I *really wanted* to be doing! I also observed other people around me, their lives and how they spent their time. I saw what they did and tried it, the bars, the social life. This was *so* not me! Working *here* was not me! I was not making major connections with others—just minor ones. I was living my life with minor connections. I wanted major ones. Here I was, 6 years into a career that I cared nothing for. I was working with numbers, inventories, and data—not dealing with people and not dealing with ideas. What I truly craved—ideas, creating, and expressing—was not even remotely present in the work I was doing 40 hours a week. I began career counseling to find my direction.

The client was still employed at her job 17 months after completing career counseling at age 32. Like so many clients, life circumstances, sporadic spurts of motivation in conflict with negative scripting tapes seeded by family and peers, an inner "providential calling," and a host of other factors played on her spirit, and Elizabeth sometimes appeared to herself (and others) to not be going anywhere—quickly or slowly.

Elizabeth completed most of her career counseling sessions in July and began her research, field interviews, and development of an action plan. During several brief telephone conversations, she indicated her desire to enroll in graphic arts classes at a well-known art institute, the one she initially wanted to attend when she graduated from high school. She enrolled that December, and in a conversation late March, she talked about her purchase of a Macintosh computer, which she bought so that "she could play with the software and get a jump on the other students." She also stated, "I want to leave the company," and was dealing with "talk from friends who think I'm crazy to even think of leaving my job." During a brief telephone conversation in June (which was now one year after her last counseling session), Elizabeth again indicated her intentions to terminate her job. That July she came in for a 1-hour session to deal with blocks (security issues and peer influence) preventing her from moving ahead with her action plan, the need to focus on "baby steps" to achieve her goals, and the possibility that remaining in her job might have been preventing other positive events from occurring in her life. The same topics had been discussed during previous counseling sessions and telephone conversations. The importance of leaving when she was truly ready to leave was emphasized. Elizabeth spoke of real hope for her future and stated with optimism that "we would be the first to know when she finally made her decision to leave."

Elizabeth called about mid-September and shared with tremendous joy, excitement, and an evidence of strength and resolve in her voice, "I just informed my company that October 4 will be my last day! I'm *so* psyched!" She also spoke with enthusiasm about "several small miracles" that happened. For example, she discovered that she would be receiving some unexpected additional sick-leave pay. Elizabeth also described leaving her keys the previous day in her car, "with unlocked doors for five hours!" "Everything was okay," she confidently asserted, in a way that seemed to acknowledge that she felt someone was watching out for her. She also spoke of a surprise call regarding an internship opportunity that fell right into her lap. During a late-October telephone conversation Elizabeth excitedly talked about the internship experience and an additional part-time job with a photographer that "just seemed to open up." As this chapter was being written, she offered the following reflections about her thoughts, perceptions, and feelings during that time in her life. Elizabeth's reference to the miracles that unfolded on the day she finally handed in her resignation is not an unusual occurrence.

> I learned a great deal about the world of work and discovered even more about myself, my own values, attitudes, likes, and dislikes as well as what I really wanted to do for my role as a worker. Through testing, conversation, questioning, list making, and reflecting, the hardest part for me was making the distinction between what I was naturally good at and what I loved to do. I realized that I was influenced by other people's views of *acceptable talents* such as management and administrative tasks; but art wasn't an accepted talent, so I relegated art to a hobby status.
>
> I took a long time to leave this job. I had fears. I was a very "earthy," grounded person, rarely taking risks. I almost had 7 years with this company. I had great benefits, good pay, and lots of seniority and vacation time. What? Was I crazy? Leave all this lovely security and take the plunge? What if it didn't work out? What if I failed? I am a responsible adult and have bills to pay. I can't do this. All sorts of fears welled up in my mind. I finished my career counseling in July. It had shaken me up so much from my situation, my routine at work. I felt I needed at least one constant, my job, plus my salary for my security. I decided to "slowly" move toward my goal by applying and being accepted at an art school where I enrolled in a graphic design program that December. I worked overtime at the "dreaded job" and saved up for a computer and printer. I learned all the latest graphics programs including design, color, and typography skills. Timing is of the essence. I felt the need to have some sort of stability in my life as I was slowly peeling off the layers of the attitudes, values, and priorities of peers, parents, and others that did not belong to me.
>
> I was making great strides personally, and the more I discovered about myself, the more I couldn't be anything but myself. I left the corporation in October, just 2 weeks shy of 7 years. One main factor

that influenced me was Princess Diana's death. Her passing screamed out at me, "Life is so damn short!" . . . To see all her potential snuffed out instantly . . . I've got tons of potential! What the hell am I doing! The climate in my work environment was unfavorable at this time. I had discovered that coworkers and management were "fixing" numbers to create desired inventories. All of this was being done behind my back as I helped out in other departments. This pushed me to the limits. Honesty is the value I hold very dear above all else. I simply couldn't work there. There was so much deceit going on. This was the final straw that propelled me into action. I left with nothing more than a great desire to be me. I had no job planned but now had no fear!

People were amazed I left my secure job after 7 years. Oddly enough, the minute I handed in my resignation paper, I received a phone call offering me an internship as a junior designer in a printing company. I worked there for four months as well as part-time with a photographer creating trivia slides for local movie theaters. While working for this photographer, I decided to make a black-and-white video for a class project involving diners. I had some of the negatives printed into slides and submitted them to a local gallery for the opportunity to display them at a show. I acquired a contract position designing Web pages at the local phone company through a temp agency. I was hired on the spot. My newly learned computer skill and the internship had provided me with the qualifications for this opportunity! To the "old me" this was totally unbelievable, but to the "new me," it was just Providence opening all the doors that I couldn't see until I had faith to change. I changed it [my life], and I found it!

During the summer of 1998 I applied for graphic design positions and interviewed quite a bit. I was contacted in the fall by a publishing company and asked to come in for an interview. I honestly didn't remember applying, but apparently did so during the summer months. Speaking briefly over the phone with the human resources director, I declined the interview opportunity based on the low salary figure that was disclosed to me. Not 5 minutes later, the director of marketing phoned me asking, "What can I do to at least get you in here for an interview?" I heard more about the position from her and decided to go in for an interview the following week. A week later I was offered the position, and at a much higher salary than I had expected.

A few weeks ago, prior to the opening of my photography exhibit (yes, I got the show!), I gave my notice to the phone company. Here I am, less than 1 year later after taking "the plunge," working in the field I love and with my beginning salary and benefits exceeding what took me 7 years to reach in the wholesale field! Career counseling has helped me identify and face the doubts, questions, fears, and attitudes that kept me from realizing my given talents. I have literally changed my life irrevocably and for the best. I recently registered to vote and I got to list my occupation. I used to list "business management." I indicated "artist/photographer." It was the biggest thrill of my life . . . a liberating moment. The woman asked me what type of photography I did. I reached into my purse and pulled out one of the specially printed postcards advertising the art show, with one of *my* photographs on it and showed it to her. I was on a natural high for days. People were constantly saying to me, "You're glowing!"

Watching my older brothers and sisters raise their children, I think about myself being a parent someday. I hope I have the continuity and insight to recognize in my child, "That's an *individual* first, and *then* my child." It's my responsibility to guide this person, not control. We shouldn't raise our children with "mental and emotional vise grips." They were created and given to you. Let them be who they were born to be, and guide them! Children are born with such a pure light and spirit—a connection with themselves, the universe, and God. There is a spiritual essence to who each of them is. They have a purpose to be here. Everything is all connected for some reason. That's what they need to hang on to. People shouldn't mess with this. Respect it, coddle it, guide it; but don't disconnect it! I often wonder, "could we *already* have had the cure for cancer?" . . . if everyone could just be who they are created to be."

As part of the career counseling, the client participated in the DOVE clarification process to elicit her implied values themes. Several days before this session, she was asked to reflect on and then list her top-ranked work values and life values. The results are listed in Figure 4.1.

Values Expressed Before the DOVE Clarification Session

A. Work Values
   1. Honesty
   2. Tolerance
   3. Intelligence
   4. Hard work
B. Life Values
   1. Honesty
   2. Loyalty
   3. Monogamy
   4. Having self-knowledge

Implied Values Themes from the DOVE Clarification Session

1. Opportunity to use my imagination, sometimes with humor to synthesize, express, and create my feelings and ideas—my inspirations—especially verbally and in written/visual ways (e.g., telling or writing short stories/columns with sketches) in ways that result in a finished product—a "communication" that gives me a sense of accomplishment and contribution.
2. Opportunity to often be alone, quiet, reflective, uninterrupted, focused, independent, and going at my own pace.
3. Opportunity to observe, explore, discover a wide variety of topics to gain insights (see all the connections), storing them for future reference, and be more universally conscious in ways that satisfy my curiosity and give me a sense of competence.
4. Opportunity to sometimes be physical, move about with some travel outdoors, and sometimes involving eye–hand coordination with full-body movement.

Figure 4.1.   Client's Top-Ranked Values.

Discussion

The dissatisfaction with work expressed by this client reflects a common theme among adult deciders across a wide age range in exploring their strengths, interests, and values as a means of discovering their life's direction or calling. The client wanted more fulfillment from work, was undecided about her career goals and "at a crossroads," expressed a need to explore and focus, and was open to considering a career change and obtaining the necessary additional education or training that would facilitate such a change. She stated that she did not receive the guidance and support from either her parents or the education system, specifically career counseling, that might have helped her make wiser choices. She seemed aware of some potential within herself, believing that she had something to contribute through her work, but had not yet fully discovered what it was or how to express it in a purposeful work role. Her desire for work with purpose and meaning is a common theme that clearly emerged throughout this investigation and with other clients. She seemed to be influenced initially by her expressed values, and she acknowledged receiving more direction and focus from the reflection process that helped her better understand the role of her implied values. Mostly, she was ready to become fully involved with making changes to improve her situation.

Readiness and Involvement

Unlike Elizabeth, some people choose not to obtain career counseling after an initial complimentary intake and overview session. Yet the same people express a need for assistance with assessment and possible further education and indicate a desire to have more meaningful work that gives them a sense of purpose. Why do some people decide not to become involved in counseling—both when they are students in college and as older adults?

We have discovered that one of the most influential factors, other than financial considerations, behind clients' not obtaining counseling is a *reluctant readiness to reflect*. The term implies some lack of motivation, perhaps influenced by a mental or emotional struggle. Realizing during the overview that the counseling process is comprehensive and requires a *willing readiness to reflect*, some people may temporarily select themselves out of the transition process into a more passive resting mode that may be less antagonistic to change in their lives. They are willing to go only so far, but their readiness is not adequate to support a full involvement with exploration and transition.

Astin's (1984) student development theory, which is based on involvement, postulates that to fully achieve the intended effects, a particular curriculum or activity (such as career counseling) must elicit sufficient student effort and investment of time and energy to bring about the desired learning and development. His 20 years of longitudinal research supports the importance of involvement as a powerful means of enhancing almost all aspects of the undergraduate student's cognitive and affective development (Astin, 1996). He acknowledges that the construct of student involvement resembles the psychological construct of motivation and prefers to use the term *involvement* because it connotes the behavioral manifestation of that state and seems to be a more useful construct for educational practitioners. "How do you motivate students?" is probably a more difficult question to answer than "How do you get students involved?" (Astin, 1984). This distinction is an important consideration for college career services providers. Numerous ways exist for encouraging students' involvement in career services, and some suggestions are described throughout this book.

Fowler's (1981) investigation of faith stages and the psychology of human development offers a reflective examination of the natural relation of transitions in psychosocial development to structural stage changes in faith development. He identifies his Stage 4 person as *individuative– reflective*, someone who is ready to interrupt external authority based on a relocation of authority to within the self and therefore become involved (p. 179). As one 26-year-old single man recently stated,

> Not knowing what to do next with my life is like a buzzing. It's getting louder and louder, and it's diminishing other aspects of my life. This inner turmoil eats away at me. I feel I am in a great transition in my life now, only I am lacking direction. I would very much like to be on a path that is productive toward my figuring out what my next step in my life will be.

Fowler sees such people as remaining open to hearing the advice from others; that advice eventually is submitted to an "internal panel of experts," who reserve the right to choose and are prepared to take responsibility for their choices—the emergence of an *executive ego*. The emergence of Stage 4 is characterized by the critical distancing from one's previous assumptive value system and the emergence of one's executive ego (Fowler, 1981). These clients appear similar to the Phase 5 adults in Riverin-Simard's (1990) investigation, who could no longer ignore their need for reflection on the actual significant vocational goals of working life.

The clients who decide to obtain career counseling appear to have a willing readiness to reflect, which is most clearly evidenced by their commitment to participate in several hours of counseling with a counselor and at least a similar amount of time on homework activities, including the DOVE clarification session, itself an intense introspection of self that loosens up the hold of Fowler's assumptive (or Rogers's conceived) values and prepares clients for taking responsibility for who they are and have been all along. Although this reflection process may cause some inner turmoil from the realization that old rules and ways of thinking and behaving are possibly ending, Houston (1982) is quick to reassure better times for clients experiencing turmoil with her farm and garden metaphor; breakdown is always the signal for breakthrough.

Breakthroughs and "Miracles"

A visible and sometimes dramatic breakthrough occurs for about 10% of our clients, and many others experience a series of subtle mini-breakthroughs, usually in a manner commensurate with their personal philosophical or spiritual faith traditions. Sometimes people who begin to listen to Fowler's executive ego (what some may call their "inner voice" or "intuition") experience moving in the "right" direction and feel that their life's purpose is being expressed more fully. Most of our clients acknowledge an awareness of a transcendence in their lives and some personal connection with a higher being or energy force—God, the Buddha within, the Holy Spirit, oneness with nature and all that is around them, or simply a real connection with something outside of themselves or deep within. Many clients report coincidences of synchronistic events that occur, sometimes referring to them as "miracles." For example, on the actual day that Elizabeth decided to finally leave her job and handed in her resignation letter, she experienced several synchronous events, which she called "several small miracles." She said,

> Oddly enough, the minute I handed in my resignation paper, I received a telephone call offering me an internship as a junior designer in a printing company. I could hardly believe it—the minute I closed that big door on the job I was tied to, everything opened up!

Some might interpret this outcome as an example of planned happenstance (Mitchell, Levine, & Krumboltz, 1999). Elizabeth's willingness to capitalize on various events and resources resulted in the creation and transformation of unplanned events into new opportunities for her further learning and growth. Planned happenstance intervention involves helping clients generate, recognize, and incorporate "chance" events into their career development. Although this step encourages counselors to teach clients to engage in exploratory activities to increase unexpected career opportunities, an important distinction should be made between chance events and events that "appear as chance" and are actually influenced by some transcendental nature or force beyond the client that somehow provides an avenue of collaboration for clients to discover and use. It is useful to consider this perspective in career counseling. As a 33-year-old married father of two small children working in the finance field stated,

> I'm not a particularly spiritual or religious person, however, I did come to believe in "miracles," although I tend to believe they're mostly self-generated. I just can't believe that God has the time to attend to such small details! My miracles started happening right away. I followed your advice and started writing. This writing that I did was a key factor in landing my current job, a step in the right direction. To top it all off, I was able to find a more enjoyable job while obtaining an 11% increase in pay! I feel I am on the right path now, and eventually I will find that "ideal job." This feels great after suffering through periodic depressions and crises regarding my career over the past 10 years.

Houston (1982) challenged people to consider what miracles really are, suggesting that they are

> the conscious activation of more patterns of reality than are usually seen in the linear-analytic Newtonian lens. . . . [a] state of high creativity, (that) sets up an organic phase-coherence with surrounding fields of reality so that the very building matrices of reality begin to organize around the creative intention. (pp. 198–199)

We interpret this as an important part of the process of receiving and collaborating with one's calling, a collaboration between personal agency and some transcendental nature, whether that nature is Houston's (1982) Essence, Ground of Being, or even God. The case of Joan helps to illustrate this process; it provides a past–present perspective that might have been lost in a case example of a currently enrolled or recently graduated traditional-aged college student. The additional life history and story of this client provides a view of what happened during and after her college years and her insights about the relevance of previous employment struggles that were appropriate for her eventual career pathway.

Case Study: Joan

Joan, age 34, single, and White, worked mostly in the investment field for 10 years and left her latest job as a property manager to look for something that was "the right direction for me and [puts] food on the table." In her freshman year of college she enrolled as a parks-and-recreation major, then switched to speech communication and public relations. Early in her work experience, she entered the financial field, primarily in sales, a common strategy for many college graduates. She took a brief sabbatical to work with young adults at a camp for 2 months and then returned to the financial industry. One of Joan's expressed needs during the intake and orientation was "to investigate and discover my career and life direction and find my own special 'niche' in life." After completing the counseling process, she focused her attention on implementing her ideal career—to become a board game developer.

   Our clients are encouraged to develop an appropriate timeline for implementing their career goals, including plans for education or training, and to be sensitive in their planning process to maintaining balance among all their career and life roles. Joan set a timeline that seemed unrealistic and, after some frustration and a brief counseling session, adjusted her timeline. She then experienced a series of 10 synchronous occurrences that propelled her ideal career forward in some amazing ways. She interpreted these events as a result of her adjusting her original implementation timeline, apparently allowing an intervention of the "highest and best" to occur for her or, as Houston (1982) might explain, an "activation of more patterns of reality than are usually seen, [that] . . . state of high creativity . . . that begins to organize around the creative intention" (pp. 198–199). Her new board game was named as one of "The Top 100 Games for 1999" by *GAMES Magazine*. Joan arranged for a booth at a major trade show in New York that year, where she debuted her game and received an offer by a company to license it. She has now sold thousands of games and is designing her next two games. She recently shared the following thoughts in a letter:

> There is a quote that says, "Love is the process of my leading you back to yourself." Over the past several years, I have been fortunate to have been led back—landing at a place where I have not only discovered my passion, but have accepted it as well. More important, I have realized that there has been (no doubt) some sort of "divine intervention" throughout my journey. As I look back over the years prior to my discovery, there were many times where frustration seemed commonplace and my goals lacked direction. I often felt lost and was apathetic. But now, having committed to my passion, and having gained the confidence to carry it out, I realize that my entire life journey has been an evolution; events and people in my past had been working to bring me to this very place in time. Responsibilities at a past job that I struggled to complete were now providing me with the prudence necessary to carry out my endeavor. And a person, who had once breezed in and out of a day's frame like an extra in a film, had suddenly re-appeared as a supporting character to aid in the development of my dream. The wonderment of coincidence and the realization of true purpose have, at times, been euphoric. Most important, I know now that I have truly found my "calling!"

It is useful to notice the patterns in clients' lives that are seeded by moments of faith, those times in one's journey when a shift in perception allows a person to turn what appears as an obstacle into an opportunity, or a stumbling block into a stepping stone. However, it also is important for counselors and clients to discern how emerging patterns of helpful and purposeful synchronous events differ from simple coincidences that may be misleading. Career counselors should work toward judicious discernment of similar unfoldings of events in clients' journeys. Transitions continually bring on endings of old rules, often accompanied by challenging beginnings and new ways of perceiving and being.

Deciders' Dilemma

A common theme among adult deciders of all ages in our practice is their desire to more fully explore and assess their strengths, interests, and values as a means of identifying and then narrowing their options and ultimately discovering their life's direction or calling. Most clients with whom we have worked, whether they are current students, recent graduates, or adults considering a return to higher education, express a need for assistance with the transitions that they are experiencing. Most of them also believe that they did not receive adequate assistance earlier in life. They generally report low job satisfaction with their current or recent employment situations, want more meaning out of work than just a paycheck, and ascribe a certain spiritual (not religious) importance to the work that they hope to someday have. Clients usually are undecided about their career goals and open to considering a job change. They also express a desire for work–family balance and sufficient time to more fully enjoy other life roles.

Clients often state a desire to earn a sufficient salary to accommodate their lifestyle and have concerns that a new job may not pay them as much as they are currently earning. Many are dealing with feelings of fear and insecurity about leaving their present employment setting, yet they are explicit and assertive in their expectations about wanting a change in the direction of their life journeys. Simply put, clients overwhelmingly state, "What I want is a *new* direction and something with more purpose—more *me!* I want to find my niche." They explain how their dilemma generates conflicting feelings and adds confusion to their lives. Many feel helpless to move on and have difficulties coping with everything that is happening in their lives. Many express self-esteem concerns; some are in or have completed therapy and have been referred by their therapist, and a few are taking medication for depression. Most report that low job satisfaction is a contributing cause of stress and affects other life roles, including the primary relationships in their lives. Some share how stress in other life roles (spouse, parent, or caretaker with aging parents) also negatively affects their work and overall job performance. Many, including younger adults, express concern that time is passing, and they are stuck and not going anywhere.

Searching for Meaning by Discovering One's Calling

We hear this main life-directive theme in the life stories of people in transition: "Help me discover my purpose. Help me hear my calling. How can I do this and live the fullness of my life with sufficient income and balance in my life roles to do what *I am here to do?*" As one 29-year-old married man recently reflected, "I want to find what's always eluded me; more of a divine purpose rather than an ego-inspired accomplishment." Many people are aware of some potential within themselves but are frustrated that they have discerned neither the specifics of it nor the appropriate avenue of optimal expression. A 27-year-old college graduate working as a grievance analyst at a health care organization wrote in her autobiographical essay, "I am struggling to find my place in this world. I am working in a job that is very unsatisfying and no longer gives me any challenges that interest me." She finished the career counseling, discovered her focus, and is completing her master's degree and preparing her application for a doctoral program. She recently wrote,

> A good deal of time and intellectual searching has given me a sense of clarity and vision regarding my interests, hopes, and dreams which I

did not have 6 years ago. I am dedicated to making my graduate studies the focal point of my life's work.

A 24-year-old woman said, "I want a clear picture in my head of what specific career niche would allow me to have a sense of purpose." This search for purpose and meaning, the recognition of values as important in work, the desire for work—family balance is clearly a focus of theorists and practitioners (Bloch & Richmond, 1997; Hansen, 1997; Super & Sverko, 1995).

In a review of medical wellness and counseling literature for insight into the nature of spirituality and purpose, Westgate (1996) uncovered four emerging dimensions of spirituality and spiritual wellness: (a) meaning and purpose in life, (b) intrinsic values, (c) transcendent beliefs or experiences, and (d) community or relationship. Of the five authors who delineated components of spirituality and spiritual wellness, all were unanimous that a sense of or search for meaning and purpose is one dimension of spiritual wellness. The emerging picture of the spiritually well person is that of someone who discovers meaning and purpose in life, who chooses to operate from an intrinsic value system that guides both life and decisions, and who has a transcendent perspective that allows an appreciation of the sacredness and mysteries of life. Westgate suggested the appropriateness of dealing with the topic of spirituality in the counseling setting using the four dimensions as guidelines for discussion and, noting the reluctance of some counselors to deal with spiritual topics, quoted Rogers's (1973) challenge to the profession:

> There may be a few who will dare to investigate the possibility there is a lawful reality which is not open to the five senses: a reality in which present, past, and future are intermingled, in which space is not a barrier and time has disappeared. . . . It is one of the most exciting challenges posed to psychology. (p. 386)

Groome (1998) was convinced of the significance of the spiritual awakening that reflects a person's wholehearted desire for something more than possessions and personal success. He interpreted it as a renewed consciousness of the hunger of the human heart that only transcendence can satisfy. Houston (1982) explained the integral level of this psychospiritual dimension—a level of awareness described as "Essence," "Ground of Being," or even God—that manifests as a kind of structuring, dynamic energy rising up from the depths to inform and energize. Most of our clients indicate that they feel that they are on this planet to live their purpose and contribute something to others or to the planet. As one 21-year-old single woman stated,

> I have definitely pondered this question at many different times in my life, and maybe we are all here to nurture this environment and planet we were given. We all do this in a different way through our jobs, relationships, family, activities, and caring for each other.

Most clients seem to truly believe that they have something to contribute and that by doing so they will somehow matter more in the great scheme of things. Yet most people claim that their college years do not sufficiently prepare them for this task.

Gardner (1999), a longtime champion of the "freshman-year experience," questioned whether today's graduates are adequately prepared to enter or reenter the world of work or graduate school, including making decisions involving family obligations and personal finance. He viewed the senior year as the last opportunity to provide specific basic competencies sought by virtually all employers, namely, critical thinking, values clarification, and decision making. He believed that these competencies are neglected in higher education and identified three primary needs of seniors: (a) the need for integration and closure, (b) the need for reflection, and (c) the need for support for their college-to-life transition. He saw an important role for campus career centers in this regard and believed that they must be a top priority of colleges and universities.

The campus career center works with what can be labeled the *historical* student (the whole career or life history that each person brings to the present) and the *present-day* student (the current conscious understandings, feelings, and perceptions each person uses to make career and life decisions). The career center becomes the staging area for how that history is reflected on, integrated, understood, and played out within the present-day client's consciousness to facilitate the evolution of the *integrated* student (the person who is capable of "becoming more like the person that she or he wants to be"; Savickas, 1997, p. 253; and making appropriate choices about college majors and career plans).

Helping students with career decisions means working with their rich and complex personal and career issues as well as the life stories that comprise who they have been, who they are, and who they are becoming. Clients share important insights that relate to career exploration experiences during their college years. Those insights—as seen in the examples presented in this chapter—give practitioners glimpses into what in the clients' pasts influences them to reach out for assistance and seek career counseling from a private practice setting.

Previous College Career Exploration Experiences

More than 90% of our clients observe that they experienced little involvement with career service providers in college settings. A few clients, however, report positive interactions with career counselors and college faculty who took the time to listen and respond to their concerns.

Many people report not being aware of any career services offered at their college (other than résumé-writing and job placement activities for students about to graduate) and indicate that they did not obtain any career counseling. A 29-year-old single woman told us about how "back then in college I may have thought of career as career/job, not career/ choice; and I wasn't ready to deal with jobs, my résumé, and interviews.

I was there to get an education and do well in my courses." The small minority of clients who report having contact and some sporadic involvement with career counselors were mostly discouraged with the quality of service and attention that they received. Some were given an interest inventory, a Myers–Briggs Type Indicator (Myers, McCaulley, Quenk, & Hammer, 1998), or were directed to sit alone and interact with a computerized guidance system. Others reported a "couple of sessions followed by a suggestion to review the books and resources in the career center. It wasn't very motivating or helpful." A bright 25-year-old client was critical of the "poor job" done by his high school guidance office, which focused mainly on "getting students through the maze of being accepted into a college." He recalled a long talk with the dean of students at his Ivy League college, during which he shared, "I have a dilemma; I don't like *any* of the majors. My friends are at least trying to choose among the several they like!" He never received any assistance and finally arbitrarily picked geography so that he could graduate and move on. He then chose the paralegal field as a temporary worker "because it was noncommittal, and I was safe and wouldn't get trapped by a high salary doing something I really didn't enjoy!" The reason he decided to do some career counseling as an adult is reflected in a statement he shared during the intake session: "I'm so sick of constantly thinking of this dilemma, not being able to choose!"

Many clients report being unclear about their career goals in college, even after they had selected a major. When asked why they did not seek assistance from a career counselor or office of career services, some clients accept full responsibility for not visiting a career counselor in college and state reasons such as, "I was more concerned with just completing my coursework, graduating, and getting on with my life" or " I was in school to get good grades; not get a job." Others explain that they thought they knew what they wanted (i.e., in terms of their major or career goal) and therefore did not bother to visit a career counselor. A 23-year-old single woman working as a nurse stated, "I felt very committed to nursing once I declared it as my major and stayed with it even though I really didn't like it. I was hoping I might find my niche. I haven't." Her mother was a nurse.

Most people are quick to add that they "did not know what they wanted during their college years and, in retrospect, could have used some career counseling back then!" Many simply see no connection between career counseling and their lack of career focus and say, "It never dawned on me to ask for help." When clients are asked whether they "would have participated in career counseling if they had been more fully aware of what was available, where the service was located, and the relevance of those services to their course selection and career goals," most clients respond in the affirmative.

Many of the issues and concerns expressed by the clients begin smoldering early in college—perhaps throughout their high school experiences. A 41-year-old divorced man recently said with sadness, "I was told by my college career counselor, 'David, you're limited in knowledge and skill. Go find a job and keep it.'" David went on to obtain two bachelors' degrees and several additional certifications and remarked during his intake session, "I guess I've been fighting him all my life—to prove him wrong!" He was recently laid off from a plant manager's job, unsatisfied with much of his work history, and stated, "It was time to assess my strengths and weaknesses, professionally and personally."

Students choosing to pursue higher education bring their need for career assistance to college and university settings and require a considerable amount of refocus or refinement in career thinking (Pascarella & Terenzini, 1991). With many deciders involved with school-to-work transition concerns, a strong need for career counseling appears to exist. A complicating factor involves evidence that professional career counselors in college settings have not provided high-quality help to most students; the need for more and better career development assistance from professional career counselors is clear (Elmhirst et al., 1994; Hoyt & Lester, 1995). It is impractical (and, most likely, impossible) to offer individual career counseling to all students who need assistance. Chapter 16 presents an approach that may alleviate the high counselor–student ratios that plague most counseling centers and possibly contribute to the overwhelm many career counselors experience as they attempt to adequately perform their responsibilities.

Vocational Counseling in the New Millennium: Assisting With Callings

The profession of career counseling started with Parsons (1909), who set forth a simple and insightful blueprint for vocational guidance, a model of matching an understanding of oneself and the world of work by a process of "true reasoning," which has influenced present-day theorists and practitioners. Important foundational trait–factor research by Dvorak and Holland (as cited in Osborne, Brown, Niles & Miner, 1997), Prediger (1982, 1999), and others have built on that initial model and provided it with strength and a structural resilience that helps define a person–environment match in ways that seem to stand the test of time and experience. Super's brilliant contributions over his lifetime, especially his life span–life space theory, have provided a context-rich functional perspective to the evolution of understanding the career development process.

To explain the twists and turns of transitions occurring throughout ages and stages, Super equipped his model with a naturally occurring and intuitively guided "search engine," the *minicycle*, which allows the person in transition to do just that—transition (Super et al., 1996). His minicycle provides a way to cope with the inevitable transitions that occur throughout a lifetime. Mitchell and Krumboltz (1996); Lent, Brown, and Hackett (1996); and others have furthered understanding of the increasingly complex role of learning and have discussed an intellectual component that improves understanding of the role of learning experiences in the career development process.

Brown (1995) and others have heard the heartbeat of values, perhaps the "true reasoning" that Parsons (1909) referred to almost a century ago, reasoning that may have at its source a values system to explain the internal motivation of a person faced with a career or life decision. This values system is similar to a beacon that guides counselors to move inside the soul to be more fully present and hear what is really happening and what is really important through a valuing process. Riverin-Simard (1988) and others raised counselors' sights to the universe of a spatial–temporal perspective and the continuous states of instability and change characterized by alternative "goals-and-means questioning" that occurs with life transitions. Fowler's (1981) sequence of faith stages and their interrelations in a rising spiral movement, where each stage represents a synthesis of earlier stages and a widening of vision, gives the lifelong journey of transitions a dynamism that increases certainty and depth of selfhood.

Super (1957) defined interest as one possible definition of motivation. Motivation also could be defined as one's calling: "a spiritual or divine summons to a special service" (Barnhart & Barnhart, 1994, p. 284). We suggest the recognition of an additional intrinsic and essential part of the career development process, namely the spiritual, that transcendent whisper that somehow gently reminds us who we are and what we are called to do—our individual callings and vocations. We have observed the importance of callings in the lives of most clients.

Callings: A Collaboration With a Transcendent Nature

Callings are the rich, simple, and complex "stuff" that move people from places deep within to a state of *being*, as opposed to a path by which people are driven in life and are constantly *doing*. Callings may become manifested during early childhood, as with Itzhak Perlman, the brilliant violinist; Bette Midler, the versatile singer and entertainer; or Michael Jordan and Larry Bird, basketball superstars. As a young child playing in the Kona coffee plantations in Hawaii, astronaut Ellison Onizuka used to wonder what it would be like to fly in space. Tony Bennett clearly knew at age five that his calling had to do with singing and painting (few people know that Bennett paints, draws, or sketches every day, even on flights to his performances). The only difference between these examples and any college student, or anyone for that matter, is that the former are well-known people discovered by the public through the media. The latter are deciders in transition—today's college students and tomorrow's hope for society and the world.

We believe that all people have callings, even multiple callings that relate, for example, to a work role and a parent role. Groome (1998) recognized that parents and teachers have a "vocation to be a humanizing educator, to teach with spiritual vision. . . . [S]uch a 'calling' (*vocatus*) is heard, indeed, from one's own depths, but also comes *from beyond the self*, as not of one's making" (p. 37). He further acknowledged the potential within all people by citing how "the greatest Greek philosopher Plato described teaching as 'turning the soul' of learners, and he meant touching and shaping their innermost 'being'—their identity and agency. . . . [F]or Aristotle, too, to educate is ultimately to nurture people's divine potential" (pp. 37–38).

Most people associate the concept of a calling with the vocational callings of the religious. History has many such accounts, such as Joan of Arc's call from God to unite France. A young Albanian woman, Agnes Gonxha Bojaxhiu, responded to her first calling at age 18 when she joined an Irish order, the Sisters of Loreto; she became the Catholic missionary nun Mother Teresa and taught at St. Mary's high school in Calcutta. She was on a train in 1946 when she received her second calling to remain in Calcutta and work with the "poorest of the poor"—"the call within the call," as she referred to it, "and when that happens the only thing you do is to say 'Yes.'" (Egan, 1985, as cited in Vardey, 1995, p. xxii). One of the most well known of all callings is evident in the relationship between God and Moses in the Old Testament. The Bible documents numerous callings in the Old Testament and specific requests from God to Adam and Eve, Noah, Abraham, and others. Similar callings can be found throughout the New Testament, the Koran and the Kabbalah.

Collective callings probably exist, as in the case of the young Chinese citizens who assembled and took a bold stand in Tiananmen Square in 1989 and were massacred or of the brave people who responded to the emerging leadership of Martin Luther King, Jr., in Montgomery, Alabama, where Rosa Parks, an African American woman, had refused to move from her bus seat in 1955 "because [she] felt [she] was being mistreated as a human being" (as cited in Chapelle, 1990, p. 57)

A person may have a primary calling, versus a secondary calling which is of lesser importance or intensity to that individual, and be able to exercise that calling over several life roles. For example, a person may devote time and energy to taking care of one's family and be fully present to child-rearing responsibilities while providing similar caring acts to people who frequent a local soup kitchen. That same person also may provide direct client services in a helping profession, such as counseling or a health-related occupation. A primary calling is felt deep from within and may take some urging to evolve and become fully manifested. Most likely, one's calling will share multiple life span–life space experiences with other callings of various importance. Based on Fowler's (1981) sequence of faith stages, a rising spiral movement perspective can be used to describe career pathways. For most people, a primary calling may be intricately woven into the fabric of a work role and balanced among other roles. For some, a primary calling may be short-lived or frustrated from its full experience for a variety of reasons, including internal psychological blocks, or physical blocks, and outside environmental obstacles. For others, a primary calling may have no relationship to earning income and may become manifested through another of Super and colleagues' (1996) life roles, just as important and contributing just as much as is necessary to fulfill a purpose and destiny.

Some people who follow a primary calling and commit to their passion may exhibit a single-mindedness of purpose, an internal focusing that is nurtured by confidence and faith in themselves, their calling and, perhaps, even some transcendental force that they interpret as guiding them. Joan, the woman who decided to develop board games, demonstrated these feelings when she stated,

> I have realized that there has been (no doubt of) some sort of "divine intervention" throughout my journey. Now, having committed to my passion, and having gained the confidence to carry it out, I realize that my entire life journey has been an evolution; I know now that I have truly found my "calling!"

There is no doubt that most of our clients over the years have had a strong desire to discover their calling. They hear some faint mumblings of this desire through the dissonance that they experience in their current work. Clients generally know more about what they do not want compared with what they do want, but they mostly want direction toward that place deep inside them that seems to have caught their attention. Environment and heredity certainly play important roles in the complex processes that shape people and, most likely, their callings. Although the debate continues as to whether environment or heredity is more influential, few people doubt the fact of their influence, given the large body of evidence that indicates the importance of genetic factors for virtually all traits that are of interest to applied psychologists (Lykken, Bouchard, McGue, & Tellegen, 1993). Some see the environment as a secondary factor, believing that it can help or hinder in the shaping of people, but it can never create (Montessori, 1909/1964).

Researchers and theorists increasingly are using new knowledge about genetic and environmental influences to further comprehend the complex mechanisms through which they affect vocational interests and values (Betsworth et al., 1994; Brown, 1995; Mitchell & Krumboltz, 1996; Spokane, 1991; Super et al., 1996). Given that many people throughout history have claimed to experience a connection with some transcendental being or force or nature, it is now reasonable for career development theory to consider the possibility that a person's interests and values, and even special abilities and talents can originate from an interaction among the environment, heredity, and a transcendent nature and manifest as a calling. One's "gifts" may be the special abilities or talents that support one's calling and which also appear with passion and focus in the context of that transcendent calling. Noted physicist-turned-Anglican priest Sir John Polkinghorne recently argued that science cannot answer metaphysical questions, such as whether the universe is designed because a creator wanted it that way, just as physics cannot explain music by describing it as vibrations. He believed that no simple answers exist for such profound questions as why science is possible at all or why the universe is intelligible and seems so special. According to Polkinghorne, belief in God (or some transcendental nature) can explain the existence of the universe, its intelligibility, the widespread phenomenon of religious experience, and the dawning of consciousness in humans, which he interprets as a "signal of meaningfulness" (as cited in Goldberg, 1999).

Perhaps in the twilight of his career Super knew how ready career counselors may be to synthesize theories to further an understanding of the complexities of the career development process. Reflecting on the true meaning of Parson's (1909) use of the term "vocational" may reestablish a commitment to a synthesized perspective on the career development process for this new millennium. This perspective envisions the idea of vocational counseling as facilitating a person's primary calling in collaboration with the transcendent awareness or belief of that person. This suggestion to reemphasize the importance of calling is made in the context of the challenges facing our profession today and the brilliant contributions of our senior scholars. As Super and Sverko (1995) closed the preface in *Life Roles, Values, and Careers*, Super seemed to be telling readers about his own primary calling:

> The central thread of the tapestry that is this volume is the observation that the various roles each contain distinctive challenges and distinctive opportunities for the fulfillment of values. The roles, and a person's ability to fulfill them, shift with development, with age and stage. The Work Importance Study spans the last phase of my own career development . . . as the work—indeed my life's work—neared completion. This too is a study in the importance of work. (p. xxi)

The following suggestions are presented to facilitate the reflection process and to encourage dialogue with students about their callings.

- Counselors should provide time and an appropriate milieu for real reflection about calling. They do not have to have all the answers; they just need to be creative and willing to raise the right questions, including discussions about the reflection process and teaching students the process so that they can use it independent of the counseling relationship. Counselors should spend time reviewing the benefits gained from reflection to raise the clients' self-efficacy concerning reflection and as an encouragement to continue the process throughout their lives.
- Counselors should be willing to consider the possibility of the transcendent or spiritual factor that this chapter discusses and be open to understanding how best to work with it in ways that are commensurate with their specific counseling orientation and the multicultural orientations of their clients.
- Counselors should be patient and sensitive to clients' readiness for intervention. Certain factors such as time and life circumstances also are at play and greatly affect clients' journeys and rate of progress. These factors often are wonderful allies and facilitators of clients' journeys, yet are often masked in a veil of impatience that makes many counselors feel uncomfortable. Counselors should offer what they can, make wise referrals when appropriate to ensure that their clients' needs will be met, and let go of any desire to "make it all happen" quickly.

- Counselors should have fun with their work and make the experience of discovering "self" and the world of work a challenging and enjoyable one that students will discuss with other students when they leave the counselor's office or classroom. Students are counselors' best (or worst) source of public relations.

Final Reflections

Bowlsbey (1996) and others have cautioned that career counseling as a profession is at a crossroads at a time when its services are more desperately needed than ever before. The profession needs a redesign in its structures, theories, and methods of providing services. There is evidence of a growing awareness of spiritual matters and an openness to exploring them within the context of counseling *and* career counseling, and for many clients spiritual issues may have an important influence on their career development (Burke et al., 1999). As theorists or practitioners, we are all educators and teachers, and we are all students. What we learn we teach, and what we teach we hopefully learn better. We grow, re-form, and transform. As educators we are reminded by Dewey (1897/1959) that every teacher should realize the dignity of her or his calling. Montessori (1909/1964), who also was transforming education during the same time period, further challenged us:

> The educator must be as one inspired by a *deep worship of life*, and must, through this reverence, *respect*, while he [or she] observes with human interest, the *development* of the child life. The child is a body that grows, and a soul which develops, these two forms, physiological and psychic, have one eternal font, life itself. We must neither mar nor stifle the mysterious powers which lie within these two forms of growth, but we must *await from them* the manifestations which we know will succeed one another. (pp. 104–105)

The authors' observations of clients have helped illuminate some of the rich career and personal issues of deciders and their desire to find work that gives them meaning and purpose and somehow ties into their calling. In an examination of the spiritual quest of Generation X, Beaudoin (1998) focused on

> one question that begins on the most intimate level possible and in the midst of profound ambiguity. Our most fundamental question is "Will you be there for me?" We ask this of our selves, bodies, parents, friends, partners, society, religions, leaders, nation, and even God. The frailty that we perceive threatening all these relationships continually provokes us to ask this question. (p. 140)

The challenge of transitions for deciders in higher education and beyond involves transforming endings into beginnings. Old rules, old ways of acting and being, old relationships, and even old values sometimes no longer seem to offer the comfort of relevance as students seek clarity and purpose. They may feel alone, misunderstood, and vulnerable to the insensitive, hypomanic world about them. Yet all these feelings matter for their important journey.

The students in career counseling are not alone. They have support with their career development process in the way that we listen to their stories and help them create a more holistic environment that offers increased opportunity for self-actualization and life balance. Perhaps our primary calling as career theorists or practitioners is to assist them in reflecting on whatever transcendent whisper beckons them to fulfill their life themes, their most precious callings.

Epilogue

Some people in the field may use the terms *vocational identity* or *self-actualization* to essentially refer to the sense of calling clients may experience. This chapter has proposed that callings may be more than that which a person is passionate about and may be rooted in what the medical wellness and counseling literature describe as meaning and purpose in life, intrinsic values, and transcendent beliefs or experiences. Passionate feelings may be a manifestation of the self-actualization one experiences when immersed in one's calling and following a true vocation. The emerging picture of the spiritually well person is one who discovers his or her meaning and purpose in life, who chooses to operate from an intrinsic value system that guides both life and decisions, and who has a transcendent perspective that allows an appreciation of the sacredness and mysteries of life (Westgate, 1996). The notion of calling may not be something counselors generally are trained to examine, but it is critical to consider when working with clients.

References

Astin, A. W. (1984). Student involvement: A developmental theory for higher education. *Journal of College Student Development, 25,* 297–308.

Astin, A. W. (1996). Involvement in learning revisited: Lessons we have learned. *Journal of College Student Development, 37,* 123–134.

Barnhart, C. L., & Barnhart, R. K. (Eds.). (1994). *The world book dictionary.* Chicago: World Book.

Beaudoin, T. M. (1998). *Virtual faith: The irreverent spiritual quest of Generation X.* San Francisco: Jossey-Bass.

Betsworth, D. G., Bouchard, T. J., Cooper, C. R., Grotevant, T. H., Hansen, J.-I. C., Scarr, S., & Weinberg, R. A. (1994). Genetic and environmental influences on vocational interests assessed using adoptive and biological families and twins reared apart and together. *Journal of Vocational Behavior, 44,* 263–278.

Bloch, D. P., & Richmond, L. J. (Eds.). (1997). *Connections between spirit and work in career development.* Palo Alto, CA: Davies-Black Publishing.

Blustein, D. L. (1997). A context-rich perspective of career exploration across the life roles. *Career Development Quarterly, 45,* 260–274.

Bowlsbey, J. H. (1996). Synthesis and antithesis: Perspective from Herr, Bloch, and Watts. *Career Development Quarterly, 45*, 54–57.

Brown, D. (1995). A values-based approach to career transitions. *Career Development Quarterly, 44*, 4–11.

Brown, D. (1996). Brown's values-based, holistic model of career and life-role choices and satisfaction. In D. Brown, L. Brooks, & Assoc. (Eds.), *Career choice and development* (pp. 337–372). (3rd ed.) San Francisco: Jossey-Bass.

Burke, M. T., Hackney, H., Hudson, P., Miranti, J., Watts, G. A., & Epp, L. (1999). Spirituality, religion, and CACREP curriculum standards. *Journal of Counseling & Development, 77*, 251–257.

Chapelle, T. (1990, January/February). Rosa Parks: From the back of the bus to the forefront of history. *The Black Collegian, 20*, 56–61.

Colozzi, E. A. (1978). *Values clarification process.* Oahu, HI: Leeward Community College.

Colozzi, E. A. (1984). *Creating careers with confidence.* Honolulu, HI: DELTA Rainbow.

Colozzi, E. A. (in press). Callings and careers: A spiritual perspective of the career development process. *Career Development Quarterly.*

Colozzi, E. A., & Haehnlen, F. P. (1982). The impact of a computerized career information system on a community college in an island state. *International Journal for the Advancement of Counseling, 5*, 273–282.

Dewey, J. (1959). My pedagogic creed. In M. Dworkin, *Dewey on Education: Classics in Education, 3.* New York: Teachers College, Columbia University. (Original work published 1897) pp. 19–32.

Elmhirst, P., Riche, N., Blais, E., Gilmone, B., Irwin, W. J., Lee, E. L., Lerner, R., Reberg, B., & Stone, J. (1994). *Putting the pieces together: Toward a coherent transition system for Canada's labour force.* Report of the Task Force on Transition into Employment to the Canadian Labour Force Development Board (CLFDB). Ottawa, Ontario: CLFDB.

Fowler, J. W. (1981). *Stages of faith: The psychology of human development and the quest for meaning.* San Francisco: Harper & Row.

Gardner, J. N. (1999). The senior year experience. *About CAMPUS, 4*, 5–11.

Goldberg, C. (1999, April 3). Crossing flaming swords over God and physics. *The New York Times*, p. D5.

Groome, T. (1998). *Educating for life.* Allen, TX: Thomas More.

Hansen, L. S. (1997). *Integrative life planning: Critical tasks for career development and changing life patterns.* San Francisco: Jossey-Bass.

Houston, J. (1982). *The possible human.* Los Angeles: J. P. Tarcher.

Holland, J. L. (1996). Exploring careers with a typology. *American Psychologist, 51*, 397–406.

Hoyt, K., & Lester, J. (1995). *Learning to work: The NCDA Gallup survey.* Alexandria, VA: National Career Development Association.

Kinnier, R. T. (1995). A reconceptualization of values clarification: Values conflict resolution. *Journal of Counseling & Development, 74*, 18–24.

Krieshok, T. S., Hastings, S., Ebberwein, C., Wettersten, K., & Owen, A. (1999). Telling a good story: Using narratives in vocational rehabilitation with veterans. *Career Development Quarterly, 47*, 204–214.

Lent, R. W., Brown, S. D., & Hackett, G. (1996). Career development from a social cognitive perspective. In D. Brown, L. Brooks, & Assoc. (Eds.), *Career choice and development* (pp. 373–421). (3rd ed.). San Francisco: Jossey-Bass.

Lykken, D. T. J., Bouchard, T., Jr., McGue, M., & Tellegen, A. (1993). Heritability of interests: A twin study. *Journal of Applied Psychology 78*, 649–660.

Luzzo, D. A. (1999). Identifying the career decision-making needs of nontraditional college students. *Journal of Counseling & Development, 77*, 135–140.

Mitchell, L. K., & Krumboltz, J. D. (1996). Krumboltz's learning theory of career choice and counseling. In D. Brown, L. Brooks, & Assoc. (Eds.), *Career choice and development* (pp. 233–280). (3rd ed.). San Francisco: Jossey-Bass.

Mitchell, K. E., Levine, A. S., & Krumboltz, J. D. (1999). Planned happenstance: Constructing unexpected career opportunities. *Journal of Counseling & Development, 77*, 115–124.

Montessori, M. (1964). *Maria Montessori: The Montessori method*. New York: Schocken. (Original work published 1909)

Morris, C. W. (1956). *Varieties of human values*. Chicago: University of Chicago Press.

Myers, I. B., McCaulley, M. H., Quenk, N. L., & Hammer, A. L. (1998). *MBTI manual: A guide to the development and use of the Myers-Briggs Type Indicator*. Palo Alto, CA: Consulting Psychologists Press.

Osborne, W. L., Brown, S., Niles, S. G., & Miner, C. U. (1997). *Career development, assessment, and counseling: Applications of the Donald E. Super C-DAC approach*. Alexandria, VA: American Counseling Association.

Parsons, F. (1909). *Choosing a vocation*. Boston: Houghton Mifflin.

Pascarella, E. T., & Terenzini, P. T. (1991). *How college affects students*. San Francisco: Jossey-Bass.

Prediger, D. J. (1982). Dimensions underlying Holland's hexagon: Missing link between interests and occupations? *Journal of Vocational Behavior, 21*, 259–287.

Prediger, D. J. (1999). Basic structure of work—relevant abilities. *Journal of Counseling Psychology, 46*, 173–184.

Raths, L. E., Harmin, M. & Simon, S. B. (1966). *Values and teaching*. Columbus, OH: Charles E. Merrill.

Riverin-Simard, D. (1988). *Phases of working life*. Montreal, Quebec: Meridian Press.

Riverin-Simard, D. (1990). Adult vocational trajectory. *Career Development Quarterly, 39*, 129–142.

Rogers. C. R. (1973). Some new challenges. *American Psychologist, 28*, 379–387.

Rogers, C. R. (1977). Toward a modern approach to values: The valuing process in the mature person. In M. Smith (Ed.), *A practical guide to value clarification* (pp. 257–267). La Jolla, CA: University Associates. (Original work published 1964)

Rokeach, M. (1977). The nature of human values and value systems. In M. Smith (Ed.), *A practical guide to value clarification* (pp. 222–245). La Jolla, CA: University Associates. (Original work published 1973)

Savickas, M. L. (1997). Career adaptability: An integrative construct for life-span, life-space theory. *Career Development Quarterly, 45*, 247–259.

Spokane, A. R. (1991). *Career interventions*. Englewood Cliffs, NJ: Prentice-Hall.

Super, D. E. (1957). *The psychology of careers*. New York: Harper and Row.

Super, D. E., Savickas, M. L., & Super, C. M. (1996). The life-span, life-space approach to careers. In D. Brown, L. Brooks, & Assoc. (Eds.), *Career choice and development* (pp. 121–178). (3rd ed.). San Francisco: Jossey-Bass.

Super, D. E. & Sverko, B. (Eds.). (1995). *Life roles, values, and careers: International findings of the work importance study*. San Francisco: Jossey-Bass.

Vardey, L. (1995). *Mother Teresa: A simple path*. New York: Random House.

Westgate, C. E. (1996). Spiritual wellness and depression. *Journal of Counseling & Development, 75*, 26–35.

Part II

Methods and Techniques

5

Determining the Appropriateness of Career Choice Assessment

Andrew D. Carson and René V. Dawis

Counselors seeking to aid college students with career-related problems frequently choose to administer some form of assessment in the context of counseling, if only to decide which type of nonassessment intervention will follow. Such assessment commonly takes the form of inventories of interests or values, self-rated abilities or skills, personality measures or, less frequently, objective tests of skills or abilities. Research generally supports the effectiveness of career assessment (see Spokane, 1991, chapters 4 and 5). However, the practical exigencies of student services in colleges and universities generally prevent the counselor from doing everything with every student that might conceivably be of assistance; the counselor and the college or university administrator must live in the world of too many students, not enough staff, too little time, and finite funding. The counselor essentially must perform triage in administering career assessment with students. Given that this situation may be obvious to both the researcher and the practitioner (not to mention the administrator of student services), it is surprising that so little practical help is available for the career counselor in performing this task.

Our goal in this chapter is to answer the question, When is career choice assessment appropriate for college students? We aim to marshal theory and assessment tools for this practical task. We might well add the question, Career choice assessment for what? The activities that most counselors associate with career development interventions include assisting clients with career choice but extend to educational concerns, such as helping clients acquire strategies, build skills, and learn information. In addition, career choice for most people, in at least the so-called First World nations, is not a one-time event, but rather a process that recurs throughout life. That being said, and allowing that career choice can be a cycling process throughout life, the essential concern of the counselor with a particular client at a particular moment remains how to help the client

The authors are grateful to Margaret G. Barton, Peg Hendershot, Dave Goodwin, and Angela Stancati for their help at various stages of this manuscript. The authors also acknowledge a potential conflict of interest in their favorable discussion of the Ball Aptitude Battery, published by The Ball Foundation, as a measure for use with college students.

make a wise career choice at that time. The educational assistance the counselor provides is to help the client make this choice. Therefore, this chapter's central concern is the use of assessment to assist clients in making wise career choices.

In addressing this central concern, Gottfredson's (1986b, p. 167; see Figure 5.1) taxonomic framework for assessing career choice problems is especially helpful as a way to organize relevant theory and research, available assessment instruments, and related counseling interventions. Using her approach, the career counselor assesses the student client on each of five successive criteria: (a) whether the student is able identify occupational options; (b) whether the student's abilities, interests, and values are appropriate for chosen occupations (we add the term *values* where Gottfredson used only *interests*); (c) the degree to which the student is satisfied with the choice; (d) whether the student's choices are unnecessarily restricted (by internal, self-imposed barriers); and (e) whether the student is realistic about the accessibility of chosen occupations. Organizing assessment around these criteria should help the counselor maximize the utility (cost–benefit) of the assessment component of career counseling with college students.

Each criterion requires its own appropriate form of assessment and has two assessment components. The first deals with whether a particular

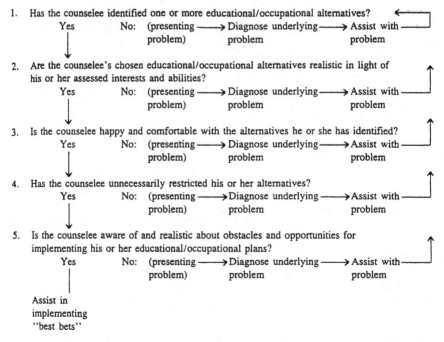

Figure 5.1. Outline of a system for assessing career choice problems. Reprinted from L. S. Gottfredson, "Special groups and the beneficial use of vocational interest inventories," in W. B. Walsh & S. H. Osipow (Eds.), *Advances in vocational psychology: Vol. 1. The assessment of interests* (p. 167), Hillsdale, NJ: Erlbaum. Copyright © 1986 by Lawrence Erlbaum. Reprinted with permission.

criterion has been met; the second involves an effort to understand why the criterion might not have been met, that is, what the nature of the "underlying problems" is (Gottfredson, 1986b, p. 168). Gottfredson differentiated these underlying problems into four broad classes: (a) lack of self-knowledge, (b) life goals and values that are in conflict (internal conflict), (c) goals and values that conflict with important people in one's life (external conflict), and (d) perceived barriers and opportunities. Career assessment with college students involves each of the five criteria, both to determine whether the criterion has been met and to understand why a criterion has not been met.

Because the focus of this chapter is on organizing theory and assessment tools within Gottfredson's criteria, it provides relatively greater attention to some theories and assessment measures than to others. In particular, it will attend in some depth to career development theories proposed by Holland (1997) and Dawis (1996; Dawis & Lofquist, 1984), and especially to the latter. These certainly are not the only two theories with applications to career development; they merely appear to reflect particularly well certain aspects of Gottfredson's criteria. The reader is referred to other sources for discussion of other major theories, such as social–cognitive career theory (Lent, Brown, & Hackett, 1996), social learning theory of career choice and counseling (Mitchell & Krumboltz, 1996), and life span approaches that originated in Super's theory (Super, Savickas, & Super, 1996). It is purely space considerations—and not an estimation of their value—that prevent our integrating those and other theories into this chapter. Although we may not mention the reader's favorite theory, that should not prevent the adaptation of that theory to practical use in the framework provided by Gottfredson's criteria. Thus, the reader should consider our reliance on Holland's and Dawis–Lofquist's theories as merely illustrative rather than either definitive or exclusionary.

Criterion 1: Can the Student Identify Occupational Alternatives?

Gottfredson's (1986b) first criterion "refers specifically to being able to name one or a small number of occupations as viable alternatives" (p. 175). Career undecidedness refers to a different issue. One can be undecided despite having generated an occupational option or set of alternatives.

For example, the Career Factors Inventory (CFI; Chartrand & Robbins, 1997; see Lewis & Savickas, 1995) measures dimensions of undecidedness (need for information, need for self-knowledge, career choice anxiety, and generalized indecisiveness) but lacks questions specifically addressing whether any occupational alternatives are being actively considered. (The CFI may be extremely useful, however, for the counselor seeking to understand why a college student is undecided; moreover, the CFI results may suggest next steps in helping the student make decisions.) Along the same lines, the Career Decision Scale (CDS; Osipow, 1987;

Osipow, Carney, Winer, Yanico, & Koschier, 1976; see Osipow & Winer, 1996) has been promoted as a measure of career indecision. However, Shimizu, Vondracek, and Schulenberg (1994) have argued that the CDS appears to measure four dimensions or factors of career indecision (diffusion, support, approach–approach, and external barriers) rather than a single general dimension. Yet, like the CFI, it appears able to tap dimensions of career indecision rather than determine whether occupational options have been identified per se. Oliver, Lent, and Zack (1998) discussed more recently developed measures of career indecision.

The most direct way to assess this criterion is to ask the student, "Have you made a choice or identified suitable occupational alternatives?" The direct approach may work well for many people. The counselor should identify what the choice is or what the alternatives are.

If the counselor wishes to quantify this criterion by using a standardized instrument, there appear to be two viable options. The first is the Career Thoughts Inventory (CTI; Sampson, Peterson, Lenz, Reardon, & Saunders, 1996; see Peterson, Sampson, Reardon, & Lenz, 1996). The CTI Synthesis Scale, with six items related to expanding and narrowing down a list of options or fields of study, appears to assess problems by addressing whether an appropriate number of options have been identified, and two of its items address whether any options have yet been identified. Other scales and items in the CTI relate to possible reasons why options might not have been identified, such as anxiety associated with identifying any options. At Florida State University, where the CTI was developed, the measure is routinely administered as a screening measure in the university's career center.

The second option is to use My Vocational Situation (MVS; Holland, Daiger, & Power, 1980; Holland, Johnston, & Asama, 1993). The MVS contains sections on occupations the student is considering, followed by a Vocational Identity Scale and ends with questions about barriers and obstacles. First, the student writes down the occupations that he or she is considering. This exercise confronts the student with whether or not he or she has made or can make an occupational choice. The Vocational Identity Scale seeks to determine whether the examinee has "a clear and stable picture of one's goals, interests, and talents. These characteristics lead to relatively untroubled decision making and confidence in one's ability to make good decisions in the face of some inevitable environmental ambiguities" (Holland et al., 1980, p. 1). Holland and his colleagues believe that this understanding should aid people in making wise vocational choices even under conditions of uncertainty about educational or vocational opportunities.

Indeed, vocational identity appears to be positively correlated with everything good (job satisfaction, decisiveness, hope, motivation to improve skills) and negatively correlated with everything bad (intolerance for ambiguity, social avoidance and distress, neuroticism; Holland, Johnston, & Asama, 1993). This is as one would expect for a measure of Gottfredson's first criterion (ability to make an occupational choice), as the likelihood of success in adequately solving the problem of career choice becomes greater after completion of each successive criterion. People who fail the first criterion are more likely to fail successive criteria. Failure in mastering these criteria increases the likelihood of difficulties in career development, which in turn increases the likelihood of negative outcomes not only in the vocational arena but also, more broadly, in other areas of functioning. Holland, Johnston, & Asama (1993) reported that the Vocational Identity Scale often is used as an initial screening measure for readiness for and likelihood of benefiting from different forms of career intervention.

This may seem like much ado about nothing. After all, one might simply query college students on the occupational options they are considering and write them down. This is an issue worthy of research, and in several studies Slaney and colleagues (e.g., Slaney, 1984; Slaney & Slaney, 1986) have used such a listing method (or a similar method using a vocational card sort; Croteau & Slaney, 1994; Slaney & Dickson, 1985; Slaney & Lewis, 1986) as measures of occupational alternatives. It underscores the need for research comparing the cost–benefit ratios of using a more formal quantitative measure (such as MVS) with a less formal qualitative one (such as just asking or using a card sort).

It is important for the career counselor to assess the degree to which the college student has met this criterion. Students face expectations from family, college, and friends that they have at least some idea of the occupation or career toward which they are pointed through their college work. This is not to say that the only purpose of college is preparation for work and career. However, students without a clue as to what they will do after college will face increasingly incredulous and possibly hostile reactions from "stakeholders" in the student's future, especially from those paying for the student's education. Such students may be considered at risk for more serious problems and, therefore, are good candidates for career interventions designed to understand the nature of the student's problem and then address it.

Criterion 2: Are the Student's Abilities and Skills, Values, and Interests Appropriate for Chosen Academic Majors and Occupations?

Much as they might desire to major in a particular field or enter a particular occupation, desire is no guarantee that the college student will succeed or be happy in that course of action. The problem of how to make reasonable predictions about the likelihood of the student's adjustment to an occupation has been a central theme across the history of research in vocational psychology and career development. Parsons (1909) outlined this in his conceptualization of wise vocational choice as the process of understanding oneself, the features of occupations, and a process of true reasoning to serve as a bridge between the two. Findings derived from many decades of research have been organized within a handful of empirically developed person–environment fit theories of career development. Familiarity with such theories and associated measurement instruments and sources of occupational information aids the counselor in evaluating whether a student's intended majors or occupations are appropriate given his or her personal characteristics. Without such a theory to serve as a guide, it is difficult for a counselor to be of much help in relation to this criterion.

Two current person–environment fit theories that one may use to guide assessment in relation to Gottfredson's second criterion are Holland's (1996, 1997) theory of vocational personalities and work environments and Dawis and Lofquist's (1984; Dawis, 1996) theory of work adjustment (TWA). Holland's theory is discussed extensively in Chapter 1 and therefore needs no further introduction. TWA is a systems model in which a person with needs encounters an environment with various kinds of reinforcements; environments have performance requirements that may be met by people with certain skills. In a sense, performance requirements are the "needs" of an environment, and the person's skills are the "reinforcers" of those environmental needs. The TWA as a systems model is shown in Figure 5.2, a flowchart emphasizing degree of satisfaction of people (reinforced needs lead to satisfaction, unreinforced ones lead to dissatisfaction) and degree of satisfactoriness of people in environments (when skill levels result in successful completion of requirements, work is satisfactory; when they are insufficient, work is unsatisfactory).

Although TWA often is assumed to apply only to job settings, one can see that this basic system can apply equally to academic and other environments. (In this sense, it is an unfortunate name for a more broadly applicable theory.) Students have needs, and courses have performance requirements. TWA therefore predicts that students whose needs are met through their courses will be more likely to experience satisfaction than those whose needs are not so met; likewise, students whose academic abilities meet or exceed those required of their courses will be more likely to exhibit satisfactory academic performance than those whose abilities less adequately meet those requirements. Support for these predictions comes from a variety of sources, such as the prediction of student performance from aptitude tests and studies of student satisfaction. One interesting study involves self-reported congruence after random assignments of students into simulated work environments that themselves resemble coursework tasks (Helms, 1996; Helms & Williams, 1973).

However, what most distinguishes the college from the workplace for most people—and this is crucial in applying either TWA or Holland's theory to the college setting—is the plethora of relevant settings in college to which students must adjust, compared with the relatively fewer and more stable ones characteristic of most postcollege jobs. Each course, club, athletic team, student publishing organization, and part-time (or even full-time) job to which students must adjust may differ in ability requirements and reinforcers. In addition, colleges differ from the workplace in that students often are left to their own devices when it comes to finding their place in the overall organizational mission, and this difference is clearest in the wide-ranging freedom that most colleges allow their students in establishing their overall courses of study. (However, the number of roles

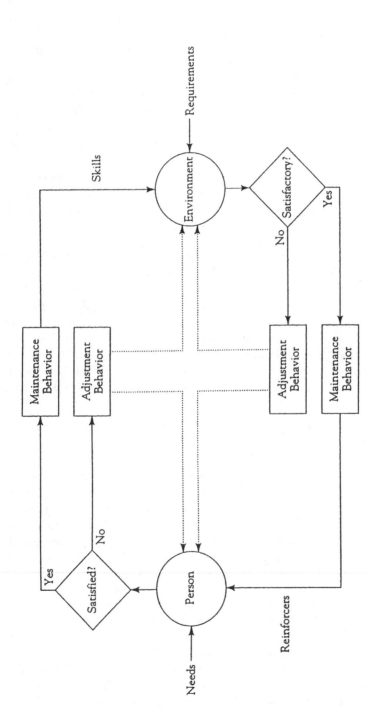

Figure 5.2. The theory of work adjustment as a process model. Reprinted from "The Theory of Work Adjustment and Person-Environment Correspondence Counseling," by R. V. Dawis, in D. Brown, L. Brooks, & Assoc. (Eds.), *Career choice and development* (3rd ed., p. 88), San Francisco, CA: Jossey-Bass. Copyright © 1996 by Jossey-Bass. Reprinted with permission.

to which workers in the modern workplace must fluidly and flexibly adjust is probably increasing [see Sennett, 1998], and therefore work environments are becoming more like college.) In applying TWA to help college students adjust, the counselor may consider separately each major environment calling for adjustment, although for practical purposes it should be sufficient to focus on college majors, which in turn correspond to occupations.

Holland's (1996, 1997) theory likewise has been applied to the prediction of academic satisfaction and performance. His theory, however, does not differentiate need-based *correspondence* (to use the term from TWA; Holland's term is *congruence*) from skill-requirement correspondence. Holland does not make this distinction. In this respect one may say that TWA, although similar to Holland's theory, is more complex. Other elements of Holland's theory also add complexity, such as the assumption that there exist moderators of the relation between congruence and vocational outcomes, such as job satisfaction.

According to Dawis (1996), career assessment based on TWA parallels the Parsons' (1909) formula: assess the person (P); assess the work environment (E); and through a process of true reasoning, determine the degree of P–E correspondence. On the E side, ability or skill-requirement patterns are provided by ability tests' occupational (criterion) validity data; for example, occupational norms have been developed using the scales of the Ball Aptitude Battery (BAB; Ball Foundation, 1998), but TWA may be operationalized through any ability measure. On the P side, measures of values and interests are used to describe a person's reinforcer requirements.

Assessment of Abilities

Counselors may wonder why they need be concerned with the abilities of their college students. After all, the students are bright enough to have made it into college. Although this may be the case for many students, it is not so for all, or at least not so for all facets of student abilities. Many of the subtle difficulties that students encounter in their chosen courses of study may reflect the influence of discrepancies between their abilities and the ability requirements of courses. The same holds true for work after college. Therefore, some appreciation on the counselor's part for how individual differences in student abilities may affect success in majors and occupations may allow the counselor to be of much greater assistance to the student. Unfortunately, most counselors are not trained in their graduate programs in the use of ability tests other than traditional intelligence tests (if even that; see Watkins, 1993; Watkins, Campbell, & Nieberding, 1994); appropriately enough, such counselors are reluctant to use measures they do not understand. We hope that the following discussion proves useful for a new generation of counselors interested in incorporating ability measurement into their work with college students.

Vocational theorists and researchers generally acknowledge the importance of abilities in career development. However, they differ in their answers to the following four questions:

1. Beyond general cognitive ability (usually called g or IQ), are there other important relevant abilities? The answer is yes (see Carroll, 1993; Jensen, 1998). Such abilities are specific, or g-free, abilities (Carson, 1998). There exist at least a small number of specific abilities, such as spatial ability, distinguishable from g that one may reliably measure with standardized tests. Counselors wishing to measure the objective abilities of their students should consider tests that tap various specific abilities; Lowman (1991) included a useful survey of ability measures.

2. Is it necessary to measure abilities and skills objectively (with tests), or are self-ratings sufficiently accurate to warrant their use in career assessment? There is controversy on this point. Recent evidence suggests that although self-ratings may provide some indication of g, they may not be good indicators of specific abilities (Carson, 1998) or may have more in common with interests than with objectively measured abilities (Carson, 1998; Luzzo & Glenn, 1997).

3. Even if abilities exist, do they matter? Why not focus exclusively on learnable skills and the acquisition—over time and through diligent effort—of expertise? Sternberg (1998) has advanced this argument. However, decades of empirical evidence show that abilities do exist and do affect educational and work adjustment (see Jensen, 1998). Whether abilities matter in a practical sense is another issue. For example, consider the case of an engineering student who has struggled with great difficulty through a major at a college, only to find out at the end of her •enior year that she has an ability pattern characteristic of people who are successful in, say, law. Regardless of whether this student had to put more hours of study into passing her courses, she has nevertheless passed them and acquired the relevant engineering skills. However, ability assessment always must be forward-looking, and the counselor must always think through questions of which course of study or work will yield the most rapid acquisition of skills or highest chance of success. Perhaps the counselor might suggest that this student consider shifting her career direction into an area of the law that would benefit from her knowledge of engineering.

4. Given that abilities matter, how much of an ability does a student need to succeed in a college major or occupation? Many researchers and theorists have used a minimum cutoff, but that is not all that matters (see Gottfredson, 1986a). One also might argue that a person could have specific abilities that are too high for optimal fit to a major or occupation. For example, consider the accounting student who can generate creative ideas at a high rate but who may find it difficult to squelch such creative impulses and focus attention on detailed accounting work. Perhaps some other option

would prove a better fit, even if the student's fit for accounting is adequate.

At any rate, counselors seeking to measure abilities (other than g) have a number of options, although each has some limitations for use with college students. The multiple ability battery with the firmest research support and the best documented set of ability profiles across occupations is the U.S. Employment Service's General Aptitude Test Battery (GATB; U.S. Department of Labor [DOL], 1970), which provides extensive data on more than 700 occupations for nine ability dimensions. GATB validity data are reported as Occupational Aptitude Patterns (OAPs; DOL, 1979) that describe a set of minimum ability requirements for the occupation. A college student's GATB pattern may be compared with the OAPs to predict satisfactoriness in performance in any occupation for which there exists an OAP. The GATB has norms ranging from grade 9 to adults, but the norms are old, and one might be concerned that any increase in the general ability level of the population over time (Flynn, 1998; Jensen, 1998, pp. 318–319) might result in overestimates of an examinee's ability level relative to the population as a whole.

Four other multiple ability tests provide crosswalks into GATB scales and therefore build on the voluminous occupational ability profiles generated through the GATB research program. The federal government has provided, through the validity research on the GATB, much of the basic research and development costs underlying the application of these measures. The first is the BAB (Ball Foundation, 1998), whose scores can be used to predict GATB scores based on conversion equations developed through coadministration of the BAB and GATB with college students. Two BAB studies (Goldman, 1987; Newhouse, Raju, & Fisher, 1999) detailed the degree to which students have met the minimum ability requirements for occupations in the Guide for Occupational Exploration (GOE; DOL, 1981). Another BAB report (Aptitude Pattern Indicator in the Ball Career System; Ball Foundation, 1998), after converting BAB to GATB score estimates, made recommendations into GOE workgroups, and then sorted the GOE workgroup recommendations into the corresponding clusters of Gottfredson's (1986a) OAP map (Carson et al., 1999).

The second instrument, the Minnesota Ability Test Battery (MATB; Dawis & Weiss, 1994), is essentially a clone of the GATB. Dawis and Weiss developed the MATB for use in vocational rehabilitation in Minnesota, and most of its use has been in that context.

The remaining batteries report GATB-associated scores and are computerized. Apticom (Harris & Dansky, 1991; reviewed by Green, 1994) has many strengths but carries a high price tag ($6,000) for the system (computer included) and requires a greater degree of counselor supervision during administration. It measures 10 of the 11 abilities provided by the GATB, including those tapping manual abilities and dexterity, with only color discrimination excluded. Because it is computerized, it offers excellent control over test administration procedures. Career Scope (Vocational

Research Institute, 1998) provides a microcomputer-based version of Apticom's tests that yields GATB-associated scores. Similarities of fit to the GOE workgroups also are reported in a manner essentially identical to that used by the BAB.

Once ability-based predictions are obtained with regard to the GOE work groups, the information may be aggregated into a number of higher order, broad categories, such as Holland's (1997) six types or the clusters of Gottfredson's (1986a) map. In fact, one may make practical use of any multiple-ability battery for which a crosswalk exists to an occupational taxonomy (see Kapes, Mastie, & Whitfield, 1994, section 6, for reviews of a variety of multiple ability and skill batteries). Some batteries, such as the BAB and the Differential Aptitude Tests (Bennett, Seashore, & Wesman, 1992; see Wang, 1995), have extensive occupational validity data for adult occupations even if they have been normed on high school students and not on college students. Other ability batteries, such as the Guilford–Zimmerman Aptitude Survey (Guilford & Zimmerman, 1981) and the Comprehensive Ability Battery (CAB; Hakstian & Cattell, 1982), have college student norms but relatively little information in the way of crosswalks to occupational ability profiles. The Armed Services Vocational Aptitude Battery (ASVAB; Defense Manpower Data Center, 1994; see Rogers, 1996; Wall, 1994) has both high school and postsecondary norms. As it was developed mainly as a selection tool for military enlisted personnel, it tends to have lower ability "ceilings" than would be optimal for college students (more on this problem below). Other objective batteries, not listed here, measure basic academic skills and are not intended to provide crosswalks to the general run of occupations.

A major problem with the multiple-ability batteries described above is that they tend to have low ceilings for their various abilities, often so low that college students achieve "high and flat" profiles across all tests in the battery. The high–flat profile suggests the presence of high g but may mask an underlying (and differentiated) profile of specific abilities. This poses a vexing problem for the counselor, one that most counselors solve by having their clients base their decisions on their interests and values. This would be a reasonable course if only minimum thresholds of abilities were important, such as is assumed within the government's system of minimum GATB cutoffs for occupations and work groups. An important goal for researchers should be to develop higher level ability tests with high ceilings for use with college students and bright adults; then it will be possible to determine whether differences in higher level ability profiles predict differential performance across college majors and occupations.

Assessment of Knowledge and Skills

Job-relevant knowledge and skills are associated with important criterion variables such as tenure, grades, and other forms of academic and work adjustment behavior (Ackerman, 1996; Ericsson, 1996). Often one wishes to know what a person can do successfully now; this is especially true when employers seek to assemble a team that must complete a task quickly. One may be less concerned with underlying abilities than with skills and knowledge already acquired because they are directly applicable to the problem at hand. Therefore, when the desired outcome is successful job performance in the short-term and long-term adjustment is of less concern, occupational decision making may be fostered most directly by providing students with more detailed information about skills required for particular jobs.

The practical problem for the counselor lies in getting information about the nature of sets of skills required for jobs. It generally is easier to get information about ability requirements. To know the skills required for a particular job requires a detailed job analysis, which rarely is available to the counselor in the college setting. An exception may be the System of Interactive Guidance and Information Plus More (SIGI-PLUS, 1997), which the counselor may use to match skills with occupations. On the horizon, counselors may look forward to the DOL's O*NET system doing much the same thing.

In addition to the sorts of cognitive skills (such as how to use a calculator) that have direct analogs to underlying (latent) abilities (e.g., numerical reasoning or finger dexterity), there has been a movement in recent years to assess so-called cross-functional skills, which tend to encompass social skills or skills in fostering teamwork and communication. Sennett (1998) outlined some of the changes in organizations—especially the focus on being fluid and flexible or on having short-term projects carried out by ad hoc teams—that have spurred the demand for such skills. However, the assessment industry has been unable to supply reliable standardized measures of such skills, either to industry or to the college counselor.

Assessment of Values

Counselors use measures of work values (and, as warranted, more general values) to identify a college student's requirements for reinforcers (needs). The counselor and student then may compare these requirements to those likely to be available in different college majors and occupations. Fit (correspondence or congruence) between values and reinforcers should predict the degree of satisfaction with an educational program or occupation.

What values are and how they differ from other constructs has been the matter of conjecture and debate for decades. The items of an early measure of values—the Study of Values (SOV; Allport, Vernon, & Lindzey, 1960)—appear to measure both values and interests. (In its current form the SOV is probably unacceptable for use by college students, as many of the items are dated or would appear sexist.) In general, interest items tend to use terms like "prefer" or "like," whereas value items tend to use terms like "important" and often require that the examinee determine clear, rank-order preference across options. Measures of interests and values tend to correlate only moderately (Dawis, 1996, p. 104). In TWA interests are thought to be the product of underlying values, abilities, skills, and reinforcement preferences. Yet measures of interests are routinely used with students and are so readily available that many counselors choose to administer them in lieu of a values measure.

Some examples of values measures receiving widespread use are the Minnesota Importance Questionnaire (MIQ; Rounds, Henly, Dawis, & Lofquist, 1981), the Rokeach Value Survey (RVS; Rokeach, 1979, 1983), the Values Scale (VS; Nevill & Super, 1989; Super & Nevill, 1985), the Career Orientation Placement and Evaluation Survey (COPES; Knapp, Knapp-Lee, & Knapp, 1995), and values modules within comprehensive computerized career guidance programs such as DISCOVER (1996) and SIGI-PLUS (1997). The MIQ, described in more detail below, comes in various forms, the most frequently used being the long form, which requires forced-choice responses in a set of paired-comparison items (untimed, usually 40 minutes or less). The RVS contains two sets of 18 values (one set more end-goal oriented, the other more about means), and the examinee rank orders each set according to their relative importance (untimed, about 20 minutes). The VS (see Nevill & Kruse, 1996) contains 106 items rated on a four-point response scale (untimed, usually 40 minutes or less). The COPES (see Knapp-Lee, 1996) consists of 128 two-choice paired comparison items, contributing to eight bipolar work values scales, themselves yielding classifications into 14 occupational clusters. COPES has mainly been used with high school students (see Oliver et al., 1998). DISCOVER and SIGI-PLUS (see Coleman & Norris, 1997) are comprehensive computerized career choice and guidance programs that include career assessment modules, including measures of work values (see Carson & Cartwright, 1997). Several other values measures might be used in vocational assessment, and the interested reader is directed to Herr and Cramer (1996, pp. 676–678), Kapes et al. (1994, section VIII), and Spokane (1991, pp. 132–135).

Values measures tend to be similar in item content, and a similar factor structure appears to underlie them (Dawis, 1996, p. 104). The MIQ provides a measure of 20 need dimensions: ability utilization, achievement, activity, advancement, authority, company policies and practices, compensation, coworkers, creativity, independence, moral values, recognition, responsibility, security, social services, social status, supervision–human relations, supervision–technical, variety, and working conditions. These 20 dimensions may be grouped into six clusters, each tapping an underlying value (Seaburg, Rounds, Dawis, & Lofquist, 1976; see Herr & Cramer, 1996, p. 588): safety, autonomy, comfort, altruism, achievement, and status (Herr & Cramer, 1996, p. 588). Shubsachs, Rounds, Dawis, and Lofquist (1978) investigated the factor structure of the reinforcer (value-satisfying) patterns of 109 occupations, finding that a three-factor solution best accounted for the data. The three factors corresponded to self (autonomy, achievement), social (altruism, status), and environmental (safety, comfort; see Dawis, 1996, p. 104). Along the lines of the philosophy of "you cannot have your cake and eat it too," to some degree each of the three fundamental values is incompatible with (or opposite from) the other two: achievement versus comfort, comfort versus altruism, altruism versus autonomy. Value conflicts are presumed to arise when both values in a bipolar pair are held to be equally important.

Inasmuch as Holland (1997) described his six vocational types partly in terms of their typical values (e.g., social types being more altruistic), it is possible to conceptualize values-based fit to occupations in terms of his theory. Unfortunately, there exists no readily available measure of values designed for this purpose. However, occupational reinforcer patterns for nearly 200 occupations have been reported by Stewart et al. (1986), and counselors using the MIQ with college students may refer to that report for help in matching values to occupations. However, a more useful resource may be the Minnesota Occupational Classification System (now in its third edition, MOCS III; Dawis, Dohm, Lofquist, Chartrand, & Due, 1987). MOCS III classifies occupations according to their ability requirements and reinforcer patterns.

Assessment of Interests

Counselors wishing to assess interests (and most do) have many well-established and well-supported measures from which to choose, although there is little new to report from recent research on interest measurement (but see Savickas & Spokane, 1999, for the latest word on vocational interests). Among measures that produce norm-referenced scores, the most widely used in college settings (generalizing from the results reported by Watkins et al., 1994) are the Strong Interest Inventory (Harmon, Hansen, Borgen, & Hammer, 1994), the Kuder Occupational Interest Survey (KOIS; Kuder, 1991; Kuder & Zytowski, 1991), and the Campbell Interest and Skills Survey (CISS; Campbell, 1994). Also receiving widespread use is the Self-Directed Search (SDS; Holland, Fritzsche, & Powell, 1994), which may be self-scored. Each of these measures may be administered and scored via personal computers.

Extensive support and reference materials have been developed for each of these measures, such as the *Kuder Book of People Who Like Their Work* (Hornaday & Gibson, 1995), which provides a database of stories about well-adjusted and satisfied workers; the *Dictionary of Holland Occupational Codes* (Gottfredson & Holland, 1996), which is a translation dictionary linking occupational titles to three-letter Holland codes and other information; and the *Dictionary of Educational Opportunities* (Rosen, Holmberg, & Holland, 1994), which provides a crosswalk between Holland codes and academic courses and majors.

Interest inventories often are incorporated into computer-assisted career guidance systems (CACGSs), both those located on PC platforms (as stand-alone programs) and those available through the World Wide Web. Interest inventories have been extensively incorporated into CACGSs and Web-based systems. For example, DISCOVER (1996) incorporates an interest inventory with crosswalks to occupational information (see Carson

& Cartwright, 1997; Hinkelman & Luzzo, 1997). The ease of access to Web-based interest inventories makes their use attractive to college students, but reliance on Web-based assessment raises understandable concerns among college career counselors. For example, how can the college counselor ensure the confidentiality of student data transferred over the Internet? Will the perceived cost–benefit of Web-based career assessment lead some administrators to reduce support for the traditional, human counselor–staffed counseling services on campus? These and related questions are addressed in chapter 9 of this book.

Criterion 3: Is the Student Satisfied With the Choices?

After determining that the student's chosen alternatives are appropriate given assessed interests, values, and abilities, the counselor then should determine whether the student is satisfied and comfortable with these alternatives. Many counselors may assume that students with appropriate alternatives will be satisfied with them, but that is not necessarily the case. Gottfredson (1986b) identified a number of reasons why people may be dissatisfied. Students may underestimate their abilities (perhaps because of low self-esteem), may have sacrificed or compromised on their life goals to achieve other ends (e.g., to take on the role of caregiver or bread-winner in a family), or may feel that they will be unable to overcome barriers on the way to their desired educational or occupational alternatives. Conversely, students who overestimate their abilities (e.g., as a result of exaggerated self-efficacy appraisal) are less likely to possess work experience against which to evaluate their occupational aspirations (DeLorenzo, 1998). Thus, it seems a wise strategy for counselors to encourage students to gain career-related work experience, if only because it serves to make self-estimates of ability more accurate.

Although a number of established measures of job satisfaction exist (e.g., the Job Satisfaction Scale in the Career Attitudes and Strategies Inventory; Holland & Gottfredson, 1994; see G. D. Gottfredson, 1996), there appears to be only one standardized measure of satisfaction or comfort with one's identified educational or occupational alternatives, the Dissatisfaction with Career Scale of the Career Barriers Inventory–Revised (Swanson & Daniels, 1995; see Swanson, Daniels, & Tokar, 1996). Another instrument that may measure this construct is the Lack of Motivation subscale in Osipow and Gati's (1998) Career Decision-Making Difficulties Questionnaire (CDMDQ). Unfortunately, these measures are now available only from their authors and not through a major publisher, so unless counselors contact the authors, they will need to rely on direct questions or inferences based on the student's behavior and self-report.

For counselors seeking to understand the reasons for lack of student satisfaction with alternatives, a variety of standardized measures come at least reasonably close to the constructs one would wish to assess, given Gottfredson's (1986b) discussion. Specifically, the CDMDQ provides two brief subscales assessing internal conflicts (incompatible preferences and other conflicts within the person, such as between interests and abilities) and external conflicts (incompatibilities resulting from the influence of others). Although the CDMDQ scales might be applied to assessment decisions made in reference to Gottfredson's five criteria, as implemented within the CDMDQ they appear especially applicable to the third criterion. Also relevant for such purposes may be the many instruments measuring self-ratings of ability and skills related to work adjustment. For this purpose we group together instruments of self-ratings of abilities and skills, such as the SDS (Holland et al., 1994). (The primary value of such measures is likely to be their usefulness as evaluation tools for this criterion [Criterion 3] and not as the primary measures of whether Criterion 2 [appropriateness of abilities, values, and interests for majors and occupations] has been met.)

Finally, it may be useful to administer a measure of self-efficacy of career decision-making abilities to people failing to experience satisfaction with identified alternatives. The major problem that some students may face is a lack of confidence in being able to make a wise career decision. Several authors report having developed measures of career decision-making measures of this sort, including the CDMDQ (Osipow & Gati, 1998) and the Career Decision-Making Self-Efficacy Scale (CDMSES; Taylor & Betz, 1983).

Criterion 4: Has the Student Unnecessarily Restricted Choices?

Even students having met Gottfredson's (1986b) first three criteria may have chosen an occupation that does "not represent as full a utilization of [their] talents and interests as might be possible" (p. 178). Such people are at risk not so much for lack of success on the job (achieving some minimum level of performance) but rather for not being sufficiently fulfilled through their work. Although people in special groups (e.g., women and minorities) may be especially at risk for unnecessarily restricted choices, people from any group may encounter this difficulty.

The key question the counselor must ask is whether the college student has erected internal, psychological obstacles that restrict the sort of choices that he or she is willing to consider. Crites (1969) was the first to distinguish such internal (psychological) barriers from external ones (which fall under the next of Gottfredson's criteria). More recently, L. Gottfredson (1996) proposed a theory—the circumscription and compromise of occupational aspirations—to account for such mental self-handicapping, and she described a growing research literature generally supporting her theory. Emerging evidence across a number of investigations (e.g., Luzzo, 1995; see London, 1998) points to internal career barriers as being an important factor in career development, especially of at-risk populations.

We located only one standardized measure available through a major publisher relating to this criterion, namely, a single item in the Barriers section of Holland et al.'s (1980) MVS. This question asked whether the client faced others who disapprove of the chosen occupation. However, one may argue that this item points not to an internal barrier (i.e., that the client only thinks that others disapprove), but rather to a real and external barrier (i.e., that others may in fact disapprove and actively block the client's movement to a chosen occupation).

Although no other standardized measures of internal career barriers per se are readily available through a major publisher, a handful of measures are available either directly through their authors or through published journal articles. If possible, the counselor could obtain the measures, evaluate their potential for use with their college students, and consider using them on a trial basis, exercising due caution given their stage of development. The first of these—already introduced in reference to Gottfredson's third criterion—is the Career Barriers Inventory–Revised (Swanson & Daniels, 1995; see Swanson et al., 1996), a 70-item inventory that yields 13 scales. This measure is well established and has good psychometric properties. The scales "cover a wide range of barriers that college students might perceive" (Swanson et al., 1996, p. 225), including the following seven that appear to relate to this criterion: (perception of) sex discrimination, lack of confidence, multiple-role conflict, conflict between children and role demands, (perception of) racial discrimination, disapproval by significant others, and discouragement from choosing nontraditional careers. (Here again, it may prove difficult to classify the barriers assessed by this sort of measure as being internal, based on perceptions, or external, based on the objective behavior of others.) The other scales may be useful in the assessment process but would appear to fall under other criteria proposed by Gottfredson.

The second measure is McWhirter's Perception of Barriers (POB; McWhirter, 1992, 1997; McWhirter & Luzzo, 1996), which in its most recent revision contains 34 items yielding two scales: career barriers and educational barriers. Individual items of the POB tap specific barriers such as family and gender.

Counselors also might consider using measures of the three components of career motivation as proposed by London and Noe (1997): *career resilience*, or the ability to adapt to changing circumstances (and similar to the construct of flexibility in TWA; see Dawis, 1996; Dawis & Lofquist, 1984); *career insight*, or the ability to be realistic about oneself and one's career and to establish reasonable goals based on those perceptions; and *career identity*, the degree to which one defines oneself through one's work. London and Noe reported research on the characteristics of three paper-and-pencil scales, including a 17-item instrument by London (1993); a 27-item measure by Noe, Noe, and Bachhuber (1990); and a 12-item measure of career commitment by K. D. Carson and Bedeian (1994). In addition, some items (especially those related to career identity) of Blau's (1985, 1988, 1989) 7-item measure of career commitment might prove similarly useful. Although the measurement of career commitment may be most relevant to clients with significant work experience, the constructs (especially career resilience and career insight) could be generally applicable to college students. People relatively low in aggregate career motivation might well fail to use their talents and interests fully in their career decisions and their work, thus providing another route to the sort of mental self-handicapping described by L. S. Gottfredson (1996).

Clinical methods that rely not on standardized paper-and-pencil measures but rather on clinical observation and expertise also are available for the counselor to use. For an example of an interview or essay-based approach to eliciting from college students information about perceived barriers—circumventing the difficulties in obtaining standardized measures—the counselor may adopt the interview method used by Luzzo (1995) in the study of career barriers of college students. His interview requires about 20 minutes, followed by coding of the student responses into one of five content categories of career barriers: family, study skills, gender, ethnic, and financial. London and Bray (1984; see London, 1985; London & Noe, 1997) described a 2-day assessment center program to study career motivation, although the cost and logistical aspects of their approach would appear to make it impractical for the college-based counselor. When the counselor uses these more clinical methods, determination of whether a person has unnecessarily restricted his or her choices is, of course, largely a matter of counselor judgment.

Having determined that the college student has unnecessarily restricted choices, the counselor should seek to uncover the causes for this problem. As a result of the lack of readily available standardized instruments to support this inquiry, the counselor must likely rely mainly on interviewing. The counselor should explore whether the student has been culturally or socially isolated, experiences that may restrict the development of self-knowledge. For example, has the student experienced a physical disability or been a primary caregiver? Does the student seek to choose a sex role–consistent academic major or occupation (e.g., nurse for a woman) because of a desire to "avoid the discomfort of being different" (Gottfredson, 1986b, p. 178) or because of the way he or she was socialized? Sex role socialization may contribute a great deal to the selection of highly sex-typed occupations by either sex. Cultural issues also may come into play regarding this issue of restriction of choice through disapproval of others, especially family members. For example, it is not uncommon for an Asian student who must please the family to pursue an occupation that personally holds little interest. (Such a situation is by no means limited to Asians.) Is the student simply ignorant of information about occupational alternatives that may be more fulfilling? It is difficult for a student to know what one does not know. Therefore, self-report measures about need for information on career decision making and occupations (such as in the Occupational Information section of the MVS; Holland et al., 1980) have inherent limitations, except as measures of the degree to which a student believes or perceives the need for more information.

Criterion 5: Is the Student Realistic About the Accessibility of Chosen Alternatives?

Students may meet the first four criteria described by Gottfredson (1986b) and yet have unrealistic expectations about how readily accessible their chosen alternatives are. This issue of accessibility is substantially the same one addressed by Crites (1969) in his concept of external barriers. An obvious instance of such a constraint is that no matter how well a student might fit a particular occupation in terms of abilities, interests, and values, such jobs simply may not be available in his or her geographical area, or severe competition may exist for a limited number of positions. For example, many (or perhaps most) students on college basketball teams wish to join (or at least fantasize about reaching) the National Basketball Association (NBA), but only a few will actually make it. In the case of aspiring NBA players, many college athletes with great talent and prospects are sidelined because of injury or may find other hurdles of college life difficult to master on the route to the professional level. The responsibility of the counselor is to help students be more aware of accessibility issues. Then, if the student still wishes to pursue an occupational dream, at least it does not stem from ignorance about the likelihood or difficulty of the effort required.

Gottfredson (1986b) noted that many restrictions based on gender, ethnicity, or physical or mental disabilities continue to pose barriers to individual career entry or success, often despite the passage of laws or the enforcement of court decisions intended to remove irrelevant barriers to accessibility. For people likely to encounter external resistance because of such factors, it may prove helpful for the counselor to gird them with the expectation that the going may be tough—not to discourage them, but rather to inoculate them against foreseeable stresses and discouragement.

In addition, people benefiting from legally mandated removal of barriers based on such factors should know that vocational success depends not just on having the right profile of psychological traits (Criterion 2) but also on having the right job-related skills and other qualities, such as will, effort, and good work habits. For all students, a realistic understanding of the accessibility of one's chosen occupation should include an understanding of the difficulties that gaining the requisite skills often may entail, and the counselor may assist the client in gaining knowledge about these skills.

Although Gottfredson (1986b) stated that this criterion is a neglected issue in the literature on career development, some measures may be applied to the assessment of individual perceptions of external barriers to employment and career development. First, Holland et al.'s (1980) MVS includes four questions under the heading of Barriers. These questions assess whether the student believes that one will face barriers related to difficulty in completing training, having enough money, lacking sufficient special talents, or facing others who disapprove of the chosen occupation. Three subscales of Krumboltz's (1991) CBI—Learning Job Skills (dislike for job training), Overcoming Obstacles, and Working Hard—all would appear to provide indicators of the degree to which a student will have difficulty in meeting Criterion 5. Other measures of the constructs of career attitudes (Woodrick, 1979) or career myths (Stead, 1991, cited in Daniels & Swanson, 1995) appear to have bearing on the assessment of Criterion 5, but the development of those instruments is still at a relatively early stage and disagreements exist about the underlying factors of such measures (Daniels & Swanson, 1995; Holland, Johnston, Asama, & Polys, 1993).

Conclusion

Vocational assessment may not guarantee an ideal choice, but it can help approximate one. The counselor with adequate time, resources, and student goodwill should use vocational assessment to assist the student in advancing toward the wisest possible career choice. The counselor's assessment efforts should be directed toward the particular problems the student brings, preferably in some logical sequence, such as in Gottfredson's (1986b) model described at the beginning of this chapter.

Implied in the foregoing conclusion is that the counselor needs to know about the various assessment instruments that can be used to measure theoretically important constructs in the course of work with students. It is likely that most master's-level training programs in counselor education and counseling psychology fail to provide adequate training in the measures reviewed in this chapter (Watkins, 1993). It also is likely that even doctoral-level training programs in these areas might similarly need to improve the depth and breadth of their coverage of career assessment measures and methods (Watkins, Campbell, & Manus, 1990; Watkins et al., 1994). The recommendations made in this chapter require the counselor to "tool up" and learn the trade better. Doing so will generate homework, such as reviewing measures, reading manuals, and surveying the published literature on instruments. The counselor will find *A Counselor's Guide to Career Assessment Instruments* by Kapes et al. (1994) especially valuable in this regard (see also Watkins & Campbell, 1990).

A related conclusion is that training programs must better prepare their students for professional practice through improved training in assessment. For example, it is not sufficient for graduate students who will counsel college students to be taught only the Wechsler Adult Intelligence Scale (WAIS; Wechsler, 1997) as the sole cognitive measure; the WAIS is probably rarely used for career assessment with college students. Counselors need to learn about ability and skill measures designed for use in career assessment. We also strongly urge training programs not to ignore measures of work values in the professional education of career counselors. Work values contribute information that interests and abilities do not provide. Furthermore, a body of literature on the usefulness of values in career assessment and career counseling is growing (see Brown, 1996; Dawis, 1996; Kapes, Matlock-Hetzel, & Martinez, 1996). Finally, counselors have to be taught how to evaluate new instruments and to judge their usefulness for the specific problems that the counselor and client are trying to solve.

Last, and perhaps most important, we remind the counselor to review the appropriate ethical and professional standards of testing, such as those embodied in the American Psychological Association's (1992) *Ethical Principles of Psychologists and Code of Conduct* and *Standards for Educational and Psychological Testing* (American Educational Research Association, American Psychological Association, and National Council on Measurement in Education, 1985). In addition to adhering to these standards, it is important for the counselor to maintain common sense, adopt sound theory, and keep current on readings of the scientific and professional literature.

References

Ackerman, P. L. (1996). A theory of adult intellectual development: Process, personality, interests, and knowledge. *Intelligence, 22*, 227–257.

Allport, G. W., Vernon, P. E., & Lindzey, G. (1960). *Manual: Study of values* (3rd ed.). Chicago: Riverside.

American Educational Research Association, American Psychological Association, & National Council on Measurement in Education. (1985). *Standards for educational and psychological testing*. Washington, DC: American Psychological Association.

American Psychological Association. (1992). Ethical principles of psychologists and code of conduct. *American Psychologist, 47*, 1597–1611.

The Ball Foundation. (1998). *Ball Career System examiner's manual*. Glen Ellyn, IL: Author.

Bennett, G. K., Seashore, H. G., & Wesman, A. G. (1992). *Technical manual: Differential Aptitude Tests* (5th ed.). San Antonio, TX: The Psychological Corporation.

Blau, G. J. (1985). The measurement and prediction of career commitment. *Journal of Occupational Psychology, 58*, 277–288.

Blau, G. J. (1988). Further exploring the meaning and measurement of career commitment. *Journal of Vocational Behavior, 32*, 284–297.

Blau, G. J. (1989). Testing the generalizability of a career commitment measure and its impact on employee turnover. *Journal of Vocational Behavior, 35*, 88–103.

Brown, D. (1996). Brown's values-based, holistic model of career and life-role choices and satisfaction. In D. Brown, L. Brooks, & Assoc. (Eds.), *Career choice and development* (3rd ed., pp. 337–372). San Francisco: Jossey-Bass.

Campbell, D. (1994). *Campbell Interest and Skill Survey manual*. Minneapolis, MN: National Computer Systems.

Carroll, J. B. (1993). *Human cognitive abilities: A survey of factor-analytic studies*. Cambridge, England: Cambridge University Press.

Carson, A. D. (1998). The relation of self-reported abilities to aptitude test scores: A replication and extension. *Journal of Vocational Behavior, 53*, 353–371.

Carson, A. D., Bizot, E. B., Hendershot, P. E., Barton, M. G., Garvin, M. K., & Kraemer, B. (1999). Modeling career counselor decisions with artificial neural networks: Predictions of fit across a comprehensive occupational map. *Journal of Vocational Behavior, 54*, 196–213.

Carson, A. D., & Cartwright, G. (1997). Fifth-generation computer-assisted career guidance systems. *Career Planning and Adult Development Journal, 13*, 19–40.

Carson, K. D., & Bedeian, A. G. (1994). Career commitment: Construction of a measure and examination of its psychometric properties. *Journal of Vocational Behavior, 44*, 237–362.

Chartrand, J. M., & Robbins, S. B. (1997). *Career Factors Inventory: Applications and technical guide*. Palo Alto, CA: Consulting Psychologists Press.

Coleman, C. L., & Norris, L. (1997, March). *Work values of university students*. Poster session presented at the meeting of the American Educational Research Association, Chicago.

Crites, J. O. (1969). *Vocational psychology*. New York: McGraw-Hill.

Croteau, J. M., & Slaney, R. B. (1994). Two methods of exploring interests: A comparison of outcomes. *Career Development Quarterly, 42*, 252–261.

Daniels, K. K., & Swanson, J. L. (1995). *An examination of career myths*. Paper presented at the meeting of the American Psychological Association, New York.

Dawis, R. V. (1996). The theory of work adjustment and person-environment-correspondence counseling. In D. Brown, L. Brooks, & Assoc. (Eds.), *Career choice and development* (3rd ed., pp. 75–120). San Francisco: Jossey-Bass.

Dawis, R. V., & Lofquist, L. H. (1984). *A psychological theory of work adjustment*. Minneapolis: University of Minnesota Press.

Dawis, R. V., Dohm, T. E., Lofquist, L. H., Chartrand, J. M., & Due, A. M. (1987). *Minnesota Occupational Classification System III: A psychological taxonomy of work*. Minneapolis: University of Minnesota, Department of Psychology, Vocational Psychology Research.

Dawis, R. V., & Weiss, D. J. (1994). *MATB: Minnesota Ability Test Battery, Technical manual*. Minneapolis, MN: University of Minnesota, Department of Psychology, Vocational Psychology Research.

Defense Manpower Data Center. (1994). *The technical manual for the ASVAB 18/19 career exploration program*. Monterrey, CA: Author.

DeLorenzo, D. R. (1998). *The relationship of cooperative education exposure to career decision-making self-efficacy and career locus of control*. Unpublished doctoral dissertation, Virginia Polytechnic Institute & State University.

DISCOVER [computer program]. (1996). Iowa City, IA: ACT.

Ericsson, K. A. (1996). The acquisition of expert performance: An introduction to some of the issues. In K. A. Ericsson (Ed.), *The road to excellence: The acquisition of expert performance in the arts and sciences, sports and games* (pp. 1–50). Mahwah, NJ: Erlbaum.

Flynn, J. R. (1998). IQ gains over time: Toward finding the causes. In U. Neisser (Ed.), *The rising curve: Long-term gains in IQ and related measures* (pp. 25–66). Washington, DC: American Psychological Association.

Goldman, S. H. (1987, February). *BAB tests and their relation to GATB, and prediction of success on 66 Occupational Aptitude Patterns* (OAP) (Tech. Rep. No. 25). Glen Ellyn, IL: The Ball Foundation.

Gottfredson, G. D. (1996). The assessment of career status with the Career Attitudes and Strategies Inventory. *Journal of Career Assessment, 4*, 363–381.

Gottfredson, G. D., & Holland, J. L. (1996). *Dictionary of Holland occupational codes* (3rd ed.). Odessa, FL: Psychological Assessment Resources.

Gottfredson, L. S. (1986a). Occupational Aptitude Patterns Map: Development and implications for a theory of job aptitude requirements [Monograph]. *Journal of Vocational Behavior, 29*, 254–291.

Gottfredson, L. S. (1986b). Special groups and the beneficial use of vocational interest inventories. In W. B. Walsh & S. H. Osipow (Eds.), *Advances in vocational psychology: Vol. I. The assessment of interests* (pp. 127–198). Hillsdale, NJ: Lawrence Erlbaum.

Gottfredson, L. S. (1996). Gottfredson's theory of circumscription and compromise. In D. Brown, L. Brooks, & Assoc. (Eds.), *Career choice and development* (3rd ed., pp. 179–232). San Francisco: Jossey-Bass.

Green, J. A. (1994). [Review of test *Apticom*]. In J. T. Kapes, M. M. Mastie, & E. A. Whitfield (Eds.), *A counselor's guide to career assessment instruments* (3rd ed., pp. 65–70). Alexandria, VA: National Career Development Association.

Guilford, J. P., & Zimmerman, W. S. (1981). *The Guilford-Zimmerman Aptitude Survey: Manual of instructions and interpretations* (rev. ed.). Palo Alto, CA: Consulting Psychologists Press.

Hakstian, A. R., & Cattell, R. B. (1982). *Manual for the Comprehensive Ability Battery (CAB)*. Champaign, IL: Institute for Personality and Ability Testing.

Harmon, L. W., Hansen, J.-I. C., Borgen, F. H., & Hammer, A. L. (1994). *Strong Interest Inventory: Applications and technical guide*. Palo Alto, CA: Consulting Psychologists Press.

Harris, J. A., & Dansky, H. (1991). *APTICOM: Operation and scoring manual*. Philadelphia, PA: Vocational Research Institute.

Helms, S. T. (1996). Some experimental tests of Holland's congruency hypotheses: The reactions of high school students to occupational simulations. *Journal of Career Assessment, 4*, 253–268.

Helms, S. T., & Williams, G. D. (1973). *An experimental study of the reactions of high school students to simulated jobs* (Report No. 161). Baltimore: Center for Social Organization of Schools. (ERIC Document Reproduction Service No. ED 087 882)

Herr, E. L., & Cramer, S. H. (1996). *Career guidance and counseling through the lifespan: Systematic approaches* (5th ed.). New York: HarperCollins.

Hinkelman, J. M., & Luzzo, D. A. (1997). Computer-assisted career guidance: Bridging the science-practitioner gap. *Career Planning and Adult Development Journal, 13,* 41–50.

Holland, J. L. (1996). Integrating career theory and practice: The current situation and some potential remedies. In M. L. Savickas & W. B. Walsh (Eds.), *Handbook of career counseling theory and practice* (pp. 1–12). Palo Alto, CA: Davies-Black.

Holland, J. L. (1997). *Making vocational choices: A theory of vocational personalities and work environments* (3rd ed.). Odessa, FL: Psychological Assessment Resources.

Holland, J. L., Daiger, D. C., & Power, P. G. (1980). *My Vocational Situation: Description of an experimental diagnostic form for the selection of vocational assistance.* Palo Alto, CA: Consulting Psychologists Press.

Holland, J. L., Fritzsche, B. A., & Powell, A. B. (1994). *The Self-Directed Search technical manual.* Odessa, FL: Psychological Assessment Resources.

Holland, J. L., & Gottfredson, G. D. (1994). *Career Attitudes and Strategies Inventory: An inventory for understanding adult careers.* Odessa, FL: Psychological Assessment Resources.

Holland, J. L., Johnston, J. A., & Asama, N. F. (1993). The Vocational Identity Scale: A diagnostic and treatment tool. *Journal of Career Assessment, 1,* 1–12.

Holland, J. L., Johnston, J. A., Asama, N. F., & Polys, S. M. (1993). Validating and using the Career Beliefs Inventory. *Journal of Career Development, 19,* 233–244.

Hornaday, J. A., & Gibson, L. A. (1995). *The Kuder book of people who like their work.* Amherst, NH: Motivation Press.

Jensen, A. R. (1998). *The g factor: The science of mental ability.* Westport, CT: Praeger.

Kapes, J. T., Mastie, M. M., & Whitfield, E. A. (1994). *A counselor's guide to career assessment instruments* (3rd ed.). Alexandria, VA: National Career Development Association.

Kapes, J. T., Matlock-Hetzel, S., & Martinez, L. (1996, April). *Contemporary measures of career interest and values: A review and synthesis of prominent instruments.* Paper presented at the meeting of the American Educational Research Association, New York.

Knapp-Lee, L. (1996). Use of the COPES, a measure of work values, in career assessment. *Journal of Career Assessment, 4,* 429–443.

Knapp, L., Knapp-Lee, L., & Knapp, R. (1995). *Career Orientation Placement and Evaluation Survey.* San Diego, CA: EdITS.

Krumboltz, J. D. (1991). *Manual for the Career Beliefs Inventory.* Palo Alto, CA: Consulting Psychologists Press.

Kuder, G. F. (1991). *Occupational Interest Survey, Form DD.* Monterey, CA: CTB McGraw-Hill.

Kuder, F., & Zytowski, D. G. (1991). *Kuder DD/PC: User's guide.* Monterey, CA: CTB Macmillan/McGraw-Hill.

Lent, R. W., Brown, S. D., & Hackett, G. (1996). The life-span, life-space approach to careers. In D. Brown, L. Brooks, & Assoc. (Eds.), *Career choice and development* (3rd ed., pp. 373–422). San Francisco: Jossey-Bass.

Lewis, D. M., & Savickas, M. L. (1995). Validity of the Career Factors Inventory. *Journal of Career Assessment, 3,* 44–56.

London, M. (1985). *Developing managers: A guide to motivating and preparing people for successful managerial careers.* San Francisco: Jossey-Bass.

London, M. (1993). Relationships between career motivation, empowerment and support for career development. *Journal of Occupational and Organizational Psychology, 66,* 55–69.

London, M. (1998). *Career barriers: How people experience, overcome, and avoid failure.* Mahwah, NJ: Erlbaum.

London, M., & Bray, D. W. (1984). Measuring and developing young managers' career motivation. *Journal of Management Development, 3,* 3–25.

London, M., & Noe, R. A. (1997). London's career motivation theory: An update on measurement and research. *Journal of Career Assessment, 5,* 61–80.

Lowman, R. L. (1991). *The clinical practice of career assessment: Interests, abilities, and personality.* Washington, DC: American Psychological Association.

Luzzo, D. A. (1995). Gender differences in college students' career maturity and perceived barriers in career development. *Journal of Counseling and Development, 73,* 319–322.

Luzzo, D. A., & Glenn, R. (1997, August). Evaluating the relationship between self-rated abilities, vocational interests, and objectively measured aptitudes. In A. D. Carson (Chair), *Self-rated and objectively measured abilities are not equivalent.* Symposium presented at the meeting of the American Psychological Association, Chicago.

McWhirter, E. H. (1992). *A test of a model of the career commitment and aspirations of Mexican American high school girls.* Unpublished doctoral dissertation, Arizona State University, Tempe, AZ.

McWhirter, E. H. (1997). Perceived barriers to education and career: Ethnic and gender differences. *Journal of Vocational Behavior, 50,* 124–140.

McWhirter, E. H., & Luzzo, D. A. (1996, August). *Examining perceived barriers, career interest-aspiration and aspiration major congruence.* Paper presented at the meeting of the American Psychological Association, Toronto, Canada.

Mitchell, L. K., & Krumboltz, J. D. (1996). Krumboltz's learning theory of career choice and counseling. In D. Brown, L. Brooks, & Assoc. (Eds.), *Career choice and development* (3rd ed., pp. 233–280). San Francisco: Jossey-Bass.

Nevill, D. D., & Kruse, S. J. (1996). Career assessment and the values scale. *Journal of Career Assessment, 4,* 383–397.

Nevill, D. D., & Super, D. E. (1989). *The Values Scale: Theory, application, and research* (2nd ed.). Palo Alto, CA: Consulting Psychologists Press.

Newhouse, N. K., Raju, N. S., & Fisher, B. M. (1999, September). *Prediction of the General Aptitude Test Battery (GATB) scores with the Ball Aptitude Battery (BAB) scores* (Technical Report). Chicago: Illinois Institute of Technology, Institute of Psychology, Center for Research and Service.

Noe, R. A., Noe, A. W., & Bachhuber, J. A. (1990). Correlates of career motivation. *Journal of Vocational Behavior, 37,* 340–356.

Oliver, L. W., Lent, E. B., & Zack, J. S. (1998). Career and vocational assessment 1995–1996: A biennial review. *Journal of Career Assessment, 6,* 231–268.

Osipow, S. H. (1987). *Manual for the Career Decision Scale.* Odessa, FL: Psychological Assessment Resources.

Osipow, S. H., Carney, C. G., Winer, J. L., Yanico, B. J., & Koschier, M. (1976). *Career Decision Scale.* Columbus, OH: Marathon Consulting and Press.

Osipow, S. H., & Gati, I. (1998). Construct and concurrent validity of the career decision-making difficulties questionnaire. *Journal of Career Assessment, 6,* 347–364.

Osipow, S. H., & Winer, J. L. (1996). The use of the Career Decision Scale in career assessment. *Journal of Career Assessment, 4,* 117–130.

Parsons, F. (1909). *Choosing a vocation.* Boston: Houghton Mifflin.

Peterson, G. W., Sampson, J. P., Reardon, R. C., & Lenz, J. G. (1996). A cognitive information processing approach to career problem solving and decision making. In D. Brown, L. Brooks, & Assoc. (Eds.), *Career choice and development* (3rd ed., pp. 423–476). San Francisco: Jossey-Bass.

Rogers, J. E. (1996). Review of the Armed Services Vocational Aptitude Battery (ASVAB) Career Exploration Program [Test review]. *Measurement and Evaluation in Counseling and Development, 29,* 176–182.

Rokeach, M. (1979). *Understanding human values: Individual and societal.* New York: Free Press.

Rokeach, M. (1983). *Rokeach Values Survey—Form G booklet.* Palo Alto, CA: Consulting Psychologists Press.

Rosen, D., Holmberg, K., & Holland, J. L. (1994). *Dictionary of educational opportunities.* Odessa, FL: Psychological Assessment Resources.

Rounds, J. B., Jr., Henly, G. A., Dawis, R. V., & Lofquist, L. H. (1981). *Manual for the Minnesota Importance Questionnaire: A measure of needs and values.* Minneapolis: University of Minnesota, Vocational Psychology Research.

Sampson, J. P., Peterson, G. W., Lenz, J. G., Reardon, R. C., & Saunders, D. E. (1996). *Career Thoughts Inventory: Professional manual*. Odessa, FL: Psychological Assessment Resources.

Savickas, M. L., & Spokane, A. R. (Eds.). (1999). *Vocational interests: Meaning, measurement, and counseling use*. Palo Alto, CA: Davies-Black.

Seaburg, D. J., Rounds, J. B., Jr., Dawis, R. V., & Lofquist, L. H. (1976, September). *Values as second order needs*. Paper presented at the meeting of the American Psychological Association, Washington, DC.

Sennett, R. (1998). *The corrosion of character: The personal consequences of work in the new capitalism*. New York: Norton.

Shimizu, K., Vondracek, F. W., & Schulenberg, J. (1994). Unidimensionality versus multidimensionality of the Career Decision Scale: A critique of Martin, Sabourin, Laplante, and Coallier. *Journal of Career Assessment, 2*, 1–14.

Shubsachs, A. P. W., Rounds, J. B., Jr., Dawis, R. V., & Lofquist, L. H. (1978). Perception of work reinforcer systems: Factor structure. *Journal of Vocational Behavior, 13*, 54–62.

SIGI–PLUS [computer software]. (1997). Princeton, NJ: Educational Testing Service.

Slaney, R. B. (1984). Relation of career indecision to changes in expressed vocational interests. *Journal of Counseling Psychology, 31*, 349–355.

Slaney, R. B., & Dickson, R. D. (1985). Relation of career indecision to career exploration with reentry women: A treatment and follow-up study. *Journal of Counseling Psychology, 32*, 355–362.

Slaney, R. B., & Lewis, E. T. (1986). Effects of career exploration on career undecided reentry women: An intervention and follow-up study. *Journal of Vocational Behavior, 28*, 97–109.

Slaney, R. B., & Slaney, F. M. (1986). Relationship of expressed and inventoried interests of female career counseling clients. *Career Development Quarterly, 35*, 24–33.

Spokane, A. R. (1991). *Career intervention*. Englewood Cliffs, NJ: Prentice Hall.

Sternberg, R. J. (1998). Abilities are forms of developing expertise. *Educational researcher, 27*, 11–20.

Stewart, E. S., Greenstein, S. M., Holt, N. C., Henly, G. A., Engdahl, B. E., Dawis, R. V., Lofquist, L. H., & Weiss, D. J. (1986). *Occupational reinforcer patterns*. Minneapolis: University of Minnesota, Department of Psychology, Vocational Psychology Research.

Super, D. E., & Nevill, D. D. (1985). *The values scale*. Palo Alto, CA: Consulting Psychologists Press.

Super, D. E., Savickas, M. L., & Super, C. M. (1996). The life-span, life-space approach to careers. In D. Brown, L. Brooks, & Assoc. (Eds.), *Career choice and development* (3rd ed., pp. 121–178). San Francisco: Jossey-Bass.

Swanson, J. L., & Daniels, K. K. (1995). *The Career Barriers Inventory Revised*. Unpublished manuscript, Southern Illinois University, Carbondale.

Swanson, J. L., Daniels, K. K., & Tokar, D. M. (1996). Assessing perceptions of career-related barriers: The Career Barriers Inventory. *Journal of Career Assessment, 4*, 219–244.

Taylor, K. M., & Betz, N. E. (1983). Applications of self-efficacy theory to the understanding and treatment of career indecision. *Journal of Vocational Behavior, 22*, 63–81.

United States Department of Labor. (1970). *General Aptitude Test Battery*. Washington, DC: U.S. Government Printing Office.

United States Department of Labor. (1979). *Manual for the USES General Aptitude Test Battery. Section II: Occupational Aptitude Pattern Structure*. Washington, DC: U.S. Government Printing Office.

United States Department of Labor. (1981). *Guide for occupational exploration*. Washington, DC: U.S. Government Printing Office.

Vocational Research Institute. (1998). *User's guide: CareerScope*. Philadelphia: Author.

Wall, J. E. (1994). An example of assessment's role in career exploration. *Journal of Counseling and Development, 72*, 608–613.

Wang, L. (1995). Differential Aptitude Tests (DAT) [Test review]. *Measurement and Evaluation in Counseling and Development, 28*, 168–170.

Watkins, C. E., Jr. (1993). Vocational assessment training in terminal master's-level counseling psychology programs: A follow-up to a previous study. *Journal of Career Assessment, 2*, 193–196.

Watkins, C. E., Jr., & Campbell, V. L. (1990). *Testing in counseling practice.* Hillsdale, NJ: Erlbaum.

Watkins, C. E., Jr., Campbell, V. L., & Manus, M. (1990). Is vocational assessment training in counseling psychology programs too restricted? *Counselling Psychology Quarterly, 3,* 295–298.

Watkins, C. E., Jr., Campbell, V. L., & Nieberding, R. (1994). The practice of vocational assessment by counseling psychologists. *The Counseling Psychologist, 22,* 115–128.

Wechsler, D. (1997). *Wechsler Adult Intelligence Scale—Third edition.* San Antonio, TX: The Psychological Corporation.

Woodrick, C. (1979). *The development and standardization of an attitude scale designed to measure career myths held by college students.* Unpublished doctoral dissertation, Texas A & M University.

6

Integrating Assessment Data into Career Counseling

Rodney L. Lowman and Andrew D. Carson

Assessment data are not the only bases from which to provide career counseling services to college students. For most populations receiving career services, however, such information is unquestionably a valuable and timesaving way to expedite the delivery of career counseling services. The results of systematically collected data that accurately describe individual traits and other career-relevant variables can facilitate greatly the process of assisting college students in making appropriate career choices or in receiving other career-related counseling. It is important that the investment in assessment be in proportion to the needs of the student, the costs and availability of assessment systems for the college, and the competence range of the assessor; thus, an important theme of this chapter is that assessors often overuse or misuse assessments in working with students.

Note that "appropriate career choice," as used in this chapter, does not necessarily mean a single solution to the question of what lifelong career the student should enter. Rather, it is possible to have multiple career choices that may be satisfying and productive at one point in the life cycle but that may need to change later.

Purposes and Principles of Assessment

Broadly speaking, career services for college students may be classified on a continuum ranging from high to low levels of student need for assistance. *Remediation services* serve students with a defined problem or set of problems and who experience relatively higher levels of career-related distress. *Enhancement services* help students seeking to optimize their career choices but who experience relatively less career-related distress. The reportedly large number of students with "undefined problems" (such as students who report being "clueless" about their career) are likely to have relatively low levels of distress and therefore might be expected to benefit from enhancement services.

Career counseling services also can be grouped roughly into two categories: (a) those that occur in the context of service delivery units (in the case of college students, most commonly in university-based counseling or student services centers) and (b) those that are delivered in the context of workshops or classes and designed for groups of students, not necessarily in a remediative way. Each population and service delivery modality can benefit greatly from the use of assessment tools, but the appropriate manner in which those tools should be used varies according to contextual factors, among other things.

Because the question of how to integrate test results into career assessment of college students hinges directly on the nature of the desired data, the choice of instrumentation for career assessment is a critically important issue. How data will be integrated depends on the purposes of the assessment and the specific nature of the data that have been collected. Successful use of career assessment data depends notably on an understanding of the nature of the problems at issue and of the student. Effective integration of assessment data requires that (a) the right questions be asked, (b) the right assessment devices be selected, and (c) the context for feedback be appropriately created so that students can understand and integrate the results of assessment into their own personal schema. Even assessment results that present ostensibly negative results (e.g., low cognitive abilities or decided mismatches with cherished career choices) can be framed in ways that the student can accept and that allow him or her to maintain self-esteem, or, in contrast, they can be sources of lifetime anxiety and consternation.

Whatever the purpose of career counseling or the particular setting in which it takes place, the choice of assessment tools must match the purposes of the assessment. The assessment problem or issue—and not the test, or even the variables to be measured—should be the first question that the career counselor considers. For a student presenting to a college service delivery unit (rather than for nonindividualized, group services), the counselor needs to determine why the student is seeking help and in what way assessment data may be relevant to the issues at hand.

Unfortunately, career assessors do not always begin at that place. Too often, in career counseling practice the assessment tool itself is taken as a given and the referral issues seem to be fitted around the tests that the assessor or counselor is accustomed to using. As an anecdotal illustration of this contention, the senior author has trained hundreds of psychologists and other professionals in career assessment; the mentality among such trainees—all of whom are full-fledged professionals—seems to be more on what to test than on what variables to measure. "What tests do I use, where do I purchase them, and how do I interpret them?" consume more of the trainees' concerns than do identifying the nature of the problems and the variables to be used. This approach may not fail, but it is not likely to succeed. Sometimes when relevant tests are selected that do address pertinent client concerns, this approach may be effective. But starting with the test rather than the measurement figure is inherently limiting.

Certain commonly used (see Spokane & Hawks, 1990) assessment tools (e.g., the Strong Interest Inventory; Harmon, Hansen, Borgen, & Hammer, 1994; and the Myers–Briggs Type Indicator; Myers, McCaulley,

Quenk, & Hammer, 1998) all too often seem to be used no matter what the student's circumstances, without any serious inquiry as to whether or how they relate to the assessment purposes at hand. Creating a context with the student from which to enhance understanding of the assessment data then can be difficult. Assume, for example, that one student comes to a college counseling center for help after failing to find a college major that seems appealing to her, and a second one comes for help with academic difficulties not explained by ability factors. Assume further that the first student is clinically depressed at the time of her initial visit and that the second one manifests with a personality disorder directly related to the experienced academic difficulties. Testing could be of use in both cases, but starting with commonly used measures of interests and personality would miss the mark in both instances. A clinical interview conducted by a perceptive counselor or psychologist would have identified the possibility of both conditions and have pointed the way to the choice of relevant assessment instrumentation. In this approach, selection of instruments would be customized to that student's specific issues.

In short, appropriate integration of assessment data into the college career assessment process requires that two important questions precede the choice of assessment instrument: (a) Why is the assessment being undertaken? and (b) What variables are germane to the assessment task at hand? Only after answering these questions is it appropriate to consider which instruments to use for a particular assessment task and, subsequently, how to present the data in a manner that will be of practical and psychological value to the student.

Remediative Career Counseling

College students obtaining career counseling services typically will be experiencing one of two major types of career-relevant problems: Students who are having some sort of academic difficulty and who seek improvement in their ability to function in their studies, or those who are having trouble identifying appropriate careers and seek assistance in identifying their best options. (Trouble with career choice often presents as having difficulty choosing a major, because deciding on a major, for most people, is metaphorically if not literally the struggle to decide the career choice.) A third possible category is that of the college student who has underlying and primary emotional problems but who presents with academic or career-related difficulties, the career issues being an emotionally safer way to present for help. Of course, many combinations of these types of problems can be encountered in routine career counseling with college students.

Career assessment instruments have important uses with all categories of college students. In deciding careers or majors, assessment of traits can be important in profiling the goodness-of-fit of various career paths. For students encountering academic difficulties, assessment measures can help determine the degree to which their difficulties derive from issues of ability limitations, personality mismatches with otherwise well-fitting careers, or emotional difficulties, to name a few common etiologies. In cases in which such explanations of school and career difficulties do not "explain" the problems, tests also can be useful in establishing the presence of underlying psychological difficulties or personality disorders that need to be addressed, sometimes before career issues can be tackled meaningfully (see, e.g., Lowman, 1993, 1996, 1997).

Making Career Assessment Data Useful

Assuming that the "right" questions have been asked and appropriate assessment methodologies have been used, the next step is to decide how to feed back the data in a way that will be most useful to the student. If the entire process of career counseling is considered a search for the client's truth, the process is necessarily a collaborative one. The most helpful data are (a) those that are relevant for assessing the student's presenting problems; (b) those that can, with competent counseling assistance, be understood and accepted by the student; and (c) those whose affective components are addressed in such a manner that the student can emotionally integrate the results.

Given that college students are commonly at the late-adolescent stage of development, certain issues occur with regularity and are likely to be relevant to positioning the assessment data. An adolescent is an adult in the making; a key adolescent developmental task is to understand and come to terms with both who one is and who one is becoming. Establishing one's career is a crucial part of that process (see Marcia, 1980; Vondracek, 1992). The college student can benefit from learning to strike a balance between high (sometimes unreasonably high) expectations and realistically possible achievements. In effect, the college student needs to learn how to negotiate successfully between a world of well-intentioned relatives and teachers who communicate "you can become anything you want to be" and cold, hard reality which, through grades and job and peer feedback, may communicate some limitations on what is possible. Career assessment data can help college students come to terms with both who they are and who they are not.

Assessment Models for Helping Clarify Career Choices

This section examines more concretely the steps entailed in the assessment and data integration process for students who present with the common problem of choosing a career. This is by no means the only type of problem with which career assessors can help college students, but it is not possible in a short chapter to consider all of the possible uses of career assessment data. The section addresses what variables need to be measured in assisting college students with career choice issues, what types of assessment data are relevant, and some of the issues entailed in making the data useful to students. Although the main focus is on how the counselor can use assessment results to suggest promising career directions, implications also are presented for the administration of assessments to groups of students, in workshops, or even for an entire student body.

For the purposes of this discussion, the student's concern is with choosing an appropriate career (or college major), and the counselor has determined that simple interviewing and face-to-face counseling techniques are insufficient and that simple self-exploration devices (such as Holland's Self-Directed Search; Holland, Fritzsche, & Powell, 1994) have been tried or have been judged to be inadequate. The student is still "stuck," and assessment data have been judged by the counselor and student to be necessary and worth the time and cost to collect and feed back. Only then should the counselor ask what needs to be measured.

The counselor's choice of theoretical models—whether or not explicitly identified—will determine the assessment devices that he or she will use. If the counselor assumes that choosing a satisfying career is just a function of occupational interests, then interest measures will suffice. If the counselor judges interests and personality traits to be relevant, then he or she will need two types of instruments. If interests, personality traits, and ability are assumed to be most relevant, a larger test battery will be needed. The point is not that "anything goes," but rather that career counselors, at a minimum, need to make their operative assumptions explicit in choosing assessment instruments.

Fortunately, several psychological theories facilitate choosing which career assessment data to collect. Although this chapter focuses on Holland's (1997) hexagonal typology, which in its inception was based on occupational interests (Holland, 1959), other relevant models exist. In particular, those concerned with ability assessment can consider use of Gottfredson's (1986a) Occupational Aptitude Patterns (OAP) map, which was created through the study of ability requirements across occupations (see also Carson et al., 1999). Practitioners especially concerned with personality traits as a starting point for integrative tasks may want to examine Jung's (1923) system of psychological types. This system has received widespread use through its operationalization in the Myers–Briggs Type Indicator (Myers et al., 1998). Any of these could serve as a model for the practitioner, although student data could be formulated around other models as well (e.g., five-factor personality theory; see Goldberg, 1992; Lowman, 1991).

The theory guiding selection of variables, however, is not a matter of personal preference or taste, even though researchers and professionals in the field have not reached consensus as to which model or theory is best for this purpose. That being said, it is probably fair to say that Holland's (1997) theory of occupational interest types is the closest practitioners have to consensus so far. Holland's theory, discussed at length in chapter 1, has generated more than 300 studies since its inception in the late 1950s, according to the references cited by Holland and Gottfredson (1990). The theory supports the integration of career assessment data on a grand scale, serving as a crosswalk not only between interests and occupations, as was its original intent, but also between interests and other domains of psychological variables, reflecting the maturing theory's expansion.

Because the authors of previous chapters in this volume introduce the general features of Holland's theory, the focus here is on its use as an integrative model. A useful tool for doing so is *Lowman's Career Assessment Matrix* (Matrix; see Table 6.1; see Carson, 1998a; Lowman, 1991, 1993), although similar matrices have been created by a number of authors (e.g., Holland, 1997; Spokane, 1996). The Matrix is a table with rows representing each of Holland's six types and columns representing a major domain of psychological traits. The cells of the Matrix show what current empirical research has found to be the traits typically associated with people with dominant interest of that Holland type. More research is needed to fine-tune the nature of the relationships and to determine the subgroups for whom they are—and are not—descriptive.

Actually, it is possible to identify the rows of the Matrix with "personal orientations" rather than with types per se. *Personal orientations* refer to people classified by dominant interest areas (see Spokane, 1996, p. 40); this concept better reflects Holland's original (1959) theoretical statement, in which he was concerned with the classification of people on the basis of dominant interests. Holland (1997) later used *vocational personality type* to refer to a more abstract, general category encompassing not only interests but also all other traits (abilities, skills, personality, values, and biographical data). This point may sound esoteric, but it has practical consequences.

It may be more difficult to unambiguously classify people at this time by vocational personality type than by personal orientation, because the variables that one might use as indicators of vocational personality type do not always agree with one another. In fact, students' career assessment data may be inconsistent across domains. Considering the vocational personality type at a purely theoretical level (within Holland's theory), no facet of personality is primary, and therefore no way exists to identify the "true" type. In practical terms, however, it is impossible to base the Matrix on anything other than scores on an interest inventory, because no one yet has developed a fully validated system for doing so on the basis of abilities, personality traits, or other characteristics.

The Matrix continues to evolve, and the version shown in Table 6.1 represents the authors' current thinking on the general properties of personal orientations. Lowman's (1991) original Matrix has been amended on the basis of results of recent empirical research, particularly work reported by Ackerman (1996; Ackerman & Heggestad, 1997), Carson (1998a, 1998b), Lowman and Palmer (1996), and Prediger (1999), among others. The model remains an interdomain (Lowman, 1991, 1997) model (i.e., it synthesizes interests, abilities, and personality).

Within the abilities/knowledge category, several complicating factors arise and need clarification. In the model's original inception (Lowman, 1991), *general intelligence* (the kind of "fluid" intelligence commonly measured on intelligence tests and which is typically referred to as g) is considered to belong in a separate category of abilities from specific abilities

Table 6.1.   An Alternative Version of Lowman's (1991) Career
Assessment Matrix

Interests	Abilities	Personality
Realistic	+Mechanical	+Reserved and introverted
	+Spatial (hands on)	+Tough minded
	+Spatial (mental)	+Masculinity
	+Inductive reasoning	−Intellectance
	−Social and interpersonal	−Ascendance
	−Idea generation/divergent thinking	−/o Adjustment and self-control
	−Writing speed	
	−Clerical speed and accuracy	
	−Language usage	
	−Spelling	
Investigative	+g	+Introversion
	+Language usage	+Self-control
	+Spelling	+Reserved
	+Spatial (mental)	+Masculinity
	+Convergent thinking	+Intellectance
	−Mechanical	−Likeability
	−Inductive reasoning	
Artistic	+g	−Adjustment
	+Vocabulary	+/−Intellectance[a]
	+Analytical reasoning	−Likeability
	−Numerical/computational	+Introversion (with exceptions)
	+Aesthetic judgment *and*	Masculinity + females − males
	+Reproductive drawing ability *and*	+/−Self-control[b]
	+Spatial *or*	+Independence
	+Musical ability *and/or*	
	+Idea generation/divergent thinking	
Social	+Social/interpersonal	+Adjustment
	+Idea generation/divergent thinking	+Ascendance[c]
	+Writing speed	+Intellectance
	−Spatial	−Introversion
	−Mechanical	+Likeability
		−Masculinity
		+Self-control
		−Tough-mindedness
		−Reserved
Enterprising	−g	+Adjustment
	−Spelling	+Ascendance
	+Organizing/managing skills	o Intellectance
	+Social/interpersonal	−Introversion
		−Reserved
		+Masculinity
		+Self-control
		+Tough-mindedness

Table continues

Table 6.1. (*Continued*)

Interests	Abilities	Personality
Conventional	+Numerical/computational +Spelling +Clerical/perceptual speed and accuracy −Idea generation/divergent thinking −Vocabulary −Writing speed −Mechanical	+Introversion +Self-control +Reserved o Adjustment −Independence −Ascendance −Intellectance −Masculinity

Note. + = high scores, − = low scores, and o = medium scores.
From *The Clinical Practice of Career Assessment: Interests, Abilities, and Personality* 186–187, by Rodney L. Lowman, 1991, Washington, DC: American Psychological Association. Copyright © 1991 by the American Psychological Association. Adapted with permission.
[a]Varies by type of artistic endeavor (e.g., writers, high; actors, average or below).
[b]+ = Self-control in work and − = in personal life.
[c]Higher interpersonal ascendance; low need for power over others.

(which are sometimes referred to as *s*). The model implies that *g* must be differentiated from more specific, or circumscribed, abilities that affect a more narrow range of performance (e.g., musical aptitudes). Most specific abilities are related to a greater or lesser extent to *g*, which unquestionably is important in a wide variety of career and job performances. Career assessment that attempts to differentiate matches with a wide range of potential careers, however, must measure across a wide spectrum of abilities.

The resulting Matrix is similar to Holland's (1997) hexagon (see chapter 1 in this volume), but several differences may be noted, most of which have to do with the relationships between abilities and interests. First, the abilities typical of the personal orientations are generally "zero-sum" across the hexagon; that is, if a given orientation is high on one ability, the orientation on the opposite side of the hexagon is likely to be relatively (not infrequently, substantially) lower.

Thus, conventional people tend to be higher on numerical abilities than artistic ones, but the reverse is the case for vocabulary ability. Investigative people tend to be higher on *g* than enterprising ones, but the reverse tends to be the case for specific memory-related abilities. Realistic people tend to be higher on spatial abilities than those who have a social orientation (see, e.g., Lowman & Ng, 1994), but the reverse is the case for abilities related to the fluency of generating words. In his original Matrix, Lowman (1991) proposed that realistic types would be low on *g*, and investigative, social, and enterprising types high on *g*. More recent findings suggest that people with investigative personal orientations (and, to a lesser degree, those with realistic or artistic orientations) tend to be higher on *g*, with enterprising people (and to a lesser degree social or conventional ones) lower on *g* (see Carson, 1998a, 1998b). Most accounts of Holland's theory suggest that investigative people are dominant over other orientations in numerical abilities, but recent research (Carson, 1998a) suggests that those who are conventional may be dominant in several specific abilities, including numerical ones, with investigative people consistently being dominant primarily on g. (The types of numerical skills at which conventional types excel are more likely to be computational rather than g-laden in nature.) Moreover, in this model (Carson's extension of Lowman's model), every orientation is dominant over others in at least one objectively measurable general or specific ability, contrary to some reports that did not differentiate general from specific ability (e.g., Ackerman, 1996). In a minor discrepancy from Lowman's original Matrix, Carson (1998a) found that people with an artistic orientation were relatively higher in the personality trait ascendance.

The practitioner seeking to integrate data across the multiple variable domains can use the Matrix to generate hypotheses about the student's personal orientation and vocational personality type. When all the data consistently point to a particular pattern as dominant and other patterns as secondary and tertiary types, the practitioner may confidently use the standard crosswalks to educational majors and occupations. However, discrepancies make using crosswalks more complicated. Lowman (1991, 1993) provided a thorough discussion of considerations in clinical decision making in the face of such discrepancies.

Ideally, the counselor would have access to detailed research data showing the psychological profiles (abilities, personality, interests, and perhaps other traits) associated with success and satisfaction in particular occupations and then compare a client's assessment results to the profiles. Unfortunately, as Lowman (1993) noted, multiple-domain data exist for relatively few occupations. Consequently, career counselors of college students may have at hand much more information about the student than about the characteristics of the educational and work environments toward which the student might consider advancing.

College career counselors may understandably try to "solve" this problem by encouraging the student to make decisions solely on the basis of interests when he or she has (or is assumed to have) a level of g adequate for the position. Because most college students have levels of g sufficient for many positions to which they may aspire, counselors may tend to rely on interest inventories and ignore the differential assessment of abilities or personality traits. This strategy has the advantage of being easy and quick to administer (and relatively inexpensive). Widely used crosswalks to occupations match individual interests to interests presumed to characterize particular occupational groups.

This strategy, however, also has limitations. There is no guarantee that the various specific abilities (or even g, for that matter) will agree with interests. Likewise, students' ability patterns may not match their career motivation (e.g., the levels to which clients aspire), no matter what their interest patterns are. Depending on the college student population, the selectivity of the admissions standards, and the like, considerably more variability may exist among college populations than one might assume to be the case. Additionally, little is known about the non-g (i.e., specific) ability requirements for success in various professional occupations. Empirical research may establish that differentiating ability profiles indeed exist among people with IQs in, say, the 120 range or above, when abilities are measured at a sufficiently high level to be differentiating. (This statement also implies, incidentally, that multidimensional aptitude tests geared for use with high school or general adult ability levels may be inappropriate for use with high-ability adults.)

As with the design of career intervention systems for large groups of students (discussed later in this chapter), the broad measurement of abilities quickly becomes a problem of cost–benefit. Providing more thorough assessment of all traits relevant to the Matrix generally becomes prohibitively expensive both from the student's and the practitioner's perspective. As Lowman (1993) has noted, however, most students may not need remediative career counseling. General populations can benefit from career guidance that is based on interests and personality because the "invisible hand" (Lowman, 1993) that directs them to reasonably appropriate careers has worked predictably well. In mass education or screening programs, a few people may be identified as needing more extensive assessment; most participants may simply find the information useful and interesting, but they will not change careers as a result.

Identifying a Career Direction for Students

The problem of understanding how to integrate complex career assessment data at an individual level, especially data cutting across multiple domains, entails the use of inductive reasoning and the integration of seemingly disparate elements of information into a meaningful whole. Essentially, the counseling task is to determine how a student is similar to other classes of people, especially people in particular academic majors or occupations. The task is to break the student's characteristics into facets for purposes of splitting a larger group of students into meaningful groupings that correspond to career clusters with ever-greater specificity, for purposes of diagnostic classification and decision making. Of course, the study of personality, broadly considered, is concerned with both integration and differentiation (Allport, 1937, chapter 5), and counselors necessarily are concerned with both processes in their work with students.

Regardless of the integrative model used, the purpose is to move beyond simple exploration of the various features of the student's test results and to integrate findings with the questions that prompted the student to obtain help in the first place. Students often seek the counselor's recommendations for particular courses of study or occupations that are "best bets." Actually, it may be sufficient to provide only a fuzzy, general sense of direction, especially early in the student's process of exploring options, but finding an appropriate (or "good-enough fitting") career direction may remain the goal. Left to their own devices, most students, given sufficient time for trial-and-error search, will perform this feat for themselves. Most students will discover a career path that provides a reasonably satisfying and satisfactory adjustment to work. A reasonable goal for career interventions with the typical college student, therefore, is to orient them more directly toward the career path to which that trial-and-error search might have led them anyway. However, for the student seeking remediative career services, that natural selection process has somehow stopped or does not work well for the student.

In short, the traditional practice of career guidance is desirable in college as well as other settings. Career counselors have both good measures of individual traits (thus permitting analytical assessment) and increasingly good theories (and empirical validation) for how those traits hang together into types that suggest academic majors and occupations.

Once the counselor opts for assessment as a goal in career intervention, and once the student has completed career assessment measures, one major problem for both counselor and student is how to handle discrepancies and inconsistencies in the data. Most problematic are discrepancies across domains (e.g., the career options—or Holland types—suggested by abilities do not appear to match those suggested by the personality traits). The counselor can explore with the student why the interdomain data appear not to match; the student surely can help in this area. The college career counselor should be forewarned, however: Such explorations all too easily can sink into the morass of trying to discover what the student's "true" vocational type is and toward discounting any inconsistent data. The problem is that the seemingly inconsistent data are just as real as the data "consistent" with the supposedly underlying pattern. Luckily, sometimes just pointing out inconsistencies across domains may be helpful to a student. Indeed, it helps for the counselor to conceptualize his or her role as facilitator and guide—the student is the one whose job it is, over time, to understand and sort through the apparent inconsistencies. Also, exploring clinical interview and biographical data with the student may uncover clues as to why discrepancies exist across interdomain data.

One way to reduce the chance of inconsistency, or at least to generate some assessment data that are consistent across domains, is to administer more than one type of measure of each major domain (Lowman, 1991). Doing so will provide the counselor with a more comprehensive picture of the student's traits. The downside is that the picture may get still murkier (e.g., additional disagreements found across measures within a trait domain.) Moreover, the time spent administering a second interest inventory could be dedicated to completing measures of abilities or personality.

Communicating Interpretations to Students

Counselors usually package their test interpretations to students in one of five ways; depending on the degree of individualization and the role of the counselor, these include: (a) an individualized report delivered orally by the counselor, (b) a written report prepared by the counselor, (c) an individualized report that to some degree automates the production of a written report that the counselor had some hand in generating, (d) an individualized written report that the counselor had no hand in generating, or (e) a generic written report. The report types essentially represent different levels of counselor involvement in the career assessment process. Greater levels of counselor involvement (e.g., orally presented, individualized results or an individualized written report authored by the counselor) are typically associated with more "costly" forms of intervention, such as individual or group counseling. Lower levels of counselor involvement (e.g., written reports in which the counselor provides little or no tailoring of content) usually are associated with less costly forms of intervention, such as workshops, classes, consulting, and stand-alone interventions (including computer-assisted career guidance systems; see Hinkelman & Luzzo, 1997; Sampson & Norris, 1997).

According to Tallent (1992), the traditional psychological report includes two sections: (a) a list of the results for each test (the "analytical" section) and (b) a discussion of the meaning of the various results and recommendations (the "inductive" section). Traditional reports frequently are formulaic, verbose, and boring. They also lend themselves to automation through computer-generated reports. Too often, written career assessment reports are exclusively computer generated, with little integration of the data to aid the student in solving his or her important problem.

Tallent (1992, pp. 204–210) suggested that a better approach to reports is the case-focused one, which is based on the clinical approach to conceptualizing cases (see also Lowman, 1991). The case-focused report identifies the main problem or problems to be addressed through assessment, and everything in the report relates to understanding and solving the problem in a unified manner. According to Tallent, "what this amounts to is that the psychological assessor should practice a mild form of caricature. We are charged with presenting a clinically useful picture, not an exact photograph" (p. 210). The counselor may develop a brief, case-focused report around the central themes of the presenting problem (probably focusing on one of Gottfredson's [1986b] criteria, as discussed in chapter 5) and how the assessment results relate to that specific problem. Among college students, it is likely that the most common problem that merits a report has to do with Gottfredson's second criterion, namely, the degree to which a student's chosen occupations reflect his or her interests and abilities. Formulated as such, a brief report (as short as a single page) may be sufficient to deal with the immediate problem. The goal is not to be a slave to a set of items to include in a report but to address the central problem as concisely as possible.

Designing a System of Career Intervention for Large Groups

The basic problem confronting the administrator charged with designing a system for career assessments or interventions for large groups of students is how to arrange investments in different intervention modalities, each of which carry not only different costs but also different levels of probable impact. Again, the common modalities are individual counseling, group counseling, workshops, classes, stand-alone interventions, and consulting. Individual career counseling can be expensive but carries substantially more potential impact, although its greatest effects now appear to occur within the first three sessions (Whiston, Sexton, & Lasoff, 1998). Group work presumably has somewhat less impact than individual counseling, but it costs less per intervention. Much lower cost-per-intention modalities include consulting or stand-alone interventions (e.g., posters or Web sites).

In some settings, such as prestigious business schools, extensive career assessment services may include individual meetings with assessors, standardized testing, videotaping of assessees, and so on. However, most settings are not so well funded, and cost–benefit considerations therefore influence how administrators design career interventions. Most assessors will find it difficult and expensive to gather the extensive data needed to create case-focused reports.

In most settings, the career assessor must make do with available resources. For example, although highly desirable, it is not essential that the assessor always meet one-on-one with the assessee. It probably helps the assessor in preparing the report to have had some direct contact with the assessee, but it is not necessary, provided that a sufficiently rich source of data regarding the assessee is available. This situation is especially true when data from tests, inventories, and life history are supplemented with behavioral observation data, such as video and audio data. The administrator of a college counseling center might reasonably strive to automate some phases of data collection and then provide the assessor with a chance to integrate the data into a case formulation around, for example, one of Gottfredson's major criteria (see chapter 5). As a first step in this direction of automating data collection, the administrator might create an assessment station in the counseling center using a computer with a microphone and video camera attached. (Although it may be impossible in many of today's centers to add electronic equipment to the career assessment process, the falling costs of such resources suggest that those facilities may eventually be within every center's reach.) Because the assessor selectively attends to the portions of the data that best relate to the problem of interest, it should be much easier to formulate the case and then write the brief report for the student.

Some counselors will make better assessors and report writers than others. The administrator, knowing this, may choose to assign report-writing tasks to the best people for that role. Other counselors may do better at other tasks and other modalities of counseling (e.g., leading workshops).

Many colleges seek to move any career intervention to the least expensive modality possible that still offers appropriate service, given the student's level of need for assistance. The debate lies in whether a service should guarantee that the staff interacting with students should always be at a level of training adequate to deal with the student's level of need. At many universities, students, even student volunteers, conduct the initial screening process with relatively little training. Only once it is determined that a student needs more assistance is he or she "bumped up" to more expensive interventions (e.g., formal paper-and-pencil testing and, if warranted, a career counseling professional with graduate degrees). This is not an unreasonable approach, provided the initial screenings or assessments are competently performed.

Another approach is for the most highly skilled professionals on a counseling center staff to always conduct the initial screening; the student then is referred to lower priced modalities if he or she is experiencing a lower level of need for assistance. The rationale here is that the expert staff member will be in a better position to quickly diagnose who needs the most help. This may or may not be the most cost-efficient or highest quality system; it also assumes that the people delivering the second phase of the service delivery process are competent.

Either extreme begets problems, because both tend to rely on human interviews to diagnose the student's problem and because the human "expert's" diagnosis, without sufficient assessment data, is likely to be subject to multiple types of bias (see Garb, 1998, chapter 5; Tallent, 1992) as well as expensive. A standardized assessment program will most quickly result in the most appropriate interventions for students needing remediative (rather than optimizing) services. However, a consistently applied system that assumes high functioning and then only by steps moves the student to higher cost modalities will generally work best from a cost–benefit perspective.

Translations to Practice

Again, the key points for counselors are as follows:

- Counselors and administrators in colleges may wish to consider *where* students encounter career interventions; it may be "beyond the counseling center," for example, in classes. For each location of intervention, counselors and administrators need to ensure that the right questions are asked, that the right assessment tools are used, and that students receive appropriate feedback.
- Counselors should not merely assign the same test or two to every student in an otherwise diverse student body. They should have a reason for the use of any assessment tools with any particular student.
- Counselors must be alert to alternative explanations when working with a student experiencing difficulties in academic and career development; such alternatives may include lack of study skills, mental or emotional disorders, physical disabilities, and substance abuse. Again, the message is to take a sufficiently broad perspective. Although use of an expert interviewer may help rule out various alternative explanations, appropriate standardized measures frequently exist that the counselor also may use for this purpose. It is important to organize the system of intervention so that stu-

dents with special assessment or intervention needs are "passed upward" through the system for more intensive (and usually more expensive) assessments and interventions.

- Counselors should not uncritically accept the notion of vocational personality type (Holland, 1997)—the concept integrates key trait domains (interests, values, and abilities) that themselves have only a weak correlation to one another. This notion is consistent with maintaining a case-focused orientation during assessment rather than a one-size-fits-all approach.
- In assessment for career counseling, if the assessment results and report are neither relevant to nor desired by the student, they have no value. One of the best ways to achieve relevance and interest is to write a case-focused report (Tallent, 1992) rather than a traditional "test-by-test" approach.

Conclusion

No field of psychology is quite as exciting as career counseling, and assessment data are an important part of the process. Assessments are valuable for both remediative and optimizing purposes. To appropriately use assessment results, college counselors must complete the proper preparatory work, including defining the nature of the presenting problems before deciding what variables to measure and which tests to use. Interpreting, or integrating, assessment data and translating them into a format useful for answering college students' questions present a significant challenge, and counselors must consider psychological factors to provide data in a format from which students can benefit.

References

Ackerman, P. L. (1996). A theory of adult intellectual development: Process, personality, interests, and knowledge. *Intelligence, 22,* 227–257.

Ackerman, P. L., & Heggestad, E. D. (1997). Intelligence, personality, and interests: Evidence for overlapping traits. *Psychological Bulletin, 121,* 219–245.

Allport, G. W. (1937). *Personality: A psychological interpretation.* New York: Henry Holt.

Carson, A. D. (1998a). The integration of interests, aptitudes, and personality traits: A test of Lowman's matrix. *Journal of Career Assessment, 6,* 83–105.

Carson, A. D. (1998b). The relation of self-reported abilities to aptitude test scores: A replication and extension. *Journal of Vocational Behavior, 53,* 353–371.

Carson, A. D., Bizot, E. B., Hendershot, P. E., Barton, M. G., Garvin, M. K., & Kraemer, B. (1999). Modeling career counselor decisions with artificial neural networks: Predictions of fit across a comprehensive occupational map. *Journal of Vocational Behavior, 54,* 196–213.

Garb, H. N. (1998). *Studying the clinician: Judgment research and psychological assessment.* Washington, DC: American Psychological Association.

Goldberg, L. R. (1992). The development of markers for the Big Five factor structure. *Psychological Assessment, 4,* 26–42.

Gottfredson, L. S. (1986a). Occupational Aptitude Patterns Map: Development and implications for a theory of job aptitude requirements [Monograph]. *Journal of Vocational Behavior, 29,* 254–291.

Gottfredson, L. S. (1986b). Special groups and the beneficial use of vocational interest inventories. In W. B. Walsh & S. H. Osipow (Eds.), *Advances in vocational psychology: Vol. I. The assessment of interests* (pp. 127–198). Hillsdale, NJ: Lawrence Erlbaum.

Harmon, L. W., Hansen, J.-I. C., Borgen, F. H., & Hammer, A. L. (1994). *Strong Interest Inventory: Applications and technical guide*. Palo Alto, CA: Consulting Psychologists Press.

Hinkelman, J. M., & Luzzo, D. A. (1997). Computer-assisted career guidance: Bridging the science-practitioner gap. *Career Planning and Adult Development Journal, 13*, 41–50.

Holland, J. L. (1959). A theory of vocational choice. *Journal of Counseling Psychology, 6*, 35–44.

Holland, J. L. (1997). *Making vocational choices: A theory of vocational personalities and work environments* (3rd ed.). Odessa, FL: Psychological Assessment Resources.

Holland, J. L., Fritzsche, B. A., & Powell, A. B. (1994). *The Self-Directed Search technical manual*. Odessa, FL: Psychological Assessment Resources.

Holland, J. L., & Gottfredson, G. D. (1990). *An annotated bibliography for Holland's theory of vocational personalities and work environments*. Unpublished manuscript, Johns Hopkins University.

Jung, C. G. (1923). *Psychological types*. London: Routledge & Keegan Paul.

Lowman, R. L. (1991). *The clinical practice of career assessment: Interests, abilities, and personality*. Washington, DC: American Psychological Association.

Lowman, R. L. (1993). The inter-domain model of career assessment and counseling. *Journal of Counseling and Development, 71*, 549–554.

Lowman, R. L. (1996). Dysfunctional work role behavior. In K. Murphy (Ed.), *Individual differences and behavior in organizations* (pp. 371–415). San Francisco: Jossey-Bass.

Lowman, R. L. (1997). Career assessment and psychological impairment: Integrating inter-domain and work dysfunctions theory. *Journal of Career Assessment, 5*, 213–224.

Lowman, R. L., & Ng, Y. M. (1994, August). *Ability, interest and personality characteristics of employed realistic males*. Paper presented at the annual meeting of the American Psychological Association, Los Angeles.

Lowman, R. L. & Palmer, L. (1996, August). An extension and test of Lowman's inter-domain (interest-ability-personality) model. In R. L. Lowman, (Chair), *New theories and empirical research on inter-domain (interest-ability-personality) relationships and applications*. Symposium presented at the annual meeting of the American Psychological Association, Toronto.

Marcia, J. E. (1980). Identity in adolescence. In J. Adelson (Ed.), *Handbook of adolescent psychology*. (pp. 159–187). New York: Wiley & Sons.

Myers, I. B., McCaulley, M. H., Quenk, N. L., & Hammer, A. L. (1998). *MBTI Manual: A guide to the development and use of the Myers-Briggs Type Indicator*. Palo Alto, CA: Consulting Psychologists Press.

Prediger, D. J. (1999). Basic structure of work-relevant abilities. *Journal of Counseling Psychology, 46*, 173–184.

Sampson, J. P., Jr., & Norris, D. (1997). An evaluation of the effectiveness of implementing computer-assisted career guidance. *Career Planning and Adult Development Journal, 13*, 75–86.

Spokane, A. R. (1996). Holland's theory. In D. Brown, L. Brooks, & Assoc. (Eds.), *Career choice and development: Applying Contemporary theories to practice* (3rd ed., pp. 33–74). San Francisco: Jossey-Bass.

Spokane, A. R., & Hawks, B. K. (1990). Practice and research in career counseling and development, 1989. *Career Development Quarterly, 39*, 98–128.

Tallent, N. (1992). *The practice of psychological assessment*. Englewood Cliffs, NJ: Prentice Hall.

Vondracek, F. W. (1992). The construct of identity and its use in career theory and research. *Career Development Quarterly, 41*, 130–144.

Whiston, S. C., Sexton, T. L., & Lasoff, D. L. (1998). Career-intervention outcome: A replication and extension of Oliver and Spokane (1988). *Journal of Counseling Psychology, 45*, 150–165.

7

Individual Career Counseling

Susan C. Whiston

As the chapters in this book indicate, many college students report difficulties with career issues and indicate that they would like assistance with career planning. The question then becomes, What are the most effective methods for assisting those students? Research over the past 50 years has indicated that the most effective method of providing career services is through individual counseling.

A recent meta-analysis (Whiston, Sexton, & Lasoff, 1998) compared the effectiveness of various career interventions (e.g., workshops, career classes, computer programs, and individual counseling) and found that individual career counseling was the most effective. Although this finding was based on only a small number of studies, the effectiveness of individual career counseling also is supported by an earlier meta-analysis. When Oliver and Spokane (1988) examined which career interventions produced the greatest gains for clients in the shortest amount of time, they found that individual career counseling produced the greatest client gain per hour or session. The Whiston et al. study also found that individual career counseling was the most expedient method for producing positive career outcomes for clients. In fact, both studies indicated that the effects of individual counseling seem to occur quickly, with the large effects being achieved in an average of 2.5 hours. Support for using individual career counseling also is indicated by the findings that the positive results that clients experience from individual career counseling tend to endure (Kirschner, Hoffman, & Hill, 1994). Given the effectiveness of individual career counseling, this chapter will focus on that treatment modality.[1]

Although many college students desire assistance with career issues, some disturbing trends indicate that counselors may be neglecting clients' career issues by focusing on other mental health issues. Numerous surveys have documented practitioners' declining interest in career counseling activities and increasing interest in psychotherapy and personal adjustment counseling (Birk & Brooks, 1986; Fitzgerald & Osipow, 1988; Watkins, Schneider, Cox, & Reinberg, 1987). This declining interest may affect the counseling services that clients with career issues receive. In examining

---

[1]It should be mentioned that career classes and workshops also have positive effect sizes (Oliver & Spokane, 1988; Whiston et al., 1998); chapter 8 addresses those types of career services.

the quality of intake evaluations, Gelso et al. (1985) found that the quality was lower for clients presenting with vocational concerns than for clients with personal concerns. In addition, others researchers have found that counselors with a preference for personal counseling were less likely to diagnose the vocational problem; to provide career counseling, job search, or occupational information; or to use an interest inventory than were clinicians with an interest in working with vocational problems (Spengler, Blustein, & Strohmer, 1990).

Although individual career counseling is the most effective method of intervening on career issues (Oliver & Spokane, 1988; Whiston et al., 1998), practitioners may not be interested or trained in how to perform effective individual counseling. This chapter is designed to address this issue by exploring the research related to effective individual career counseling with college students. As Astin (1993) stressed, college students have distinct needs, which include career development issues. It is important that clinicians understand the unique needs of college students and provide career services that are effective for this group.

This chapter has an empirical base and provides a summary of the research related to effective individual career counseling, rather than a model of individual career counseling. The first section discusses the similarities and differences between individual career counseling and personal counseling. The second section provides an overview of process variables (e.g., client characteristics, counselor behaviors) that are related to effective career counseling outcomes, and the third section focuses on specific interventions that have been shown to influence positive outcome for college students. Because college students vary in their needs and attributes, the fourth section provides an overview of the research related to matching specific career treatments or interventions with client attributes or characteristics.

Individual Career Counseling versus Personal Counseling

Some practitioners may not be interested in individual career counseling because they see it as something separate from personal counseling. Opinions vary on the degree of overlap between career and individual counseling. Rounds and Tracey (1990) and Richardson (1996) argued that a false dichotomy is drawn between psychotherapy-type counseling and career counseling and suggested that career counseling falls within the broader category of psychotherapy and counseling. Conversely, Spokane (1991) argued that although some overlap exists between career counseling and psychotherapy, career counseling should be distinguished from psychotherapy. Spokane contended that career counseling is not just the application of counseling skills to vocational issues. Hackett (1993) stated that on rare occasions, a clinician might be able to focus on "pure" career or personal issues, but more often the two are intertwined in a complex manner. Although overlap may exist between personal counseling and career counseling, a unique set of knowledge and skills is necessary in counseling college students on career issues.

The intertwining of career and personal counseling is supported by Anderson and Niles's (1995) findings that noncareer concerns frequently arise in career counseling with adults. Lucas (1992) found few differences between college students seeking counseling for career issues and students seeking assistance with other issues; both groups have concerns about study habits, emotional distress, and relationships. Although some practitioners may believe that career clients are less distressed than clients with personal concerns, Gold and Scanlon (1993) found that career counseling clients and noncareer clients had similar levels of psychological distress. Some evidence shows that clients' satisfaction with counseling is not related to whether the focus is more on career or personal issues (Phillips, Friedlander, Kost, Specterman, & Robbins, 1988). The similarity of personal and career counseling also is supported by Kirschner et al.'s (1994) findings that a counselor's behaviors were similar in both career and personal counseling. The few differences in behavior that they found were related to the psychologist using more intentions of setting limits and giving information and fewer intentions of cognition and self-control in career counseling compared with personal counseling.

Given that career and personal counseling are intertwined, two bodies of knowledge exist that can assist clinicians in providing effective career counseling to college students. First, clinicians have 100 years of theoretical and empirical exploration of career development and career interventions. Second, in providing effective individual career counseling, the clinician must also be an effective counselor. This requirement leads to the suggestion that career counselors also be knowledgeable with a second body of research, which is the research related to effective counseling and psychotherapy. Niles and Pate (1989) suggested that practitioners need skills in both career and mental health counseling to address the complexities of client concerns effectively. Readers unfamiliar with counseling and psychotherapy outcome research are directed to sources such as Bergin and Garfield (1994); Luborsky, Crits-Christoph, Mintz, and Auerbach (1988); and Sexton, Whiston, Bleuer, and Walz (1997). This chapter assumes that the practitioner is a skilled clinician with knowledge about effective personal counseling and focuses on how clinicians can build on that clinical base to provide effective individual career counseling.

Process and Outcome

Although the research indicates that individual career counseling is one of the most effective methods of providing services to clients with career issues, the research is somewhat limited on the process that should occur in this counseling. The terms *process* or *process variables* typically refer to what happens in the counseling sessions. Not as much is known about the process of career counseling as is known about personal counseling and psychotherapy (Meir, 1991; Spokane, 1991). Currently, researchers are beginning to explore the process of career counseling and identify the factors within the process that influence outcome. Often client and counselor characteristics are considered part of process research because they influence what occurs. Specific interventions (e.g., computer interventions or interest inventories) are addressed later in this chapter because such strategies are not always part of the general career counseling process.

Client Characteristics

Neither Oliver and Spokane (1988) nor Whiston et al. (1998) identified any client characteristics that predicted successful outcome in career counseling. Interestingly, neither the age nor the type of client (e.g., those seeking counseling, nonclient volunteers, convenience samples) was related to outcome. In addition, researchers who have examined differences in the career counseling outcomes among ethnic and racial groups have yet to find significant differences. The lack of differences in outcome also is true for both men and women receiving career counseling. These findings, however, should not be interpreted to mean that it is appropriate for all clients to receive the same generic career counseling. Because college students vary in their stage of career development and related career issues, many researchers have contended that career counseling needs to be geared toward the individual client (Fretz, 1981; Whiston et al., 1998).

Client Preferences and Expectations

College students' expectations about career counseling need to be taken into account when the practitioner is making decisions about the counseling process. Practitioners may need to work to engage clients who have low expectations of counseling. Tinsley, Tokar, and Helwig (1994) found that clients with relatively positive expectations about career counseling were more involved in the first session of career counseling than were those with less positive expectations. It also appears that college students have fairly clear ideas about what they want from career counseling. Galassi, Crace, Martin, James, and Wallace (1992) found that college students anticipated devoting about three sessions to the process. What they most frequently hoped to achieve during the counseling involved clarifying career goals, career direction, and methods for achieving their goals. Students also frequently reported that they wanted the counseling to confirm either a college major or a career choice. This study (Galassi et al., 1992) explored students' preferences for activities during sessions and what they anticipated would occur in the career counseling. Their results showed that students preferred talking about specific careers and decision making but that they expected to explore those possibilities themselves or take tests during the sessions. Thus, there appeared to be some mismatch between what the students would prefer to take place and what they expected to occur in sessions. The prospective clients were unsure of what the counselor would do but preferred that the counselor give advice, opinions, and answers. The clients also indicated that they were willing to participate between sessions by being involved in activities such as reading, collecting information, and interviewing people. For practitioners interested in measuring clients' attitudes toward career counseling, the Attitudes Toward Career Counseling scale (Rochlen, Mohr, & Hargrove, 1999), a new instrument, shows promise in measuring clients' perceptions of the expected value and stigma related to career counseling.

Session and Counseling Factors

Kirschner et al. (1994) reported one study that provides unique insights into the process of career counseling. Using a case study approach, the researchers found that career counseling sessions could be described in three stages: (a) establishing rapport and obtaining information, (b) interpreting tests, and (c) consolidating career choices. Kirschner and her colleagues examined which counselor intentions were most helpful in individual career counseling. Counselor intentions were used because they are associated strongly with actual behaviors in counseling and reflect counselors' subjective reasoning about their choices of interventions (Hill et al., 1988). The two components that most often were identified as being helpful were insight and challenge. These results suggest that career counseling needs to involve complex counseling skills, whereby the practitioner facilitates client insight and uses skills that are challenging and confrontive. Although challenging and confrontation interventions may increase anxiety, they may not be detrimental to the client; Hill and Spokane (1995) found that increases in anxiety were associated with increases in information gathering. It may be that discomfort is a necessary precursor to instituting constructive behavioral change. Spokane (1991) argued that a decline in anxiety during career counseling may be unrealistic and, in fact, detrimental to obtaining a positive outcome.

Other intentions that Kirschner et al. (1994) found to be helpful were giving information, focusing on feelings, focusing on change, and focusing on the relationship. Once again, the results reflected that the intentions or skills found to be associated with effective career counseling are intentions typically associated with personal counseling. Nagel, Hoffman, and Hill (1995) also found that successful career counselors tended to be active in their approach and primarily used information giving, direct guidance, paraphrase, and closed-question techniques during the middle stage of counseling. In another study (Nevo, 1990), Israeli students reported that the most significant factors contributing to their satisfaction with career counseling were assistance in organizing their thinking and help in identifying their interests and abilities. The same students ranked discussions with counselors as being more important than using objective tests, interest inventories, or vocational information. It also appears that explaining the parameters of the career counseling in the first session increases perceptions of counselors' credibility (Miller, Mahaffey, Wells, & Tobackyk, 1995). Although all the findings indicate that an active approach in career counseling is generally effective, practitioners should consider that the process should vary with the needs of individual clients (Heppner & Hendricks, 1995).

Relational Factors

In the area of psychotherapy, the research has consistently shown that the quality of the therapeutic relationship or alliance has one of the most significant influences on successful outcome (Horvath & Symonds, 1991; Orlinsky & Howard, 1986; Sexton & Whiston, 1994). The importance of the relationship or working alliance in career counseling is not as well researched, but Heppner and Hendricks (1995) have found that the relationship is important to career counseling clients and the process. Meara and Patton (1994) suggested that counselors communicate both verbally and nonverbally and that career counseling will proceed more effectively if both parties work collaboratively to identify problems and search for solutions. Clinicians need to encourage client participation and empathize with client concerns and issues. Explaining interventions (e.g., interest inventories, computer-assisted information systems) so that clients understand their purposes also may bolster the relationship. Meara and Patton contended that the career counseling process and relationship can be affected adversely when the client is confused about the goals of the counseling, the tasks in the process, and the type of relationship between the client and counselor.

Length of Counseling

Oliver and Spokane (1988) found that the only significant predictor of outcome in career counseling was "treatment intensity," a measure of the length or amount of career counseling that involved both the number of sessions and hours of treatment provided to the clients. They concluded that longer, more thorough career counseling consistently would produce a more effective outcome. Although this finding was not supported by Whiston et al.'s (1998) analysis of more recent research, practitioners should consider that more comprehensive career counseling has been found to be associated with better outcomes. Spokane (1991) suggested that career counseling should involve at least 10 sessions. This conclusion is supported by research specific to college students; Pickering and Vacc (1984), for example, found that long-term career interventions were more successful than short-term interventions. In college settings, however, providing 10 sessions may be somewhat unrealistic. Although practitioners may want to consider methods for providing thorough career counseling services, they also should remember that both Oliver and Spokane (1988) and Whiston et al. (1998) found large effect sizes for individual career counseling even when the average amount of time clients spent in counseling was less than 2.5 hours. Wilson, Mason, and Ewing (1997) examined whether the number of counseling sessions on a variety of life issues had any impact on student retention. They found that the largest incremental gains in terms of student retention occurred in the first six counseling sessions, with few additional gains after that point. Therefore, it seems that counselors should focus on the quality of the initial sessions in order to have the greatest effect on the outcome of the career counseling.

Treatment Interventions and Outcome

A variety of treatments under the umbrella of individual career counseling may influence the effectiveness of career counseling. For example, clinicians sometimes wonder whether to incorporate formal testing instruments or computer applications in their individual counseling. This section addresses the effectiveness of certain treatments or interventions within the broader area of individual career counseling.

Using Assessment Interventions

Spokane (1991) proposed that the purposes of career assessments are to unearth congruent career possibilities, assess conflicts and problems, motivate constructive behavior, acquire a cognitive structure for evaluating career alternatives, clarify expectations and plan interventions, and establish the range of abilities. Although the research is somewhat limited, general findings indicate that clients who receive test interpretations, regardless of the format, experience greater gains in counseling than those who do not receive an interpretation (Goodyear, 1990). In their meta-analysis of career interventions, Oliver and Spokane (1988) found an effect size of .62 for individual test interpretation. Clients report more satisfaction, clarity, and helpfulness when the interpretation is performed individually compared with other formats, such as groups (Goodyear, 1990). If, however, the cost of test interpretation is considered, then the evaluation of whether individual or group is more effective changes somewhat. Krivasty and Magoon (1976) found that individual interpretations were six times more expensive than group interpretations.

Interest inventories are commonly used assessment tools in career counseling. In reviewing the past 70 years of research related to vocational interest, Betsworth and Fouad (1997) found that interests were correlated with career choice. They also found that the relationship between interest and satisfaction was relatively low but suggested that the small correlations could be partially a result of methodological problems. Besides providing useful information for career counseling, Randahl, Hansen, and Haverkamp (1993) found that students who used an interest inventory were involved in more career exploration activities in the year following the test administration than were students who did not take an interest inventory. This finding suggests that career counselors should use an interest inventory routinely with freshmen and sophomores seeking assistance to facilitate career exploration activities. In addition, Lowman (1993) argued that career assessment should be broader than interest assessment. He suggested that practitioners assess patterns of interest, abilities, and personality characteristics. His suggestion concerning abilities assessment is supported by the research indicating that abilities assessment is a good predictor of occupational success (Hunter, 1986; Hunter & Schmidt, 1983). Prediger (1999) argued that ability tests are not the gold standard and that clients' "informed" self-estimates of their abilities also are valid indicators. Furthermore, Prediger found evidence that the basic structure of work abilities corresponds to Holland's (1997) hexagonal model of interest and occupational types. Interested readers are directed to Prediger's study, which shows the interrelationship of interests and abilities. If other research supports Prediger's findings, it will allow for coordinated interpretations of interests and ability assessments, which would facilitate the integration of self-knowledge.

Some clinicians may have concerns about how to use interest inventories and other career assessment tools appropriately with ethnic and racial minority clients. Early research raised some questions about using instruments that were based on Holland's hexagonal model with ethnic minority samples (Rounds & Tracey, 1996); however, more recent research has supported a common vocational-interest structure among racial and ethnic groups (Day & Rounds, 1998; Fouad, Harmon, & Borgen, 1997). Day and Rounds's results are particularly noteworthy because their sample size was greater than 49,000 and involved large groups of minority students. Their multidimensional scaling analysis provided support for traditional methods of assessing career interests by indicating that people from diverse ethnic groups use the same cognitive map or structure of preference when examining career interests. Although these results (Day & Rounds, 1998; Fouad et al., 1997) provide support for using interest inventories with ethnic and racial minority clients, clinicians still need to evaluate any instrument's psychometric qualities to ensure that it is appropriate for the specific client and desired purposes.

Some research provides information on how to best integrate career assessment into the counseling process. Hanson, Claiborn, and Kerr (1997) found some differences between career counseling clients who received an interactive interpretation and those who received a delivered interpretation. The clients who received the interactive interpretation considered their sessions to be "deeper" and rated the counselor as being more expert, trustworthy, and attractive. Goodyear (1990), however, found mixed results on whether clients who participated more in an interpretative process had better outcomes. In addition, some findings indicate that clients perceive interpretations that are tentative as being more helpful than interpretations that are more absolute (Jones & Gelso, 1988). In using assessment results, Hanson and Claiborn (1998) suggested that the counselor should take time to "optimize" the power of the test (e.g., "This test is useful in particular ways, within particular limits"), rather than allowing the client to "maximize" it (e.g., "The test speaks the truth").

Computer Applications

Computer-assisted career-guidance systems (CACGS) serve thousands of clients daily (Sampson & Reardon, 1990); yet, questions remain about how to effectively use these systems. Whiston et al. (1998) found that CACGS were significantly more effective than no treatment but not as effective as individual counseling. CACGS, however, were more cost-effective than individual counseling, which led Whiston et al. to conclude that a combination of individual and computer interventions may be the most efficacious and cost-effective method for delivering career services. Their conclusion is reinforced by numerous studies that have found that computer-plus-counseling is more effective than computer interventions only (Garis & Niles, 1990; Marin & Splete, 1991; Niles & Garis, 1990).

Building on the research showing that the combined effect of computer use and counseling is more effective than using only computer systems, Niles (1993) investigated when it might be most effective for counselors to intervene when using one of the systems. He examined the differences among strategies designed to prepare clients to use the system ("preintervention"), interventions that occurred during the use of the computer system ("enroute"), and strategies that focused on planning after using the system ("postintervention"). The "enroute" group, with whom the counselor intervened during the use of the computer system, reported a higher level of enjoyment in using the system than the postintervention group. The postintervention group, who received counseling after using the computer, however, reported less career indecision than the control group, which did not receive any career counseling services. Thus, it may be better for counselors to intervene both while clients are using a CACGS and after clients have completed working with the system. Additional discussion of many of the issues associated with using CACGS with college students appears in chapter 9 of this book.

Social–Cognitive Approaches

In recent years, social–cognitive theory has had a significant influence on the field in terms of both theoretical applications (e.g., Lent, Brown, & Hackett, 1994) and extensive empirical inquiry (Lent & Hackett, 1987). Social–cognitive theory in general, and self-efficacy in particular, has been the subject of intensive study during the past 20 years, and researchers are learning more about how to apply this theory in career counseling. As discussed in chapter 2, the social–cognitive model holds that each person's career development is influenced by person factors (e.g., race, gender, interests), experiences or experiential sources (e.g., success in certain activities), and contextual determinants (e.g., opportunities, environmental influences) that interact and mutually influence one another. Within this triadic causal system, the variable of person factors is intricately linked to individual self-efficacy beliefs,[2] outcome expectations, and personal goals. It often is important to examine college students' perceptions about their abilities to perform certain tasks because some students may eliminate certain careers on the basis of faulty self-efficacy beliefs. Luzzo, Funk, and Strang (1996) found that self-efficacy in career decision making increased as a result of attributional retraining for students who initially exhibited an external locus of control.[3] Hackett and Betz (1981) theorized that sex role stereotyping would affect self-efficacy beliefs and that women would have lower self-efficacy beliefs in activities such as mathematics and other activities typically thought of as "masculine." Researchers accordingly have found gender differences in factors such as mathematics self-efficacy (Betz & Hackett, 1983; Lent, Lopez, & Bieschke, 1991) and occupational self-efficacy (Post-Kammer & Smith, 1985). In addressing self-efficacy beliefs in career counseling, Juntunen (1996) found that a feminist approach to career counseling can influence career self-efficacy beliefs.

Attribute–Treatment Interactions

It has been suggested (Fretz, 1981; Rounds & Tinsley, 1984; Savickas, 1989) that the important question is no longer whether career counseling is effective, but rather what works with which clients and under what circumstances. Fretz (1981) argued that clients vary and that to identify effective modes of career counseling, researchers need to focus on client attribute-by-treatment interactions. The past 20 years have seen an increase in nontraditional students entering higher education, and college students are no longer a homogenous group. It is, therefore, important that researchers provide information about which career counseling techniques work with which types of students. Research progress on client attribute–treatment interactions has been somewhat slow (Phillips, 1992), but researchers are beginning to identify some of the trends in this area.

Demographic Factors

Over the past two decades, an abundance of research related to gender differences in career development has taken place, and entire texts have been devoted to the career development of women (Betz & Fitzgerald, 1987; Walsh & Osipow, 1994). It is interesting that voluminous research exists on women's career development and work issues, but little of this rich body of information has been transformed into research examining the effect of career counseling or interventions on women's career development. A few studies, such as Kivlighan, Johnston, Hogan, and Mauer

---

[2]Self-efficacy beliefs concern people's perceptions about their abilities to perform certain tasks or behaviors.

[3]Students who generally believe that career development is influenced primarily by chance and factors outside themselves are said to have an external locus of control.

(1994), have examined how gender may interact with treatment. Interestingly, they found that men and women did not vary in the amount of gains in vocational identity as a result of using SIGI PLUS. In an intervention designed specifically for women reentering the work force, Slaney and Dickson (1985) failed to find a significant change in identity as a result of a card-sort exercise. In career counseling with women, counselors should consider issues related to multiple roles, internal barriers, external barriers, and gender stereotypes (Fitzgerald, Fassinger, & Betz, 1995; Fitzgerald & Rounds, 1994).

Many authors are calling for career counselors to be aware of ethnic and racial differences among clients and to vary their counseling to meet the needs of minority clients (Fouad & Bingham, 1995; Leong, 1995). Research support exists for adjusting career counseling interventions to account for the fact that ethnic and racial minority clients consistently report more perceived career barriers (Luzzo, 1993; McWhirter, 1997), lower self-concept (Burke & Hoelter, 1988), and different attitudes toward career decision making (Luzzo, 1992) than do White students. Competent multicultural career counseling is a complex skill that requires clinicians to be aware of their own cultural values, to have an understanding of the worldview of culturally different clients, and to develop and use appropriate intervention strategies (Sue, Arredondo, & McDavis, 1992). Fouad and Bingham (1995) proposed a culturally appropriate model for career counseling, which involves the following seven steps:

1. establishing rapport and a culturally appropriate relationship
2. identifying career issues
3. assessing effects of cultural variables
4. setting counseling goals
4. making culturally appropriate counseling interventions
6. making decisions
7. implementing the decisions and following up.

Although this model has not been tested empirically, it expands on the earlier work of Bingham and Ward (1994) and Ward and Bingham (1993). In working with ethnic and racial minority clients, particularly women, practitioners may benefit from using the checklist that Ward and Bingham developed. The checklist is designed for the counselor to assess whether he or she has the appropriate attitudes and background information to enter career counseling with a client who is culturally different from the practitioner. Designed to stimulate the counselor's awareness of cultural issues, the checklist includes items such as "I am familiar with the minimum cross-cultural competencies," "I have information about this client's ethnic group's history and local sociopolitical issues and the client's attitude toward seeking help," and "I am aware of the importance that interaction of gender and race or ethnicity has in my client's life" (Ward & Bingham, 1993, pp. 250–251).

Counselors also should consider adjusting the career counseling process for clients with disabilities. College students with disabilities are not always fully aware of the various ways in which their disabilities may be influencing their career decision making (Hitchings, Luzzo, Retish, Horvath, & Ristow, 1998). In comparing the career activities of students with disabilities and students without disabilities, Hitchings et al. found that those with disabilities were less likely to have used career materials and career inventories or to have attended a career fair. Furthermore, students with disabilities underused opportunities such as job shadowing and volunteering. The counselor may need to examine the previous career exploration activities of students with disabilities to determine whether the counseling process needs to be supplemented with additional career exploration activities.

Decision-Making Factors

The label of *undecided* typically is applied to students who are developmentally appropriate in being undecided, whereas *indecisive* applies to students who have a chronic problem with indecision (Salomone, 1982). Heppner and Hendricks' (1995) findings supported the case for varying the treatment for undecided and indecisive clients. Using a case study approach, Heppner and Hendricks found that the most important session for an indecisive client was one in which they discussed the client's relationship with his family and the feelings of being overwhelmed with responsibility toward the family. In contrast, the undecided client reported that the most helpful aspects of the career counseling were events that related to aspects of himself or occupations. Heppner and Hendricks also concluded that six sessions may not have been sufficient for the indecisive client and that different interventions may have produced a better outcome with that client. Counselors therefore may want to assess whether students have chronic problems with decision making early in the career counseling process to determine whether brief intervention or in-depth counseling to address the issues around indecision is more appropriate.

Client Personality and Styles

Concerning the interaction between clients' personalities and career counseling interventions, most research has involved Holland's (1985, 1997) typology. Kivlighan and Shapiro (1987) found that investigative and realistic people were more likely than other personality types to benefit from a test feedback intervention rather than an interactive exploration of personality factors. Lenz, Reardon, and Sampson (1993) investigated the effects of selected client characteristics (i.e., gender, personality, level of identity, and degree of differentiation) on clients' evaluation of SIGI-PLUS. Surprisingly, only personality had a significant influence on their ratings; as scores on the social and enterprising scales increased, individual ratings of the system's contribution to their self- and occupational knowledge decreased. Thus, clients with more of a people orientation seemed to prefer more interactions with another person rather than with a computer-assisted program. Earlier research also supported matching the format of the intervention (i.e., interactional vs. individual) to the personality type of the college students (i.e., social and enterprising vs. realistic and investigative; Kivlighan, Hageseth, Tipton, & McGovern, 1981).

Blustein (1987) argued that to provide effective career counseling to college students, one must understand the relationship between decision-making styles and career development. As Holland, Magoon, and Spokane (1981) indicated, the rational assumptions underlying many career interventions may not be appropriate for all clients. Harren (1979) proposed three career decision-making styles in college students. *Rational* decision makers are those who typically use logical deliberations and objective self-appraisal in their career decisions, whereas *intuitive* decision makers rely more on personal self-awareness, emotions, and fantasies in their career decisions. Finally, those with a *dependent* style rely heavily on the opinions of others while making career decisions. A number of studies have examined the interaction between different treatments and clients' decision-making styles. Krumboltz, Kinnier, Rude, Scherba, and Hamel (1986) found that a rational intervention was most effective with dependent decision makers. Conversely, Rubinton (1980) found rational interventions to be most successful with rational decision makers and intuitive interventions to be most successful with intuitive decision makers. Niles, Erford, Hunt, and Watts (1997) found that college students who had a more systematic or rational decision-making style also had accomplished more career development tasks.

Another study (Mau & Jepsen, 1992) examined the interactions between teaching decision-making strategies and clients' decision-making styles. The researchers compared a control group with two groups of students (rational decision makers and nonrational decision makers), who were taught either the elimination-by-aspects strategy (EBA) or the subjective expected-utility strategy (SEU). With the EBA strategy, the decision maker is taught to look for a choice of action that is "good enough," rather than best, and to eliminate options. The SEU approach involves having the decision maker specify desired outcomes and evaluate each alternative until the right choice is made. The researchers found no interaction between decision-making style and the decision-making strategy taught, with rational decision makers benefiting the most regardless of the decision-making strategy they used.

Practitioners should note the research evidence showing that students' decision-making styles will influence the ways in which they make career decisions (Daniels, 1982; Rubinton, 1980). Some clients may not be aware of their typical decision-making style; identifying their style may facilitate greater self-awareness. Many common interventions seem to be of most benefit to the rational decision makers, rather than to those who use a more intuitive or dependent style. Therefore, it is important that counselors consider using alternative methods with clients whose style is intuitive or dependent. For example, if a client has an intuitive style, the counselor might assist the client in identifying information to be used in making the intuitive decision, and then move on to analyzing the benefits and liability of the decision. Interventions also could be tailored to the dependent style by helping the client identify people on whose opinion the client relies in making decisions. The counseling then can progress to the dynamics surrounding the decision and the effects of the dependency.

Other Factors

Kivlighan, Johnston, Hogan, and Mauer (1994) studied the interaction between client characteristics and a CACGS. They found that clients with relatively more stable goals showed the most change in vocational identity. They also found that clients who had a greater desire to do things by and for themselves reported more satisfaction with the system. The results appear to indicate that clients with more independence and stable goals may be able to use a CACGS with little additional services, whereas other clients will need additional career counseling and assistance.

Numerous researchers (e.g., Oliver & Spokane, 1988; Rounds & Tinsley, 1984) have voiced a need for a diagnostic system for career issues that would assist clinicians in selecting the appropriate career interventions. Researchers have yet to develop a commonly used diagnostic system, but some initial efforts have been made in this area. One example is the research of Lucas and Epperson (1988, 1990), which classified undecided students. The classification of undecided students may be particularly helpful because Gordon's (1981) research indicated that even by the time students reach their senior year, about 20% to 50% are still undecided. Lucas and Epperson identified five types of undecided students:

1. students who seem close to deciding on a career and whose only task seems to be an integration of plans and priorities
2. students who seem to have difficulty deciding whether to concentrate on work, relationship, or leisure activities
3. students with undecided and limited interest, who seem to lack motivation and feel helpless
4. students who feel distressed and unclear about goals
5. students who show little interest in work activities and perceive little control over the decision-making process.

Practitioners may benefit from this categorization because it can help them tailor the process of the career counseling rather than provide a generic service to all undecided students.

Research on client attribute-by-treatment interactions certainly would benefit from a well-developed career diagnostic system. It would be much easier to identify trends in the research if researchers consistently used a diagnostic system to identify client issues and attributes. A diagnostic system also could help practitioners by providing a framework to identify issues and needs of the client. Furthermore, the matching of treatment to client characteristics could be facilitated by a sound career diagnostic system.

Practical Applications

The preceding sections described research related to the effectiveness of individual career counseling approaches and studies that identified potent factors within the process. In concluding this chapter, it may be useful to tease out the pertinent variables to career counseling practice. The research on career interventions has indicated that the most effective method of providing career services is through individual career counseling. Hence, practitioners working with college students on career development issues may want to consider strategies for incorporating individual counseling into the services they provide.

In general, it appears that individual career counseling should be an interactive process in which the clinician plays an active role. It may be helpful to start the process by explaining the parameters of the career counseling to the client. Galassi et al.'s (1992) findings indicated that clients most frequently hoped to clarify their career goals and direction and identify methods for achieving those goals. In attempting to help clients achieve their goals, the clinician would be advised to use interventions that challenge and facilitate insight. Although the clinician plays an active role in the counseling process, the client also must be encouraged to actively participate. In addition, some research indicates that the environment needs to be collaborative, whereby the client and counselor strive to form a working alliance.

Although the findings are not conclusive, it seems that compared with shorter interventions, longer and more intense career counseling will produce greater client gains. Large numbers of counseling sessions may not be possible in some college settings, in which case counselors should focus on strategies for making the first few sessions engaging and productive. In addition, practitioners may want to consider incorporating computer applications with counseling, because counseling-plus-computer applications have been shown to be more effective than only having the client use a CACGS. Clinicians also may want to consider incorporating career assessment instruments into the counseling process. When incorporating assessment tools into career counseling, however, practitioners need to consider the characteristics of the client and whether the instrument is appropriate. Recent research indicates that many of the interest inventories that are based on Holland's theory can be appropriate for ethnic and racial minority clients.

General consensus exists that the client's attributes and characteristics should influence the choice of interventions. Current research on client attribute-by-treatment interactions provides some indications about which treatments work with which clients. Section III of this book, which focuses on the career development needs of special populations, provides information on working with diverse groups of clients and how to adapt career counseling to meet their needs. In addition, practitioners need to consider the personality and other psychological factors of the clients. The development of a diagnostic system would be helpful to career counselors by providing a systematic method for evaluating client factors that could facilitate the selection of effective career interventions.

References

Anderson, W. P., & Niles, S. G. (1995). Career and personal concerns expressed by career counseling clients. *Career Development Quarterly, 43*, 240–245.

Astin, A. W. (1993). *What matters in college: Four years revisited.* San Francisco: Jossey-Bass.

Bergin, A. E., & Garfield, S. L. (Eds.). (1994). *The handbook of psychotherapy and behavior change* (4th ed.). New York: Wiley.

Betsworth, D. G., & Fouad, N. A. (1997). Vocational interests: A look at the past 70 years and a glance at the future. *Career Development Quarterly, 46*, 23–47.

Betz, N. E., & Fitzgerald, L. F. (1987). *Career psychology of women.* Orlando, FL: Academic Press.

Betz, N. E., & Hackett, G. (1983). The relationship of mathematics self-efficacy expectations to the selection of science-based college majors. *Journal of Vocational Behavior, 23*, 329–345.

Bingham, R. P., & Ward, C. M. (1994). Career counseling with ethnic minority women. In W. B. Walsh & S. H. Osipow (Eds.), *Career counseling for women* (pp. 165–199). Hillsdale, NJ: Lawrence Erlbaum.

Birk, J. M., & Brooks, L. (1986). Required skills and training needs of recent counseling psychology graduates. *Journal of Counseling Psychology, 33*, 320–325.

Blustein, D. L. (1987). Decision-making styles and vocational maturity: An alternative perspective. *Journal of Vocational Behavior, 30*, 61–71.

Burke, P. J., & Hoelter, J. W. (1988). Identity and sex-race differences in educational and occupational aspiration formation. *Social Science Research, 17*, 29–47.

Daniels, M. H. (1982). The heuristic value of Harreh's career decision-making model for practitioners. *Journal of College Student Personnel, 23*, 18–24.

Day, S. X., & Rounds, J. (1998). Universality of vocational interest structure among racial and ethnic minorities. *American Psychologist, 53*, 728–736.

Fitzgerald, L. F., Fassinger, R. E., & Betz, N. E. (1995). Theoretical advances in the study of women's career development. In W. B. Walsh & S. H. Osipow (Eds.), *Handbook of vocational psychology: Theory, research, and practice* (2nd ed., pp. 67–109). Mahway, NJ: Lawrence Erlbaum.

Fitzgerald, L. F., & Osipow, S. H. (1988). We have seen the future but is it us? The vocational aspirations of graduate students in counseling psychology. *Professional Psychology: Research and Practice, 19*, 575–583.

Fitzgerald, L. F., & Rounds J. (1994). Women and work: Theory encounters reality. In W. B. Walsh & S. H. Osipow (Eds.), *Career counseling for women* (pp. 327–354). Hillsdale, NJ: Lawrence Erlbaum.

Fouad, N. A., & Bingham, R. P. (1995). Career counseling with racial and ethnic minorities. In W. B. Walsh & S. H. Osipow (Eds.), *Handbook of vocational psychology: Theory, research, and practice* (pp. 331–365). Mahwah, NJ: Lawrence Erlbaum.

Fouad, N. A., Harmon, L. W., & Borgen, F. H. (1997). The structure of interests in employed adult members of U.S. racial/ethnic minority groups and nonminority groups. *Journal of Counseling Psychology, 44*, 339–345.

Fretz, B. R. (1981). Evaluating the effectiveness of career interventions [Monograph]. *Journal of Counseling Psychology, 28*, 77–90.

Galassi, J. P., Crace, R. K., Martin, G. A., James, R. M., & Wallace, R. L. (1992). Client preferences and anticipations in career counseling: A preliminary investigation. *Journal of Counseling Psychology, 39*, 46–55.

Garis, J. W., & Niles, S. G. (1990). The separate and combined effects of SIGI and DISCOVER and a career planning course on undecided university students. *Career Development Quarterly, 39*, 291–274.

Gelso, C. J., Prince, J. P., Cornfield, J. L., Payne, A. B., Royalty, G., & Wiley, M. O. (1985). Quality of counselors' intake evaluations for clients with problems that are primarily vocational versus personal. *Journal of Counseling Psychology, 32*, 339–347.

Gold, J. M., & Scanlon, C. R. (1993). Psychological distress and counseling duration of career and noncareer clients. *Career Development Quarterly, 42*, 186–187.

Goodyear, R. K. (1990). Research on the effects of test interpretation: A review. *The Counseling Psychologist, 18*, 240–257.

Gordon, V. N. (1981). The undecided college student: A developmental perspective. *Personnel and Guidance Journal, 59*, 433–439.

Hackett, G. (1993). Career counseling and psychotherapy: False dichotomies and recommended remedies. *Journal of Career Assessment, 1*, 105–117.

Hackett, G., & Betz, N. E. (1981). A self-efficacy approach to the career development of women. *Journal of Vocational Behavior, 18*, 326–339.

Hanson, W. E., & Claiborn, C. D. (1998). Providing test feedback to clients: What really matters. In C. Claiborn (Chair), *Test interpretation in counseling: Recent research and practice*. Symposium conducted at the conference of the American Psychological Association, San Francisco.

Hanson, W. E., Claiborn, C. D., & Kerr, B. (1997). Differential effects of two test-interpretation styles in counseling: A field study. *Journal of Counseling Psychology, 44*, 400–405.

Harren, V. A. (1979). A model of career decision making for college students. *Journal of Vocational Behavior, 14*, 119–133.

Heppner, M. J., & Hendricks, F. (1995). A process and outcome study examining career indecision and indecisiveness. *Journal of Counseling & Development, 73*, 426–437.

Hill, A. L., & Spokane, A. R. (1995). Career counseling and possible selves: A case study. *Career Development Quarterly, 43*, 221–232.

Hill, C. E., Helms, J. E., Tichenor, V., Spiegel, S. B., O'Grady, K. E., & Perry, E. (1988). Effects of therapist response modes in brief psychotherapy. *Journal of Counseling Psychology, 35*, 222–233.

Hitchings, W. E., Luzzo, D. A., Retish, P., Horvath, M., & Ristow, R. (1998). Identifying the career development needs of college students with disabilities. *Journal of College Student Development, 39*, 23–32.

Holland, J. L. (1985). *Making vocational choices: A theory of vocational personalities and work environments* (2nd ed.). Englewood Cliffs, NJ: Prentice-Hall.

Holland, J. L. (1997). *Making vocational choices: A theory of vocational personalities and work environments* (3rd ed.). Odessa, FL: Psychological Assessment Resources.

Holland, J. L., Magoon, T. M., & Spokane, A. R. (1981). Counseling psychology: Career interventions, research, and theory. *Annual Reviews of Psychology, 32*, 279–305.

Horvath, A. O., & Symonds, B. D. (1991). Relation between working alliance and outcome in psychotherapy: A meta-analysis. *Journal of Counseling Psychology, 38*, 139–149.

Hunter. J. E. (1986). Cognitive ability, cognitive aptitudes, job knowledge, and job performance. *Journal of Vocational Behavior, 29*, 340–362.

Hunter, J. E., & Schmidt, F. L. (1983). Quantifying the effects of psychological interventions on employee performance and work-force productivity. *American Psychologist, 38*, 473–478.

Jones, A. S., & Gelso, C. J. (1988). Differential effects of style of interpretation: Another look. *Journal of Counseling Psychology, 35*, 363–369.

Juntunen, C. (1996). Relationship between a feminist approach to career counseling and career self-efficacy beliefs. *Journal of Employment Counseling, 33*, 130–143.

Kirschner, T., Hoffman, M. A., & Hill, C. E. (1994). Case study of the process and outcome of career counseling. *Journal of Counseling Psychology, 41*, 216–226.

Kivlighan, D. M., Hageseth, J. A., Tipton, R. M., & McGovern, T. V. (1981). Effects of matching treatment approaches and personality types in group vocational counseling. *Journal of Counseling Psychology, 34*, 326–329.

Kivlighan, D. M., Johnston, J. A., Hogan, R. S., & Mauer, E. (1994). Who benefits from computerized career counseling? *Journal of Counseling & Development, 72*, 289–292.

Kivlighan, D. M., & Shapiro, R. M. (1987). Holland type as a predictor of benefit from self-help career counseling. *Journal of Counseling Psychology, 34*, 326–329.

Krivasty, S. E., & Magoon, T. M. (1976). Differential effects of three vocational treatments. *Journal of Counseling Psychology, 23*, 112–118.

Krumboltz, J. D., Kinnier, R. T., Rude, S., Scherba, D. S., & Hamel, D. A. (1986). Teaching a rational approach to career decision making: Who benefits most? *Journal of Vocational Behavior, 29*, 1–6.

Lent, R. W., Brown, S. D., & Hackett, G. (1994). Toward a unifying social cognitive theory of career and academic interest, choice, and performance [Monograph]. *Journal of Vocational Behavior, 45*, 79–122.

Lent, R. W., & Hackett, G. (1987). Career self-efficacy: Empirical status and future directions. *Journal of Vocational Behavior, 34*, 347–382.

Lent, R. W., Lopez, F. G., & Bieschke, K. J. (1991). Mathematics self-efficacy: Sources and relations to science-based career choices. *Journal of Counseling Psychology, 38*, 424–430.

Lenz, J. G., Reardon, R. C., & Sampson, J. P. (1993). Holland's theory and effective use of computer-assisted career guidance systems. *Journal of Career Development, 19*, 245–253.

Leong, F. T. L. (1995). Introduction and overview. In F. T. L. Leong (Ed.), *Career development and vocational behavior of racial and ethnic minorities* (pp. 1–4). Mahwah, NJ: Lawrence Erlbaum.

Lowman, R. L. (1993). The inter-domain model of career assessment and counseling. *Journal of Counseling & Development, 71*, 549–554.

Luborsky, L., Crits-Chrostoph, P., Mintz, J., & Auerbach, A. (1988). *Who will benefit from psychotherapy? Predicting therapeutic outcomes.* New York: Basic Books.

Lucas, M. S. (1992). Problems expressed by career and non-career help seekers: A comparison. *Journal of Counseling & Development, 70*, 417–420.

Lucas, M. S., & Epperson, D. L. (1988). Personality types in vocationally undecided students. *Journal of College Student Development, 29*, 460–466.

Lucas, M. S., & Epperson, D. L. (1990). Types of vocational undecidedness: A replication and refinement. *Journal of Counseling Psychology, 37*, 382–388.

Luzzo, D. A. (1992). Ethnic group and social class differences in college students' career development. *Career Development Quarterly, 41*, 161–173.

Luzzo, D. A. (1993). Ethnic differences in college students' perception of barriers to career development. *Journal of Multicultural Counseling and Development, 21*, 227–236.

Luzzo, D. A., Funk, D. P., & Strang, J. (1996). Attributional retraining increases career decision-making self-efficacy. *Career Development Quarterly, 44*, 378–386.

Marin, P. A., & Splete, H. (1991). A comparison of the effect of two computer-based counseling interventions on the career decidedness of adults. *Career Development Quarterly, 39*, 360–371.

Mau, W. C., & Jepsen, D. A. (1992). Effects of computer-assisted instruction in using formal decision-making strategies to choose a college major. *Journal of Counseling Psychology, 39*, 185–192.

McWhirter, E. H. (1997). Perceived barriers to education and career: Ethnic and gender differences. *Journal of Vocational Behavior, 50*, 124–140.

Meara, N. M., & Patton, M. J. (1994). Contributions of the working alliance in the practice of career counseling. *Career Development Quarterly, 43*, 161–177.

Meir, S. T. (1991). Vocational behavior 1988–1990: Vocational choice, decision-making, career development interventions, and assessment. *Journal of Vocational Behavior, 39*, 131–181.

Miller, M. J., Mahaffey, S. H., Wells, D., & Tobackyk, J. (1995). Effects of structuring on students' perceptions of career counseling. *Career Development Quarterly, 43*, 233–239.

Nagel, D. P., Hoffman, M. A., & Hill, C. E. (1995). A comparison of verbal response modes used by master's-level career counselors and other helpers. *Journal of Counseling & Development, 74*, 101–104.

Nevo, O. (1990). Career counseling from the counselee perspective: Analysis of feedback questionnaires. *Career Development Quarterly, 38*, 314–323.

Niles, S. G. (1993). The timing of counselor contact in the use of a computer information delivery. *Journal of Employment Counseling, 30*, 2–12.

Niles, S. G., Erford, B. T., Hunt, B., & Watts, R. H. (1997). Decision-making styles and career development of college students. *Journal of College Student Development, 38*, 479–488.

Niles, S. G., & Garis, J. W. (1990). The effects of a career planning course and a computer-assisted career guidance program (SIGI PLUS) on undecided university students. *Journal of Career Development, 16*, 237–248.

Niles, S. G., & Pate, R. H. (1989). Competency training issues related to the integration of career counseling and mental health counseling. *Journal of Career Development, 16*, 63–71.

Oliver, L. W., & Spokane, A. R. (1988). Career-intervention outcome: What contributes to client gain? *Journal of Counseling Psychology, 35*, 447–462.

Orlinsky, D. E., & Howard, K. I. (1986). Process and outcome in psychotherapy. In S. L. Garfield & A. E. Bergin (Eds.), *Handbook of psychotherapy and behavior change* (3rd ed., pp. 361–381). New York: Wiley.

Phillips, S. D. (1992). Career counseling: Choice and implementation. In S. D. Brown & R. W. Lent (Eds.), *Handbook of counseling psychology* (2nd ed., pp. 513–547).

Phillips, S. D., Friedlander, M. L., Kost, P. P., Specterman, R. V., & Robbins, E. S. (1988). Personal versus vocational focus in career counseling: A retrospective outcome study. *Journal of Counseling and Development, 67*, 169–173.

Pickering, J. W., & Vacc, N. A. (1984). Effectiveness of career development interventions for college students: A review of published research. *Vocational Guidance Quarterly, 32*, 149–159.

Post-Kammer, P., & Smith, P. L. (1985). Sex differences in career self-efficacy, considerations, and interests of eighth and ninth graders. *Journal of Counseling Psychology, 32*, 551–559.

Prediger, D. J. (1999). Basic structure of work-relevant abilities. *Journal of Counseling Psychology, 46*, 173–184.

Randahl, G. J., Hansen, J.-I. C., & Haverkamp, B. E. (1993). Instrumental behaviors following test administration and interpretation: Exploration validity of the Strong Interest Inventory. *Journal of Counseling and Development, 71*, 435–439.

Richardson, M. S. (1996). From career counseling to counseling/psychotherapy and work, jobs, and career. In M. L. Savickas & W. B. Walsh (Eds.), *Handbook of career counseling theory and practice* (pp. 347–360). Palo Alto, CA: Davies-Black.

Rochlen, A. B., Mohr, J. J., & Hargrove, B. K. (1999). Development of the Attitudes Toward Career Counseling Scale. *Journal of Counseling Psychology, 46*, 196–206.

Rounds, J. B., & Tinsley, H. E. A. (1984). Diagnosis and treatment of vocational problems. In S. D. Brown & R. W. Lent (Eds.), *Handbook of counseling psychology* (pp. 137–177). New York: Wiley.

Rounds, J. B., & Tracey, T. J. (1990). From trait and factor to person-environment fit counseling: Theory and process. In W. B. Walsh & S. H. Osipow (Eds.), *Career counseling* (pp. 1–44). Hillsdale, NJ: Erlbaum.

Rounds, J., & Tracey, T. J. (1996). Cross-cultural structural equivalence of RIASEC models and measures. *Journal of Counseling Psychology, 43*, 310–329.

Rubinton, N. (1980). Instruction in career decision making and decision-making styles. *Journal of Counseling Psychology, 27*, 581–588.

Salomone, P. R. (1982). Difficult cases in career counseling: II. The indecisive client. *Personnel and Guidance Journal, 60*, 496–500.

Sampson, J. P., & Reardon, R. C. (Eds.). (1990). *Enhancing the design and use of computer-assisted career guidance systems*. Alexandria, VA: National Career Development Association.

Savickas, M. L. (1989). Annual review: Practice and research in career counseling and development. *Career Development Quarterly, 38*, 100–134.

Sexton, T. L., & Whiston, S. C. (1994). The status of the counseling relationship: An empirical review, theoretical implications, and research directions. *The Counseling Psychologist, 22*, 6–78.

Sexton, T. L., Whiston, S. C., Bleuer, J. C., & Walz, G. R. (1997). *Integrating outcome research into counseling practice and training*. Alexandria, VA: American Counseling Association.

Slaney, R. B., & Dickson, R. D. (1985). Relation of career indecision to career exploration with reentry women: A treatment and follow-up study. *Journal of Counseling Psychology, 32*, 355–362.

Spengler, P. M., Blustein, D. L., & Strohmer, D. C. (1990). Diagnostic and treatment overshadowing of vocational problems by personal problems. *Journal of Counseling Psychology, 37*, 372–381.

Spokane, A. R. (1991). *Career intervention*. Englewood Cliffs, NJ: Prentice-Hall.

Sue, D. W., Arredondo, P., & McDavis, R. J. (1992). Multicultural competencies and standards: A call to the profession. *Journal of Counseling and Development, 70*, 477–486.

Tinsley, H. E. A., Tokar, D. M., & Helwig, S. E. (1994). Client expectations about counseling and involvement during career counseling. *Career Development Quarterly, 42*, 326–336.

Walsh, W. B., & Osipow, S. H. (Eds.). (1994). *Career counseling for women*. Hillsdale, NJ: Lawrence Erlbaum.

Ward, C. M., & Bingham, R. P. (1993). Career assessment of ethnic minority women. *Journal of Career Assessment, 1*, 246–257.

Watkins, C. E., Jr., Schneider, L. J., Cox, J. R. H., & Reinberg, J. A. (1987). Clinical psychology and counseling psychology: On similarities and differences revisited. *Professional Psychology: Research and Practice, 18*, 530–535.

Whiston, S. C., Sexton, T. L., & Lasoff, D. L. (1998). Career-intervention outcome: A replication and extension of Oliver and Spokane (1988). *Journal of Counseling Psychology, 45*, 150–165.

Wilson, S. B., Mason, T. W., & Ewing, M. J. M. (1997). Evaluating the impact of receiving university-based counseling services on student retention. *Journal of Counseling Psychology, 44*, 316–320.

8

Career Planning Workshops and Courses

Thomas J. Halasz and C. Bryan Kempton

I am a very indecisive person, and I'm afraid to make the wrong decision when choosing a career goal, or even my major.

—Student in Career Planning Course

Colleges and universities long have experimented with the use of group interventions as a meaningful way to affect the career development of students. Early versions of career courses can be traced back to the Great Depression (Hoppock, 1932). At that time, most group-oriented career workshops and courses were not based on theoretical models or empirical studies relating to career development. They primarily focused on helping students learn more about various occupations and comparing their "own qualities with the demands of these vocations and thus more adequately adjust [themselves] to a vocation as a life work" (Hoppock, 1932, p. 366).

Since that time, many career centers have continued the use of group interventions through workshops and career courses. Devlin (1974) found that 10% of surveyed colleges and universities had career planning courses. Later, Haney and Howland (1978) noted that nearly 40% of 916 colleges and universities that they surveyed had career courses for students. More recently, statistics in a 1997 survey from the National Association of Colleges and Employers (Collins, 1998) indicated that roughly

---

The definition of the terms decidedness, career decidedness, indecision, and indecisiveness, vary slightly from one discussion to another in this chapter. These variations are due to the fact that we have not been able to find an authoritative resource to concretely define these terms. Generally, we use different terms because a source we referenced has used that term. The following may help further explain our usage of these terms. Herr and Cramer (1992) explain that in "indecision there may be lack of information and knowledge of how to sort through alternatives; in indecisiveness a generally dysfunctional personality orientation may cause such choice anxiety that an individual is rendered incapable of making a decision. Seldom are these distinctions made explicit when, for example, counselors speak of decided and undecided students" (p. 610).

four out of every five career centers provided group-oriented career counseling interventions and workshops. Furthermore, credit-bearing career planning courses were offered at 29% of institutions surveyed, and courses without academic credit were offered at 23% of institutions. The proportion of institutions offering non-credit-bearing career courses has remained constant for more than a decade (Collins, 1998).

Current statistics indicate that the use of group interventions and career courses is likely to continue to increase as colleges and universities work toward a more comprehensive and responsive preparation of students for future society and the global work force (Smith & Gast, 1998). State and federal governments, as well as parents, continue to demand greater accountability for services provided by colleges and universities. Interested parties demand to know how their tuition money or tax dollars are being used to improve and enhance students' educational experiences, retention, and success after graduation. Furthermore, the onus of responsibility is being placed on career centers to assist students in early major selection so that graduation in 4 or 5 years is a possibility.

In response to the demand for greater accountability within higher education, professional organizations such as the National Career Development Association (NCDA), the National Occupational Information Coordinating Committee (NOICC), and the Council for the Advancement of Standards have developed guidelines and established standards for professional practice within the field of career services. The NCDA Professional Standards Committee (1992), for example, has outlined minimal competencies for individual and group counseling, assessment and program management, and implementation. The NOICC guidelines (1996) identify adult competencies and indicators for the areas of self-knowledge, career planning, and educational and occupational exploration. The skills and competencies that dictate the quality of career workshops and courses are found within these specific categories.

Given the rising use of career workshops and courses and the development of professional standards governing their implementation, why are so many career centers moving toward offering these types of services for students? Furthermore, what specific factors are prompting career centers to present an average of 98 workshops a year for more than 1,400 students (Collins, 1998)? Unlike the Depression-era career courses and group workshops, the answer to these questions are grounded in numerous studies of the effectiveness of group interventions and career courses compared with other vehicles for career services delivery.

This chapter summarizes the theory, research, and practice behind the use of career courses and workshops in career services. It also reviews research on the effectiveness of career interventions with groups. The chapter identifies trends in service delivery and provides ideas for the integration of theory-based and empirically sound group career interventions into student affairs practices. However, most research on group interventions in career services focuses on the use of career courses and counseling groups rather than programmatic group workshops.

Research

I am just not confident that my major will lead me to a career that will be stable and make me "happy" at the same time. I feel like there is just so much I'm unaware of.

—Student in Career Planning Course

When considering the use of career-oriented group interventions with students, Corey (1990) provided a clear explanation of their popularity:

> One of the main reasons for the popularity of the group as a primary therapeutic tool in many agencies and institutions is that it is frequently more effective than the individual approach. This effectiveness stems from the fact that group members can practice their new skills both within the group and in their everyday interactions outside of it. There are practical considerations, too, such as lower cost and broader distributions of the available counselors and therapists. (p. 4)

Additional reasons for the popularity of group interventions include their effectiveness in disseminating information, providing motivation, teaching, practicing attitude development, promoting exploration, and general counseling purposes (Herr & Cramer, 1992).

Similarly, past research on the effectiveness of group interventions has focused primarily on group counseling in relation to individual counseling. Davis and Horne (1986) found that career courses and small-group career counseling interventions were equally effective in furthering students' career decidedness and maturity. They also found that career courses could affect large groups of undecided students and were cost-effective. Johnson and Smouse (1993) furthered this research by showing that a career class was successful in improving the career decidedness, comfort, and self-clarity of college students. Other areas, such as decisiveness and motivation, were not affected in their study and warranted a different level of intervention. As Fretz's (1981) work tells us, this study's limited results underscores the importance of tailoring group interventions (in whatever form) to the specific career development needs of the clients involved.

Kivlighan (1990) provided a telling summary of literature on career-oriented group interventions, including the observation that such interventions emphasized self-understanding, self-disclosure, guidance, and interpersonal action, virtually ignoring areas such as catharsis, universality, and instillation of hope—three crucial variables affecting group process and outcome. Furthermore, Kivlighan (1990) mentioned a pervasive lack of attention to group composition. For example, Schroer and Dohn (1986) noted that gender composition has significant effects on career group successes: Women seek to experience or become aware of a greater range of options, whereas men seek to experience a "confirmation of career plans." Research such as this provides us with substantive guidelines for the development of career courses and workshops and a framework in which to develop further research.

Various researchers also have produced studies comparing the effectiveness of group career development interventions that were based on a variety of theories. Stonewater and Daniels (1983) examined a career guidance course that was based on Chickering's theory and found that career-related content enhanced students' psychosocial development. Orndorff and Herr's (1996) research refuted a central assumption of career choice theory, which states that students make educated decisions on the basis of adequate knowledge of the career options available to them. Rather, as Orndorff and Herr pointed out, with more than 20,000 occupations available to them, most declared as well as undeclared students have limited knowledge about available career options.

Carver and Smart (1985) provided empirical tests on several theory-based assumptions on career development in higher education. Their research supported the work of Ginsberg, Super, Tiedeman, and O'Hara (cited in Carver & Smart, 1985) by showing that people in late adolescence begin to explore career options seriously while making tentative choices toward occupational goals. Their research also supported the work of Crites (cited in Carver & Smart, 1985) by demonstrating that "structured career planning programs can have a positive impact on the career development of college students" (pp. 41–42).

For the purposes of examining the effect of family systems and Adlerian ideas, Bradley and Mims (1992) conducted research on a career development course that used a lecture and small-group counseling format. They found that family system and Adlerian ideas could be applied in a career development course. Freshmen and sophomores who participated in the course advanced further in vocational developmental stages than did students participating in individual career counseling. In similar research, Henry (1993) supported Holland's work on vocational identity when he examined the effects of a career development course on the professional identity of premedical students. Career development courses geared toward the needs of the students were found to significantly affect their vocational identity, knowledge of occupational information, and understanding of barriers.

Orndorff and Herr (1996) evaluated the effectiveness of a career course on traditional career development areas such as career decidedness, academic major certainty, reduction of career indecision, and career maturity. Their research also examined the impact of the career course on students' self-esteem, use of academic and student services, and involvement in student organizations. The results showed that declared students needed assistance with occupational exploration as much as undeclared students and that undeclared students needed greater assistance in self-assessment. Furthermore, Orndorff and Herr noted that students in general might need "observational and experiential modes of career exploration to clarify their existing perceptions of various occupations" (p. 637).

Hardesty's (1991) meta-analysis focused on summarizing other previous studies of career interventions and confirmed the effectiveness of undergraduate career courses offered for credit. Specifically,

> students completing career courses were 40% more capable of making realistic career decisions than were students that did not complete these courses. Similarly, students completing these courses were 48% closer or more certain of their choices than they were at the beginning of the courses. (p. 185)

A Study of a Career Planning Course

I'm just very uninformed about different majors and careers and would like to be more knowledgeable.
—Student in Career Planning Course

In recent research designed to measure the effects of a credit-bearing career course on students' career development, Halasz and Kempton (1997) compared a career course with two non-career-related academic courses. The course, Exploring Careers, was housed within the psychology department of a large midwestern university and offered as a section of Project Outreach, a series of courses designed to provide students with experience-based learning opportunities (Miller, 1993). Increasing pressure from psychology faculty to provide justification for the course precipitated research evaluating its effectiveness.

The course met for 2 hours once per week for 14 weeks; the first hour of each class was dedicated to interactive lecture topics and the second hour to small-group interaction and group processing. Goals for the course included helping students develop a greater understanding of their interests, skills, and values and how they related to majors and careers. Other important goals involved exploring university majors and careers, making career decisions, and developing job- and internship-search strategies. The course also included sections on identifying and marketing personal strengths and the socialization process in career development, and it featured professional panels of speakers from the community, who discussed career-related topics. Exploring Careers was cotaught by a staff member from the career center and a doctoral psychology student.

The course was designed to be both developmental and experiential for the students enrolled in the class. Developmentally, the course subscribed to Holland's (1997) theory of careers, with the experiential focus coming into play as an outgrowth of its connection with the psychology-based Project Outreach. To meet this experiential goal, Exploring Careers provided students with a workplace observation exercise, the professional panels described above, and informational interview assignments.

The researchers evaluating the course hypothesized that students participating in Exploring Careers would show a more significant positive effect on a measure of career certainty and decidedness than students from the non-career-oriented control classes. The Career Decision Scale (CDS;

Osipow, Carney, Winer, Yanico, & Koschier, 1980) was used to test the hypothesis because of its ability to measure levels of career certainty and indecision, its low cost, and its ease of administration. For similar reasons, Cooper (1986) used the CDS to show significant decreases in students' career indecision following individual and group interventions.

The CDS consists of 18 Likert-type questions and 1 open-ended item, which gives students an opportunity to provide more information or clarify responses from earlier items. The instrument is further divided into the certainty and indecision subscales. High-certainty subscale scores indicate a greater level of career choice and major certainty. Low-indecision sub-scale scores indicate comfort with the career exploration and decision-making process. Total test time for the CDS is approximately 15 minutes, and its overall test–retest coefficients range from .70 to .90. Most inter-item correlations range from .60 to .70 (Osipow et al., 1980).

The CDS was administered the first and last weeks of class for both the experimental and the control courses. Sixty-three of the 79 students registered for Exploring Careers participated in both the pre- and posttest administrations of the CDS. In the two control groups (an upper-level communications course and another psychology course within Project Outreach), 55 of 70 students and 32 of 50 students, respectively, completed both the pre- and posttests.

The results showed that students in Exploring Careers had a significant positive change in pre- and posttest scores for the certainty and indecision subscales of the CDS. In other words, students indicated that they were more comfortable with the career decision-making process and more certain of their career and major choices after completing the class. Students in the psychology control group showed a significant positive effect for the certainty subscale and no significant change in scores on the indecision subscale. Students in the communications class showed no significant change on either CDS subscale.

Practitioner Survey

Finding out about careers in a planned and orderly way through this class is opening my eyes to many options and helping me decide what I do and don't want to do.

—Student in Career Planning Course

Although Halasz and Kempton (1997) and other researchers suggest that career courses and group interventions in career development have a positive effect on students, the authors of this chapter wanted to benchmark the types of group interventions and career courses being used in career centers today. If nothing else, this benchmarking would help us ascertain whether career services practitioners are incorporating career course and group intervention theory and research into their daily practice of providing services for students.

During the summer and fall of 1998, we surveyed 40 career services offices. A short survey was developed and transmitted electronically through various listservs subscribed to by career professionals at those offices. The goal of the survey was simply to obtain specific information regarding the types of group career interventions and courses currently provided for students. The results were noteworthy in a few areas.

A little more than two thirds of the respondents indicated that they offered some sort of career course for students at their institution. This proportion is slightly higher than other recently reported data mentioned earlier in this chapter (Devlin, 1974; Haney & Howland, 1978; Collins, 1998). The 28 institutions that reported having a career course responded to questions regarding the specifics of their course. When questioned about their course's theoretical basis, most career services professionals mentioned the work of John Holland. Other respondents mentioned drawing theoretical frameworks for their class from the work of Super, Krumboltz, Bandura, and Jung. Interestingly, a few did not identify a theoretical base, rather they mentioned phrases such as "basic career development A–Z," which included self-assessment, career exploration, and decision making skills. Finally, 12 respondents indicated that they were not sure of the theoretical basis of their career course. Some respondents said our question was a "good question" and that developing a theoretical base was "one of the main concerns [that they] have." Twenty-three respondents noted that they had "no real basis" for their career course.

Most respondents reported that their career courses were credit bearing, with one-credit offerings having the highest frequency. Class sizes ranged from 15 to 20 to more than 200 students. Career services professionals of various titles taught nearly all the career classes described in this survey, with an academic department's collaborative assistance. Some career courses began in the 1960s, whereas others had started as recently as the fall semester of 1998. Many in the sample reported the use of a career development text in their career course. A list of those texts and texts mentioned in various journal articles and research is in Appendix A.

One of the most telling aspects of the survey came from the question "What factors affected your decision whether or not to offer a career class?" For the most part, answers to this question fell into two groups. The first group of answers were related to the simple notion that "students needed it." Furthermore, some respondents saw a career class as a way to meet the career development needs of students in "ongoing consistent meetings" that ultimately seek to "further integrate academic and career development."

The second group of answers referenced administrative and faculty support as a key issue that, more often than not, decided the fate of a career course initiative. Regardless of whether a career course was currently being offered at their institution, many respondents cited faculty and administrative support or resistance as a significant determining factor. In a similar career course survey, Mead and Korschgen (1994) reported that career courses at surveyed institutions, although deemed successful by students, faced opposition from faculty. Respondents from our survey indicated that the nonexistence of a career course at their institution was largely a result of faculty opposition and concern over granting academic credit for the course. It seems that the long battle for collaboration between student and academic affairs departments is still being waged in the area of career services.

Career courses cited in our survey reflected previous research in that they could be classified into three primary categories: (a) career decision making, (b) career exploration, and (c) job-search skills and strategies. Mead and Korschgen (1994) also found that respondents reported offering courses that represented three broad categories: (a) career decision making, (b) job-search skills and preparedness, and (c) college-specific courses (e.g., business or technical). Their research indicated that students enrolled in these classes were distributed nearly equally by academic year. In our survey, some career courses were specific to an individual college or major, whereas others were open to certain class levels or, in some cases, designed for at-risk students. Most classes targeted either first-year students or seniors. Additionally, some classes were limited to women (e.g., women in engineering, women in business). A small number of courses were part of the required core curriculum for students.

Although not mentioned in our survey or that of Mead and Korschgen (1994), other research reveals the increased use of capstone career development courses for students graduating from a college or university. Smith and Gast (1998) described in detail the purpose and organization behind courses of this nature. Dodson, Chastain, and Landrum (1996) went further to explore the results of combining a capstone course with an academic focus on psychology. They found that their course was effective in providing much needed information on career and graduate study options in an organized and systematic fashion.

Finally, in our survey most colleges and universities with career courses indicated that they used one or more of 20 self-assessment tools in those courses. The Strong Interest Inventory (SII; Harmon, Hansen, Borgen, & Hammer, 1994), the Myers–Briggs Type Inventory (MBTI; Myers, McCaulley, Quenk, & Hammer, 1998), the Self-Directed Search (Holland, Fritzsche, & Powell, 1994) and the Campbell Interest and Skills Survey (Campbell, Hyne & Nilsen, 1992) were some of the most frequently mentioned. Computerized assessments, such as the System of Interactive Guidance and Information, Plus More (SIGI PLUS; Educational Testing Service, 1998) and DISCOVER (ACT, 1995), also were cited. A summary of the various instruments used for individualized career assessment in career courses mentioned in this survey is provided in Appendix B.

Most respondents replied that they did not use a standardized assessment of the effectiveness of their career courses outside of departmental and instructor evaluations. A small percentage mentioned efforts at gauging individual student career development through pre- and posttest administrations of inventories, such as My Vocational Situation (Holland, Daiger, & Power, 1980). Research cited in this chapter, including Carver and Smart (1985), Cooper (1986), Halasz and Kempton (1997), Henry (1993), Stonewater and Daniels (1983), and Orndorff and Herr (1996), suggests that more career professionals should consider evaluation of this sort for ethical reasons as well as for the continued justification of the career courses' existence amid faculty and/or administrative pressures.

Aside from questions regarding career courses, we also asked the same institutions for information on their use of group-oriented workshops. All career services practitioners reported providing the standard fare of résumé and cover-letter writing, interviewing, networking, and job-search workshops. In addition, 35 indicated that they provided Internet job-searching workshops, career panels, and "Choosing a Major" and "What Can I Do With a Major In" workshops. A smaller number, 10, offered group interpretations of inventories such as the MBTI and SII. Numerous other workshops for special student populations, such as etiquette dinners for business majors and private-school job searching for education majors, also were mentioned.

An interesting finding was that 15 of the 40 respondents reported enlisting the help of employers in providing career workshops for students. In this way, according to respondents, career centers could help employers develop their presence on campus while enhancing collaborative employer relationships with the career center and student attendance through pre-program publicity. A few institutions indicated that employers were the sole presenters of some workshops, whereas others mentioned that they presented various career-related topics collaboratively.

A larger than expected group of survey respondents, 20, mentioned that they had recurring problems with low student attendance at group-oriented workshops and programs. Many of the centers in this group indicated that they recently had decided not to offer this service, deciding instead to provide it in programs and workshops for academic classes and organizations and on the Internet. Most reported evaluating workshops and programs through the use of simple departmental evaluations, if at all. Not surprisingly, hardly any journal-based information exists on the use or effectiveness of these types of group interventions.

Recommendations

> I have investigated my interests and assessed my abilities, and I believe that I am in the process of pursuing a career suitable for me, and I even have grad school as a back-up plan.
> —Student in Career Planning Course

On the basis of the results of our survey of career centers and review of published research, it seems certain that more institutions are experimenting with various offerings of career courses and workshops. It also is apparent that most career centers do not use standardized assessments to evaluate the impact of career courses or workshops on students' career development. Rather, many career centers report the continued use of assessments for individualized career development purposes.

When developing an effective career course that takes into account the end goal of positively affecting students' career development, it is important to pay particular attention to the staffing of the course, regardless of the theoretical base or design of the class. Most career centers have trained counselors on staff, but do they have educators? Unlike traditional academic courses, career courses require instructors who can attend to students' developmental and practical career development needs. In other words, career courses require instructors who can translate theory and research into practical applications for students. Career course instructors also need to be trained to use standardized assessments, to screen participants, and to understand referral procedures.

Additionally, institutional support is needed for expanding career centers' services. When support is lacking, starting from the ground up may be necessary. For example, career centers may build collaborative efforts with other departments by creating programs to provide group interventions for a limited time and with a limited scope. Small groups for skills building or groups designed for career exploration can be effective. As time passes and the need for a greater number of groups develops, faculty and staff support is easier to generate and group career interventions can be established. Having career center personnel coteach with faculty or staff can help develop collaborative relationships, thereby increasing the likelihood of acceptance and accountability of a career course. Consequently, it also is important to pay attention to current literature that addresses key accountability issues, such how to grade career courses (Filer, 1986) and the effective promotion of the course to university faculty (Brooks, 1995).

Last, but perhaps most important for developing a career course or workshop, is the need to identify a target population. Meeting the needs of a target population can be accomplished only by developing a clear understanding of that population's needs and tailoring the group intervention accordingly. To determine appropriate interventions, we strongly support the increased use of intake procedures and the use of standardized assessments to measure the intervention effectiveness of the course. Additionally, Blustein's (1992) seven theory-into-practice suggestions, which are based on Snyder's (1981) work in social cognition, may prove helpful in developing group interventions in career courses. Specifically, career courses could be instrumental in improving students' competence in self- and environmental exploration as well as modeling the appropriate means for decision making (Blustein, 1992).

Given the issues inherent in developing a career course, practitioners must rely on research and other resources for guidance. However, a great need exists for further research on the use of career courses and group-oriented workshops with college students. For example, a longitudinal study to examine the impact of career courses on timely issues such as student retention, involvement in experiential learning opportunities, and postgraduation placement rates would be useful. Another area for possible research would be to use career courses as recruitment tools. With schools that attract special populations, such as nontraditional-aged students, offering career courses and group interventions or workshops might possibly result in greater numbers of such students attending those schools. Finally, research comparing variations of career courses or group interventions and their effectiveness is needed to continue benchmarking innovations in this area of career services delivery.

Career-oriented group interventions can effectively provide career education in the form of information about the world of work, self-exploration, and career-search skills. Using Vacc and Loesch's (1987) concept of career education, the integration of career development concepts and activities into education curricula provides "organized and systematic provision of information about various aspects of the world of work so that individuals can make 'informed' and therefore, theoretically, 'intelligent' job, occupation, and career choices" (p. 117). If we are to assist students in becoming savvy job searchers and work with students experiencing significant developmental challenges, a new model of career assistance is needed. Although it capitalizes on current career development theory and research, this model also should incorporate career courses and group interventions that use a wide variety of approaches for students with different needs.

References

ACT, Inc. (1995). *DISCOVER for Colleges and Adults.* Iowa City, IA: Author.

Blustein, D. L. (1992). Applying current theory and research in career exploration to practice. *Career Development Quarterly, 41*, 174–184.

Bradley, R. W., & Mims, G. A. (1992). Using family systems and birth order dynamics as the basis for a college career decision-making course. *Journal of Counseling and Development, 70*, 445–448.

Brooks, J. E. (1995). Guide to developing a successful career course. *Journal of Career Planning and Employment, 55*, 29–33.

Campbell, D. P., Hyne, S. A., & Nilsen, D. L. (1992). *Campbell Interest and Skill Survey.* Minneapolis, MN: National Computer Systems.

Carver, D. S., & Smart, D. W. (1985). The effects of a career and self-exploration course for undecided freshmen. *Journal of College Student Personnel, 26*, 37–42.

Collins, M. (1998). Snapshot of the profession. *Journal of Career Planning and Employment, 41*, 32–36, 51–55.

Cooper, S. E. (1986). The effects of group and individual vocational counseling on career indecision and personal indecisiveness. *Journal of College Student Personnel, 27*, 39–42.

Corey, G. (1990). *Theory and practice of group counseling* (3rd ed.). Belmont, CA: Wadsworth.

Davis, R. C., & Horne, A. M. (1986). The effect of small-group counseling and a career course on career decidedness and maturity. *Vocational Guidance Quarterly, 34*, 255–262.

Devlin, T. C. (1974). Career development courses. *Journal of College Placement, 34*, 62–68.

Dodson, J. P., Chastain, G., & Landrum, R. E. (1996). Psychology seminar: Careers and graduate study in psychology. *Teaching of Psychology, 23*, 238–240.

Educational Testing Service. (1998). *System of Interactive Guidance and Information, Plus More (SIGI PLUS).* Princeton, NJ: Author.

Filer, R. D. (1986). Assigning grades in career-planning courses: A neglected issue. *Career Development Quarterly, 35*, 141–147.

Fretz, B. R. (1981). Evaluating the effectiveness of career interventions [Monograph]. *Journal of Counseling Psychology, 28*, 77–90.

Halasz, T. J., & Kempton, C. B. (1997, March). *Bridging theory to practice: Student learning in career exploration courses.* Symposium conducted at the annual meeting of the American College Personnel Association, Chicago.

Haney, T., & Howland, P. (1978). Career courses for credit: Necessity or luxury? *Journal of College Placement, 38,* 75–79.

Hardesty, P. H. (1991). Undergraduate career courses for credit: A review and meta-analysis. *Journal of College Student Development, 32,* 184–185.

Harmon, L. W., Hansen, J.-I. C., Borgen, F. H., & Hammer, A. L. (1994). *Strong Interest Inventory: Applications and technical guide.* Palo Alto, CA: Consulting Psychologists Press.

Henry, P. (1993). Effectiveness of career-development courses for nontraditional premedical students: Improving professional identity. *Psychological Reports, 73,* 915–920.

Herr, E. L., & Cramer, S. H. (1992). *Career guidance and counseling through the lifespan: Systematic approaches* (4th ed.). New York: HarperCollins.

Holland, J. L. (1997). *Making vocational choices: A theory of vocational personalities and work environments* (3rd ed.). Odessa, FL: Psychological Assessment Resources.

Holland, J. L., Daiger, D. C., & Power, P. G. (1980). *My Vocational Situation.* Palo Alto, CA: Consulting Psychologists Press.

Holland, J. L., Fritzsche, B. A., & Powell, A. B. (1994). *The Self-Directed Search technical manual.* Odessa, FL: Psychological Assessment Resources.

Hoppock, R. (1932). Courses in careers. *Journal of Higher Education, 3,* 365–368.

Johnson, D. C., & Smouse, A. D. (1993). Assessing a career-planning course: A multidimensional approach. *Journal of College Student Development, 34,* 145–147.

Kivlighan, D. M. (1990). Career group therapy. *The Counseling Psychologist, 18,* 64–80.

Mead, S., & Korschgen, A. J. (1994). A quick look at career development courses across the country. *Journal of Career Planning and Employment, 54,* 24–25.

Miller, J. (1993). Psychology in the community. In P. L. Howard (Ed.), *Praxis I: A faculty coursebook on community service learning* (pp. 123–134). Ann Arbor, MI: Office of Community Service Learning Press.

Myers, I. B., McCaulley, M. H., Quenk, N. L., & Hammer, A. L. (1998). *MBTI Manual: A guide to the development and use of the Myers-Briggs Type Indicator.* Palo Alto, CA: Consulting Psychologists Press.

National Career Development Association. (1992). Career counseling competencies. *Career Development Quarterly, 40,* 378–386.

National Occupational Information Coordinating Committee. (1996). *K-Adult handbook, national career development guidelines.* Washington, DC.

Orndorff, R. M., & Herr, E. L. (1996). A comparative study of declared and undeclared college students on career uncertainty and involvement in career development activities. *Journal of Counseling and Development, 74,* 632–639.

Osipow, S. H., Carney, C. G., Winer, J. L., Yanico, B., & Koschier, M. (1980). *The Career Decision Scale* (3rd rev.). Odessa, FL: Psychological Assessment Resources, Inc.

Schroer, A. C. P., & Dohn, F. J. (1986). Enhancing the career and personal development of gifted college students. *Journal of Counseling and Development, 64,* 567–571.

Smith, D. D., & Gast, L. K. (1998). Comprehensive career services for seniors. In J. N. Gardner, G. Van der Veer, & Assoc. (Eds.), *The senior year experience* (pp. 187–226). San Francisco: Jossey-Bass.

Snyder, M. (1981). Seek and ye shall find: Testing hypotheses about other people. In E. T. Higgins, C. P. Herman, & M. P. Zanda (Eds.), *Social cognition: The Ontario symposium* (pp. 277–303). Hillsdale, NJ: Erlbaum.

Stonewater, J. K., & Daniels, M. H. (1983). Psychosocial and cognitive development in a career-decision-making course. *Journal of College Student Personnel, 24,* 403–410.

Vacc, N. A., & Loesch, L. C. (1987). *Counseling as a profession.* Muncie, IN: Accelerated Development.

Appendix A
Career Course Texts

Bolles, R. N. (1996). *How to find your mission in life*. San Francisco: Ten Speed Press.

Campbell, D. T. (1974). *If you don't know where you are going you will probably end up some place else*. Niles, IL: Argus.

Chapman, E. N. (1976). *Career search*. Chicago: Science Research Associates.

Ellis, D. (1990). *Career planning*. Boston: Houghton Mifflin.

Ferguson, J. (1974). *The career guidance class*. Camarillo, CA: T. Metcalf.

Gillingham, W. H., & Hornak, J. (1980). *Career planning and you*. Mt. Pleasant: Central Michigan University.

Hartel, W. C., Schwartz, S. W., Blume, S. D., & Gardner, J. N. (1994). *Ready for the real world*. Belmont, CA: Wadsworth.

Krannich, R. (1993). *Careering and recareering for the 1990's*. Manassas, VA: Impact.

Lock, R. D. (1992). *Taking charge of your career direction*. Pacific Grove, CA: Brooks/Cole.

Luzzo, D. A. (1997). *Making career decisions that count: A practical guide*. Upper Saddle River, NJ: Prentice-Hall.

Michelozzi, B. N. (1988). *Coming alive from nine to five: A career search handbook*. Mountain View, CA: Mayfield.

Montelongo, R., & Gerrish, S. (Eds.). (1996). *Choices and challenges: Foundations for career planning* (3rd ed.). Bloomington: Indiana University, Bloomington Career Development Center.

Powell, C. R. (1990). *Career planning today*. Dubuque, IA: Kendall/Hunt.

Sukiennik, D., Raufman, L., & Bendat, W. (1998). *The career fitness program: Exercising your options* (3rd ed.). Upper Saddle River, NJ: Prentice-Hall.

Yenna, D. (1996). *Career directions*. (3rd ed.). New York: McGraw-Hill.

This list is a compilation of career course texts mentioned by respondents in our survey and texts mentioned in journal articles and does not constitute the authors' endorsement of the listed materials.

Appendix B
Career Course Assessments

Assessment of Career Decision Making
Harren, V. A. (1978). Department of Psychology. Southern Illinois University, Carbondale, IL 62901

Career Decision Scale
Psychological Assessment Resources, P.O. Box 998, Odessa, FL 33556

Career Maturity Inventory
CTB/McGraw-Hill, 20 Ryan Ranch Rd., Monterey, CA 93940

DISCOVER
ACT, Inc., 2201 North Dodge St., P.O. Box 168, Iowa City, IA 52243

My Vocational Situation
Phychological Assessment Resources, P.O. Box 998, Odessa, FL 33556

Myers–Briggs Type Indicator
Consulting Psychologists Press, 3803 East Bayshore Rd., Palo Alto, CA 94303

Self-Directed Search
Psychological Assessment Resources, P.O. Box 998, Odessa, FL 33556

SIGI PLUS
Educational Testing Service, Rosedale Road, Princeton, NJ 08541

Strong Interest Inventory
Consulting Psychologists Press, 3803 East Bayshore Rd., Palo Alto, CA 94303

Survey of Career Development
Rayman, J. R. (1989). Career Development and Placement Services, University Park, PA 16802

This list is a compilation of career course assessments mentioned by respondents in our survey and does not constitute the authors' endorsement of the listed materials.

Part III

Special Populations and Issues

9

Computer-Assisted Career-Guidance Systems

Greg Iaccarino

For the past 30 years, computer-assisted career guidance systems (CACGSs) have played a fundamental role in the career development of a variety of clients, from secondary to postsecondary students as well as nonstudents. For the purposes of this chapter, *CACGSs* are defined as software packages or other computerized tools that people use to engage in tasks that mirror or complement those inherent in the career exploration process. Sampson (1997) similarly defined a CACGS as a "system of interrelated assessment, generation of options, and information dissemination subsystems, often coupled with counseling interventions and various print and media-based support resources, that are used within organizations to assist individuals in making career decisions" (p. 2).

The aim of this chapter is to explore the issues and practices of CACGSs in the work of career services practitioners and their college student clientele. It includes a brief history of the development of CACGSs; discusses their practice, application, and criteria for selection; reviews different programs; and notes some issues affecting their use.[1] A discussion of the Internet and its impact on career development also is included.

History, Development, and Theoretical Foundations of CACGSs

CACGSs date to the late 1960s, when interactive mainframe technology was funded by state, federal, and foundation grants; they were originally intended for use by secondary and community college students (Harris-Bowlsbey, 1992). Early programs emphasized career information. The Career Information System (CIS) was developed from 1969 to 1971 as a model program using funds from the U.S. Department of Labor (DOL). It had four important features:

---

[1]Additional information about CACGSs is presented in several of the other chapters of this book, including a discussion of their role in career assessment (chapter 5), an evaluation of their efficacy (chapter 7), their integration in career planning workshops and courses (chapter 8), issues associated with their use with ethnic minority students (chapter 13), and their use as part of a systematic approach to career guidance (chapter 16).

1. use of the most current state labor market data and the latest survey data on education and training opportunities in the state
2. a permanent staff to update information on an annual cycle, to train users of the system, and to deliver the system on state-of-the-art computer systems
3. use of "friendly," interactive software and user materials that would make access possible by a variety of users in different institutional settings
4. a commitment to be self-supported rather than grant-supported by charging fees to user agencies.

In 1975, the Employment and Training Administration of the DOL granted funding to eight states to set up computerized career information systems—first in Oregon, followed by Colorado, Massachusetts, Minnesota, Wisconsin, Ohio, Alabama, and Michigan. The state-funded systems contained state-specific vocational information. The Association of Computer-Based Systems for Career Information (ACSCI) was subsequently formed as a professional organization for the advancement of career information and delivery (Clyde, 1979).

Guidance and career development became the paradigm in the 1970s, led in part by the creation of the System of Interactive Guidance Information (SIGI; Clyde, 1979), which was based on Martin Katz's theory of career guidance (cited in Sampson, Shahnasarian, & Reardon, 1986). Users of the original SIGI software explored their interests and values, formulated plans and career decisions, and developed various options (Wilhelm, 1978). DISCOVER, a comprehensive information and guidance system based on Harris-Bowlsbey's career guidance theory, soon followed (Sampson et al., 1986). The development of additional CACGSs, some of which will be profiled in this chapter, emerged later.) The 1990s saw the growth of multimedia systems, videos, CD-ROMs, and the Internet as resource tools that are increasingly being used to supplement traditional CACGSs (Sampson, 1997).

CACGSs serve two basic functions: (a) as resources for career and occupational information and (b) as tools for career decision making and exploration of alternatives (Gati, 1996). Clients use them in either standalone settings at career services offices or with the assistance of a career services professional. Any CACGS should assist users with developing their career decision-making skills; clarifying their values, interests, and abilities as they relate to career decision making; identifying potentially satisfying occupations congruent with their values, interests, and abilities; acquiring an understanding of the world of work; integrating their understanding of self and the world of work, such that they are capable of making a tentative occupational choice that is both rewarding and realistic; and formulating a systematic plan of action for implementing their occupational choice (Peterson, Ryan-Jones, Sampson, Reardon, & Shahnasarian, 1994; Sampson et al., 1993).

Practice and Application of CACGSs:
An Online Survey of Career Counselors

Both a literature review and a summary of responses from an online survey of 50 career services professionals conducted by the author show that CACGSs are widely used and that a variety of issues surround their use. The survey consisted of 14 short-answer questions and was administered in 1998 by inviting subscribers of the JOBPLACE electronic listserv to participate. The listserv includes more than 2,000 career services professionals and administrators in higher education. Respondents were asked to list which CACGSs they use and why, define the intended use of their CACGSs and their actual use, discuss issues regarding use of CACGSs among special populations, describe the costs associated with their CACGSs, summarize the effectiveness (pros and cons) of CACGSs, compare and contrast CACGSs with resources and tools available online, and describe any ethical issues in the use of CACGSs. Following are summaries of the survey results.

Appropriate Selection

Survey respondents reported that cost was the primary motivator for selection of a CACGS. Additional reasons for selection (other than program content in a few cases) were not mentioned.

To assist practitioners, a number of professional organizations list guidelines for appropriate CACGS selection. The National Career Development Association's (NCDA's) selection and evaluation guidelines, at *http://ncda.org/aboutsofteval.html*, contain 67 criteria under five categories: program content, compatibility with career development theories, user interaction with the program, technical aspects of the software and hardware, and vendor technical support. The criteria are comprehensive and provide practitioners with useful details that initially might be overlooked. ACSCI also has guidelines, which are available at *http://www. acsci.org/acsi_pubs1.html*. Zunker (1986) commented that when selecting programs, practitioners should examine how a particular CACGS will benefit users, obtain relevant information about the systems being considered (e.g., costs, hardware requirements, and recommended user populations), obtain a demonstration copy of the program, and determine the approximate cost per user.

Intended and Actual Uses

CACGSs are used for career exploration, major selection, occupational information, and job search strategies. They often are in accessible locations in career resource centers or libraries of career services and employment centers. Some also are on campus networks in stand-alone locations in computer labs, libraries, and residence halls. One survey respondent described CACGSs as "fast-food career service," because users can quickly obtain career and educational information. No differences were apparent between the intended use of CACGSs and the actual use of the systems as described by survey respondents.

Ethical Issues

Some survey respondents expressed concern that CACGSs might be used in stand-alone locations without counselor intervention. Users might disagree with some of the "findings" from the program (e.g., an occupation or major that does not fit with their original interests). Information overload might result from long sit-down sessions without supporting help (Gati, 1994; Sampson et al., 1993). Given these potential concerns, practitioners should use CACGSs as part of a regular individual or group advising session (an approach that is supported by the survey results). The American Counseling Association advises practitioners that when they use CACGSs as part of counseling, they must ensure that the client is intellectually, emotionally, and physically capable of using the computer application (Howland & Palmer, 1992). The system's content should be current, accurate, and nondiscriminatory, as noted both by the National Board of Certified Counselors (NBCC) and NCDA (Howland & Palmer, 1992).

Budget Issues

Most of the surveyed practitioners noted that budgetary reasons and technical workstation capabilities, not CACGS program content, affected the decision to switch from one CACGS to another. According to the surveys, licensing costs range from $300 to $1,500, and the latest program versions require comprehensive workstations. Startup costs can run high as well: As Hinkelman and Luzzo (1997) stated, "The CD-ROM/Multimedia versions of CACG are already being marketed, with costs for such systems beginning at well over $3,000 for necessary equipment and software" (p. 42).

Types

A summary of the types of CACGSs used by the survey respondents follows. The purpose of this listing is not to endorse any one program or to list specific costs but to provide an overview of unique features. More comprehensive information (e.g., costs, ordering information) is available from the Web site for each program. (See Offer, 1997, for a description of CACGSs available in Europe.) In addition, histories of the development of many programs (including some of the programs described below), along with empirical research studies and bibliographic information, can be found at the Web site of Florida State University's Center for the Study of Technology in Counseling and Career Development (http://www.career.fsu.edu/techcenter).

Career Finder Plus (www.eurekanet.org/cfinder.html). A CD-ROM package, Career Finder Plus, uses multimedia technology to show videos of people on the job in several occupations. It provides a database of 1,109 occupations. Users answer up to 18 questions on numerous topics (i.e., using words, using numbers, understanding science, understanding people, using art, attending to details, leading others, making things, growing things, physical activity, change, meeting people, travel, drive, independence, style, training and helping people) and then receive a list of the 20 best matching occupations.

Career Information Delivery Systems (www.noicc.gov). Career Information Delivery Systems (CIDSs; National Occupational Information Coordinating Committee, 2000) are information oriented and contain occupational and labor market, educational, military, and apprenticeship information within a state. Approximately 9 million people use CIDSs at some 20,000 sites nationwide on an annual basis. State CIDSs have been supported by the National Occupational Information Coordinating Committee (NOICC), a federal interagency committee responsible for career market information and career development needs of clients. CIDSs are operated by State Occupational Information Coordinating Committees, other state agencies, or universities. More than half of the 48 state CIDSs now in operation were developed originally with NOICC funding. Special features of these programs are in development, including career information for people with disabilities as well as general résumé and interview information. In relation to the Internet, Sampson (1999) noted that CIDSs "are increasingly providing links in information files to related web sites in an attempt to provide a less overwhelming method for users to locate relevant Internet-based career resources and services" (p. 7).

CareerLeader (www.careerdiscovery.com). CareerLeader (2000) helps users define their interests in business careers through an interest module (the Business Career Interest Inventory), a values module (the Management and Professional Reward Profile), and an abilities assessment inventory (the Management and Professional Abilities Profile). After using the modules, users can determine how their results fit into 23 business career profiles. Each profile contains a comprehensive overview of the work people do in that career, descriptions of the typical interests of those people, the work rewards available in the career, and the abilities necessary to succeed in it.

The Career Key (www.ncsu.edu/careerkey/index.html). Developed by Lawrence K. Jones (1998), professor of counselor education at North Carolina State University, The Career Key (internet version) can be downloaded from the Internet as a paper-and-pencil version using Adobe Acrobat Reader. The instrument, which is based on Holland types, allows users to measure their personality (interests, values, abilities, and skills associated with an occupation that interests them), find corresponding occupations, and then look up descriptions in the *Occupational Outlook*

Handbook (DOL, 1998). This program has a section on its intended use (i.e., it is a tool to be used in the beginning of the career planning process), and it advises users to seek career counseling[2] (see Jones, 1999, for more information on the reliability and the validity of the Career Key).

CareerScope (www.vri.org). Distributed by the Vocational Research Institute (VRI), CareerScope (2000) is a self-administered aptitude battery and interest inventory that can run on either a Windows® or Macintosh platform. It addresses the issue of possible reading difficulties; "All that's needed is a fourth-grade reading level," the VRI Web site claims. It also teaches the user how to use a computer mouse. The CareerScope assessment comprises an interest inventory and multiple aptitude tasks. A counselor can control the order of the batteries as well as the traits that can be assessed. "Administration templates" can be created and saved that control the delivery of the assessment tasks. Different templates then can be assigned to different evaluees or candidate pools to achieve targeted assessment objectives. The program makes available user assessment profiles and counselor reports for follow-up intervention. Counselors can generate a series of reports by date of administration or user ID number. The reports can then be tailored to address the respective needs of the user or counselor (Kapes & Martinez, 1998, discuss the application of CareerScope in school-to-work programs).

Career Visions (www.cdsways.com/products/cvisions.html). Career Development Systems researched and developed this CACGS at the Center on Education and Work at the University of Wisconsin–Madison. It is known for incorporating a number of multimedia and video technologies into the career search process. Quick Time movies about occupations, audio-visual instruction, and charts and graphs are part of this comprehensive system, as are data on occupations, industries, employers, programs of study, and educational institutions. Online tutorials also are available. The most extensive change to the latest version of Career Visions is found in the programs-of-study database and its interconnection to institutions. This change includes the use of a generic list of program names, which enables users to locate programs of interest, find institutions that offer the programs, and obtain actual program titles as used by individual institutions (see Sampson, Norris, Barrett, & Reardon, 1998, for a bibliography of this program).

CareerWAYS (www.cew.wisc.edu/cew/groups/carways.htm). CareerWAYS (1997) teaches students to develop a career plan consistent with their interests, skills, preferences, and aptitudes by helping them develop

---

[2]The program states "Consider seeing a professional career counselor. Deciding on a career, finding a job, or working out a problem at work is often difficult. It can be confusing and stressful. Problems like these can have a negative impact on your physical and mental health. They can also affect your relationships with friends and family. Most people find career counseling helpful."

and maintain their own computerized portfolio. As they work with the program, they develop a career plan that gradually evolves as they mature, assess and reassess their experiences, and relate those experiences to the planning process. Furthermore, CareerWAYS stores a complete record of students' transactions with the program, including their course work, interests, values, work preferences, career goals, and plans for achieving those goals. It also provides tools for creating résumés, cover letters, and lifestyle budgets and has audio, video, and other interfaces for effective use. The goal of CareerWAYS is to make students "owners" of their career plan. Ownership relates to increasing motivation to explore options, seek information, and succeed in a career.

CHOICES CT (www.can.ibm.com/ism/client_operations.html career-ware). Choices CT gives adults in career transition new ways to consider their experiences and to relate their transferable skills, interests, and priorities to career and education options. The Choices CT RoadMap guides job seekers with a step-by-step approach to career exploration. Users can identify their transferable skills with an online Work Content Skills Checklist and assess interests through a 144-item online Interest Checklist. Reports show related occupations. The program also has direct Internet linkages to America's Job Bank. An electronic portfolio and planner help adults organize information about themselves, identify education and training routes for target occupations, and document employability skills. Interactive modules focus on job search, interviewing, writing a skills-based résumé, dealing with challenges and barriers to employment, and making a career action plan (see Sampson, Reardon, & Rudd, 1998a, for a bibliography of CHOICES CT).

Compute a Match System/Pesco 2001 (www.pesco.org). The Compute a Match System/Pesco 2001 has assessment modules that measure aptitudes such as finger dexterity, eye–hand and eye–hand–foot coordination, spatial ability and perception, and general learning ability and styles. It also has an interest inventory, temperament assessment, and work attitude survey as well as a job title list for further career exploration. Language and math tests are available, as are job skills tests, which enable the user to simulate various aspects of a work environment (e.g., tests on various office software products—Access, Corel Presentations, Excel).

DISCOVER (www.act.org/discover). One of the pioneering CACGSs, DISCOVER is a comprehensive program that takes the user through various modules (such as beginning the career journey, learning about the world of work, learning about yourself, finding occupations, learning about occupations, making educational choices, planning next steps, planning your career, and making transitions; Ramey & Splete, 1995). Users then integrate their profiles with the World-of-Work map, which is based on Holland's types. Educational, military, apprenticeship, internship, and job placement information also is available. The Windows® 95 version and CD-ROM multimedia version for Macintosh have multimedia capabilities and contain video clips, audio clips, and photos. Links to Internet career information are a relatively new feature of DISCOVER (see Sampson, Reardon, & Rudd, 2000, for a comprehensive bibliography on DISCOVER).

Embark.com (www.embark.com). Embark.com (2000) is a version of a CACGS on the Internet. It contains career interest information (including a Web version of the Self-Directed Search) as well as undergraduate, graduate, and professional educational and financial aid information. Users can access a database that also is accessible by admissions recruiters, and they can save a profile for repeat usage of the program. They also can connect directly to college Web sites and apply online (see Sampson, 1999, for more information).

Focus II (www.focuscareer.com). Developed by Frank Minor at IBM, Focus II helps users assess their interests, skills, values, and work experience needs; explore and analyze occupational and educational paths compatible with their personal attributes; map out realistic occupational goals and educational plans to support their goals; and identify training and development needs. Diagnostic reports for practitioners also are available, which summarize users' career planning deficiencies, occupational and educational aspirations and concerns, and personal development needs. Users complete the program through the following phases, as listed by the program (see Sampson & Reardon, 1998, for a Focus II bibliography):

- Phase 1: Analyze career planning status
- Phase 2: Self-assess interests, values, and skills
- Phase 3: Explore and analyze occupations based on interests and work values
- Phase 4: Explore and analyze occupations based on educational areas of study, education level, training, and skills
- Phase 5: Explore and analyze occupations based on type of work
- Phase 6: Find information for a specific occupation
- Phase 7: Your personal development needs.

System of Interactive Guidance and Information (SIGI PLUS) (www. ets.org/sigi). SIGI PLUS is a comprehensive guidance and information system that enables users to complete the following 9 sessions:

1. Introduction
2. Self assessment
3. Search
4. Information
5. Skills
6. Preparing
7. Coping
8. Deciding
9. Next steps

As mentioned in chapter 5 of this book, SIGI PLUS enables users to match skills with occupations (see Sampson, Reardon, & Rudd 1998b, for a SIGI PLUS and SIGI bibliography).

Which Is Most Effective?

After reading the preceding descriptions of CACGSs, readers may want to know which ones are the most effective. The literature suggests that it is difficult to determine one best system, given the diversity of practitioner environments and user needs (Gati, 1990). Perceived effectiveness of CACGSs often may depend on the state of career decidedness of users and their need for career information (Peterson et al., 1994). In terms of diversity of users by Holland type, for example, Lenz, Reardon, and Sampson (1993; see also chapter 7 of this book) found that Holland's social and enterprising types, compared with realistic and investigative types, rated SIGI PLUS lower with respect to acquiring self- and occupational knowledge. Users looking for occupational information may rate one relevant program higher than users looking for a program that has more of a guidance focus. As Sampson and Reardon (1990) also noted,

> The interaction of CACG system features and costs with varied client populations and organizational variables is too complex to allow one "best" system to exist for all situations. A better approach would involve practitioners asking themselves, "Given our client population, organizational structure, financial resources, staff (time and skills), and historical/theoretical approach to service delivery, which CACG system provides the features that we need at an acceptable cost, and has been shown to be effective for clients under these operating conditions?" We believe that this is the proper type of question to be addressed—there is no professionally responsible alternative. (p. 146)

Although Gati (1990) noted that more research should be done on the effectiveness of systems, doing so might be difficult because the aims of the systems vary. A review of research for this chapter did not reveal any consistent findings regarding which programs are used more than others. The common variable that appears to determine selection is cost. Several respondents to the online survey noted that Focus II is one of the more affordable programs (and well-liked by users) and is similar in quality to some of the more expensive systems. DISCOVER was the most recommended CACGS for adult student populations.

The Internet and the Career Development Process

Although this chapter has focused on stand-alone CACGSs, the discussion would be incomplete without mention of the rapid growth of the Internet as a part of the career development process. The Internet has existed almost as long as stand-alone CACGSs, but its role in the career development process did not escalate until the early 1990s (with the development of Web browsers and other technologies). It continues to develop today as a standard tool for practitioners and users (Anderson, 1996).

Every part of the career development process, from planning to placement, is represented on the Internet in thousands of forms. A novice Internet user accustomed to an organized structure of traditional CACGSs will at first be overwhelmed by the apparent "disorganization" of career information on the Web. Using "jobs and careers" as search keywords in the Altavista search engine, for example, recently yielded 7,759 pages on this topic; the keyword "employment" generated more than 9 million pages. Internet career reference books, abstracts of which would require another chapter in this book, are found at every conventional and virtual retailer. The successful practitioner's office now has online placement programs (such as Jobtrak) that allow candidates to post résumés and employers to view them. Traditional print copies of the *Dictionary of Occupational Titles* (DOL, 1991) and *Occupational Outlook Handbook* (DOL, 1998) and many other standards of the practitioner's bookshelf are now readily accessible on the Internet. Web pages are vital for employers today for standard business; many employers have links on their sites to job listings and accept résumés through e-mail.

An Internet Authority: Margaret Riley Dikel

A leading Internet authority is Margaret Riley Dikel, an independent consultant, author, and columnist. Riley Dikel (1998) has claimed that the Internet can help users through online assessment instruments and skill inventories (e.g., the Keirsey Temperament Sorter; Keirsey, 2000), database searches of occupational (*Occupational Outlook Handbook*; DOL, 1998) and educational (*Peterson's Guides*, 1998) information, and communication tools (e-mail discussion lists, online résumé-posting services, employer Web sites with reference information about the employer).

Riley Dikel developed a widely acclaimed, centralized, online resource guide, "Employment Opportunities and Job Resources on the Internet," accessible at *www.rileyguide.com*. The guide has links to employment listings, industry and occupational information, and job-search resources. What makes the guide most effective for practitioners and users is its educational emphasis (e.g., "dos and don'ts" of online résumé posting, Internet etiquette, and tips on effective online and traditional job searching). Rather than just list Internet sites, Riley Dikel offers a short review and critique of each site in the guide, including recommended off-line print resources. A section is included for people who are new to the Internet. More important, the guide is commercial free, and its text-based structure allows for easy downloading onto any platform.

The Internet as an Integral Part of Traditional CACGSs

As noted earlier, many stand-alone CACGSs now incorporate links to career information on the Internet. The new role of CACGSs is to continue providing the organized structure while becoming an integral part of the Internet. As Harris-Bowlsbey (1998) stated,

> The advantage of this general approach is that the Internet sites can be accessed in conjunction with the material provided in the system and thus be folded into the career planning process offered by that system. After the user accesses and explores the website, he or she is returned to the place within the system from which the launch took place. In this way the best of the system itself and the best of the Internet can be combined to provide assistance on a given topic. (p. 46)

Advantages, Challenges and Future Issues for CACGSs and the Internet

Advantages of CACGSs. Sampson (1997) noted that the benefits of CACGSs include the following:

- improved generation of occupational alternatives (e.g., enhanced capacity to relate self-knowledge to occupational alternatives)
- enhanced occupational knowledge (e.g., awareness of the world of work, awareness of appropriate career exploration resources, acquisition of relevant occupational and educational information)
- improved career certainty (e.g., increasing specificity of occupational alternatives)
- improved vocational maturity (e.g., awareness of the need for planning, increased concern with vocational choice, improved attitude toward career choice, greater perceived ability to make career decisions)
- positive user perceptions of computer use (e.g., perception that the computer was easy to use and understandable, computer use perceived as an interesting and enjoyable experience)
- enhanced service delivery (e.g., time savings for the user and the counselor, positive counselor attitude about using computers in service delivery). (p. 3)

Results of the surveys cited in this chapter generally support Sampson's (1997) points. CACGSs are comprehensive, multifaceted, career guidance tools that help clients in various aspects of the career decision-making process. They can provide large lists of occupational and educational information that might not be readily available in a practitioner's career library. As a result, practitioners are not the sole providers of career information and can focus on helping users interpret the results and explore alternatives beyond the systems. Users not only gain more awareness about their career development, they also become more skilled at navigating through career reference resources in the world of work (Sampson, 1997).

The video chips available on some of the previously discussed systems enable clients to see role plays (e.g., interviews) as well as live profiles of people in a particular career as a supplement to text-based information. As Mariani (1996) stated, "In CACGS, the counseling profession has found its paints, palette, and brushes. The artistry of today's counselor lies in providing the tools to clients and then helping them paint their own workscapes" (p. 24). As mentioned in chapter 7 of this volume, CACGSs are best used as part of the counseling process, rather than separate from it.

The organizational, sequential structure of many CACGSs enables users to develop a plan through the career decision-making process. Having a plan results in increased self-confidence and satisfaction with the process (Sampson, 1997). Users who are intimidated with the random nature of the Internet initially should work with a structured CACGS that is linked to the Internet, examples of which are mentioned earlier in this chapter.

Advantages of the Internet. Advantages of the Internet include wide accessibility of employer information; reduced costs for practitioners who previously bought hard-copy reference materials; convenient sources of job listings; and faster, efficient means of communication. In addition, networking is made easier through listservs of professional organizations; users are no longer physically required to attend professional meetings at distant sites. Career information, dissemination, and retrieval have become more streamlined as a result of the Internet. Users can access the Internet on a 24-hour basis and are not tied to a certain location or computer.

Challenges to CACGSs: Special Populations. CACGSs should be used with appropriate client groups, and practitioners should be aware of value differences between special populations and CACGSs. For example, one of the online survey respondents noted that CACGSs' use of U.S. theoretical orientations may present a challenge to Asian users, who may have specific career options as a result of their upbringing. Krumboltz (1985) further advised practitioners to note differing perceptions of occupational adjectives. A CACGS, for example, may describe a corporate CEO as a high-pressured occupation, when such may not be the case in various areas of the world. In addition, practitioners should be prepared to work with populations who may not have the reading, language, interpretative, and analytical skills that are required by many text-based CACGSs. Alternative resources, if necessary, should be readily available for such populations (Haring-Hidore, 1984).

With the exception of the single online survey respondent who mentioned the issues of using CACGSs with Asian populations, the results of the online survey did not reveal issues of concern regarding CACGS use with special populations. Similarly, a review of the literature did not reveal any significant ethnically or racially based concerns. Nevertheless, as the authors of chapter 13 of this book discuss, additional empirical research is warranted in this area. How do Asian or African American users, for example, perceive the effectiveness of CACGSs in their career development? Do the theoretical orientations of CACGSs apply to diverse cultures? As Hinkelman and Luzzo (1997) stated,

> There is a great need in the CACGS literature for the use of large and diverse samples of participants. Much of the CACGS research to date has suffered from the typical, white college sophomore male sampling dilemma found frequently in the psychological literature. More studies are needed that examine the effectiveness of CACGSs with under represented populations, such as racial and ethnic minorities, older adults, and persons with disabilities. (p. 43)

Challenges facing the Internet. Unlike traditional CACGSs, which have a history of empirical research, the Internet is still developing in this area. Some survey respondents prefer CACGSs to the Internet because of the CACGSs' structure, organization, and theoretical foundations. Sampson (1999) cited some of the Internet's limitations:

- A limited selection of validated assessments are available (exceptions are the Self-Directed Search at *www.self-directed-search.com/* and the *Occupational Outlook Handbook* at *stats. bls.gov/ocohome.htm*).
- Most Internet resources do not list recommendations on when counseling is needed.
- The Internet may still be inaccessible to people who cannot afford a computer or who live in rural areas with limited access to Internet service providers.
- Users may become overwhelmed with the vast array of resources, especially if they use them where professional assistance is not available to help them navigate the system. Many CACGSs, however, "provide implementation sources, customer service, and training to institutions, agencies, and organizations" (Sampson, 1999, p. 14) in a structured fashion. Standards, as previously discussed, also apply to CACGSs.

In addition, there is the ethical issue of engaging in Internet career exploration from the user's workplace computer. Many employers now have policies regarding use of the Internet at work (Iaccarino, 1996). Still, the ease of accessing the Internet at break time is tempting to many employees. Another issue arises when users post their résumé on their personal Web pages, where photographs or other personal items may inadvertently interfere with the person's chances of finding employment. Confidentiality and privacy issues also are a concern, as discussed by Carson and Dawis in chapter 5. A highly recommended source for further reading about effective uses of the Internet are guidelines produced by the NCDA (*http://www.ncda.org*) and the NBCC (*http://www.nbcc.org*).

Like any career development tool, the Internet is only one source to use in the career exploration and planning process. As David Kass of the Israel National Employment Service said on a November 28, 1998, JOBPLACE listserv e-mail posting:

Both Richard Bolles and Margaret Riley Dikel warn the potential job hunter not to use the Internet as the sole tool in the job hunt, but rather as an additional tool. They note that one should spend no more than 20–25% of search time on the Internet—but if job hunters are technically inclined they raise this estimate up to 50% search time. In general it would seem that the net is a valuable tool for researching the job or the company, but that the actual success in landing the job may have nothing to do with the Internet per se.

Conclusion and Recommendations for Practice

CACGSs will continue to be a fundamental part of the career development of college students and other populations. Once the only technological resource available to assist college students in the career decision-making process, CACGSs are now part of the multimedia and Internet revolutions. Practitioners should consider carefully the needs and personality characteristics of users when using CACGSs. Lenz et al. (1993), for example, found that users with high social and enterprising scores on Holland's My Vocational Situation and Vocational Preference Inventory prefer a face-to-face appointment immediately after using a CACGS, whereas realistic and investigative types seek more information directly from the system. Practitioners also may want to administer assessment instruments such as the Myers–Briggs Type Indicator or Strong Interest Inventory to users before encouraging the use of a CACGS (Mariani, 1996).

Practitioners also should take cultural background of users into consideration when using systems. Attributes of a certain profession, such as independence or teamwork, as "defined" by a CACGS, might differ from the users' interpretation of those attributes (Gati, 1996). A CACGS that does not ask questions about family background might be detrimental to users whose families play a significant part in their career development. Practitioners should discuss any possible discrepancies with students before inviting their use of the systems.

As previously discussed in the chapter, budget and costs are the main factors considered when selecting a particular CACGS. Practitioners should be reminded to look at many complex items when selecting and evaluating CACGSs. An excellent resource is Sampson's (1994) feature–cost analysis, in which several CACGSs are evaluated according to the following criteria:

- *Performing assessment.* Does the CACGS allow for input of scores from popular assessment instruments?
- *Identifying occupational alternatives.* Are there modules on skills and abilities, education and training? Can multiple searches be conducted?
- *Obtaining occupational information.* Are multiple sources used to develop occupational information? How often is the material updated? Is the information arranged categorically (e.g., by DOT number, SIC code)? Does the system include career ladder, employment outlook, and income information?

- *Identifying educational alternatives and obtaining educational information.* Can users easily search for educational, military, and financial aid information? Is there clear demographic information about institutions?
- *Coping with adult transitions.* Are issues relevant to adult populations addressed, such as financial aid, time management, and child care?
- *Decision making.* Is there a description of a career decision-making model? Is feedback provided to users about their choices according to a decision-making matrix?
- *Employment planning.* Are there lists of career reference books related to job searching? Does job placement (e.g., résumé writing, interviewing) information exist?
- *Working on user exit.* Does the CACGS provide a history of current and past user sessions? Can the user complete an optional evaluation of the system?
- *Offering user-friendly features.* Are graphics clearly displayed? Are menu-driven command features available? Is the user's name listed on the printout? Is there an orientation to the function keys?
- *Collecting data for accountability and research.* Can practitioners compile empirical reports and draw generalizations and conclusions from system use?
- *Providing support materials for users.* Are printed guides available to users? Do posters exist?
- *Providing support materials for institutions.* Are training manuals available with case study examples? Does the CACGS have a theoretical basis for system design and use? Is a monthly newsletter available from the vendor?
- *Providing demonstration resources.* Can practitioners receive a demonstration copy of the CACGS?
- *Generating counselor or administrator reports.* Can reports be generated easily?
- *Explaining budget and costs.* Are costs easily spelled out? (pp. 12–26)

As noted earlier, budget and costs are only one of a long list of items that practitioners should consider in the evaluation and selection of programs. As Sampson (1994) stated, "The ultimate effectiveness of this feature–cost analysis . . . can be measured by the willingness of professionals to . . . move beyond basic surface level evaluations to more theory-based, context-specific, comprehensive evaluations of CACG system performance" (p. 7).

CACGSs will continue to be a fundamental part of the career decision-making process for practitioners and users. This chapter has highlighted some of the current issues associated with the systems. Practitioners who wish to obtain more information on CACGS research and applications are urged to contact Florida State University's Center for the Study of Technology in Counseling and Career Development at *www.aus.fsu.edu/ techcntr/*.

References

ACT, Inc. (2000). DISCOVER. [On-line]. Available: www.act.org/discover.

Anderson, B. (1996). The Internet in the workplace: Issues of implementation and impact. *Thresholds in Education, 22*(3), 17–22.

Career Development Systems. (1997). *Career visions*. [On-line]. Available: www.cdsways. com/products/cvisions.html.

Clyde, J. S. (1979). *Computerized career information and guidance systems. Information series No. 178*. Columbus, OH: Ohio State University, Columbus. National Center for Research in Vocational Education. (ERIC Document Reproduction Service No. ED 179 764)

Educational Testing Service. (1999). *Focus II*. [On-line]. Available: www.ets.org/sigi.

Embark.com. (2000). *Embark.com*. [On-line]. Available: www.embark.com.

EUREKA. (2000). *Career finder*. [On-line]. Available: www.eurekanet.org/cfinder.html.

Gati, I. (1990). The contribution of differential feature-cost analysis to the evaluation of computer-assisted career guidance systems. *Journal of Career Development, 17*, 119–128.

Gati, I. (1994). Computer-assisted career counseling: Dilemmas, problems and possible solutions. *Journal of Counseling and Development, 73*, 51–56.

Gati, I. (1996). Computer-assisted career counseling: Challenges and prospects. In M. L. Savickas & W. B. Walsh (Eds.), *Handbook of career counseling theory and practice* (pp. 169–190). Palo Alto, CA: Davies-Black.

Haring-Hidore, M. (1984). In pursuit of students who do not use computers for career guidance. *Journal of Counseling and Development, 63*, 139–140.

Harris-Bowlsbey, J. A. (1992). *Building blocks of computer-based career planning systems*. Ann Arbor, MI: ERIC Clearinghouse on Counseling and Personnel Services. (ERIC Document Reproduction Service No. ED 363 824)

Harris-Bowlsbey, J. A. (1998). Models of use of the Internet in career planning. In J. A. Bowlsbey, M. R. Dikel, & J. P. Sampson (Eds.), *The Internet: A tool for career planning* (pp. 11–29). Columbus, OH: National Career Development Association.

Hinkelman, J. M., & Luzzo, D. A. (1997). Computer-assisted career guidance: Bridging the science-practitioner gap. *Career Planning and Adult Development Journal, 13*, 41–50.

Howland, P., & Palmer, R. (1992). Ethics and computer guidance: Uneasy partners? *Journal of Career Planning and Employment, 52*(4), 38–41, 43–45.

Iaccarino, G. (1996). A look at Internet privacy and security issues and their relationship to the electronic job search: Implications for librarians and career services professionals. In E. A. Lorenzen (Ed.), *Career planning and job searching in the information age* (pp. 107–113). New York: The Haworth Press.

IBM Global Services. (1999). CHOICES CT. Available: www.can.ibm.com/ism/client_operations.html careerware.

Jones, L. K. (1998). *The career key*. [On-line]. Available: www.ncsu.edu/careerkey/index.html.

Jones, L. K. (1999). The career key: An investigation of the reliability and validity of its scales and its helpfulness to college students. *Measurement and Evaluation in Counseling and Development, 23*, 67–76.

Kapes, J. T., & Martinez, L. (1998, December). *Career assessment: Recently developed instruments useful for school-to-work programs*. Paper presented at the American Vocational Association Convention, New Orleans, LA. (ERIC Document Reproduction Service No. ED 427 208)

Keirsey, D. M. (2000). *Keirsey temperament sorter*. [On-line]. Available: http://keirsey.com.

Krumboltz, J. D. (1985). Presuppositions underlying computer use in career counseling. *Journal of Career Development, 12*, 165–175.

Lenz, J. G., Reardon, R. C., & Sampson, J. P. (1993). Holland's theory and effective use of computer-assisted career guidance systems. *Journal of Career Development, 19,* 245–253.

Mariani, M. (1996). Computer-assisted career guidance: Ride the rising tide. *Occupational Outlook Quarterly, 39*(4), 16–27.

National Occupational Information Coordinating Committee. (2000). *Career information delivery systems.* [On-line]. Available: www.noicc.gov.

Offer, M. (1997, March). Supporting career guidance in the information society: A review of the use of computer-assisted guidance and the Internet in Europe. Unpublished manuscript: Advice Guidance and Training, Winchester, United Kingdom.

Peregrine Partners. (2000). Careerleader. [On-line]. Available: www.careerdiscovery.com.

Pesco International. (2000). *Compute a match / Pesco 2001.* Available: www.pesco.org.

Peterson, G. W., Ryan-Jones, R. E., Sampson, J. P., Reardon, R. C., & Shahnasarian, M. (1994). A comparison of the effectiveness of three computer-assisted career guidance systems: DISCOVER, SIGI, and SIGI PLUS. *Computers in Human Behavior, 10,* 189–198.

Peterson's Guides, Inc. (1998). *Peterson's graduate & professional programs: An overview.* Princeton, NJ: Author.

Ramey, L., & Splete, H. (1995). *Adult career counseling center. Twelfth annual report.* Rochester, MI: Oakland University Adult Career Counseling Center. (ERIC Document Reproduction Service No. ED 390 989)

Riley Dikel, M. (1998). Sample websites. In J. A. Harris-Bowlsbey, M. R. Dikel, & J. P. Sampson (Eds.), *The Internet: A tool for career planning* (pp. 11–29). Columbus, OH: National Career Development Association.

Sampson, J. P. (1994). *A differential feature-cost analysis of seventeen computer-assisted career guidance systems: Technical report number 10* (5th ed.). Tallahassee: Florida State University, Center for the Study of Technology in Counseling and Career Development. (ERIC Document Reproduction Service No. ED 383 982)

Sampson, J. P. (1997). *Enhancing the use of career information with computer-assisted career guidance systems.* Paper presented at the meeting of the Japan Institute of Labor, Tokyo.

Sampson, J. P., Jr. (1999). Effective design and use of Internet-based career resources and services. *IAEVG (International Association for Educational and Vocation Guidance) Bulletin, 63,* 4–12.

Sampson, J. P., Jr., Lumsden, J. A., Carr, D. L., & Rudd, E. A. (1999). *A differential feature-cost analysis of internet-based career information delivery systems (CIDS): Technical report no. 24.* Tallahassee: Center for the Study of Technology in Counseling and Career Development, the Florida State University.

Sampson, J. P., Jr., Norris, D. S., Barrett, K., & Reardon, R. C. (1998). *Computer-assisted career guidance: Career visions bibliography.* [On-line]. Available: www.career.fsu.edu/techcenter/cvbibnew.html.

Sampson, J. P., Jr., Reardon, R. C., Lenz, J. G., Ryan-Jones, R. E., Peterson, G. W., & Levy, F. C. (1993). *The impact of DISCOVER for Adult Learners and SIGI PLUS on the career decision making of adults (technical report No. 9).* Tallahassee: Florida State University, Center for the Study of Technology in Counseling and Career Development. (ERIC Document Reproduction Service No. ED 363 824).

Sampson, J. P., Jr., Reardon, R. C., & Rudd, E. (1998a). *Computer-assisted career guidance: Choices bibliography.* [On-line]. Available: www.career.fsu.edu/techcenter/chbibnew.html.

Sampson, J. P., Jr., Reardon, R. C., & Rudd, E. (1998b). *Computer-assisted career guidance: SIGI PLUS and SIGI bibliography.* [On-line]. Available: www.career.fsu.edu/techcenter/sigibibnew.html.

Sampson, J. P., Jr., Reardon, R. C., & Rudd, E. (2000). *Computer-assisted career guidance: DISCOVER bibliography.* [On-line]. Available: www.career.fsu.edu/techcenter/disbibnew.html.

Sampson, J. P., Jr., & Reardon, R. C. (1990). Evaluating computer-assisted career guidance systems: Synthesis and implications. *Journal of Career Development, 17,* 143–149.

Sampson, J. P., Jr., & Reardon, R. C. (1998). *Computer-assisted career guidance: Focus II bibliography*. [On-line]. Available: www.career.fsu.edu/techcenter/focusbibnew.html.

Sampson, J. P., Jr., Shahnasarian, M., & Reardon, R. C. (1986). *A comparison of the use of DISCOVER and SIGI (technical report no. 2)*. Tallahassee: Clearinghouse for Computer Assisted Career Guidance Systems. (ERIC Document Reproduction Service No. ED 272 677).

U. S. Department of Labor, Bureau of Labor Statistics. (1998). *Occupational outlook handbook, 1998–1999 edition*. Washington, DC: U.S. Government Printing Office.

U. S. Department of Labor, Employment and Training Administration. (1991). *Dictionary of occupational titles, 4th edition*. Lanham, MD: Bernan Press.

Vocational Research Institute. (2000). *Careerscope*. [On-line]. Available: www.vri.org.

Wilhelm, S. J. (1978). Computer-based guidance systems: Are they worth it? *Journal of Career Placement, 38*(2), 65–69.

Wisconsin Center for Education and Work. (1997). *Careerways*. Available: www.cew.wisc.edu/cew/groups/carways.htm.

Zunker, V. G. (1986). *Career counseling: Applied concepts of life planning*. Monterey, CA: Brooks/Cole.

10

Career Development of Returning-Adult and Graduate Students

Darrell Anthony Luzzo

Between one third and one half of today's college students are returning adults—people over age 25 who have decided to return to school after spending several years outside the educational arena (Griff, 1987; Hirschorn, 1988; Rathus & Fichner-Rathus, 1997). In addition, many university campuses have a large contingent of graduate students, most of whom tend to be people who are older than the traditional undergraduate population. More than 20 million returning-adult and graduate students are expected to be enrolled in college-level studies within the next several years (Luzzo, 1999).

For a significant proportion of returning-adult and graduate students, the decision to pursue higher education is a matter of economic circumstance. It may be that seeking additional academic credentials will ensure greater job security. Or perhaps the loss of one's job includes a severance package that covers the costs of additional education. For someone who is transitioning from public assistance, pursuing postsecondary education may be the first step toward economic self-sufficiency. These examples illustrate a significant pressure on many returning-adult and graduate students to pursue college studies. Simply put, economic factors (e.g., enhancement of career development, expansion of job opportunities) often are the primary reason for adults to return to school (Ashar & Skenes, 1993).

Unfortunately, most college and university career development and career counseling programs focus on the needs of traditional-aged undergraduate students, even while the need to respond to the expanding population of returning-adult and graduate students is growing (Ginter & Brown, 1996; Griff, 1987; Mounty, 1991). This chapter discusses characteristics differentiating traditional and nontraditional students, identifies the career development needs of graduate and returning-adult students, and provides career counselors with practical suggestions for effectively addressing the career-related issues and concerns of older student populations.

Characteristics Differentiating Traditional and Nontraditional Students

Researchers and student affairs personnel recognize a variety of characteristics that differentiate students of traditional age (i.e., those under age 25) and older students, often referred to in the literature as *nontraditional* students (Ashar & Skenes, 1993; Chartrand, 1992; Chickering & Havighurst, 1981; Miller & Winston, 1990).

> Among these differences is the realization that nontraditional students usually have work, family, and community responsibilities outside of the college or university environment. Such students are often less concerned with establishing an identity or engaging in university-sponsored social activities. Nontraditional students, unlike many traditional students, usually work full-time and focus on occupational and family goals as salient factors in their lives. (Luzzo, 1999, pp. 137–138)

Furthermore, researchers and theorists who study college student development have argued that nontraditional students possess more of an instrumental educational orientation, in contrast to the expressive orientation traditionally exhibited by younger students (Chickering & Havighurst, 1981). This trait suggests that acknowledging the importance of economic issues and trends in the lives of adult students might be more important to ensuring their academic retention and persistence than focusing on their intellectual and social integration.

Chartrand (1992) argued that widely accepted models of student development, most of which focus almost exclusively on developmental factors relevant to late adolescence, may not be as relevant to the development of nontraditional student populations. Returning-adult students, whether undergraduates or graduate students, make up a population that has considerably different developmental needs and tasks than students of traditional college age. Because older students are at different developmental levels, "it is important that psychosocial assessment strategies and instrumentation be geared to the special characteristics and life patterns of these different age cohorts" (Miller & Winston, 1990, p. 109).

Identifying Career Decision-Making Needs of Graduate Students

As discussed in chapter 1 of this book, Super (1984) hypothesized five stages of lifelong career development. Following the *growth stage*, which usually occurs in late childhood and early adolescence, people experience the *exploration stage*. During this stage, college students engage in tasks such as assessing job-related skills, learning more about occupations of interest, selecting among the most preferable career alternatives, and determining the education and training required for entry into particular career fields. Following the exploration stage, people enter the *establish-*

ment stage, which involves achieving stability in an occupational choice, improving one's chances of advancement within a career field, and becoming increasingly proficient in that career (McCaffrey, Miller, & Winston, 1984). The developmental stages of *maintenance* within and *disengagement* from one's work then follow.

College students do not all progress through the stages of career development in exactly the same manner or at exactly the same pace. It therefore would be incorrect to assume that all graduate students—just because they are enrolled in graduate studies—are at the same level of career development. An adult career changer with a bachelor's degree in one field of study may decide to make a career change by earning a master's degree in another field. A middle-aged woman may return to college following a divorce and, having received a bachelor's degree earlier in life, work toward an advanced degree in the same field. Some graduate students are retirees looking for a second career or simply working toward the accomplishment of a personal goal.

It may be common to assume that all graduate students seek advanced degrees primarily to obtain training for a previously made career choice. Yet, as faculty and student affairs personnel regularly observe, many graduate students—especially those who enter graduate school directly after undergraduate studies—possess limited knowledge of the profession that they expect to enter. Consequently, a significant proportion of students enter graduate school each year with unclear career goals (McCaffrey et al., 1984) and enroll in graduate studies more as a way to explore career options than as a means of further commitment to a previously chosen career. Many undergraduate students apply for and enroll in graduate school because of faculty or parental pressure or because they believe—often mistakenly—that an undergraduate degree is not marketable. This line of reasoning may create problems for relatively younger graduate students, who quickly discover that they are in graduate school more as a method for deciding which career field to enter than as part of their career establishment or maintenance.

Despite these observations, however, it is probably true that most graduate students—especially those who are older than traditional-aged college students—are at either the latter stages of career exploration or the initial stages of career establishment. Yet with the diversity of career-related concerns that graduate students exhibit, it is important that college career counselors increase their understanding of the needs of this population. Empirical research can play a valuable role in that process.

Several journal articles address the career development of graduate students; most provide descriptions of programs carried out at individual campuses. One of the primary limitations associated with such program descriptions is that they tend to lack empirical support to justify their implementation on a widespread basis. Furthermore, the programs presented in the literature tend to be either specific to a particular career field (e.g., Davis & Minnis, 1993; McGovern & Tinsley, 1976; Passmore & Swanson, 1981; Richmond & Sherman, 1991) or geared to undergraduates who are considering graduate education (e.g., Wessel, 1995), rather than to students who are already admitted to or attending graduate programs.

Fortunately, one noteworthy investigation provides at least some empirical evidence supporting hypothesized differences in career development between undergraduate and graduate students. McCaffrey et al. (1984) designed a study to determine whether graduate students' career maturity is significantly different from the career maturity of undergraduates. McCaffrey et al. analyzed survey data from randomly selected samples of 60 first-year students, 60 seniors, and 60 graduate students at a large southeastern university. Equal numbers of women and men were included in each student group.

Results indicated that first-year students exhibited significantly lower levels of career maturity than the senior and graduate students. Findings also revealed that graduate students, although aware of the tasks involved in achieving stability in a job choice and planning for future development, had not accomplished those tasks. Additional mean comparisons showed many similarities between the career development of graduate students and that of seniors. In particular, graduate students were similar to college seniors in their perceived need to determine career-related skills, learn about career options, and use effective career decision-making techniques. On the basis of their results, McCaffrey et al. supported a claim made earlier in this chapter: Graduate-level education—at least for some students—appears to be "an opportunity to crystallize a career decision rather than a chance to gain advanced training to achieve a previously determined career goal" (p. 130).

Clearly, additional research is needed in this area. Studies designed to increase career counselors' awareness of the particular career decision-making needs of graduate students are especially warranted. It also will be important to evaluate the effectiveness of various career intervention strategies among graduate student populations.

Recognizing the Career Development Needs of Returning-Adult Students

It is important that career counselors recognize that returning-adult students represent diverse backgrounds and motivations for returning to the higher education environment. A downsized factory worker may need an undergraduate degree to qualify for management positions in his or her field or to enter a new field with more promising occupational opportunities. A successful, long-term employee may be unable to receive a promotion without a bachelor's degree. Returning-adult students often have graduated from high school, have worked for several years in or out of the home, and have decided to return to school to pursue a professional degree.

With people of such diverse motivations all referred to as "returning-adult students," it seems critical that career counselors increase their ability to provide effective services for this growing population. Developing treatment strategies for returning-adult students requires an increased understanding of some of the differences between traditional and non-traditional students.

One might expect returning-adult students to experience substantially different career development needs from undergraduates of traditional age (Miller & Winston, 1990). Super (1984) provided theoretical support for those differences. He believed that nontraditional students are likely to be engaged in *recycling*, the process of reexperiencing earlier stages of career development. Because returning-adult students are expected to use their accumulated knowledge from previous career decision-making experiences, it often is assumed that they will be much more effective and efficient in repeating earlier stages of career development (Healy & Reilly, 1989).

Despite this theoretical and intuitive rationale, several researchers have reported a number of career decision-making similarities between traditional-aged and returning-adult students. For instance, various studies conducted since the early 1980s have revealed that the age of college students apparently has little influence on their knowledge of career decision-making principles (Healy, Mitchell, & Mourton, 1987; Luzzo, 1993a), knowledge of preferred occupation (Greenhaus, Hawkins, & Brenner, 1983), and level of career indecision (Slaney, 1986; Zagora & Cramer, 1994).

At the same time, however, significant differences between traditional and nontraditional students have been found for several characteristics associated with career development. For example, numerous investigations have revealed that age is positively correlated with college students' attitudes toward career decision making (Blustein, 1988; Guthrie & Herman, 1982; Healy, O'Shea, & Crook, 1985; Luzzo, 1993b). Older students report attitudes that reflect relatively low levels of anxiety and fear, whereas younger students tend to possess attitudes more reflective of insecurity and a general sense of concern related to making career decisions (Blustein, 1988; Healy et al., 1987; Healy & Mourton, 1987; Luzzo, 1993b).

Evidence also supports the notion that traditional undergraduates and returning-adult students differ in terms of career commitment, vocational identity, career decision-making self-efficacy, and perceived career decision-making needs (Colarelli & Bishop, 1990; Greenhaus et al., 1983; Haviland & Mahaffy, 1985; Luzzo, 1993a; Peterson, 1993). Results of this research have shown that returning-adult students tend to be more committed to their identified career choice than traditional students are. Research also has revealed that returning-adult students are more likely to cite substantial numbers of barriers to reaching their chosen occupational goal (e.g., economic barriers, multiple-role conflict) than are traditional-aged undergraduates. As Luzzo (1993a) and Peterson (1993) discovered, returning-adult students also tend to display higher levels of career decision-making self-efficacy than their traditional-student counterparts. These findings suggest that nontraditional students are more likely than traditional students to possess confidence in their ability to engage in the career decision-making process.

Healy and Reilly (1989) conducted one of the most comprehensive analyses of the career decision-making differences between younger and older college students. Nearly 3,000 traditional and nontraditional college students completed a survey about career counseling needs and services. Participants rated their needs in seven career areas: (a) knowing more about interests and abilities, (b) understanding how to decide on career goals, (c) becoming more certain of career plans, (d) exploring careers related to interests and abilities, (e) selecting courses relevant to career goals, (f) developing job-finding skills, and (g) obtaining a job. For each career area, students rated their perceived need for assistance.

Although the results of the study indicated a general decline in career decision-making needs with age, Healy and Reilly (1989) discovered that many career decision-making tasks were reported as major needs by 25% to 35% of adults over age 30. In fact, most of the nontraditional students in Healy and Reilly's study reported at least minor needs in each career area.

> The lowest needs for the older cohorts were in deciding upon career goals, becoming more certain of plans, and in obtaining jobs, while their highest needs were in exploring jobs related to talents and interests and in selecting courses related to goals. (p. 544)

Healy and Reilly concluded that many nontraditional students seem to adopt an exploratory posture toward the ever changing employment opportunity structure. As a result, it is likely that returning-adult students seek opportunities to discover and develop their career potential.

Practical Career Counseling Implications

Several recommendations for providing effective career counseling services to returning-adult and graduate student populations can be inferred from the research and theoretical arguments reviewed in this chapter. Although not all strategies will be effective on every college and university campus, they do provide counselors with hands-on suggestions to help improve services to nontraditional students.

One of the clearest messages that emerges from a review of the literature is that returning-adult and graduate students are not so advanced in their career development that they need considerably less guidance in career planning and decision making (Healy et al., 1987; Healy & Reilly, 1989; Luzzo, 1999; McCaffrey et al., 1984). What is important, however, is that college and university career counselors recognize the specific career decision-making needs of this group of students. Older undergraduate students in particular appear to have specific needs associated with career exploration and academic assistance, such as learning more about specific academic requirements for careers and determining appropriate courses in which to enroll (Healy & Reilly, 1989).

For graduate students, practitioners may want to provide opportunities to explore career goals and learn effective career decision-making strategies. Departmental seminars, faculty mentoring programs, and small-group workshops are just a few of the strategies that career counselors might want to consider implementing. McCaffrey et al.'s (1984) findings indicate that it is likely that many graduate students would benefit from career exploration and planning activities that emphasize a comprehensive self-evaluation of skills and values and an orientation to fundamental career decision-making principles.

Equally important to consider when developing career development programs for graduate students is the issue of institutional type. Graduate students at private, liberal arts colleges may have different career decision-making needs from graduate students attending a regional state university or a major research institution. Additional research could be designed to evaluate the role of institutional type in the career development of graduate students.

By coordinating career-related services with other campus agencies, counselors can establish a network of resources that might be particularly relevant to many returning-adult and graduate students. Similarly, by establishing ongoing liaison relationships with their institution's vocational and academic departments, career counselors can keep abreast of the content of courses and help ensure that timely information is available to returning-adult students who seek career counseling services (Luzzo, 1999).

Psychological characteristics can have a meaningful influence on the career development of returning-adult and graduate students. When working with such populations, counselors need to consider the role that factors such as the perception of occupational barriers and role conflicts play in students' career decision making. Integrating a discussion of psychological characteristics into the career counseling process can serve a valuable purpose by helping older students consider the interaction between personal and career-related issues in their lives.

As the number of nontraditional students increases, it is important that counselors determine whether traditional career counseling interventions (e.g., small-group interpretation of assessments, one-on-one counseling) are appropriate for older student populations. Experimental research by career counseling practitioners is especially warranted in this area. Such research will help determine whether traditional career counseling interventions are as effective for returning-adult and graduate students as they are for the younger students for whom they were originally developed. Career counselors might want to consider collaborating on research projects with faculty members at their institution who are knowledgeable about research methodology and statistical analysis.

Finally, resourceful and creative career intervention strategies need to be considered for returning-adult and graduate students, such as the following possibilities:

- By expanding career placement and counseling service hours to include evenings and weekends, counselors can help ensure that working adult students are able to access career counseling services.

- Evening and weekend orientation sessions can acquaint returning-adult and graduate students with the many adjustments and life changes that often take place when reentering school.
- Counseling workshops and seminars for returning-adult and graduate students should include well-planned strategies for addressing career-related concerns identified by students themselves. Counselors can rely on previous research that has identified such concerns (e.g., Haviland & Mahaffy, 1985; Healy & Reilly, 1989; McCaffrey et al., 1984), or they can conduct investigations at their own campus to ensure that students' needs are met through program offerings.
- Career counselors should consider integrating a discussion of perceived barriers into their work with returning-adult students. Counselors can assist their clients with developing effective strategies for addressing and overcoming career-related barriers, such as encouraging clients to keep a journal of barriers encountered to identify how they tend to handle barriers in their lives. Clients could then be encouraged to list additional ways in which specific barriers might be managed or prevented in the future.
- It may be particularly helpful for career centers to hire counselors who have expertise in working with the unique problems and concerns of older student populations (McCaffrey et al., 1984). Counselors who are keenly aware of the career-related issues common to nontraditional students will be respected and appreciated by such clients.
- Career counselors also can play an important role in helping undergraduate students consider the advantages and disadvantages of attending graduate school. Workshops in which graduate students share their experiences with undergraduates who are considering graduate school may prove particularly effective in this regard.
- Many graduate students who seek doctoral degrees plan to obtain an academic position following completion of their program. Career counselors may want to advise doctoral students who are planning to work in academia to develop alternative employment opportunities in nonacademic settings in case academic employment opportunities are difficult to find.

Need for Continued Research

Additional research efforts are needed to address many of the unanswered questions regarding the ways in which traditional students and returning-adult and graduate students engage in the career decision-making process. Some of those questions are as follows:

- Do younger and older students explore careers through the same or different means? Do they ask the same or different questions about possible careers and courses that will assist them in preparing for careers?
- Are returning-adult students and those of traditional age equally concerned about economic issues? Do they exhibit a comparable degree of understanding of the world of work and current employment trends?
- Do graduate students possess unique career decision-making needs?
- Do traditional methods of career counseling work as effectively when applied to returning-adult and graduate student populations?

By answering these and other important questions through empirical research, career counselors and vocational psychologists can develop useful models to help college career counselors conceptualize and implement age-appropriate treatments for diverse student populations.

Career counselors are encouraged to conduct the research that is needed to improve understanding of returning-adult and graduate students' career decision-making processes. Furthermore, counselors are urged to present the results of their research at relevant professional conferences (e.g., the annual conferences of the American College Personnel Association, the National Career Development Association, the National Association of Student Personnel Administrators, and the American Counseling Association) and to publish their results in professional journals (e.g., the *Journal of College Student Development, NASPA Journal, Career Development Quarterly*). In this way, college and university career counselors can help their colleagues provide effective career counseling services to all students.

References

Ashar, H., & Skenes, R. (1993). Can Tinto's student departure model be applied to nontraditional students? *Adult Education Quarterly, 43*, 90–100.

Blustein, D. L. (1988). A canonical analysis of career choice crystallization and vocational maturity. *Journal of Counseling Psychology, 35*, 294–297.

Chartrand, J. M. (1992). An empirical test of a model of nontraditional student adjustment. *Journal of Counseling Psychology, 39*, 193–202.

Chickering, A. W., & Havighurst, R. J. (1981). The life cycle. In A. W. Chickering & Assoc. (Eds.), *The modern American college* (pp. 16–50). San Francisco: Jossey-Bass.

Colarelli, S. M., & Bishop, R. C. (1990). Functions, correlates, and management. *Group and Organizational Studies, 15*, 158–176.

Davis, W. E., & Minnis, D. L. (1993). Designing a program to prepare graduate students for careers as college teachers. *Innovative Higher Education, 17*, 211–224.

Ginter, E. J., & Brown, S. (1996, August). *Lifestyle assessment and planning utilizing Super's C-DAC model and a life-skills model.* Paper presentation made at the 3rd International Congress on Integrative and Eclectic Psychotherapy, Huatulco, Mexico.

Greenhaus, J. H., Hawkins, B. L., & Brenner, O. C. (1983). The impact of career exploration on the career decision-making process. *Journal of College Student Personnel, 24*, 494–502.

Griff, N. (1987). Meeting the career development needs of returning students. *Journal of College Student Personnel, 28*, 469–470.

Guthrie, W. R., & Herman, A. (1982). Vocational maturity and its relationship to vocational choice. *Journal of Vocational Behavior, 21*, 196–205.

Haviland, M. G., & Mahaffy, J. E. (1985). The use of My Vocational Situation with nontraditional college students. *Journal of College Student Personnel, 26*, 169–170.

Healy, C. C., Mitchell, J. M., & Mourton, D. L. (1987). Age and grade differences in career development among community college students. *Review of Higher Education, 10*, 247–258.

Healy, C. C., & Mourton, D. L. (1987). The relationship of career exploration, college jobs, and grade point average. *Journal of College Student Personnel, 28*, 28–34.

Healy, C. C., O'Shea, D., & Crook, R. H. (1985). Relation of career attitudes to age and career progress during college. *Journal of Counseling Psychology, 32*, 239–244.

Healy, C. C., & Reilly, K. C. (1989). Career needs of community college students: Implications for services and theory. *Journal of College Student Development, 30*, 541–545.

Hirschorn, M. W. (1988, March 30). Students over 25 found to make up 45 percent of campus enrollments. *The Chronicle of Higher Education*, p. A35.

Luzzo, D. A. (1993a). Career decision-making differences between traditional and nontraditional college students. *Journal of Career Development, 20*, 113–120.

Luzzo, D. A. (1993b). Value of career decision-making self-efficacy in predicting career decision-making attitudes and skills. *Journal of Counseling Psychology, 40*, 194–199.

Luzzo, D. A. (1999). Identifying the career decision-making needs of nontraditional college students. *Journal of Counseling and Development, 77*, 135–140.

McCaffrey, S. S., Miller, T. K., & Winston, R. B., Jr. (1984). Comparison of career maturity among graduate students and undergraduates. *Journal of College Student Personnel, 25*, 127–132.

McGovern, T. V., & Tinsley, H. E. A. (1976). A longitudinal investigation of the graduate assistant work-training experience. *Journal of College Student Personnel, 17*, 130–133.

Miller, T. K., & Winston, R. B., Jr. (1990). Assessing development from a psychosocial perspective. In D. G. Creamer (Ed.), *College student development: Theory and practice for the 1990s* (pp. 89–126). Washington, DC: American College Personnel Association.

Mounty, L. H. (1991). Involving nontraditional commuting students in the career planning process at an urban institution. *Journal of Higher Education Management, 6*, 43–48.

Passmore, D. L., & Swanson, R. A. (1981). A model personal career development plan for graduate students. *Journal of Industrial Teacher Education, 19*, 19–25.

Peterson, S. L. (1993). Career decision-making self-efficacy and institutional integration of underprepared college students. *Research in Higher Education, 34*, 659–685.

Rathus, S. A., & Fichner-Rathus, L. (1997). *The right start*. New York: Addison Wesley Longman.

Richmond, J., & Sherman, K. J. (1991). Student-development preparation and placement: A longitudinal study of graduate students' and new professionals' experience. *Journal of College Student Development, 32*, 8–16.

Slaney, F. M. (1986). Career indecision in reentry and undergraduate women. *Journal of College Student Personnel, 27*, 114–119.

Super, D. E. (1984). Career and life development. In D. Brown, L. Brooks, & Assoc. (Eds.), *Career choice and development* (pp. 192–234). San Francisco: Jossey-Bass.

Wessel, R. D. (1995). Graduate studies awareness: A career services program. *Career Development Quarterly, 43*, 296–301.

Zagora, M. Z., & Cramer, S. H. (1994). The effects of vocational identity status on outcomes of a career decision-making intervention for community college students. *Journal of College Student Development, 35*, 239–247.

11

Career Decision Making and Student–Athletes

Edward A. Martinelli, Jr.

Previous chapters introduced the theoretical bases and techniques of career counseling. Working with any person regarding his or her career issues will require the use of foundational models of career development, theory, assessment, and interventions. This base, along with the information found in other chapters on special populations, will be helpful in working with student–athletes.

This chapter begins with a description of student–athletes and their common experience. Next, it discusses career options, followed by the National Collegiate Athletic Association (NCAA) regulations pertinent to career development. The chapter concludes with a review of important student–athlete career research and theory, with an emphasis on career maturity; a discussion of the involvement of professionals with student–athletes and programs, particularly the CHAMPS/Life Skills program; and specific career counseling suggestions for counselors.

The Student–Athlete

The student–athlete population is vast and growing. It is as diverse as it is large. Women and men of a variety of cultural and ethnic backgrounds participate in college athletics; these differences can affect the delivery of effective career services. In 1990–1991 the NCAA reported that nearly 277,371 college students participated in NCAA-sponsored sports. By 1996–1997 that number had risen 20%, to 331,282. Female participant growth outdistanced male participant growth both in raw numbers and by percentage, a likely consequence of recent federal law (Title IX) regarding male and female involvement (NCAA, 1998a).

Like all college students, student–athletes face life transitions, developmental tasks, and personal needs and desires (Chickering, 1969). They come to college with hopes and dreams, problems and difficulties, strengths and talents. However, student–athletes often find that they must function in an environment unlike that of most other college students. The most prominent of the differences may be how they are perceived because of their student–athlete designation (Ferrante & Etzel, 1991).

As the descriptor indicates, these students are both students and athletes. At different times of the year, it may be difficult to distinguish which role has priority. Student–athletes must prepare for practices, tryouts, and competition while managing their responsibilities in class. The most important competitions often occur at the same time of year as class tests and finals. Many student–athletes work under pressure to excel at both endeavors. Many cope with this challenge successfully; others stumble and lose their way. This difficult struggle of effort and identity has a potential negative impact on college student–athletes' personal development (Blann, 1985; Chartrand & Lent, 1987; Ferrante & Etzel, 1991; Nelson, 1983).

Research has indicated that student–athletes, particularly football and basketball players, may be less prepared academically than many other students (American Institute for Research [AIR], 1988; Purdy, Eitzen, & Hufnagel, 1982). These difficulties are compounded because many student–athletes are first-generation college students (Sellers, Kuperminc, & Waddell, 1991). Many books directed at supporting the student–athlete discuss strategies for improving academic skills. Because of the academic difficulties that many student–athletes encounter, a substantial portion of the student–athletes' time (and the time of those who work with them) is spent dealing with academic concerns (Brooks, Etzel, & Ostrow, 1987).

Role duality often affects time use among student–athletes. AIR (1988) has indicated that, depending on the sport, nearly 30 hours per week may be spent in a sport-related activity. Course work and athletic preparation or competition both occur during typical career center office hours. Consequently, student–athletes might not participate in career counseling or associated activities simply because they may not have the time or because such services may not be available when student–athletes do have the time (e.g., in the evenings or on weekends). Numerous authors have noted that student–athlete use of campus services is minimal (e.g., Ferrante & Etzel, 1991; Pinkerton, Hinz, & Barrow, 1987).

Some sports (e.g., football and basketball) have a greater following and have a greater number of fans who attend competitions. They engender large support structures and offer the possibility of professional involvement. These sports are most likely to be revenue-generating enterprises for the sponsoring institution; hence, they often are referred to as "revenue" sports. The remaining sports are often referred to as "Olympic" sports. Although the actual statistics vary by sport, NCAA statistics and others have indicated that about 1% of student–athletes will have a professional career in athletics (Figler & Figler, 1984; Muczko & Thompson, 1994). For the few who do reach professional status, the average length of their professional involvement is 3 to 4 years (Dietzel, 1983; Holtz, 1993; Muczko & Thompson, 1994). The need for career counseling among this group of students is as great, if not greater, than that of the rest of the college student population.

Etzel, Barrow, and Pinkney (1994) posited that more similarities than differences may exist between student–athletes and other students, but they also argued that "with student athletes . . . concern about the role of sport in future career/life planning may significantly flavor the need for career development services" (p. 41). Many authors have shared this concern (Blann, 1985; Nelson, 1983; Pearson & Petitpas, 1990; Remer, Tongate, & Watson, 1978; Wooten, 1994). One reason that student–athletes may benefit from career counseling is the frequency with which student–athletes delay or ignore career planning. This avoidance can become increasingly problematic because of NCAA (1998b) regulations that tie competition eligibility to progress toward a degree. The later a student–athlete begins active involvement in career exploration and planning activities, the more restricted her or his career options are likely to be.

Many student–athletes have some initial career goals when they enter college. Many hope for a professional career in athletics. Initially, the choice may be between becoming a professional athlete or pursuing a career related to their college major, which may be more a vague idea than a specific goal. The decision, though, often is out of the hands of student–athletes. First, athletes get injured; the injury can either delay or ruin the opportunity to rise to professional status. Second, student–athletes can become ineligible to play, which typically involves difficulties with academic progress (which will be discussed later).

Whether the student–athlete intends to play professionally on leaving college or not, the issue of the realism of that goal needs to be addressed. Some football players intend to "go pro," even as they near the end of their eligibility, having never played a significant amount of time. There is nearly no chance that scouts will notice them or that tryouts will be successful. Others, although starting for the team, do not demonstrate the same level of athletic talent as others in their conference or across the nation. They fail to recognize the limited number of openings in their career field and how many others will be vying for these few positions. Because of the specialized nature of some positions in certain sports, their ability to adapt to a new position or develop transferable skills on the playing field may be questionable.

The abruptness of potential career changes also plays a significant role in a student–athlete's career decision making. As indicated earlier, an injury can take a player from stellar possibilities to the sidelines in a fraction of a second. If the student–athlete has built an identity around his or her role in competitive sports, the physical inability to participate can have serious psychological and career implications. The lack of control in this area is one of the most pressing concerns for an athlete (Blinde & Stratta, 1991; Parker, 1994). Career counseling and planning for this eventuality can be framed to the student–athlete as a way to prepare for and maintain some control over the potential hazards of their activities.

Hill (1993) pointed out that because of the typical short duration of a professional career in athletics, retirement from competition is a short-term reality for every student–athlete. Hill suggested that many student–athletes lack role models in professions other than athletics and that this limits the career options they tend to consider. This reality suggests that student–athletes should consider other career options early in college. Direct interventions and considerations will be discussed later in the chapter regarding this and similar issues.

NCAA Rules and Regulations

It is important to realize the different expectations and rules for maintaining eligibility that organizational bodies like the NCAA place on student–athletes, coaches, and universities. Article 14 of the *NCAA Division I Manual* bylaws (1998b) most directly affects the work of career counselors and other faculty and staff involved with student–athletes. The NCAA not only defines the criteria for academic standing, eligibility, effects of high school competition and outside competition, it also defines full-time enrollment, length of competitive involvement, "satisfactory-progress" standards (which includes choice of major, hours earned, and grade point average [GPA] requirements), and transfer-student regulations. Career counselors must be knowledgeable about the constraints and guidelines within which a student–athlete must function. To the career counselor, these regulations serve two purposes: (a) They underscore the need for earlier intervention and counseling with the students, and (b) they inform the counselor about environmental factors that influence the student's available choices of college major and subsequent career choices.

The NCAA monitors a student–athlete's progress on both a quarter/semester and annual basis. During the competitive season, full-time enrollment is defined by the NCAA as 12 semester or quarter hours during that particular semester or quarter. Student-athletes must also complete annually, prior to each fall term, 24 semester or 36 quarter hours of academic credit. Of this total, 75% of the hours must be completed during the regular academic year. Consequently, the summer term is only to augment the student's progress towards the degree, not act as a major component. Completion of these requirements meets the initial criteria for academic progress. A secondary part of the requirements relates to the amount of progress towards the completion of a college major and the baccalaureate degree.

Recently, regulating bodies such as the NCAA and sponsoring institutions have taken a more active role in facilitating student–athlete graduation. Recent reports from the NCAA indicate that student–athlete graduation rates are rising and compare favorably with graduation rates for nonathletes (NCAA, 1997). Consistent with its effort to encourage graduation, the NCAA also has instituted policies about choosing a major and progressing toward its completion. The student–athlete must choose a degree program by the fifth semester or seventh quarter. She or he must also have 25% of the chosen degree completed by the end of the second year of enrollment; 50% by the end of the third year; and 75% by the end of the fourth year (NCAA, 1998b). Although many general education and core curriculum classes can be used to meet the various percentages of degree completion, the student–athlete's ability to change majors while maintaining eligibility decreases over time.

The NCAA requirements present two critical issues for the career counselor working with the student–athlete. First, they must choose a college major within a shorter time frame; student–athletes therefore have less time than most other students to explore options and take classes in an attempt to match abilities with interests. Second, the NCAA regulations state that should the student decide to change his or her major, the same percentages must be met in the new major. This policy significantly limits the options for change available to a student–athlete. Therefore, a clear need exists for career exploration early in a student–athlete's tenure at an institution. The NCAA regulations also apply to transfer students. Although it may seem daunting to track such stringent requirements, typically at least one person in the athletic department is responsible for maintaining eligibility and compliance with NCAA regulations. This person can be a tremendous source of information for a counselor unfamiliar with NCAA policy and should be consulted frequently, because the NCAA regulations change often.

It is not uncommon for college students to work while in school. Financial concerns are a pressing matter for many students. Working can meet the monetary needs of the student as well as help them develop transferable skills for use in the world of work. Many students take advantage of experiential learning opportunities in their chosen major or career field. For the student–athlete, this type of learning can be virtually impossible for two reasons. First, and most important, the amount of time that experiential learning requires may be unmanageable. Second, NCAA regulations govern the amount of money a student–athlete may earn during each academic year.

During the 1997 NCAA Convention, the Division I Management Council and Board of Directors addressed the question of whether scholarship student–athletes could work for wages and, if so, with what restrictions. The NCAA decision, incorporated into the 1998–99 bylaws in Article 15 which discusses financial aid, allows student–athletes on full grants-in-aid to work without affecting their eligibility with a $2,000 cap above the full-scholarship value that such student–athletes receive. This can only be done after the student–athlete has spent one year in residence and as long as the student–athlete is academically eligible. Student-athletes must also a) be certain that the payment for employment is not due to "value or utility" to the employer based on the student–athlete's "publicity, reputation, fame or personal following;" b) be paid for "work actually performed;" and c) be paid at "the going rate in that locality for similar services" (NCAA, 1998b, p. 187). The NCAA appears to be trying to find a compromise between financial and career concerns and discouraging student–athletes from receiving monies due to their affiliation with a particular institution or athletic program.

It seems that the NCAA understands that student–athletes, like most college students, have financial concerns. They may also be aware of the benefit that experiential learning has in future career planning. At the same time, the NCAA wants to set a fair and equitable standard. They may want to avoid the potential dilemma of student–athletes receiving funds from individuals or entities that would not require actual "labor" for a payment of funds. There have been many instances where alumni, agents and others have given money to athletes for a variety of reasons and needs that have not required the student–athlete to engage in any sort of employment activity. Although this new NCAA policy may present new opportunities for student–athletes, it may be difficult for many scholarship athletes to take full advantage of the regulation.

Scheduling employment under the conditions most student–athletes experience is nearly impossible. Young and Sowa (1992) surveyed African American student–athletes ($n = 136$) and found that an average of 30.5 hours were spent each week in their sport, an hour higher than the mean time reported for attention to academic concerns. AIR (1988) conducted a national survey of 4,083 female and male Division I athletes and found similar results (see also Young & Sowa, 1992). Student–athletes spent nearly 60 hours per week in academic or sports-related activities. For many, athletic participation is viewed as employment: They are required to be at a specific location at a specific time; wear a particular type of attire; and often spend hours studying playbooks, watching films, or in some other way trying to improve their performance and ability.

Career Research and Theory

Because the focus of this book is on melding research and theory with career counseling practice, it would be helpful to consider numerous studies evaluating the effectiveness of career interventions with college student–athletes. Unfortunately, that research base does not yet exist. Many professionals have called for increased attention to this population (Etzel et al., 1994), but only recently has there been movement in that direction. Studies available for review have tried to capture the essence of what the student–athlete population is like and have developed models for working with this expanding group of students. Etzel et al. (1994) indicated that the current literature contains speculation, summaries, and recommendations, but little data-based literature exists on student–athletes. Nevertheless, the few empirical studies that have been conducted provide at least some insight into the career decision making of this population of college students.

In the areas of career development and choice, Sowa and Gressard's (1983) work showed that student–athletes' career plans were not clear. They surveyed 48 student–athletes and 43 nonathletes and asked them to complete the Student Developmental Task Inventory (Winston, Miller, & Prince, 1979), which measures progress in developmental task achievement. Two of its subscales measure appropriate educational plans and career plans. Results indicated statistically significant differences ($p < .05$) between athletes and nonathletes on three of the subscales: the two previously mentioned and a scale measuring mature relationships with peers.

Sowa and Gressard concluded that the results implied that "athletes have difficulty in formulating well-defined educational goals and gaining personal satisfaction from educational experiences" (p. 238).

Etzel et al. (1994) used a 54 self-report item instrument to survey 170 male and female student-athletes and 300 "general students" at an NCAA Division I university. A total of 201 surveys were returned. The results, grouped by expressed need, revealed differences between student-athletes and general students on several factors, including career concerns. Findings showed that student-athletes were more concerned with career-related issues than were general students. The athletes also preferred one-on-one counseling as a delivery method, whereas the general student population preferred a group approach.

Career maturity has been defined as an indication of a person's completion of appropriate vocational developmental tasks (Zunker, 1998). Several researchers have indicated that the career maturity levels of student-athletes have been lower than those of nonathletes (Blann, 1985; Stuart, 1985). Kennedy and Dimick (1987) surveyed the entire membership of the football and men's basketball teams and a similar number of nonathletes at a midwestern university. The entire group completed the Career Maturity Inventory (Crites, 1978). Although the scores did not reveal statistically significant differences, the group means were consistently lower for the student-athlete group. Kennedy and Dimick (1987) suggested that student-athletes, particularly those participating in revenue sports, might have less mature career plans than college students in general.

Smallman and Sowa (1996) studied the career maturity levels of revenue and Olympic sport athletes. They administered the Career Development Inventory (CDI; Super, Thompson, Lindemann, Jordaan, & Myers, 1981) to a total of 125 male student-athletes, 76 Olympic and 49 revenue. Comparisons revealed no significant differences between revenue and nonrevenue student-athletes' career maturity. However, results revealed that student-athletes' reported scores were in the bottom 25th percentile compared to the norm group of college students in general, indicating lower levels of career maturity than would be expected.

Brown and Hartley (1998) surveyed 114 male student-athletes from 5 universities. The sample included Division I and Division II football and basketball athletes. They investigated the relationship between athletic identity and career maturity. They also administered the CDI (Super et al., 1981) to student-athletes and looked at the five individual scales: Career Planning, Career Exploration, Career Decision Making, World of Work Information, and Knowledge of Preferred Occupational Group, and their relationship to their scores a measure of athletic identity. Although they hypothesized that high athletic identity would be associated with lower career maturity, the results did not indicate such a relationship.

An important consideration in this study is that 81% of the students were not planning on a professional sport career. Those student-athletes that were aspiring to a professional sport career had lower career maturity. Perhaps career aspirations instead of identity are more closely asso-

ciated with career maturity. Brown and Hartley (1998) argued that, because their sample had such an uncharacteristic level of professional
aspiration, the results might indicate that student–athletes were beginning to understand the difficulties of having a professional sport career
and were changing their career aspirations. It may be important to begin
looking at what careers are being considered by student–athletes with
high athletic identity, rather than assuming that student–athletes' career
aspirations focus primarily on professional sports.

Nelson (1982) conducted one of the most significant studies regarding
career counseling and student–athletes. Although the focus of the study
was on academic success, the results have implications for career development. As suggested earlier, athletic departments are concerned about
the academic success of student–athletes because of the direct impact
on competition eligibility. Nelson worked specifically with 132 first-year
student–athletes and found that a five session career counseling program
was associated with a higher grade point average (GPA) at the end of the
first semester for those who participated in the program (n = 65) relative
to those in the control group (n = 67) who did not participate in the career
counseling treatment. This effect seemed to continue into the subsequent
quarter as well.

Nelson's (1982) findings are important for two reasons. First, they suggest a way of helping student–athletes improve their GPAs, thereby helping them remain eligible for competition, which in turn may lead to
greater support for such programs from athletic departments. The results
also show how a career counseling program can help both the student and
the department. Second, the results provide evidence that career interventions can assist student–athletes with making changes in major selection early in their academic career. As discussed earlier, changes in major
have a significant effect on eligibility as the student–athlete progresses
through school.

Career Counseling With Student Athletes

When considering appropriate career services for student–athletes, two
questions seem especially relevant: "Who works with student–athletes?
and How do they work with them?" Brooks et al. (1987) addressed those
questions and found some intriguing results. The researchers surveyed
134 NCAA Division I athletic advisors and counselors and found that most
(87%) were employed by the university's athletic department. Nearly two
thirds (64%) of their time was spent with revenue athletes—not surprisingly, most of their time (73%) was devoted to male athletes.

One of the most telling descriptors concerning the allocation of the
survey respondents' time is that only 8% of their work was self-described
as "vocational counseling." They indicated that approximately 14% of their
time involved dealing with "personal–social counseling" and that 45% of
their time was spent on "academic advising." A conflict of interest may
exist among counselors who work for an athletic department, where the

primary need may be to keep athletes eligible rather than to focus efforts on developmental programming (Brooks et al., 1987; Sellers et al., 1991).

More research-based evaluations of the career counseling of student–athletes may be on the horizon. The NCAA's recent (1994) addition of the Challenging Athletes Minds for Personal Success/Life Skills program (CHAMPS/Life Skills) may signal an opportunity for broader views of the career development needs and processes of student–athletes. Instead of career needs being seen in terms of graduation rates, eligibility, grade point averages, and other peripheral issues, actual career development and guidance has become a fundamental and articulated part of the program. As of July 1998, the program had been implemented at nearly 250 institutions with the greatest number being Division I-A schools ($n = 112$; NCAA, 1998a).

The CHAMPS/Life Skills program comprises five areas supporting student–athlete development: (a) academic excellence, (b) athletic excellence, (c) personal development, (d) career development, and (e) service. Participating institutions receive needs assessments, administration manuals, and teaching materials from the NCAA to help implement the program. Each area is divided into "focus segments." The career development area, for example, has segments in general career development, tasks for each year in school, working with agents, and the alumni career network and includes a seminar on life after sports. The suggested career development programs appear to be consistent with the recommendations made by the studies cited in this chapter. The program materials sent to institutions that join include programs that have been designed and used at other institutions and have been deemed appropriate to be shared with schools joining the program, to be used as presented or modified to meet the specific needs of the institution.

The NCAA also offers a leadership training conference and newsletter. More information regarding applications, training, resources, and history are available from the NCAA and can be accessed through its Web site (*www.ncaa.org*). Although the program has a scope broader than just career development, it provides a semistructured program for working with student–athletes.

Counseling Suggestions and Future Possibilities

The student–athlete faces a variety of challenges in attempting to succeed in both academics and sports. Time is a critical factor in work with student–athletes, and it is difficult to find time for student–athletes to explore career options without overburdening an already tight schedule. Nevertheless, a variety of programs for student–athlete development have been suggested, although many lack an empirical foundation.

The CHAMPS/Life Skills program has the potential to add to the knowledge base about student–athletes. Programs could be evaluated on larger populations than has been possible in the past. The CHAMPS/Life Skills program also may help raise awareness of the career needs of student–athletes. Because the program is designed for both revenue and Olympic student–athletes, more student–athletes may be served than in other sport-specific programs.

A number of researchers and those interested in the development of student–athletes have suggested various programs to meet student–athlete needs. Because many of these suggestions were offered before the CHAMPS/Life Skills program was initiated, little if any research has been offered evaluating the CHAMPS/Life Skills program's specific potential and ability to meet student–athletes' career development needs. Consequently, much of the literature about programs needs to be considered against the framework of the NCAA's program. It would be helpful to have research designs specifically evaluating the effectiveness of CHAMPS/Life Skills programs. This is especially important given that the inclusion of the CHAMPS/Life Skills program is a direct response to earlier calls for career development programming.

Alternately, many of the programs suggested by others might adequately meet the needs of student–athletes without having to design such an involved program, like CHAMPS/Life Skills, thereby setting up a convenient comparison of "treatments." Certainly overlapping interventions exist, and, as indicated earlier, some of the materials used in the CHAMPS/Life Skills program come from existing successful programs.

The literature about student–athletes and their career development needs typically stresses two concepts: (a) that programming be more formal and intentional in presentation and (b) that it occur early in student–athletes' enrollment. For example, in describing the University of Kentucky's program, Sanders (1992) suggested that an important first step is the approval and encouragement of the coaching staff, which can increase credibility and influence student–athlete participation. The first semester of the University of Kentucky's program involves an orientation that includes assessment of academic skills and the administration of the Self-Directed Search (SDS; Holland, 1985). In the second semester, student–athletes are matched with alumni and community professionals for a "job shadowing" experience. A written summary of the experience is required. A series of seminars on social issues is included to broaden exposure to the community and world of work. Finally, job-search strategies and interviewing skills are taught, and opportunities to mentor younger students are offered.

Wooten and Hinkle (1994) suggested and implemented a 3-semester-hour course for student–athletes that was divided into the three areas of exploration, assessment, and job skills. The course included a textbook, guest speakers, written assignments, experiential activities, and access to computer-assisted career guidance systems (CACGSs). The course instructors used a variety of career development assessment instruments that they believed met the needs of the student–athlete population with whom they worked. Graduate interns taught the course and were an excellent resource to work with student–athletes. (Graduate students are more willing to work the hours in the evening in which student–athletes typically are available.) The course offered counseling to the student–athletes both individually and in small groups.

Gabbard and Halischak (1993) suggested scheduling structured career work early in a student–athlete's enrollment through an "introductory career workshop." Although they did not specifically delineate how their program was delivered, Gabbard and Halischak indicated that both career exploration and job skills work were important parts of their program. They suggested that there be more consultation and interaction between athletic, academic, and student services departments on campus. Doing so, they argued, allows for better service delivery and introduces student–athletes to services from which they might not otherwise benefit.

Street and Schroeder (1996) worked with 19 freshmen football players during the fall and spring semesters. Two small groups received a career exploration and planning program in bi-weekly, 1-hour meetings. Session attendance was mandatory, and the athletes received study hall credit for attending. The SDS (Holland, 1985) was administered, and the students worked with the SIGI-PLUS (1997) CACGS. When preassessment and final assessment values were compared, statistically significant differences ($p < .05$) were found in career decidedness, in comfort level about choice of major, and in knowledge about selecting a major or career. Street and Schroeder also found that the number of students choosing a professional football career as their first, second, or third career choice decreased from 40% to 15% over the course of the program.

Hill (1993) suggested that those who work with student–athletes must be aware of the perceived obstacles that this client population faces. Although Hill did not delineate the exact nature of the obstacles, he gave particular attention to minority and multicultural issues. Counselors therefore should both elicit perceived obstacles and discuss additional barriers that may not be readily apparent to student–athletes who are members of minority groups. Coleman and Barker (1992) suggested a number of internal and external barriers that could be addressed with multicultural student–athletes. The list included such barriers as level of self-esteem, expectations, locus of control, previous work experience, schedule restrictions, racism and discrimination, peer pressure, and family and public expectations.

Nelson (1982) worked with 132 first-year student–athletes from 22 sports. The treatment she used (for which statistically significant effects on the student–athletes' GPA were revealed) included a weekly 2-hour career counseling group that lasted for 5 weeks. Notably, the sessions were offered three times each week to make them more amenable to the student–athletes' practice and game schedules. Sessions included work in career dreaming, peer and parental values, abilities, transferable skills, career assessment, individual review of career information (including possible majors), and an introduction to the on-campus career center.

Wooten (1994) suggested focusing on coping skills "in response to or in anticipation of transition from sport" (p. 3). Because student–athletes may become dependent on others for decision making, he suggested a model that included developing decision-making skills. He also suggested that career counseling be part of a more holistic model that would include "emotional and cognitive aspects involved in the transition from sport" (p. 3). Wooten illustrated the model with a discussion of two case studies, but no large-scale evaluation of the model has been done. Given the preponderance of student–athletes who will not have a professional sports career, this would seem to be an important focus for career development work.

Similarly, Petitpas and Schwartz (1989) developed information about transferring skills learned as a student–athlete to other career areas. They used the *Athlete's Guide to Understanding and Identifying Transferable Skills* (Schwartz, 1988) with small groups of 6 to 8 members. Three questions were asked in the sessions to help direct the discussion:

1. What kinds of personal characteristics and skills have you developed through sports that might be equally valuable in a work setting?
2. What skills have you developed through sports participation that will help you succeed in your job search and career?
3. What are the costs and benefits of your personal style and how do they relate to various work environments? (pp. 39–41)

Although no data regarding the effectiveness of the program in changing student–athletes' perceptions or skills are available, it seems likely that discussions with student–athletes introducing these questions may promote overall student–athlete development.

One interesting recent idea in career development theory is the notion of career adaptability (Savickas, 1997). The student–athlete's dilemmas may be particularly suited for this concept's focus on the ability to prepare for change. Encouraging student–athletes to consider the importance of adaptability—in their career choices as well as on the playing field— might have a profound influence on their career development. As measures of career adaptability become available, college student–athletes may be an ideal population with whom to evaluate both the instruments and the theoretical underpinnings of the adaptability construct.

Removing ambiguity about career decisions, setting career goals, and focusing energies on achieving academic and sport-related goals may affect the student–athlete's overall development. This potential is resonant to the perspective, shared by the NCAA and many coaches, that student–athletes are building not just competitive athletic skills, but skills for life. Both areas have much to offer toward student development. It also is evident that communication between athletic departments and campus services needs improvement; putting what counselors can accomplish into language that is more suited to the athletic department's needs would be helpful. Indicating to coaches and staff that the work of career development could facilitate and positively affect student–athlete eligibility is likely to be warmly received.

Thus, strategies for career development work with student–athletes should include the following:

- support from coaches and other institutional service units
- knowledge of the NCAA regulations pertaining to career development and an awareness of whom to contact in the athletic department
- early intervention in response to programmatic and regulatory concerns
- formal and intentional programming at times that are convenient for student–athletes
- a focus on realities of professional sport participation
- attention to transferable skills
- activities to explore careers and avoid foreclosure of options
- availability to all student–athletes regardless of gender, sport, or grant status.

Career needs of student–athletes are receiving a more focused approach than in the past. Programs and interventions are now being applied to the needs of student–athletes across a variety of demographic groups and sports programs. While much has been offered to understand the needs and desires of this population, the changing nature of college athletics and the world of work serve as a reminder of the opportunities for continued translation of theory and research into career counseling practice.

References

American Institutes for Research. (1988). *Summary results from the 1987–1988 national study of intercollegiate athletics*. Palo Alto, CA: Center for the Study of Athletics.

Blann, W. (1985). Intercollegiate athletic competition and students' educational and career plans. *Journal of College Student Personnel, 26*, 115–118.

Blinde, E., & Stratta, T. (1991). The "sport career death" of college athletes: Involuntary and unanticipated sport exits. *Journal of Sport Behavior, 15*, 3–20.

Brooks, D. D., Etzel, E. F., & Ostrow, A. C. (1987). Job responsibilities and backgrounds of NCAA Division I athletic advisors and counselors. *Sport Psychologist, 1*, 200–207.

Brown, C., & Hartley, D. L. (1998). Athletic identity and career maturity of male college student–athletes. *International Journal of Sport Psychology, 29*, 17–26.

Chartrand, J. M., & Lent, R. W. (1987). Sports counseling: Enhancing the development of the student–athlete. *Journal of Counseling and Development, 66*, 164–167.

Chickering, A. W. (1969). *Education and identity*. San Francisco: Jossey-Bass.

Coleman, V. D., & Barker, S. A. (1992). Counseling multicultural student–athletes: An examination of barriers. *Academic Athletic Journal, 6*, 26–33.

Crites, J. O. (1978). *Career Maturity Inventory administration and use manual*. Monterey, CA: CTB/McGraw-Hill.

Dietzel, P. F. (1983). There is life after football. *Physical Educator, 40*, 161–162.

Etzel, E. F., Barrow, J., & Pinkney, J. W. (1994). Career counseling and student–athletes: A needs assessment. *Academic Athletic Journal, 8*, 37–46.

Ferrante, A. P., & Etzel, E. F. (1991). Counseling college student athletes: The problem, the need. In E. F. Etzel, A. Ferrante, & J. Pinkney (Eds.), *Counseling college student athletes: Issues and interventions* (pp. 1–18). Morgantown, WV: Fitness Information Technology.

Figler, S., & Figler, H. (1984). *Athlete's game plan for college and career*. Princeton: Peterson's Guides.

Gabbard, C., & Halischak, K. (1993). Consulting opportunities: Working with student–athletes at a university. *Counseling Psychologist, 21*, 386–398.

Hill, T. L. (1993). Sports psychology and the collegiate athlete: One size does not fit all. *Counseling Psychologist, 21*, 436–440.

Holland, J. L. (1985). *The Self-Directed Search: Professional manual*. Odessa, FL: Psychological Assessment Resources.

Holtz, L. (1993, June 3). Notre Dame coaches to succeed in life. *USA Today*, pp. 11C.

Kennedy, S., & Dimick, K. (1987). Career maturity and professional sports expectations of college football and basketball players. *Journal of College Student Personnel, 28*, 293–297.

Muczko, J. P., & Thompson, M. A. (1994). Career preparation and the college football player. *Academic Athletic Journal, 8*, 18–23.

National Collegiate Athletic Association. (1997). *NCAA graduation-rate disclosure*. Overland Park, KS: Author.

National Collegiate Athletic Association. (1998a). *Participation statistics*. Overland Park, KS: Author.

National Collegiate Athletic Association. (1998b). *1998–99 NCAA Division I manual*. Overland Park, KS: Author.

Nelson, E. (1983). How the myth of the dumb jock becomes a fact: A developmental view for counselors. *Counseling and Values, 27*, 176–185.

Nelson, E. S. (1982). The effects of career counseling on freshman college athletes. *Journal of Sports Psychology, 4*, 32–40.

Parker, K. B. (1994). "Has-beens" and "wanna-bes:" Transition experiences of former major college football players. *Sport Psychologist, 8*, 287–304.

Pearson, R., & Petitpas, A. (1990). Transitions of athletes: Pitfalls and prevention. *Journal of Counseling and Development, 69*, 7–10.

Petitpas, A., & Schwartz, H. (1989). Assisting student–athletes in understanding and identifying transferable skills. *Academic Athletic Journal, 3*, 37–42.

Pinkerton, R., Hinz, L., & Barrow, J. (1987). The college student athlete: Psychological considerations and interventions. *Journal of American College Health, 37*, 218–226.

Purdy, D., Eitzen, D., & Hufnagel, R. (1982). Are athletes also students? *Social Problems, 29*, 439–448.

Remer, R., Tongate, F., & Watson, J. (1978). Athletes: Counseling the overprivileged minority. *Personnel and Guidance Journal, 56*, 626–629.

Sanders, E. J. (1992). Implementing a career development program for student–athletes. *Academic Athletic Journal, 7*, 24–29.

Savickas, M. L. (1997). Career adaptability: An integrative construct for life-span, life-space theory. *Career Development Quarterly, 45*, 247–259.

Schwartz, H. (1988). *The athlete's guide to understanding and identifying transferable skills*. Unpublished manuscript, Springfield College, Springfield, MA.

Sellers, R. M., Kuperminc, G. P., & Waddell, A. S. (1991). Life experiences of black student–athletes in revenue-producing sports: A descriptive empirical analysis. *Academic Athletic Journal, 6*, 20–38.

SIGI PLUS [computer software]. (1997). Princeton, NJ: Educational Testing Service.

Smallman, E., & Sowa, C. J. (1996). Career maturity levels of male intercollegiate varsity athletes. *Career Development Quarterly, 44*, 270–277.

Sowa, C. J., & Gressard, C. F. (1983). Athletic participation: Its relationship to student development. *Journal of College Student Personnel, 24*, 236–239.

Street, J. M., & Schroeder, C. (1996). Developing a structured career orientation program for first-year football players. *Academic Athletic Journal, 11*, 8–19.

Stuart, D. L. (1985). Academic preparation and subsequent performance of intercollegiate football players. *Journal of College Student Personnel, 26*, 124–129.

Super, D. E., Thompson, A., Lindemann, R., Jordaan, J. J., & Myers, R. (1981). *The Career Development Inventory*. Palo Alto, CA: Consulting Psychologists Press.

Winston, R. B., Miller, T. K., & Prince, J. S. (1979). *Assessing student development*. Athens, GA: Student Development Associates.

Wooten, H. R., Jr. (1994). Cutting losses for student–athletes in transition: An integrative transition model. *Journal of Employment Counseling, 31*, 2–9.

Wooten, H. R., Jr., & Hinkle, J. S. (1994). Career life planning with college student–athletes. *TCA Journal, 22*, 35–39.

Young, B. D., & Sowa, C. J. (1992). Predictors of academic success for black student–athletes. *Journal of College Student Development, 33*, 318–324.

Zunker, V. G. (1998). *Career counseling: Applied concepts of life planning* (5th ed.). Pacific Grove, CA: Brooks/Cole.

12

The Career Development Needs of Students With Learning Disabilities

William E. Hitchings and Paul Retish

People with learning and other disabilities have been part of higher education for many years, but two factors have contributed to a surge in enrollments in four-year institutions over the past 15 years. First, as Conyers and Szymanski (1998) reported, students with learning disabilities, like their peers without disabilities, are now seeking a college degree because it has become an important requirement for employment. In the last quarter of the 20th century, the economy of the United States shifted from a manufacturing to a service base (McDaniels, 1989). Global competition and technology are dominating the changes, resulting in new and redesigned jobs with skills that require education beyond high school (Gerber, 1997). Therefore, students with learning disabilities hope to improve their career options and, ultimately, their future economic opportunities by pursuing further education.

Second, people with learning disabilities historically have been less economically successful than their peers without disabilities. For example, Gerber (1997) identified follow-up studies of people with disabilities reporting unemployment rates ranging from 21% to 89%. Other studies have been less pessimistic, finding unemployment rates comparable to people without disabilities. But people with learning disabilities have higher levels of underemployment when compared with their peers without disabilities who have similar educational levels. As a result, students with learning disabilities have some unique needs, including the need for assistance with gaining or refining skills needed to obtain their first job as well as to reach their future career goals.

This chapter is intended to provide readers with a better understanding of the career development needs of college students with learning disabilities and recommendations for strategies to use when providing career counseling services to this client population. The chapter provides vignettes containing information on the preparation of students for the postsecondary experience, research findings on the career development of college students with learning disabilities, and findings on the career development of successful adults with learning disabilities. Although the focus is on college students with learning disabilities, the recommendations can be extended to people who have health, sensory, and physical disabilities.

Vignettes

Vignette 1: Woman, Sophomore, Speech Therapy Major

I'd like to be a speech therapist and work in a clinic or hospital. Nobody actually sat down with me and talked about it. I read a coupla books. Also, there are a couple friends of the family who are speech pathologists, so I talked to them. I have a difficult time comprehending reading. It takes me longer to [read] something. When writing an essay, I need time to gather and process my thoughts. Memory is a problem, and I am a visual learner. I need to have things written down. When the speaker is talking, I can't listen and take notes . . . something gets lost along the way! I used the resource room from elementary school through junior high, but between my freshman year and 10th grade, I decided I wanted to do it on my own. I didn't need all that assistance, just extended time on tests. I reported to a case manager [CM] or she checked on me at mid-terms and finals. I used CM and college counselor when I was looking for colleges. The counselor just helped with colleges. I don't know if my disability will be a problem in the future. I don't know much about the field [speech therapy]. If I have deadlines, it could be a problem. My language problems could be a problem, but I don't know!

Vignette 2: Man, Junior, Education Major

I am going to teach elementary school, but my real goal is to teach history in high school. My strengths are my age and maturity. I was terrible in high school and never thought about going to college. In high school my counselor suggested that I take a health occupations class, but it had nothing to do with my problem. I've not used any of the opportunities through the college's career office. I'm LD. It's a learning disability. I can't spell. I read real, real slow. I don't really know what it's called. I have a problem with abstract processing things like algebra, or . . . Somebody said that word to me. I don't know what it really means. I know the things I can't do, I'm not really sure, somebody said it though. My learning disability has not been a major problem in the jobs that I have done in the past. I managed an office for my father and ran a pediatric clinic while in the service. In the future, it will be a problem, but I'll keep trying to figure out how to do things better.

Vignette 3: Woman, Senior, Business and Public Relations Major

I have problems with understanding what I read. I read slow, very, very slow. I'd rather listen to somebody. I can follow what they say and don't have to worry about how to pronounce the words. I also take a long time to write things, like, ah, ah, [papers] for my classes. I need help organizing and with spelling and commas. I've had these problems since I can remember. In school, I had tutors, then a resource teacher in high school. Here I use the tutors or try to get help from my profs. I want a job, but nothing with writing.

The people in these vignettes participated in a series of studies examining the impact of disability on college students' career decision making (e.g., Hitchings, Luzzo, Retish, Horvath, & Ristow, 1998; Hitchings et al., 2000; Luzzo, Hitchings, Retish, & Shoemaker, 1999). They represent a small but growing population in postsecondary education, specifically at four-year colleges and universities. In the past 15 years, the proportion of college students reporting at least one disability has increased from 2% to more than 10% of students, or approximately 1.3 million (Hartman, 1993; Henderson, 1999).

Like their peers without disabilities, students with learning disabilities are continuing their education to improve their future financial security and independence, to accomplish personal goals, and to respond to peer pressure and parents' expectations (Cooper, 1987; Marshall & Kreston, 1989). As one student explained to the authors of this chapter, "Just something between $40,000 and $50,000 would do just fine so long as I can buy a car, travel, and not have to live with my parents." Their future depends on having the skills necessary for employment in an economy less reliant on manufacturing and based more on services and technology, jobs that require increased skills. Many of those skills can be obtained through postsecondary education (Brown, 1989; Hallahan, Kauffman, & Lloyd, 1998; White, 1992).

Impact of a Disability

The students in the vignettes have learning disabilities that vary by subtype, severity, and age of onset (Baggett, 1993; Rojewski, 1992). Although two students have learning disabilities that are similar in subtype and degree, the impact differs as a result of previous educational experience, family response, and personal attributes. Some people have obvious disabilities, such as those with sensory or physical impairments who may require accommodations to write, talk, or travel. But learning disabilities can be subtle, affecting the person only at certain times or in certain situations (e.g., at work). People with learning disabilities may have inefficient reading, writing, mathematics, or problem-solving skills that result in limitations similar to those with sensory problems (Biller, 1985; Sitlington, Clark, & Kolstoe, 2000; White, 1992).

For people between ages 15 and 24, the impact of a learning disability may extend beyond their academic and social experiences to career development efforts. Super (1990) described this period as a time for exploration, but people with learning disabilities may have to spend time learning to compensate for their disability. Thus, they may have less time to explore possible career options or determine their strengths and weaknesses. Furthermore, they may not have an opportunity to determine the impact of their disability on possible career choices (Brandt, 1994; Humes, Szymanski, & Hohenshil, 1989; Smith, 1998). Those wanting to continue their education often focus on strengthening academic skills and meeting graduation requirements. Students with disabilities may have little or no time to take career-oriented electives, because they are strongly encouraged or required to use special academic-support programs. For example, in the course of their research the authors met a student who had earned 4 credits in "Resource" out of 20 possible credits toward a high school diploma. The remaining 16 credits were in core academic areas—English, mathematics, social studies, and science. He had no career-oriented electives in business, which was his interest and major in college. The student actively participated in school activities and sports and thus did not have time to work during high school.

Impact of Federal Mandates

At one time, the students in the vignettes would have gone directly to work and not have considered further education (Dowdy, Carter, & Smith, 1990). If they did go on, they had few opportunities or accommodations to be successful in higher education. In the mid-1970s, two federal laws led to increased access to postsecondary education and improved secondary special education. First, Section 504 of the Rehabilitation Act of 1973 (P.L. 93-112, 29 U.S.C. § 794, amended in 1992) opened the door for people with disabilities to continue their education beyond high school if they were "otherwise qualified" to be admitted to postsecondary institutions. The initiative mandated that colleges and universities receiving federal funds provide equal access for people with disabilities to all programs and services (Aune & Friehe, 1997). Although some universities (e.g., the University of Illinois) provided equal access to students with disabilities, most institutions were reluctant to accommodate students with any type of impairment (i.e., physical, health, mental, or learning).

Second, the Individuals with Disabilities Education Act (IDEA; 1990) mandated transition planning and services. Studies showed that after leaving high school, people with learning disabilities were significantly underemployed or unemployed, with many in low-paying, low-status jobs (Adelman & Vogel, 1993; Aune & Friehe, 1997; Aune & Kroeger, 1997; Danek, 1992; Gajar, Goodman & McAfee, 1993). IDEA describes transition as a coordinated set of activities "designed within an outcome oriented process, which promotes movement from school to post-school activities including postsecondary education" and "shall be based upon an individual student's needs, taking into account the student's interests and preferences" (§ 602a). Successful transition programs for students with learning disabilities would have a range of career development activities, such as assessment, exploration, and counseling (Rojewski, 1992). In addition, programs would provide self-advocacy training, including disability awareness (Aune & Friehe, 1997; Ness, 1989; Rojewski, 1992; Thompson, 1994).

The mandate to assist students with disabilities can be coupled with the School-to-Work Opportunities Act (STWOA) of 1994 (P.L. 103-239). STWOA requires a school-based learning component with a program that includes the following:

> (1) career awareness and career exploration and counseling (beginning at the earliest possible age, but no later than the 7th grade) in order to help students who may be interested to identify, and select or reconsider, their interests, goals, and career majors.... (6) procedures to facilitate the entry of students participating in a school-to-work opportunities program into additional training or postsecondary education. (§ 6103(4))

The expectation for individuals with learning disabilities to continue their education has been fueled not only by the dramatic changes in the economy and future occupational needs, but also as a result of studies on the employment status of individuals with learning disabilities, the impact of federal legislation on higher education, and improvement of special educational services in secondary schools. If high school students with a learning disability are in transition programs with career counseling and self-advocacy as suggested by Rojewski (1992), then students should continue on to higher education with better career decision-making skills and clearer career goals. Specific instruction in the career decision-making process is not an important element in the education of their peers without disabilities. Because of such instruction, students with learning disabilities might enter higher education with a better understanding of their learning disability and how it may impact their future career options.

Career Development and Successful Adults With Learning Disabilities

Research investigating the career-related issues of students with learning disabilities has generally concluded that they face many of the same career issues as their nondisabled peers (Aune & Kroeger, 1997). They use the same career decision-making process as those without disabilities but have the additional need to consider their disability and its role in career exploration and planning (Egly, Geis, Leuenberger, & Morris, 1987).

Over the past 10 years, researchers have studied successful adults with learning disabilities. Like their peers without disabilities, these adults have a vision for the future. They reach their goals through active career development efforts (Gerber, Ginsberg, & Reiff, 1992) and can assess their strengths, weaknesses, and effects of their disability (Adelman & Vogel, 1990; Egly, Leuenberger, Morris, & Friedman, 1985; and Smith, 1998). In addition, their acknowledgment and understanding of their disability allows them to better understand people and situations (Egly et al., 1985).

Career Development and College Students With Learning Disabilities

Unfortunately, many college students with learning disabilities were either not eligible for services or were terminated from services in high school by their junior year (Hitchings et al., 1998, 2000; Luzzo et al., 1999). As a result, the students did not engage in transition planning and appear not to have acquired the necessary skills and information to do so, such as an understanding of their disability and its impact on career choice and personal strengths and limitations. In addition, they have had limited opportunity to explore careers of interest to help achieve their expressed career goals. Other research findings also illustrate such students' general lack of disability awareness and career development skills (Aune & Kroeger, 1997; Dowdy et al., 1990; Mangrum & Strichart, 1988; Ness, 1989).

Recent studies (Hitchings et al., 1998, 2000; Luzzo et al., 1999) have shown that people with learning disabilities have a range of entry-level work experiences (many part-time) in recreation, food service and hospitality, telemarketing, manufacturing, child care, and construction. Participants in a study by Dowdy et al. (1990) reported that they worked in entry-level jobs for 2 or fewer years. One fourth of the participants in the Dowdy study believed that their disability would not be an issue in their future work. Hitchings et al. showed that even with work experiences related to their career goal, 72% of students with disabilities do not believe that their learning disability will affect their future career. Hitchings and colleagues' participants, despite greater work experience (three to six jobs over 5 or more years), did not appear to have a clear understanding of their disability and its impact on work.

The findings are attributable, in part, to the types of work in which the students have routinely engaged. They tend to be employed in occupations whose essential functions may not require people to read, write, or problem solve at the same level or in the same way as in an academic setting. With the exception of education and health sciences majors, many students who participated in the research of Hitchings and his colleagues were not employed in occupations related to their careers of interest. Also, those who did have problems related to their learning disability avoided jobs they perceived as challenging. As one student said, "I worked at [name of company], because I don't want to look dumb." As a result, if people with disabilities develop work histories similar to the participants described in Hitchings et al. (1998, 2000), they may be underestimating the impact of their disability on their future career choice. Unfortunately, on graduation and entering the real work world, many students may find themselves above entry level, in positions that require higher level reading, communication, and problem-solving skills (Hallahan et al., 1998). The impact of their disability then may be a more serious impediment.

Hitchings et al. (1998, 2000) found that less than 50% of their participants, with or without learning disabilities, were planning to use the college's or university's career development services in their senior year, and none planned to do so earlier than the second semester of their junior year. The students reported that they would seek information on employment related to their major, assistance in developing a résumé, and improving their job-search or interviewing skills. A number of sophomores and juniors reported that they found little or no connection between a career interest inventory taken as part of orientation seminars during their first semester of college, their choice of their major, and their career goals. Career development staff members have reported that less than 20% of all students schedule follow-up appointments to discuss inventory results, career activities, and selecting majors. Others studies have reported similar results (Aune & Kroeger, 1997; Morningstar, 1997; Rabby & Croft, 1991).

Hitchings et al. (1998, 2000) found that 90% of the students with learning disabilities were not actively engaged in the career development process. They had limited knowledge of the impact of their disability on their future goals, like the student in Vignette 1. As a result of their limited understanding of their disability, students were unsure whether they would reach their expressed career goal. In addition, the students believed that they had little control over the career decision-making process. One third of the students indicated their parents were active in major decision making from the time the students became involved in special education. These findings led to an examination of a similar group of students regarding their career self-efficacy, or the belief that one can accomplish one's career goal (Luzzo et al., 1999), and attributional style for career decision making. More than 100 college students, including 50 who had a learning disability, completed the Career Decision-Making Self-Efficacy Scale–Short Form (Betz, Klein, & Taylor, 1996) and the Assessment of Attributions for Career Decision Making (Luzzo & Jenkins-Smith, 1998). The career decision-making self-efficacy score for students with learning disabilities ($M = 168.92$, $SD = 22.46$) was significantly lower than for their peers without disabilities ($M = 192.21$, $SD = 21.04$), effect size = 1.04. In terms of attributional style for career decision making, students with learning disabilities were more likely than students without disabilities to believe that external factors were responsible for career-related outcomes in their lives.

We believe that such differences may be attributed to the parents' and teachers' perceptions that students—because of their disability—are inadequately prepared to make career decisions. As a result, many parents (hoping to protect the student from failure and disappointment) tend to make most of the educational and career decisions for their children. The ongoing actions of parents and teachers may lead students to believe that they have little control over or responsibility for their career decisions.

How Can Students Achieve Their Career Goals?

In regard to career development efforts for college students with learning disabilities, Hoffman (1980) characterized efforts by colleges as too little and too late for many students and suggested they are "left to their own resources" (p. 60). Fifteen years later, the career development needs of students with learning disabilities were still not being met by institutions of higher education (Ohler, Levinson, & Sanders, 1995). Career development personnel may lack the knowledge to work with students who have disabilities and may rely on disability service staff to deal with "their" students.

A broader issue may center on the perception of the role of career development at the college or university level. It would appear that many students consider the career decision-making process a side activity to be engaged in during the senior year. During the final two semesters, they expect to learn interview skills, put together a résumé, and begin their job search. This perception of career decision making might change if the career development process were integrated with academic advising and, when appropriate, with disability services during the students' first year on campus (Asmundson, 1992).

Career counselors in colleges and universities sometimes believe that students with learning disabilities have such unique needs that only specially trained people can work effectively with them. Although that may be true in some cases, most counselors could work with students who have disabilities, provided the counselors refer students to information on successful adults with disabilities and, perhaps, reviewed their own knowledge of late-adolescent and young-adult development. Counselors need to recognize that while in high school, students with learning disabilities probably did not engage in any systematic career planning. They should not have to refer students back to the disability service staff, as often as now happens, but they may need to modify their approaches to career development planning (Aune & Kroeger, 1997; Rabby & Croft, 1991). In doing so, counselors may want to consider the following six elements:

1. Students with learning disabilities, like those without disabilities, need to understand that career development activities are not limited to the first job after graduation. Although many college students with learning disabilities have used elementary search skills to obtain their first part-time or summer positions, these skills may not be sufficiently developed to obtain higher level positions. Furthermore, students with disabilities need to realize that they are developing skills and learning a process that can be used throughout their life as they encounter or seek to make career changes (Egly et al., 1987).

2. Most students with learning disabilities would benefit from gaining a better understanding of their strengths and weaknesses, especially of the impact that their disability may have on their career choice. Such knowledge can be developed through a variety of exploratory activities, especially first-hand employment experiences in their careers of interest (Adelman & Vogel, 1990; Aune & Friehe, 1997; Hartman, 1993; Ryan & Heikkla, 1988; Thompson, 1994). Those who have identified and can explain their per-

sonal strengths and weaknesses are not only able to provide more accurate information to employers, coworkers, and employment agencies, but also can make more informed career choices (Ryan & Price, 1992). Furthermore, the knowledge gained from successful exploration opportunities may help students become more actively involved in the career decision-making process (Rojewski, 1992). As a result, people may feel that they have greater control over their destiny (Bos & Vaughn, 1998; Ohler et al., 1995), have improved self-confidence (Enright, Conyers, & Szymanski, 1996; White, 1992), and believe that they can achieve their long-term career goals (Rojewski, 1992). Ultimately, such experiences may reduce the risk of the student ending up in a less-than-satisfying employment situation (Egly et al., 1987).

3. People with learning disabilities need to find the right match between their expressed interests and career choice (Adelman & Vogel, 1990). Successful people have chosen careers that capitalize on their strengths and minimize their weaknesses (Gerber et al., 1992; Hutchinson & Freeman, 1994; Smith, 1998).

4. Students with learning disabilities may have organizational and planning skills inadequate for the career development process (Biller 1985; Smith, 1998). Consequently, a systematic approach should be taken, one that includes activities designed to enhance decision-making skills, assessments of work-related values, and introduction to labor market data (Thompson, 1994), coupled with specific tasks to engage the individual in active learning practices (Betz & Voyten, 1997). All of these activities may be incorporated into a career plan designed by the individual student in concert with a career counselor and a disability services staff member (Baggett, 1993).

5. Because of their lack of work experiences in their career of interest, few students with learning disabilities have had contact with a successful role model in their career area. With this in mind, Asmundson (1992) proposed linking students with mentors drawn from alumni as well as local or regional employers. These resources are not limited to mentoring: In working with students who have learning disabilities, New York's Fashion Institute of Technology uses alumni and other contacts in the industry not only to mentor but also to participate in workshops that are based on the students' needs. The topics for workshops have included disability issues such as employers' responsibilities and accommodations (Ballard, 1995).

6. If students with limited experiences in their careers of interest attend college, then they should have opportunities throughout college to have direct contact with people working in those career areas. This message needs to be publicized. The authors are involved in a study of career activities of college students who are within two semesters of graduation. In spite of on-campus marketing of the value of internships and cooperative opportunities,

less than 30% of the students with disabilities in the study have completed or are planning an internship. More than 75% of their peers without disabilities have completed or were scheduled for an internship (Goodman, 1999).

St. Ambrose University: A Model Approach

Disability services staff members at St. Ambrose University, students and faculty associated with the university's graduate program in postsecondary disability service, and staff working at the Career Development Center (CDC) are collaborating to provide both individual and group career counseling to students with disabilities by using existing CDC services (Exhibit 12-1) and Reekie's (1995) Action Planning for people with learning disabilities. Reekie's model is based on an integration of research by Bandura (1977) and Betz (1992), which incorporates most of the recommendations found in the previous section.

St. Ambrose University's CDC is revising its plan for helping students become more involved in their own career decision-making process. In past years, CDC representatives led one session of the seminar for new students to explain the purpose of the CDC and the resources available to students. During the session, the students completed a career interest inventory and received the results at a later date, along with an invitation to have the inventory interpreted. Unfortunately, many students at the university waited until late in their junior year or the beginning of their senior year to use CDC's services again.

The process is being revised so that students can make a link between their career interests and their selection of an academic major, ultimately obtaining a cooperative placement or internship in their career interest areas. The single-session "orientation" visit is being expanded to five sessions, with four additional components. First, students are given the opportunity for self-evaluation (i.e., students assess their values, attitudes, skills, and personal strengths and weaknesses). Second, they explore the role of work and learning in society. Third, they assess their career interests using commercially available inventories. Fourth, using the profile from the inventories, students can begin to explore their interests through reading, interviewing people working in those careers, and job shadowing. Finally, a career plan is developed with the student for use over the next six or seven semesters.

The career plan uses Reekie's (1995) Action Planning process, which attempts to modify a person's belief system to enable them to believe that they can perform the behaviors necessary to achieve a specific outcome (i.e., to develop and apply career decision-making skills toward achieving a career goal). The model, based on the work of Bandura and others, assesses the person's past experiences (previous performance), their ability to observe others carrying out the expected behaviors (vicarious experience), levels of emotional arousal as they attempt to engage in a task related behavior upon request, and responsiveness to verbal encourage-

Exhibit 12-1. Career Development Center: Career-Building Checklist

Check off these career-building options as you use them.

First-year students: Get acquainted with yourself first.
_____ Consider career assessment using a computerized program.
_____ Visit the Career Resources Library to explore career possibilities.
_____ Consult with career staff and advisor on choices of majors.
_____ Check part-time job listings at the CDC or on the campus network.
_____ Join campus organizations and actively seek leadership responsibilities.

Sophomores: Explore your options.
_____ Open a credential file at the CDC.
_____ Plan a work experience related to your major or career goal.
_____ Apply for an internship.
_____ Develop a résumé.
_____ Attend an interviewing seminar.
_____ Sign up for available internship or cooperative interviews.
_____ Begin internship, cooperative or part-time positions related to your major or career goal.

Juniors: Focus on your goals.
_____ Attend a cover-letter seminar.
_____ Consider having a mock interview.
_____ Sign up for available internship interviews.
_____ Attend Fall Career Expo for internships and networking.
_____ Sign up for available internship or cooperative interviews.
_____ Begin internship, cooperative, or part-time positions related to your major or career goal.

Seniors: Present yourself professionally.
_____ Update and finalize résumé.
_____ Check full-time listings regularly.
_____ Research companies of interest.
_____ Sign up for on-campus interviews.
_____ Attend Fall Career Expo for internships and networking.
_____ Register for Direct Referral Program in your last semester.

All Students: Available any time.
_____ Visit the Career Resources Library to explore career possibilities.
_____ Attend Fall Career Expo for internships and networking.
_____ Attend seminars: writing cover letters, interviewing, preparing a résumé.
_____ Use the computer-assisted career guidance program.
_____ Open a credentials file.

ment from others as well as self (verbal persuasion; Reekie, 1995). Students are assigned specific tasks in the career decision-making process, such as locating and using sources for career information or analyzing the impact of their disability on a job or portions of a job. Modeling by peers with disabilities and successfully employed people with disabilities provides students with vicarious experiences. Students receive verbal and written feedback throughout each phase.

To assist students with disabilities, modules have been added on disability awareness, legal rights and issues, and self-determination and self-advocacy skills (Rumrill, Roessler, & Brown, 1994). Each module is designed to actively involve the students. For the exploration and disability modules, the disability services staff is seeking the participation of graduates working in careers in which undergraduates have expressed interest. The alumni will serve as sources of information on the world of work and on specific jobs within career fields, and they will share their experiences with regard to the impact of their disability and accommodations.

The faculty, students, and staff involved in the new career development effort have agreed to evaluate the impact of the changes beginning with the class of 2003. Each student's career decision-making self-efficacy and attributional style will be assessed before and after the New Student Seminar course. Using logs that were based on the activities in their plans, researchers will follow a random sample of the students as they carry out their career plans over the succeeding semesters. An attempt will be made to assess the quality of the students' résumés and interview skills when they seek to obtain an internship and when they begin the formal process of seeking employment in their field or career of interest. This phase is now under consideration to determine whether the resources are available to carry out such an ambitious plan. Ultimately, a dramatic increase is expected in the number of students (up to 75%) seeking internships in their careers of interest by the end of their sixth semester.

Ten years ago, St. Ambrose University extended its commitment to students with learning disabilities who are otherwise academically qualified to attend college. Now it will further extend its commitment to help students become career qualified as well. The revisions made by CDC will help all students reach their future goals.

Success in our society is in part measured by our success at work. It is more than just keeping a job; it includes being satisfied with one's job and advancing through promotion (Shapiro & Rich, 1999). Individuals with learning disabilities seek the same success in employment as their peers without disabilities, but the disability that presents a unique challenge to learning also presents a similar challenge to employment.

Colleges and universities are responding to the academic challenges faced by students with learning disabilities, but institutions are just beginning to consider the career development needs of the students as more students move toward graduation and the world of work. We are beginning to understand that having a degree is not enough to succeed in the world of work if one also has a learning disability.

Individuals with learning disabilities need to gain an understanding of the disability, understand how the disability may impact their career(s) of interest, and must be able to identify and use potential accommodations that may enable them to be successful on the job. If colleges and universities provide the resources to help students gain this information, then students with learning disabilities may have a brighter future and achieve the success they seek.

References

Adelman, P. B., & Vogel, S. A. (1990). College graduates with learning disabilities: Employment attainment and career patterns. *Learning Disability Quarterly, 13*, 154–166.

Adelman, P. B., & Vogel, S. A. (1993). Issues in the employment of adults with learning disabilities. *Learning Disability Quarterly, 16*, 219–232.

Asmundson, S. J. (1992). Career counseling with college students in science and engineering. In D. H. Montross & C. J. Shirkman (Eds.), *Career development: Theory and practice.* (pp. 121–127). Springfield, IL: Charles C. Thomas.

Aune, B., & Friehe, S. A. (1997). Transition to postsecondary education: Institutional and individual issues. *Topics in Language Disorders, 16*, 1–22.

Aune, B., & Kroeger, S. A. (1997). Career development of college students with disabilities: An interaction approach to defining the issues. *Journal of College Student Development, 38*, 344–356.

Baggett, D. (1993, October). *An individual career plan for students with disabilities in higher education.* Paper presented at the international meeting of the Division of Career Development and Transition of the Council for Exceptional Children, Albuquerque, NM.

Ballard, G. (1995). *Career placement for learning disabled students: Final performance report.* New York: Fashion Institute of Technology. (ERIC Document Reproduction Service No. 381 973).

Bandura, A. (1977). Self-efficacy: Toward a unifying theory of behavioral change. *Psychological Review, 84*, 191–215.

Betz, N. E. (1992). Counseling uses of career self-efficacy theory. *Career Development Quarterly, 41*, 22–26.

Betz, N. E., Klein, K., & Taylor, K. M. (1996). Evaluation of a short form of the Career Decision-Making Self-Efficacy Scale. *Journal of Career Assessment, 4*, 47–57.

Betz, N. E., & Voyten, K. K. (1997). Efficacy and outcome expectations influence career exploration and directedness. *Career Development Quarterly, 46*, 179–189.

Biller, E. F. (1985). *Understanding and guiding the career development of adolescents and young adults with learning disabilities.* Springfield, IL: Charles C. Thomas.

Bos, C. S., & Vaughn, S. (1998). *Strategies for teaching students with learning and behavior problems* (4th ed.). Needham Heights, MA: Allyn & Bacon.

Brandt, J. E. (1994). *Assessment and transition planning: A curriculum for school psychologists and special educators.* Biddeford, ME: University of New England. (ERIC Document Reproduction Service No. 375 548)

Brown, D. S. (1989). Workforce composition in the year 2000: Implications for clients with learning disabilities. *Rehabilitation Counseling Bulletin, 33*, 80–84.

Conyers, L. M., & Szymanski, E. M. (1998). The effectiveness of an integrated career intervention for college students with and without disabilities. *Journal of Postsecondary Education and Disability, 13*, 23–34.

Cooper, R. J. (1987). What an admission counselor needs to know about learning disabled students. *Journal of College Admissions, 116*, 14–19.

Danek, M. M. (1992). The status of women with disabilities revisited. *Journal of Applied Rehabilitation Counseling, 23*, 7–13.

Department of Education (1992). *Federal Register 34, CFR Parts 300 & 301: Assistance to States for the Education of the Children with Disabilities Program and Preschool Grants for Children with Disabilities*; Final Rule, 57(189), 44804–44815.

Dowdy, C. A., Carter, J. K., & Smith, T. E. C. (1990). Differences in transitional needs of high school students with and without learning disabilities. *Journal of Learning Disabilities, 23*, 343–348.

Egly, N. J., Geis, J. M., Leuenberger, J. E., & Morris, M. J. (1987). *Career development for persons with learning disabilities, Postsecondary intervention model for learning disabilities; Study manual #5.* Lincoln: University of Nebraska. (ERIC Document Reproduction Service No. ED 286–312).

Egly, N. J., Leuenberger, J. E., Morris, M. J., & Friedman, B. G. (1985). Postsecondary intervention model for learning disabilities. Lincoln, NB: University of Nebraska, Barkley Memorial Center.

Enright, M. S., Conyers, L. M., & Szymanski, E. M. (1996). Career and career-related educational concerns of college students with disabilities. *Journal of Counseling and Development, 75,* 103–114.

Gajar, A., Goodman, L., & McAfee, J. (1993). *Secondary schools and beyond: Transition of individuals with mild disabilities.* New York: Merrill.

Gerber, P. J. (1997). Life after school: Changes in the workplace. In P. J. Gerber & D. S. Brown (Eds.), *Learning disabilities and employment.* (pp. 3–18). Austin, TX: Pro-Ed.

Gerber, P. J., Ginsberg, R., & Reiff, H. B. (1992). Identifying alterable patterns in employment success for highly successful adults with learning disabilities. *Journal of Learning Disabilities, 25,* 475–487.

Goodman, M. L. (1999). *Motivation and career planning activities of junior and senior college students with and without disabilities.* Unpublished master's thesis, St. Ambrose University, Davenport, Iowa.

Hallahan, D. P., Kauffman, J. M., & Lloyd, J. W. (1998). *Introduction to learning disabilities* (2nd ed.). Boston: Allyn & Bacon

Hartman, R. C. (1993). Expanding opportunities for students with disabilities: Who are we talking about? *Journal of College Admission, 9,* 8–10.

Henderson, C. (1999). *College freshman with disabilities. A biennial statistical profile.* Washington, D.C.: American Council on Education. Health Resource Center.

Hitchings, W. E., Luzzo, D. A., Retish, P., Horvath, M., & Ristow, R. (1998). Identifying the needs of college students with disabilities. *Journal of College Student Development, 39,* 23–32.

Hitchings, W. E., Luzzo, D. A., Retish, P., Horvath, M., Ristow, R., & Tanners, A. (2000). *College students with disabilities, their transition and career decision making needs: In their own words.* Manuscript submitted for publication.

Hoffman, E. G. (1980). Career counseling of the disabled. In J. P. Hourihnan (Ed.). *Disability: The college's challenge.* (pp. 59–66). New York: Columbia University.

Humes, C. W., Szymanski, E. M., & Hohenshil, T. H. (1989). Roles of counseling in enabling persons with disabilities. *Journal of Counseling & Development, 68,* 145–150.

Hutchinson, N., & Freeman, A. (1994). *Pathways.* Toronto, CA: Nelson.

Individuals with Disabilities Education Act of 1990, 20 U.S.C. § 602a. (Reed. 1990).

Luzzo, D. A., Hitchings, W. E., Retish, P., & Shoemaker, A. (1999). Evaluating differences in college students' career decision making on the basis of disability status. *Career Development Quarterly, 48,* 142–156.

Luzzo, D. A., & Jenkins-Smith, A. (1998). Development and initial validation of the Assessment of Attributions for Career Decision Making. *Journal of Vocational Behavior, 52,* 224–245.

Mangrum, C. T., & Strichart, S. S. (1988). *College and learning disabled students: Program development, implementation, and selection.* Philadelphia, PA: Grune & Stratton.

Marshall, C., & Kreston, R. (1989). Career counseling and women with disabilities: A research project to facilitate higher learning. *Journal of Postsecondary Education and Disability, 7,* 4–5.

McDaniels, C. (1989). *The changing workplace: Career counseling for the 1990s and beyond.* San Francisco: Jossey-Bass.

Morningstar, M. E. (1997). Critical issues in career development and employment preparation for adolescents with disabilities. *Remedial and Special Education, 18,* 307–320.

Ness, J. E. (1989). The high jump: Transition issues of learning disabled students and their parents. *Academic Therapy, 25,* 33–39.

Ohler, D. L., Levinson, E. M., & Sanders, P. (1995). Career maturity in young adults with learning disabilities: What employment counselors should know. *Journal of Employment Counseling, 32,* 64–79.

Rabby, R., & Croft, D. (1991). Working with disabled students: Some guidelines. *Journal of Career Planning and Employment, 51*, 49–54.

Reekie, F. A. (1995). Strategic action plans with clients who have learning disabilities. *Journal of Employment Counseling, 32*, 165–180.

Rehabilitation Act Amendment of 1992, 29 U.S.C. § 701 *et seq.* (Lexis Law Publishing, 2000).

Rojewski, J. W. (1992). Key components of model transition services for students with learning disabilities. *Learning Disability Quarterly, 15*, 135–150.

Rumrill, P. D., Roessler, R. T., & Brown, P. L. (1994). *Self-advocacy: A training manual.* Project Career. Fayetteville: University of Arkansas.

Ryan, A. G., & Heikkla, M. K. (1988). Learning disabilities in higher education: Misconceptions. *Academic Therapy, 24*, 177–192.

Ryan, A. G., & Price, L. (1992). Adults with LD in the 1990s. *Intervention in School and Clinic, 28*, 6–20.

School-to-Work Opportunities Act of 1994, 20 U.S.C. § 6103 (Lexis Law Publishing).

Shapiro, J., & Rich, R. (1999). *Facing learning disabilities in the adult years. Understanding dyslexia, ADHD, assessment, intervention, and research.* New York: Oxford University Press.

Sitlington, P. L., Clark, G. M., & Kolstoe, O. P. (2000). *Transition education and services for adolescents with disabilities* (3rd ed.). Needham Heights, MA: Allyn and Bacon.

Smith, C. R. (1998). *Learning disabilities: The interaction of learner, task, and setting* (4th ed.). Boston: Allyn & Bacon.

Super, D. E. (1990). Career and life development. In D. Brown, L. Brooks, & Assoc. (Eds.), *Career choice and development* (2nd ed., pp. 192–234). San Francisco: Jossey-Bass.

Thompson, A. R. (1994). *Career development project: Postsecondary education programs for individuals with disabilities.* Final report. Starkville: Mississippi State University, Department of Counselor Education and Educational Psychology. (ERIC Document Reproduction Service No. ED 377 670)

White, W. J. (1992). The postschool adjustment of persons with learning disabilities: Current status and future projections. *Journal of Learning Disabilities, 25*, 448–456.

13

Career Development of Ethnic Minority Students

Susan B. DeVaney and Aaron W. Hughey

In the year 2000 minorities are expected to account for over one third of all entrants to the national workforce and 25% of workers.
—Luzzo, 1993, p. 227

Vocational development theory involves an understanding of occupational choice, vocational identity, evolution of personal identity in regard to career, and adjustment to the world of work. Most theorists view vocational behavior as a continuing process of growth and learning, with emphasis on individual self-concept, developmental experiences, personal history, and the psychosocial environment (Morales, 1996). According to Super's (Super, Savickas, & Super, 1996) life span–life space approach to careers, for example, people often choose occupations that allow for maximum integration of one's vocational self-concept. Culturally based messages received from significant people and institutions in one's environment greatly affect these perceptions and expressions of self (Hollinger, 1996).

According to Arbona (1996), contemporary developmental theories, formulated largely through the study of White, middle-class males, may apply to people from all classes and ethnic groups if they exhibit at least average academic achievement, desire stable and meaningful employment, and have access to educational opportunities. Yet traditional models of career development, when applied to ethnic minorities, may overemphasize patterns associated with White middle-class career development and discount varied and divergent beliefs about work. Coupled with the unavailability of career guidance and prejudicial barriers to employment faced by ethnic minorities, these factors may negate theories that are based on assumptions that career development is a continuous process and that all people have the means to implement their choices (Hendricks, 1994; Leong & Brown, 1995). In addition, traits required for occupational success may vary for people outside the majority culture. Some ethnic minorities, for example, may advance more fully if they possess certain characteristics not required of White males (i.e., the ability to deal with discrimination).

Although ethnic groups are the primary units of focus in explaining economic stratification, it is clear that most people living in poverty with little education lack vocational maturity and focus (Arbona, 1996). Traditional theorists such as Holland (1973) often fail to explain how culturally based factors can restrict occupational access. Influences deriving from cultural milieu, such as the meaning of ethnic group membership, also may have measurable effects on career development (Arbona, 1989). More acculturated people seem to have a greater probability of vocational success as measured by White, middle-class standards. Racial identity influences the vocational process in terms of career maturity, perceptions of racial climate, work adjustment, and work satisfaction but has little impact on content variables such as needs, interests, or college major.

Theoretically, as people move into the stage of social evaluation, they reject occupations that they perceive to be inappropriate in terms of race and class (Gottfredson, 1986). When people encounter circumstances that lead them to believe that their ethnicity limits work options, they abandon higher aspirations and resort to traditional, less prestigious, occupations with limited power and autonomy. In addition, families exert strong influences to live out culturally determined career myths, traditions, and rules. Students from minority groups whose historical affiliation has been with the land (Native American, Black) or physical labor (Asian, Latino) may find themselves unsupported by family and community when preparing for more lucrative occupations (Herring, 1998). Ethnic minority women trained as scientists, for example, reported that their families, although supportive of educational advancement in general, considered scientific pursuits unfeminine and incompatible with family vocational heritage (Malcolm, Hall, & Brown, 1976).

Ethnic Minority Career Development

For the purposes of this chapter, *ethnic group* refers to a societal cluster whose members regard themselves as distinct on the basis of shared sociocultural characteristics or identification with an ancestral nation. Note that this chapter does not specifically address the characteristics and career needs of international students, recent immigrants, or other more generic groups that fall outside this definition. The four ethnic groups considered here are African American (Black), Asian American/Pacific Islander (Asian), Latino (Hispanic), and Native American (American Indian). Although a limited amount of general background information will be provided for each group, the primary focus is on career development variables. The macroculture, usually identified as White but also can be referred to as European American, Caucasian, and Anglo, will serve as the basis for group comparisons. (For more information related to culture and ethnic groups, readers should consult Sue & Sue, 1990.)

Although it is important to understand the general characteristics associated with an ethnic group to which a college student may technically belong, it is equally important to recognize that individual members of that group may exhibit those attributes to varying degrees—or they may not exhibit them at all. Generalizations about ethnic groups are only useful to the extent that they do not distract from the uniqueness of the individual. Caution always should be exercised regarding how the career counselor uses this information (i.e., students must be viewed first as people).

Many questions regarding the career development of ethnic minority college students remain unanswered. Few studies involving Asian Americans and Native Americans exist. In comparison, more is known about Hispanic and African American student populations, even though much of this information is anecdotal. As a result, the sections describing Asian and Native American college student vocational development are regrettably much shorter than the sections devoted to Black and Hispanic students. Furthermore, there are no distinct theoretical statements regarding the career development of minorities, and relatively few attempts have been made to incorporate ethnic vocational development into existing models.

Researchers often quantify outcomes such as employment and educational attainment in terms of ethnicity, yet the factors that influence career development generally are considered apart from ethnicity. Most theories take into account genetics, place in time and history, financial status, social class, and gender role socialization, but they do not integrate those factors to explain ethnic group career development. Traditional career development theories are not likely to incorporate encounters with racial discrimination, the meaning of work from a cultural perspective, or the availability (actual or perceived) of career guidance information. For the career counselor, theoretical questions arise when attempting to explain the vocational behavior of ethnic individuals who also happen to be poor, female, or otherwise at risk for lower occupational attainment (Robinson, Butler, & Glennen, 1996). It is generally known that gender inequities exist in salary, educational and occupational access, and family support for career advancement, but the extent to which vocational outcomes are a result of ethnicity is largely unexplained.

With the exception of Asian Americans, ethnic minorities are underrepresented in fields offering the greatest opportunities for financial reward and advancement. Native Americans, Black people, and Latinos tend to lack the academic preparation needed to pursue scientific and technical careers. Arbona (1989) used Holland's RIASEC typology to evaluate relative levels of occupational presence among Hispanics, Blacks, and Whites. Among Holland's six categories (realistic, investigative, artistic, social, enterprising, and conventional), occupations classified as realistic require the least education, offer the least prestige, and provide the fewest advancement opportunities. Seventy-one percent of Hispanic, 68% of Black, and 54% of White men worked in realistic jobs; 41% of Hispanic, 37% of Black, and 24% of White women worked in the same. When considering the ethnic representation in enterprising occupations, the type associated with greatest prestige and advancement, only 6% of Hispanic men and 10% of Black men, as opposed to 23% of White men, worked in those jobs. Fewer women sought enterprising occupations, but proportionally 15% of White women, compared with 10% of Hispanic and 7% of Black women, could be found in more entrepreneurial lines of work.

College Students and Career Development

The college student population is heterogeneous in terms of age, wealth, motivation, skills, experience, and social class. According to Zunker (1998), 45% of college students are now older than 25, placing them in adult developmental stages and life circumstances. A competitive academic market and the availability of loans and grants have made higher education accessible to students with a wide range of personal and academic characteristics.

A National Career Development Association (NCDA) survey (Brown, Minor, & Jepsen, 1991) indicated that Americans thought more attention should be directed toward helping students choose careers and prepare for college. The NCDA survey also found that college graduates are more likely than high school graduates (62% vs. 32%) to plan a career. Seventy-nine percent of African Americans and 75% of Hispanics reported that they would seek more career information if they could start their careers over again. Black participants in the study reported selecting the first job available as opposed to engaging in a more considered job-search process.

Although affluence seems to be a greater career determinant than ethnicity, educational underachievement tends to characterize many ethnic minorities. Ethnic minorities are less likely than European Americans to attend college, complete college degrees, and enter professional training programs (Brown et al., 1991; Herring, 1998). Among the major ethnic groups, Asian Americans are most likely to enroll in college (Brown et al., 1991; Herring, 1998).

In terms of career development, ethnic minorities fall into the same categories as other college students on the basis of family and work responsibilities, academic preparation, and financial aid status. They differ in their individual willingness to self-assess, explore, experiment, and plan. In addition, students' ethnic identity development influences their psychosocial development (Pope, 1998). Arbona (1996) suggested that minorities may have greater need for cognitive and social preparation than for traditional career choice interventions. Moreover, within-group differences in terms of learning style and disability affect career development interventions for all groups. Counseling techniques specifically geared to auditory, kinesthetic, or visual learners may circumvent barriers related to reading level and insufficient academic preparation. Career guidance at the college level must be broad and flexible enough to address the needs of all students.

Persistence in College

Graduation rates for ethnic minorities are well below those of White students at both public and private institutions (Reyes, 1997). Student persistence is closely related to past and current academic performance, but academic endangerment is not a factor for well over a third of all students who drop out. Most of these students simply do not develop a sense of engagement with the institution (Blinne & Johnston, 1998). Eimers and Pike (1997) found that the probability of retention increased with the degree of social and academic integration students experienced on campus. They suggested that White students generally place a higher value on fitting in socially on campus, whereas minority students tend to be more concerned with academic matters.

Ethnic minority students also are more likely to perceive a lack of campus career planning resources, experience instances of prejudice, and sense alienation than are White students (Eimers & Pike, 1997; Mohr, Eiche, & Sedlacek, 1998). However, minority students who persist in their educational endeavors tend to interact more extensively with faculty than do White students. Brown and Kurpius (1997) observed that academic preparation and aspirations, academic performance, and interactions with faculty and staff best differentiated between Native Americans who persisted in college and those who did not. Other strategies for coping with college life include incorporating students' cultural community into the campus community and depersonalizing prejudicial incidents (Padilla, Trevino, Gonzalez, & Trevino, 1997; Taylor & Howard-Hamilton, 1995).

African American/Black College Students

In general, African Americans at all levels exhibit lower levels of career maturity than do their White counterparts. Black children have fewer out-of-school learning experiences, are less likely to be able to envision themselves in particular occupations, perceive a more limited range of appropriate jobs, and are less likely to take ownership of their career decisions (Sharf, 1997). Black adolescents are disproportionately represented among the unemployed and underemployed of their age group and often aspire to prestigious occupations for which they have little preparation. Parmer (1993) reported that 32% of inner-city 11th and 12th graders thought they were likely to become professional athletes within 10 years, despite the fact that the actual probability of their doing so was 1 in 50,000.

As adolescents, Black females tend to have higher educational and occupational aspirations than do Black males (Brown et al., 1991). By the time they enter college, however, the reverse is true. Black women do better scholastically and are more likely to be employed in professional positions but ultimately earn less than either Black men or White women. Hackett and Byars (1996) found significant self-doubt and discouragement among Black women that could be traced to the differential application of school reward structures. African American women, unlike other minority women, expected to work in traditional occupations as well as to support themselves throughout their lives. For these women, skills for coping with racial and gender barriers, life planning, and decision making are crucial in determining whether their priorities will revolve primarily around a career or around personal relationships.

The slower rate of career development among African Americans may be precipitated by a lack of positive work experiences, low expectations of success, low career satisfaction, and restricted occupational aspiration (Luzzo, 1992). Occupational stereotyping by guidance counselors, few perceived opportunities, lack of visible role models, poor academic preparation, underdeveloped interests, and a lack of career planning may result in restrictive career choice patterns (Dunn & Veltman, 1989).

What might be perceived as career immaturity among African Americans also can be explained as a cultural preference for cooperation over individual effort (Cheatham, 1990). Commitment to work and education, as opposed to socioeconomic status, has been shown to predict career maturity in African American students. Naidoo (1994) found that Black people tend to demonstrate more participation, commitment, and value expectations in the home and family role than in the work role. Women in Naidoo's study expressed more commitment to the work role and more career maturity than did men. Jackson and Healy (1996) confirmed that Black women participated to a greater extent than Black men in home and family life and had more knowledge of the work world. Dawkins (1980) reported that Black men in their study valued money, freedom from supervision, and leadership to a greater extent than did Black women, who placed greater importance on helping others. By contrast, Thomas and Shields (1987) found that Black women valued financial reward more than did Black men.

White and Black college students' career attitudes and concerns are comparable to other groups, but Black students are more likely to perceive prejudicial treatment and financial barriers to career development (Henry et al., 1992; Keller, Piotrowski, & McLeod, 1992; Luzzo, 1993). Several colleges have developed retention programs tailored to African American students that are based on the elements of career planning: self-knowledge, exploration of career options, decision-making strategies, résumé development, interviewing skills, and lifelong career options (Keller et al., 1992; Reyes, 1997). Faculty–student mentoring programs have had a positive impact on academic achievement and retention; contact frequency and duration seem to be more salient success factors than either gender or ethnicity of mentors (Campbell & Campbell, 1997).

One successful program tracked the career development of 61 Black premedical students over a 3-semester period (Henry et al., 1992). During this time students explored individual work values, personal attributes, and barriers to success in a supportive, small-group environment. In addition to providing information about decision making, application procedures, and interviewing, the seminar used guest speakers and student reports to increase knowledge of school policies, curriculum, evaluation methods, and support services. An optional follow-up program consisted of "job shadowing" with minority physicians. Both male and female participants exhibited significant gains with respect to individual skills as well as total vocational development.

Although colleges can do much to facilitate the career development of African American students on campus, many use "reach-down" programs to recruit and prepare promising students for postsecondary education, particularly in science and math (Lloyd & Miller, 1989). Incorporating structured programs at the high school level can address concerns about the slow career development of African Americans in particular and the general lack of adequate occupational resources for ethnic minorities (Hackett & Byars, 1996; Hollinger, 1996; Keller et al., 1992; Rodriquez, 1997b). These programs can help identify unrealistically high or low efficacy beliefs, assess applicable skill levels, emphasize test-taking skills, and teach application procedures for financial aid and admission.

For African Americans, improving educational attainment generally remains the most important career development concern. Promoting student accountability and responsibility for personal career development involves fostering student-generated knowledge as opposed to counselor-driven knowledge. By increasing motivation for career planning, students can avoid unconscious counselor stereotyping and unintentional restriction of career choices. In addition, placing career knowledge and skills within the context of a broader life-planning process, rather than a narrow occupational focus, can foster transfer of planning skills to the career arena and integration of worker, student, and family roles (Jackson & Healy, 1996).

Asian American/Pacific Islander College Students

Asian American college students come from families originating in India, Vietnam, Cambodia, China, Japan, Malaysia, and the Philippines. Although their cultures and physical characteristics are distinct from each other, they share a common worldview that is based on centuries of Confucian, Shinto, Buddhist, and even Muslim thought (Leung, 1995). Herring (1998) found that most Asian Americans immigrated to the United States voluntarily; maintained ties with the homeland; and retained a tight-knit, hierarchical family unit. The generally high value placed on occupational prestige, financial success, and financial and job security causes Asian Americans more than other groups to view education as a means to a vocational end (Herring, 1998; Leong, 1991). At the same time, however, high school graduation rates vary significantly by national subgroup and family financial status. Among Asian Americans, the Vietnamese have the lowest graduation rate; Asian Indians and Filipinos, the highest (Leung, 1995). Asian American college graduates are overrepresented in the physical and behavioral sciences and underrepresented in teaching, law, and politics. This restricted career choice pattern reflects an appreciation of structure and prestige and also explains the lower-than-average verbal SAT scores, exhibited even by third-generation students. Chinese American undergraduates typically have relatively high self-imposed and perceived parental educational and career expectations (Liu, 1998).

A more dependent decision-making style and greater appreciation for tradition in occupational choice may diminish the applicability of current career maturity models to Asian Americans. Women of Asian heritage tend to seek traditional occupations, operate from an external locus of control, and suffer from a lack of occupational role models (Yang, 1991). Career indecision may stem from a lack of vocational information and role models (Sharf, 1997). Asian women often experience internal conflict as they consider career fields that are personally appealing but culturally inappropriate. Abandoning traditional interfamilial hierarchies wherein the female occupies a position of subservience may bring prestige and security, but it can precipitate significant cognitive dissonance in the family (Yang, 1991).

Asian American college students are more likely than other ethnic groups to expect and encounter study-skills barriers (Luzzo, 1993). The perception of Asian Americans as a successful minority overrepresented in higher education sometimes has resulted in restricted admissions as well as limited scholarship and vocational assistance (Leung, 1995). Luzzo (1992) observed lower career maturity scores and greater vocational incongruence among Filipino and other Asian American college students when compared with Latino, African American, and White students.

The good news is that 37% of Asian Americans/Pacific Islanders use college career information centers (Brown et al., 1991). Because their culture relies on the concept of saving face and avoiding shame, Asian American students may prefer the privacy of individual counseling to group interventions. Individual counseling may enable students to resolve academic and vocational conflicts influenced by a fatalistic orientation, the shame of lower-than-expected performance in school, or aspirations incongruent with cultural and familial expectations. Career counselors can help these students develop study and decision-making skills, build confidence, and consider a broad range of occupational alternatives. Career counselors should be attuned, however, to the dependent decision-making style and deferential personal demeanor of many Asian Americans, which can lead to a lack of spontaneous and accurate feedback in the counseling and advisement process (Rojewski, 1997). For example, many Asian Americans present academic and career issues to their faculty advisors when the real concerns are interpersonal in nature (Leong, 1986). Reaching to the underlying issue requires perception by the counselor and sufficient time for a trusting relationship to develop.

Latino/Hispanic College Students

The terms *Latino* and *Hispanic* are used to describe a diverse group that shares a history of Spanish colonialism in Latin America and includes as countries of origin Mexico, Puerto Rico, Cuba, and those of Central and South America (Arbona, 1990). Latinos belonging to various social, educational, and economic strata have immigrated to North America both to escape political unrest and to gain financial advantage through improved employment opportunities.

Latino and European Americans subscribe to similar views of occupational success. They believe that a college education can lead to a good job and a middle-class lifestyle. They have similar attitudes toward work, career strategies, and occupational expectations, and they express similar needs for achievement and career progression behaviors. Despite these similarities, however, Hispanics have generally lower expectations for success than their European American counterparts, and occupational aspiration among Hispanic students typically declines during college. Even though Latino students exhibit a level of career maturity similar to European American students (Arbona, 1996), only one in 20 Hispanic first-graders graduates from college (Cervantes, 1988).

Educational attainment for Latinos appears to be more closely related to socioeconomic status and school variables than to cultural traits. Second-generation students are more likely to attend and finish college, are more bicultural, and ultimately earn higher incomes (Arbona, 1990). Luzzo and Jenkins-Smith (1996) found that Mexican American students rarely cited ethnic discrimination, gender, or age as barriers to college success. Rather, study skills, employment-related competition, and finances were listed most often as major concerns. In a second survey, Latina women reported that the number of hours spent in domestic labor were likely to interfere with their academic progress, although men in the study did not see the number of hours worked or home responsibilities to be barriers to college success (Chacon, Cohen, & Strover, 1986).

Family members tend to exercise substantial influence over Latino students' educational aspirations. Morales (1996) reported that the less assimilated into the macroculture a student is, the more influential the family is in the student's decision making. In addition, parental perceptions of availability of jobs held greater sway on choice of major with Hispanic students than with Anglo students. Successful students, those with higher vocational identity, were generally older and more influenced by family to attend college and to enter a particular field of study. Including families in career development interventions and programs and encouraging life-planning may improve retention among this group.

Familial expectations, such as those concerning early marriage and child bearing, are significant factors in the career development of Hispanic students and can be inconsistent with academic success. Once in college, Latina women tend to demonstrate feminist work values and more assertiveness, self-sufficiency, and comfort in both cultures than do Latino men (Arbona, 1996). The typical Latina college woman has supportive working-class parents with little education, prefers a combined worker–homemaker role, and espouses values of equality and satisfying work. Latino men often underestimate the amount of preparation necessary to enter particular fields. For academically talented Hispanic students, developing an identity as a member of a middle-class may constitute a step in the career development process not required of European American students.

Because Hispanic students tend to possess a more field-dependent and cooperative learning style, they may benefit from instruction in study and verbal skills (Jackson & Healy, 1996). In addition to benefiting from tutoring and mentoring services, students for whom English is a second language could be channeled into courses that do not require high English proficiency such as math and computer science. Successful programs at the University of West Florida, North Carolina State, and the University of Michigan have used precollege orientation, freshman advising, academic and personal counseling, mentoring, and tutoring to reach Latinos (Keller et al., 1992; Reyes, 1997). The University of South Carolina (Keller et al., 1992) implemented a course to teach freshmen students the importance of education, how college is different from high school, and use of the Internet. Other schools, such as San Francisco State (Reyes, 1997), have increased Hispanic faculty presence to draw more students of color into the sciences.

For Hispanics a more important issue than retention may be attracting students to college. MESA (Mathematics, Engineering, and Science Achievement) relies on corporate support to help Hispanic middle and high school students identify specific academic and career interests (Rodriguez, 1997b). Retention rates for Mexican American engineering students enrolled in the MESA program were 57%, as opposed to 21% for non-MESA students. Other reach-down programs, such as Academic Preparation for Excellence, Algebridge, and Testskills have taught students to be better test takers and have promoted enrollment in advanced mathematics courses (Rodriquez, 1997b).

Once enrolled in college, Hispanics to tend to complete their programs of study when their needs, interests, skills, and social and intellectual expectations are met by the institution (Arbona, 1996). Junior colleges and other two-year institutions have been instrumental in providing access to higher education for Latinos, who often prefer local, practically oriented educational programs. Historically, however, these institutions have not successfully articulated the transfer for Hispanic students either to four-year schools or to prestigious and remunerative occupations (Arbona, 1996). Furthermore, college completion often comes at the expense of traditional cultural values. In general, many Latinos matriculate locally and at a relatively low level to maintain family connections. For the career counselor serving Hispanic clients, acculturation variables and family orientation are among the most potent considerations.

Native American/American Indian College Students

Native Americans live in approximately equal numbers on and off reservations. Much more information is available, however, regarding tribal groups (Leung, 1995). American Indians have the lowest standard of living of any ethnic group, with some tribal communities experiencing as much as 90% unemployment. Twenty-four percent of the American Indian population lives below the poverty level (Herring, 1998). The boarding school phenomenon of the late 19th century through the 1950's, whereby European American people removed Native American children from their homes and forced them to abandon their culture, also made education a symbol of European American oppression to many Native Americans (Rodriguez, 1997a).

Because so few Native Americans enter college, many institutions do not keep enrollment data on this population (Leung, 1995; Rodriguez, 1997a). Of those who do enroll, half leave within the first year. Others drop out temporarily and return several times without completing a degree. For many American Indians, successful adjustment to college appears to be a function of communal support. Those who have the blessing of their tribal communities, who have a "leaving ceremony" for example, tend to make more successful adjustments. In addition, older students and those who commute from outlying reservations often are more connected to their communities and thus more likely to remain in school.

Vocational issues for Native Americans living in tribal communities differ from those of more assimilated people (Leung, 1995). The primary form of work on a reservation is manual labor (Sharf, 1997). The cycle of poverty and unemployment characteristic of many Native Americans on reservations is related to a limited exposure to the world of work (particularly high-status jobs), a lack of occupational information, and inadequate job-search and work maintenance skills. Tribal mores often conflict with such mainstream work values as punctuality, competition, and individual initiative. Strong ties to the peer group make separation from the tribe a difficult matter and contribute to general ill-preparedness for higher education and employment.

Native American retention and vocational preparation interventions take various forms. Support systems designed to "replace" the tribe can be creatively implemented by inviting families, elders, and artisans to campus; recognizing and celebrating Native American heritage; or establishing a Native American support group or intertribal council (Rodriguez, 1997a). Stanford University (Rodriguez, 1997a) has offered a 6-week summer orientation program for American Indians during which students meet professors, discuss academic expectations, and apply for financial aid. In another successful effort, the University of New Mexico (Rodriguez, 1997a) has hired a significant number of American Indian professors, thus providing academic role models and drawing students to campus.

Given that many Native American students arrive on campus with little understanding of the world of work, comprehensive program efforts or a freshman seminar course involving career self-assessment, computer-assisted exploration, job shadowing, information interviewing, and job try-outs can offer much to prepare them (Leung, 1995). Apparently, many Native American students experience personal isolation in the college milieu and guilt at having left the tribe, entered the European American world, and thus ostensibly abandoned their people. Pressure to return to the tribe can be extraordinarily strong, even for doctoral students (Napier, 1996). Helping Native Americans overcome these obstacles presents a significant challenge for career counselors.

Suggestions for Practice

In terms of career aspirations, a college degree may hold greater meaning for ethnic minorities than for European Americans (Zunker, 1998). Nevertheless, occupational success can be a double-edged sword. The tangible attributes associated with vocational success (higher salaries, greater prestige, more responsibility, prestigious titles) may require adoption of the behaviors and value system of a macroculture in which goods are bought rather than produced, time is a commodity, and career decisions are made by the individual rather than the family. Career counselors are obliged to discuss the trade-offs that college attendance, independent vocational choices, and breaks with tradition invariably produce. In addition, the counselor should develop a clear understanding of the student's family orientation and social behavior, self-awareness and insight, motivation to learn and change, and coping mechanisms. Given these considerations, the authors offer the following suggestions for career counselors in their work with ethnic minority college students.

Demystify the Career Counseling Process

Ideally, career development intervention begins as soon as students arrive on campus (if not before) and continues as an integral part of the educational process. To dispel the myth that career counseling is appropriate only for those who are undecided or confused about vocational choices, counselors can make themselves and the career center visible by means of an organized marketing program. Personal appearances at orientation programs, introductory courses, group advisement sessions, student organizations, and faculty and residence hall meetings can create campus-wide awareness of career services and staff. Counselors can increase visibility and decrease the stigma often associated with the counseling process by holding open houses for minority students each semester. Actively disseminating printed material, posters, and videos through targeted departments and courses can inform students of the benefits of various degrees in terms of increased earnings, occupational status, and professional advancement (Black, Paz, & DeBlassie, 1991).

Network With Other Student Services Organizations

A comprehensive referral network is a career counselor's most powerful tool. Counselors should possess a comprehensive knowledge of student services on and off campus and should freely disseminate brochures, handouts, and personal guidance related to the programs and services provided at those locations. Counselors should schedule time to network with staff in departments of financial assistance, minority student support, women's studies, human resources, Americans With Disabilities Act compliance, tutoring, and technological assistance. Private organizations, such as the local chamber of commerce, minority business alliance, the National Association for Female Engineers, the National Coalition Building Institute, and the African American Society actively promote minority career development through mentoring, scholarships, internships, and work–study opportunities.

Develop a Role as Student Advocate

Minority students enjoy a higher probability of academic success when campus programs for minorities are coordinated through a central office staffed by highly visible, credible people (St. John, 1997). Administrative blessing for minority recruitment and retention efforts often takes the form of a steering committee consisting of faculty, student affairs personnel, administrators, students, families, and community members. Career counselors should lobby for the establishment of such a group and request ongoing career center presence in it. Possible roles for the steering committee include increasing collaborative arrangements and smoothing the transition between feeder community colleges and four-year institutions as well as promoting reach-down programs, such as Upward Bound, Talent Search, Student Support Services, and Educational Opportunities Centers, all of which serve large numbers of minorities and together have produced more than 2 million college graduates (Rodriguez, 1997b).

Involve Faculty as Mentors

All young people need attention from caring adults who advocate for them. For ethnic minority students entering college, this care and advocacy can enhance career development during the college period and beyond. In successful mentoring programs, trained faculty meet regularly with students for support, information giving, and guidance. Luzzo and Jenkins-Smith (1996) recommended integrating a discussion of perceived barriers to success into the mentoring process. Counselors can help students develop strategies to overcome these obstacles by discussing how students overcame similar difficulties in the past. In addition, thoughtful use of well-trained peer counselors can give minority students an additional social and academic anchor on campus.

Recognize Family and Cultural Influences on Decision-Making Style

Career counselors should be cognizant of the fact that not all cultures place equal value on counseling as a legitimate process. Some students come from backgrounds in which their elders or religious leaders served as counselors and advisers. Cultural traditions may block college completion or entry into certain fields or occupations. Career development specialists must recognize the primacy of cultural belief systems and integrate this knowledge into their counseling approach.

Some counselors assume that clients make their decisions either unilaterally or with the assistance of a trained professional. In reality, many people affect client decisions: spouses, parents, grandparents, relatives, guardians, close friends, and significant others. Independent decision making by the student may not be appreciated or even tolerated in the family. The counselor can help clients identify the role that others play in their career development process and then assist in developing the strategies and skills necessary to engage in meaningful conversation about occupational matters.

Choose Appropriate Career Counseling Interventions

The group format can provide a safe environment in which to practice social skills and receive feedback. In many instances, work with ethnic minority students can best be accomplished using groups involving peers, families, and members of other cultural minorities. Increasing outreach to parents, establishing regular drop-in hours, and performing counseling services at different sites are effective marketing strategies. These efforts should be integrated thoughtfully into the entire counseling program, not treated as add-ons.

In general, the type of counseling intervention used should be related to the individual student's personality characteristics. That is, it should be based on a careful assessment of the student's developmental level, decision-making style, and sense of control. Many ethnic minority students, for example, believe that they have internal control of their decisions but recognize that many environmental factors prevent their taking full responsibility for their actions (Sue & Sue, 1990). Understanding this belief system can influence counselors in their choice of intervention. In addition, counselors should have a clear understanding of a student's past social behavior, ability to develop insight, and motivation to learn and change.

Wisely Incorporate Technology Into the Career Counseling Process

The Internet is fast becoming a primary source of information for both career development specialists and students. Because this is an area in which many ethnic minorities lack skills, counseling interventions using the Internet can serve a dual purpose: for career information and learning the skills to use the Internet. In addition to online assessments and electronic exchange of information, career counselors can develop and maintain Web sites that are specifically designed for ethnic minority clients. These sites should contain links to professional organizations, financial assistance centers, minority specialty publications, job-search engines, local newspapers, and résumé-preparation sites. Computers should be available for use by all students; courteous, trained staff should check frequently to make sure students know how to use the various programs and can get the most out of their sessions.

Computer-assisted career guidance programs also can be helpful as sources of information regarding students' interests, courses of study, graduate programs, and financial aid opportunities. CHOICES (1996), for instance, includes in its database every two- and four-year school in the country as well as financial aid and programs of study for those schools.

It contains an interest inventory and a powerful occupational search capacity, but it may require staff assistance for optimal operation. SIGI PLUS (1997) can be operated with minimal instruction and independent of staff interpretation. SIGI PLUS allows the student to make occupational comparisons using values and interests as discriminating variables, although not at the same level of detail as CHOICES. DISCOVER (1996), however, often is used in high schools and may be most useful for students with a low level of career awareness. In any event, students must be directed to these options, properly instructed in their use, informed of the amount of time necessary to work through the program, and offered the opportunity both before and after to discuss their concerns and results.

Use Appropriate Career Instruments

The career counselor has hundreds of assessment instruments from which to choose. Many career centers neglect evaluating their instrumentation regularly in light of increased minority presence on campus, technological advancements, and diversity of measurement needs. Zunker (1998) recommended consulting the National Occupational Information Coordinating Committee's list of competencies and indicators to determine whether instruments currently in use are accurately and consistently providing desired information on ethnic minority students. A quick check of the administration manual to ascertain the basic features of the norm groups is always a good idea.

Wholesale administration of assessments for large groups of students may provide little information beyond that already available from admission records. Established instruments, such as the Strong Interest Inventory (Harmon, Hansen, Borgen, & Hammer, 1994) or the Self-Directed Search (Holland, Fritzsche, & Powell, 1994), provide excellent information but are somewhat expensive compared with most computer-assisted guidance programs, which include an interest inventory as part of a much broader and deeper assistance package. The Myers–Briggs Type Indicator (MBTI; Myers & McCaulley, 1985) often is used to open discussion of how one uses one's personality in social and work environments. A form of the MBTI is now available free of charge online (http://keirsey.com). Other no-cost instruments, such as The Career Key (Jones, 1998; www.ncsu.edu/careerkey), sponsored through North Carolina State University, can be used. For either small-group or individual counseling for minority career development, the authors recommend the Career Beliefs Inventory (CBI; Krumboltz, 1991). The CBI identifies personal beliefs regarding social issues, family expectations, differences between cultural work values, and locus of control and highlights how these variables may block career advancement. This instrument meshes well with the Career Maturity Inventory (Crites & Savickas, 1995), which assesses knowledge of occupations and attitudes toward work.

Evaluate Social Preparation

Social skills are inherently important to preparation for both college and the workplace. To be successful in either setting, students must be able to communicate effectively, deal with conflict and disappointment appropriately, and know how to present themselves positively in a variety of situations. Knowing how to conduct oneself in a social context is increasingly essential for career advancement. This is especially true for minority students, who must struggle to compete in an environment governed by potentially unfamiliar standards and rules. For this reason, it is important that career counselors address with tact any deficiencies they observe in these areas. Assertiveness training, public speaking, interviewing simulations, job shadowing, and résumé development are all excellent mechanisms for enhancing social skills.

Stress the Importance of Networking

Internships provide students with excellent opportunities to learn more about specific careers while still in college. The combination of academic course work and practical experience can be a potent learning and networking tool. Career counselors should be able to recommend internships on campus and at various local and regional companies and agencies holding the greatest potential benefit for minority students. Alumni career networks, established on some campuses through the career center and on others through the alumni office, can provide access to successful graduates who are willing to mentor students, provide information interviews, and permit shadowing experiences.

Employ More Minorities as Career Counselors

All students need people to whom they can look for inspiration and guidance, either in a formal sense or on a more informal level. This is especially true for minorities, who find fewer such models in all venues. Ethnic minority students tend to prefer counselors who are members of their group. Minority counselors often are adept at using a pluralistic counseling model that recognizes the client's culturally based beliefs, values, behaviors, and degree of adaptation to the current cultural milieu. In one innovative professional development program, Ohio State created a model career development training program for minority staff as a way to encourage their entry into the field of career planning and placement (Campbell & Hadley, 1992).

Conclusion

Students are people first and only secondarily members of cohort, gender, ethnic, and cultural groups. Regardless of ethnicity, students with greater *career decision-making self-efficacy*, defined as positive judgments regarding one's ability to choose and adjust competently, may have little difficulty with college career choices. Many minority students, however, may not regard a particular occupation as a source of intrinsic satisfaction and self-expression (Hendricks, 1994). Members of ethnic groups may deliberately choose not to adopt European American majority attitudes, values, and behaviors as they make career choices (Cheatham, 1990). Little has been done to design career development systems with the needs of ethnically diverse populations in mind, who often have greater need of career services than mainstream college entrants (Spokane & Hawks, 1990).

The ever-expanding use of technology, changing perspectives on work, increasing social and cultural diversity in U.S. society, and fundamental shifts in how people relate to one another both individually and collectively are precipitating unprecedented difficulties for educational institutions in this country (Nugent, 1994). A primary challenge facing career counselors is to develop a working model of practice for ethnic minority students. As Herring (1998) suggests, empowering minority students involves dispelling career myths, negotiating power differentials, acknowledging family history and learned behavior, and respecting the student's search for meaning and insight. The career counselor works to instill a genuine desire for positive change, develops competence with respect to testing and social labels, appreciates the power of coping mechanisms, and nurtures examination of internal and external loci of control. The counselor provides opportunity for the acquisition of academic and job skills, but more important, models an appreciation for all cultures and the ability to work with people from any ethnic group. Clearly, the door is open for college career counselors to profoundly influence the campus environment and to promote career development in students of all backgrounds.

References

Arbona, C. (1989). Hispanic employment and the Holland typology of work. *Career Development Quarterly, 37*, 257–268.

Arbona, C. (1990). Career counseling research and Hispanics: A review of the literature. *Counseling Psychologist, 18*, 300–323.

Arbona, C. (1996). Career theory and practice in a multicultural context. In M. L. Savickas & W. B. Walsh (Eds.), *Handbook of career counseling theory and practice* (pp. 45–54). Palo Alto, CA: Davies-Black.

Black, C., Paz, H., & DeBlassie, R. R. (1991). Counseling the Hispanic male adolescent. *Adolescence, 26*, 223–234.

Blinne, W. R., & Johnston, J. A. (1998). Assessing the relationships between vocational identity, academic achievement, and persistence in college. *Journal of College Student Development, 39*, 569–575.

Brown, D., Minor, C. W., & Jepsen, D. A. (1991). The opinions of minorities about preparing for work: Report of the second NCDA national survey. *Career Development Quarterly, 40*, 5–19.

Brown, L. L., & Kurpius, S. E. (1997). Psychosocial factors influencing academic persistence of American Indian college students. *Journal of College Student Development, 38*, 3–12.

Campbell, N. K., & Hadley, G. B. (1992). Creating options: A career development training program for minorities. *Journal of Counseling and Development, 70*, 645–647.

Campbell, T. A., & Campbell, D. E. (1997). Faculty student mentor programs: Effects on academic performance and retention. *Research in Higher Education, 38*, 727–742.

Cervantes, O. F. (1988). *What universities and counseling centers can do to address the problem of low admission, attrition, and retention of minority students*. Washington, DC: U.S. Department of Education. (ERIC Document Reproduction Service No. 304 049)

Chacon, M. A., Cohen, E. G., & Strover, A. (1986). Chicanas and Chicanos: Barriers to progress in higher education. In M. A. Olivas (Ed.), *Latino college students* (pp. 296–324). Hillsdale, NJ: Teachers College Press.

Cheatham, H. E. (1990). Africentricity and career development of African Americans. *Career Development Quarterly, 38*, 334–345.

CHOICES [computer software]. (1996). Montreal, Canada: Careerware.

Crites, J. O., & Savickas, M. L. (1995). *Career Maturity Inventory*. Montreal, Canada: Careerware.

Dawkins, M. P. (1980). Educational and occupational goals: Male versus female seniors. *Urban Education, 15*, 231–242.

DISCOVER [computer software]. (1996). Iowa City, IA: ACT.

Dunn, C. W., & Veltman, G. C. (1989). Addressing the restrictive career maturity patterns of minority youth: A program evaluation. *Journal of Multicultural Counseling and Development, 17*, 156–164.

Eimers, M. T., & Pike, G. R. (1997). Minority and non-minority adjustment to college: Differences or similarities. *Research in Higher Education, 38*, 77–97.

Gottfredson, L. S. (1986). Special groups and the beneficial use of vocational interest inventories. In W. B. Walsh & S. H. Osipow (Eds.), *Advances in vocational psychology, Volume I: The assessment of interests* (pp. 127–198). Hillsdale, NJ: Lawrence Erlbaum.

Hackett, G., & Byars, A. M. (1996). Social cognitive theory and the career development of African American women. *Career Development Quarterly, 44*, 322–340.

Harmon, L. W., Hansen, J.-I. C., Borgen, F. H., & Hammer, A. L. (1994). *Strong Interest Inventory: Applications and technical guide*. Palo Alto, CA: Consulting Psychologists Press.

Hendricks, F. M. (1994). Career counseling with African American college students. *Journal of Career Development, 21*, 117–126.

Henry, P., Bardo, H. R., & Henry, C. A. (1992). The effectiveness of career development seminars on African American premedical students: A program evaluation using the medical career development inventory. *Journal of Multicultural Counseling and Development, 20*, 99–112.

Herring, R. D. (1998). *Career counseling in schools: Multicultural and developmental perspectives*. Alexandria, VA: American Counseling Association.

Holland, J. L. (1973). *Making vocational choices: A theory of career*. Englewood Cliffs, NJ: Prentice-Hall.

Holland, J. L., Fritzsche, B. A., & Powell, A. B. (1994). *The Self-Directed Search technical manual*. Odessa, FL: Psychological Assessment Resources.

Hollinger, C. (1996). An examination of the lives of gifted Black young women. In K. D. Arnold, K. D. Noble, & R. F. Subotnik (Eds.), *Remarkable women: Perspectives on female talent development* (pp. 133–148). Cresskill, NJ: Hampton Press.

Jackson, G. C., & Healy, C. C. (1996). Career development profiles and interventions for underrepresented college students. *Career Development Quarterly, 44*, 258–269.

Jones, L. K. (1998). *The Career Key*. Raleigh, NC: North Carolina Occupational Information Coordinating Committee and North Carolina State University, *www.ncsu.edu/careerkey*.

Keller, J. W., Piotrowski, C., & McLeod, C. R. (1992). The evolution of a career development program. *Education, 112*, 470–473.

Krumboltz, J. D. (1991). *Career Beliefs Inventory*. Palo Alto, CA: Counseling Psychologists Press.

Leong, F. T. L. (1986). Counseling and psychotherapy with Asian Americans: Review of the literature. *Journal of Counseling Psychology, 33*, 196–206.

Leong, F. T. L. (1991). Career development attributes and occupational values of Asian American and White American college students. *Career Development Quarterly, 39*, 221–230.

Leong, F. T. L., & Brown, M. T. (1995). Theoretical issues in cross-cultural career development: Cultural validity and cultural specificity. In W. B. Walsh & S. H. Osipow (Eds.), *Handbook of vocational psychology: Theory, research, and practice* (2nd ed., pp. 143–180). Mahwah, NJ: Lawrence Erlbaum.

Leung, S. A. (1995). Career development and counseling: A multicultural perspective. In F. T. L. Leong (Ed.), *Handbook of multicultural counseling* (pp. 549–566). Thousand Oaks, CA: Sage.

Liu, R. W. (1998). Educational and career expectations of Chinese-American college students. *Journal of College Student Development, 39*, 577–588.

Luzzo, D. A. (1992). Ethnic group and social class differences in college students' career development. *Career Development Quarterly, 41*, 161–173.

Luzzo, D. A. (1993). Ethnic differences in college students' perceptions of barriers to career development. *Journal of Multicultural Counseling and Development, 21*, 227–236.

Luzzo, D. A., & Jenkins-Smith, A. (1996, Spring). Perceived occupational barriers among Mexican American college students. *TCA Journal, 24*, 1–9.

Malcolm, S. M., Hall, P. O., & Brown, J. W. (1976). *The double bind: The price of being a minority woman in science.* [Report No. 76-R-3]. Washington, DC: American Association for the Advancement of Science.

Mohr, J. J., Eiche, K. D., & Sedlacek, W. E. (1998). So close, yet so far: Predictors of attrition in college seniors. *Journal of College of Student Development, 39*, 343–354.

Morales, P. (1996, August). *Acculturation and vocational identity: The influence of Hispanic familism.* Paper presented at the meeting of the American Psychological Association, Ontario, CA.

Myers, I. B., & McCaulley, M. H. (1985). *Myers–Briggs Type Indicator.* Palo Alto, CA: Consulting Psychologists Press.

Naidoo, V. A. (1994). Factors affecting the career maturity of African American university students: A causal model (Doctoral dissertation, Ball State University, 1993). *Dissertation Abstracts International, 54*, 2770-A.

Napier, L. A. (1996). Nine native women: Pursuing the doctorate and aspiring to positions of leadership. In K. D. Arnold, K. D. Noble, & R. F. Subotnik (Eds.), *Remarkable women: Perspectives on female talent development* (pp. 133–148). Cresskill, NJ: Hampton Press.

Nugent, F. A. (1994). *An introduction to the profession of counseling* (2nd ed.). New York: Macmillan.

Padilla, R. V., Trevino, J., Gonzalez, K., & Trevino, J. (1997). Developing local models of minority student success in college. *Journal of College Student Development, 38*, 125–135.

Parmer, T. (1993). The athletic dream—but what are the career dreams of the African American urban high school students? *Journal of Career Development, 20*, 131–145.

Pope, R. L. (1998). The relationship between psychosocial development and racial identity of Black college students. *Journal of College Student Development, 39*, 273–282.

Reyes, N. (1997). Holding on to what they've got: A look at programs designed to keep college students in college. *Black Issues in Higher Education, 38*, 36–41.

Robinson, L. F., Butler, E. R., & Glennen, R. E. (1996). The changing roles and functions for offices of minority student affairs. *College Student Affairs Journal, 16*, 70–76.

Rodriguez, R. (1997a). Learning to live a warrior's life: Institute seeks to improve Native American education. *Black Issues in Higher Education, 14*(20), 38–40.

Rodriquez, R. (1997b). Reaching out, but in which direction? The future focus of academic outreach programs. *Black Issues in Higher Education, 13*(26), 16–21.

Rojewski, J. W. (1997). Cultural diversity and its impact on career counseling. In *The Hatherleigh guide to vocational and career counseling.* (The Hatherleigh Guides Series No. 9, pp. 178–208). New York: Hatherleigh.

Sharf, R. S. (1997). *Applying career development theory to counseling* (2nd ed.). Pacific Grove, CA: Brooks/Cole.

SIGI PLUS [computer software]. (1997). Princeton, NJ: Educational Testing Service.

Spokane, A. R., & Hawks, B. K. (1990). Annual review: Practice and research in career counseling and development, 1989. *Career Development Quarterly, 39*, 98–128.

St. John, E. (1997). Smith: Making way for more sisters. *Black Issues in Higher Education, 14*(20), 38–40.

Sue, D. W., & Sue, D. (1990). *Counseling the culturally different: Theory and practice* (2nd ed.). New York: John Wiley and Sons.

Super, D. E., Savickas, M. L., & Super, C. M. (1996). The life-span, life-space approach to careers. In D. Brown, L. Brooks, & Assoc. (Eds.), *Career choice and development: Applying contemporary theories to practice* (3rd ed., pp. 121–178). San Francisco: Jossey-Bass.

Taylor, C. E., & Howard-Hamilton, M. F. (1995). Student involvement and racial identity attitudes among African American males. *Journal of College Student Development, 36,* 330–335.

Thomas, V. G., & Shields, L. C. (1987). Gender influences on work values of Black adolescents. *Adolescence, 22,* 37–43.

Yang, J. (1991). Career counseling of Chinese American women: Are they in limbo? *Career Development Quarterly, 39,* 350–359.

Zunker, V. G. (1998). *Career counseling: Applied concepts of life planning* (5th ed.). Pacific Grove, CA: Brooks/Cole.

14

Career Counseling With College Women: A Scientist–Practitioner–Advocate Model of Intervention

Ruth E. Fassinger and Karen M. O'Brien

Alena, age 21, Asian American, and majoring in economics, sought career counseling 3 months before graduation from college. Her parents are encouraging her to go to law school, and her boyfriend is pressuring her to get married. She knows that she would like to take time off to travel and do volunteer work. Her parents have threatened to cut off financial support, and Alena does not think she can survive without their support, financially as well as emotionally. She reluctantly admits that she does not want to marry her boyfriend, because she feels that children would soon follow, and she could not then pursue a career.

Tamara, age 19, African American, and an engineering major, attended a career workshop after being told by a White engineering professor that few Black women complete a major in engineering and succeed in the field. He suggested that she change her major to teaching, as she did a good job with her class presentation. She had been experiencing doubts about her major before this incident, but now wonders if she ought to persist, just to spite him and prove herself. Tamara's grades are marginal in all of her classes, but she admits that she has to work much harder in her engineering courses than in other courses and sees this as a possible sign that she does not belong in this major.

Kathleen, age 20, White, lesbian, an elementary education major, and in the college honors program, sought career counseling because her recent student teaching evaluation, while otherwise positive, suggested that she should not make her sexual orientation known to her students. She refuses to be "closeted," but she is distraught that being open about her lesbianism may cost her the career that she has dreamed of and worked so hard to attain. She does not know any lesbian or gay professors and is certain that there are no lesbian or gay teachers in her school or students in her program, so she has no one to talk to about these matters.

For more than three decades, theory and research related to women's career development have comprised some of the most vigorous and exciting work in vocational psychology and counseling (Fitzgerald, Fassinger, & Betz, 1995). Early work focused on identifying vocational differences and similarities between men and women and differentiating career-oriented from home-oriented women. More recent efforts have begun to explore critical vocational issues for diverse subgroups of women created by the varying contexts in which they live, work, and are educated; these subgroups include lesbians, women of color, poor and working-class women, and women with disabilities, in addition to middle-class, college-educated White women (e.g., Betz & Fitzgerald, 1987, 1993; Bingham & Ward, 1994; Fassinger, 1996; Fitzgerald & Betz, 1994; Fitzgerald et al., 1995). However, this field has yet to clearly articulate the most helpful theory-and research-based interventions for the three women described in the cases at the beginning of this chapter.

The purpose of this chapter is to translate the rich literature on women's career development into recommendations for interventions and strategies for addressing the vocational needs of college women. For college-bound youth and college-educated young adults, it is generally agreed that one of the developmental tasks to be addressed during the college years is the clarification of vocational goals and preparation for entry-level behaviors (e.g., job hunting, applying to graduate school) that will lead to realization of goals (e.g., Chickering & Reisser, 1993; Super, 1990). Institutions of higher education facilitate this process through offering the various kinds of resources and services that are outlined in the chapters in this book (e.g., individual career counseling, computer-assisted career guidance interventions, workshops). However, it is well documented that the vocational needs, motivations, goals, and problems of college women often are considerably different from those of college men (Fitzgerald et al., 1995; Fitzgerald & Weitzman, 1992). This chapter addresses the unique issues facing college women in selecting careers and implementing choices. It also offers recommendations for addressing those issues both in individual counseling as well as in the wider arenas of institutional change and social policy.

Issues in Career Choice and Implementation for Women

What are the issues unique to the career development and planning process of women? Two central themes characterize discussions of the differences between female and male vocational patterns and issues. The first is a pervasive and persistent underutilization of women's abilities and talents, characterized by vocational segregation into jobs or positions that are low in status, pay, and opportunity for advancement relative to those of men. The second is the high level of participation in family roles for most women and the concomitant problems of role overload and compromised career aspirations as a result of combining family and career pursuits. Thus, although the *extent* of women's participation in the labor force is increasingly similar to that of men, the *nature* of that participation differs markedly because of the difficulty for women of accessing desirable careers and balancing the responsibilities of work and personal lives (Betz, 1994; Fitzgerald & Weitzman, 1992).

A number of problems contribute to the patterns described above. Betz and Fitzgerald (1987), in their now-classic book on women's vocational development, dubbed these issues "barriers" and categorized them as external (or environmental) and internal (or individual) barriers. External barriers are those that exist in the environment or the social context; they can be imposed by people but are rooted in societal structures (e.g., laws, policies, workplace norms, gender ideologies, educational practices). Some examples of contextual or structural barriers are occupational stereotypes; gender role stereotypes; gender bias in education; barriers in higher education; a "null" environment that fails to encourage women to pursue careers; lack of role models and mentors; gender-biased career assessment and counseling; and direct discrimination related to gender, race or ethnicity, or other kinds of diversity (e.g., pay inequities, workplace harassment, the glass ceiling; Betz, 1994; also see Fassinger, in press). For many women, blatant discrimination has been replaced by a seemingly benevolent tolerance of their presence characterized by a general lack of support or encouragement. For example, women may no longer be formally or overtly excluded from particular majors or fields, but they still experience difficulties accessing mentors, acquiring financial support, and obtaining encouragement for their career pursuits (e.g., Tamara's discouraging professor in the opening example).

Lest the reader assume that widespread solutions to external barriers already have occurred, it is useful to examine one example of so-called progress. In the field of chemistry, a hard science that prides itself on its "influx" of women, the top university departments (i.e., Harvard, Stanford, MIT, Columbia, and the University of Chicago) each had one or no women faculty in 1980. In 1997, almost 20 years later, the same departments each had one woman on their faculties, suggesting that little change had occurred in two decades of public efforts to increase the representation of women in academic positions in science (Brennan, 1998)—and chemistry is one of the more positive examples.

A recent study (Carr et al., 1998) investigating the productivity of female and male faculty at U.S. medical schools found that women with children were significantly less productive and less satisfied with their career progress than their male peers with children (averaging 18 published articles compared with their male peers' average of 29). The study attributed differences not only to women's greater responsibility for children but also to the lack of institutional support (e.g., research funding, administrative support) for the work of women faculty. Endless examples could be presented here; suffice it to say that there is considerable agreement among contemporary scholars of women's career development that contextual and structural barriers to women's vocational choice, implementation, and success are pervasive and largely intractable (Betz, 1994; Fassinger, in press; Fitzgerald et al., 1995; Harmon & Meara, 1994).

Internal barriers, as defined by Betz and Fitzgerald (1987), are manifested in individual women and are thought to be the result of gender socialization that has been translated into internalized beliefs and representations of the self (Betz, 1994). Some examples of individual barriers are home–career conflict, math avoidance, low self-esteem, low self-efficacy expectations, and low expectations for success. Betz (1994) noted that individual barriers are those that traditionally have been the focus of vocational counseling and intervention, whereas contextual or structural barriers most often are addressed through social change efforts.

Because the individual or internal barriers are created by a sociocultural indoctrination and socialization process that places women at a disadvantage (relative to men) in the educational system, the workplace, and the family (Betz, 1994; Betz & Fitzgerald, 1987; Fassinger, in press), it is important for career counselors to remain aware of the critical role that society plays in all of women's vocational difficulties, whether they are expressed as contextual problems (e.g., the outright discrimination faced by Kathleen) or as internal distress related to societal messages (e.g., Alena's belief that career and family are mutually exclusive). Thus, vocational counseling focused solely on helping individual women cope with their own untenable circumstances, without an explicit analysis and articulation of the sociocultural factors that create those circumstances, in effect supports the status quo and ignores the need for sweeping social change that would make work a more viable enterprise for women. Women's vocational problems are problems of context: therefore, only solutions—that is, vocational interventions—that recognize and incorporate elements of contextual change will be truly effective in addressing women's vocational needs (Fassinger, 1998, in press; Harmon & Meara, 1994). Accordingly, career counselors must not only devote greater attention to contextual issues in individual counseling, but also become more actively involved in direct advocacy and social change efforts in their academic institutions and communities.

Recommendations for Intervention: Contextual Barriers

What contextual elements might be a focus of intervention by career counselors? Foremost is the need for onsite child care for returning students and working parents as well as workplace policies such as liberal family leave allowances, job sharing, domestic partner benefits, and flexible schedules for both work and classes. Career counselors who are interested in research might document the evidence that child care programs and alternative work arrangements benefit both institutions and individuals (e.g., Bond, Galinsky, & Swanberg, 1998) and ensure that this information is disseminated widely throughout the institution. Career counselors also might offer presentations throughout their colleges and universities about the importance of workplace issues, such as child care, and can place themselves on important institutional committees that might work toward such changes (e.g., campus climate committees, academic excellence task forces). Interventions can be offered to students directly, in the form of workshops in which participants might learn about institutional and workplace realities (e.g., that few work sites—including, perhaps, their own academic institution—offer onsite child care). In addition, participants can be taught how to engage effectively in efforts to change existing policies.

A second goal for contextual change involves educational and policy efforts to address the problem of sexual and gender harassment in the classroom and in the workplace. This is an area of burgeoning concern in academic institutions (e.g., see Fitzgerald, 1993), and because career counselors often have experience counseling individuals who have experienced harassment, they can offer an invaluable perspective to informing campus initiatives. Again, career counselors can position themselves on college or university committees (judicial boards and human relations committees are critical in this area), and they also can offer presentations and workshops on sexual and gender harassment to faculty, staff, and students. One effective way to educate the often-resistant university community about sexual harassment is to include discussion of harassment in the context of other, more generic presentations, such as "Gender Issues in Workplace Communication."

A third target of contextual change is the preservation of affirmative action goals and practices. Career counselors, who have extensive knowledge of the world of work and excellent connections with employers in their communities, can contribute a great deal to debunking some of the myths and misunderstandings that have arisen regarding affirmative action (including local practices) and can educate the university community —particularly students—about the fair and appropriate use of policies and practices aimed at equity in hiring and promotion. It is critical that career counselors be involved in policy decisions in their own institutions, partly because their own institutions are accessible and therefore amenable to intervention, but more important, because colleges and universities feed the labor market and shape public opinion about the kind of vocational preparation that is competent, reasonable, and fair. In addition, career counselors who work closely with employers can offer their expertise to those constituencies as well, particularly in terms of the ways in which practices in their institutions affect the vocational preparation and availability of prospective new workers.

The last suggestion regarding social change is that career counselors, as experts in one of the most critical areas of human development, assume a more active, preventive role throughout the educational system. This role might range from involvement in career education activities in local schools (e.g., organizing job fairs or field trips to the college for middle school and high school students, staging a "Career Day" for elementary school students) to offering expertise to teacher preparation programs within one's own college or university (e.g., offering special workshops or guest lectures on gender issues in education and career development). Career counselors might offer in-service presentations and workshops to local teachers, using their important knowledge base regarding career development to address the need for gender-fair, female-affirming classrooms, educational practices, resources, and programs. A career counselor might, for example, present an in-service workshop for local school librarians, discussing the importance of acquiring library materials that depict women in a wide variety of occupations and perhaps offering lists of appropriate materials. Of course, career counselors also must ensure that vocational materials in their own career centers are gender-fair and representative of diverse women.

An argument might be made that advocacy and preventive roles are not within the purview of career counselors' institutionally dictated job responsibilities. It must be acknowledged that the capacity to engage in such activities outside the confines of one's office depends on myriad factors, including current job demands, individual commitment to social justice issues, individual interest in campuswide training and outreach activities, institutional support, and individual interest in campus–community connections. It is likely that not all college career counselors will engage in the activities suggested above. Career counselors, however, by virtue of their training, expertise, and access to local community institutions (e.g., schools and businesses), make up a potentially powerful force that might more effectively improving the context in which women's career development occurs. Given that social change is slow, however, career counselors will necessarily be involved in individual change efforts for a long time to come. Suggestions for interventions aimed at individuals or small groups in the college setting are presented in the following sections.

Individual Approaches to Vocational Intervention for Women

Despite the vast literature on barriers to women's vocational development, scholarly work examining the process and outcome of career interventions with and for women has been much slower to appear in the literature (Phillips & Imhoff, 1997). In fact, Phillips and Imhoff noted the "conspicuous gap" between the extensive documentation of problems for women in their career development and the paucity of research describing and evaluating interventions to address the problems. This is unfortunate, because evidence shows that practitioners have been incorporating considerations of gender into their work for some time (Brooks & Forrest, 1994; Harmon & Meara, 1994), yet most of this important intervention work remains unexplored and untested.

So where does one begin in developing career interventions for college women? Traditional wisdom dictates that theory be the starting point. However, most vocational psychologists and career counselors begin discussions of women and work by asserting that traditional theories of career development and their concomitant approaches to assessment are based on the experiences of educated White men and therefore do not necessarily apply to women, particularly when diversity among women (e.g., ethnicity, sexual orientation, social class) is taken into account. Moreover, there is a current shift in focus from sex to gender in psychology, that is, moving from a focus on differences (and sometimes similarities) between women and men to examining the effects of societally determined, contextual notions of gender and gender roles on both women and men (Anselmi & Law, 1998). This shift in focus raises questions about whether the traditional emphases of theories and assessment devices are fair to or appropriate for men as well, especially insofar as existing practices reinforce masculine gender roles focused on achieving, competing, and providing without regard for men's personal needs and values. Even contemporary gendered frameworks of career development, while promising, have been criticized for inadequate inclusion of diversity in terms of race, class, ethnicity, sexual orientation, disability and the like (see Fitzgerald et al., 1995, for a review).

This situation presents an interesting conundrum: If counseling intervention is supposed to be derived from and built on solid theory, and it is not clear that existing theories are as solid as assumed, then interventions (including practices related to individual career counseling) are suspect as well. Although the existing literature may not offer incontrovertible theories or strategies for intervention, it does provide consistent themes and issues around which interventions can be built—and which clearly suggest the need for a new approach to career counseling and other vocational interventions with college women.

What are the distinguishing features of this new approach? It would, of course, incorporate all of the components of effective interpersonal counseling and communication: active listening; empathic responding; sensitive and skillful probing, questioning, clarifying, and interpreting; building a solid rapport and sound interpersonal alliance; creating an environment characterized by both challenge and support; assessing thoroughly; setting mutually agreed-on goals; providing information and resources as needed; soliciting ongoing client feedback counseling and intervention effectiveness, including at termination; working to ensure the transfer of learning beyond the counseling itself; and ending the counseling in a sensitive and caring way. These components are critically important, whether the intervention involves individual counseling or a workshop for a dozen students.

Sociopolitical Consciousness Raising

The proposed approach has several major additional features. The first is its deliberate focus on consciousness raising and sociopolitical analysis of contextual factors in individual career development and career problems and decisions. Thorough assessment includes focused attention to contextual factors, which are carefully explored in relation to existing structures of power and privilege in the client's immediate environments (including counseling) as well as in society at large.

Consider, for example, Tamara, who is struggling with her decision about her major and who admits that engineering is difficult but feels that she must stick with it to prove herself. Administering interest inventories and proceeding to help her find alternative career options are unlikely to be successful intervention strategies in the absence of a clear understanding of the ways in which gender and cultural issues are at play in her career decisions. Effective career counseling with Tamara, therefore, would include careful exploration of what it means to be an African American woman in a predominantly White society and a woman in a predominantly male major and career field. Analysis of context must include the counseling relationship itself, because it, too, contains potential for misuse of power and privilege. Tamara may believe that she has to prove herself to the counselor (perhaps especially if the counselor is White or male), or she may look to the counselor for the answer to her dilemma. Truly empowering Tamara will include conscious efforts to minimize the power differences between counselor and client as much as possible, so that not just counselor words, but also counselor actions are communicating to Tamara that she is strong, competent, capable of solving her problems, and worthy of treatment as an equal. Tamara would be included as an active participant in generating knowledge about her test results and possible career options. She would be encouraged to generate a "career search action plan," in which she would outline steps (e.g., informational interviewing, locating successful African American women to serve as role models) that would empower her to decide on a career that fits her values and needs. She would be encouraged to examine how society influences her views of herself (as an African American woman) and her career choices, including the issue of remaining in a major to prove her professor wrong. A positive outcome of career counseling with Tamara would be her increased ability to accurately sort out societal messages and demands (contextual forces) from her own judgments and self-reflections (internal motivations) in making career decisions.

The False Work–Home Dichotomy

A second feature of a contextualized approach to career intervention for college women includes conscious and consistent tearing down of the false dichotomy between work and home or personal life. If there is one overarching truth in the literature on the vocational psychology of women, it is that for most contemporary women, career and personal concerns are inextricably linked and that it is impossible to consider one without thinking about the other (Betz, 1994; Fitzgerald & Weitzman, 1992; see O'Brien, Friedman, Tipton, & Linn, in press, and Richie et al., 1997, for empirical examples). The arbitrary dichotomizing of the two realms, a legacy from late 19th-century sociopolitical shifts that relegated men to the public, work sphere and women to the private, home sphere (Unger & Crawford, 1996) is patently unhealthy for women (and, one might add, for men and society as well). This split prevents women from effectively integrating their work and personal lives without feeling stressed, guilty, and inadequate, and it traps young women like Alena into believing that it is impossible to have both a family and a career. Operating under such a belief system, young women may be inclined (as Alena certainly seems to be) to forego either family or career or to compromise career pursuits out of fear and doubt. The dichotomizing of work and home constricts men's choices as well, because it reinforces in men a single-minded dedication to providing and achieving and ignores the possibility that men might want greater involvement in home and children.

Career counselors are in an excellent position to intervene in issues relating to the work-home interface. They can offer workshops for students (as well as faculty and staff) on managing career and family, emphasizing both the struggles and the benefits of multiple roles. Moreover, they can highlight patterns of gender socialization that create imbalances in heterosexual two-job families and can provide resources that showcase working couples who successfully manage home and family. Panels of working couples are particularly effective in this regard and should include lesbian and gay couples, whose perspectives often include highly creative, non-gender-stereotypic solutions to problems in managing the work–home interface. In individual counseling, career counselors can bridge the dichotomy between the vocational and the personal by routinely inquiring about both career and personal concerns, modeling for clients the recognition that the issues are interdependent and mutually influential.

The dichotomizing of the vocational and the personal may have particularly pernicious effects on a woman like Kathleen, who already is being directed to conceal her personal life because of homonegativity of others in her professional environment. In the absence of unambiguous support from her counselor and other lesbian- or gay-affirmative professionals and peers, Kathleen may give up her goal of becoming a teacher. Even more likely (given how far along she is in her educational progress) is that she will finish her degree but will not seek a teaching job, or that she will obtain a teaching job and resign herself to a life of secrecy, shame, and fear.

A career counselor can help Kathleen articulate her concerns and sort out what is based on workplace realities and what is rooted in her fear and internalized homonegativity. The counselor can connect Kathleen with lesbian and gay educators who can serve as role models for the healthy integration of work and identity. The career counselor also can provide skills training to equip Kathleen to navigate her entry into her chosen career; examples of important skills include assertiveness, accessing legal resources, establishing collegial support systems, conflict management, and stress management. In addition, if Kathleen has a partner, the career counselor can provide resources and referrals to help the women with the unique issues that they face as a dual-career lesbian couple (see Fassinger, 1996). The counselor thus challenges the dichotomy between work and personal life being encouraged by Kathleen's supervising teacher, through open acknowledgment of the need for Kathleen to integrate her identities as a worker and a lesbian. The counselor is empowering Kathleen to plan for the difficult situations she is likely to encounter as a lesbian worker and to engage in actions that challenge workplace realities insensitive to her needs.

Interventions With Men

The third critical factor in a contextualized career counseling approach is the recognition that most women's lives will include significant interactions with men—at school or work, at home, and in their communities. Therefore, college men must be targeted for intervention efforts aimed at education and consciousness raising. It is not enough to empower women to challenge patriarchal structures and the nonegalitarian attitudes of individual men, because such an approach still places the burden for social and political change squarely on the shoulders of individual women. Young men must be taught that effective support of women in school or in the workplace does not consist of complimenting them on their appearance, and men (and women) also must be taught that truly egalitarian relationships in the home are not embodied in men "helping" with household chores and child care that are consistently planned, organized, and managed by their female partners.

Returning to the opening cases, a counselor might find, for example, that Alena's reticence about marrying her boyfriend is really rooted in the realization that he expects a more traditional, nonegalitarian relationship than is acceptable to her. Assuming that she may actually want to marry him if her fears can be addressed, then career counseling might assist Alena in articulating her beliefs and fears about both relationships and careers, by uncovering and addressing constrictive messages she may have learned from society or from her Asian culture (e.g., single career women are unfulfilled, a woman's place is with her children, men have the right to an orderly home maintained by their wives). In addition, her boyfriend could be encouraged to explore his own relationship and career expectations through individual career counseling, bibliotherapy, and workshops on dual-career issues, thereby challenging his attitudes sufficiently that this young couple might build a more egalitarian relationship together (within, of course, the context of cultural values that they both hold).

Incidentally, it has been the authors' experience that little, if any, campus educational programming on dual-career issues specifically targets men. Given that research indicates that neither college women nor men think about or plan realistically for futures involving multiple roles (e.g., McCracken & Weitzman, 1997), career counselors who wish to engage in important advocacy work might consider providing such programming. It can be an effective strategy for consciousness raising, and the focus on educating men as well as women is an important element of the contextualized approach to career counseling.

Recommendations for Training Career Counselors

If vocational psychologists and career counselors are to be prepared to deliver contextually sensitive career counseling and to assume advocacy roles in their academic institutions and communities, then changes are needed in the training of new professionals. First, the scientist–practitioner model of training and professionalism must be augmented to include preventive and advocacy roles—thus creating a scientist–practitioner–advocate model of training. Courses in legal and policy issues would be incorporated into the model, and students would be trained in consultation, program development, and program evaluation. Because many faculty currently teaching in graduate-level career counseling training programs also lack relevant expertise and experience, extensive in-service opportunities must be made available for the further development of professional skills.

Second, in addition to the infusion of gender issues into the entire graduate curriculum, at least one course in gender would be made mandatory in graduate training, and national and state licensing and certification exams would be modified to reflect this necessary knowledge. Similarly, basic competence in diversity and multiculturalism would be considered necessary for conferral of a degree and licensure or certification to ensure that professionals were competent to address the needs of diverse women (and men). Lest the reader assume that many or most graduate curricula already are infused with attention to gender, data suggest that this is not the case. Fifteen years after the American Psychological Association's Division 17 Committee on Women developed and published the *Principles Concerning the Counseling and Therapy of Women* (1979), a study indicated that more than half of a national sample of internship-level doctoral counseling and clinical psychology students had never heard of the *Principles* (Mintz, Rideout, & Bartels, 1994). This study reported that only about 15% of their sample had taken a graduate-level course in counseling women or in the psychology of women, that most (83%) of that 15% reported that the course had been an elective, and that more than half (58%) of the total sample reported that no course related to women or gender was offered in their training program. Clearly, much work remains to be done in reforming curricula—they are inadequate for training students in gender-sensitive interventions of any kind.

Third, to serve women (and men) effectively, conscious integration of educational and work issues into counseling that is not expressly focused on career concerns must occur. Counselors must pay greater attention to personal issues in career-focused interventions, so that career counselors do not unconsciously reinforce the pernicious and false dichotomy between work life and personal life that is so harmful to women. Moreover, attention to the integration of the vocational and the personal should extend to the climate and practices within graduate training programs, and advising might include attention to helping students achieve and maintain balanced lives. Of course, faculty must model balance in their own professional lives, and sharing their interests and commitments outside the program with students can be an effective means of modeling this kind of integration.

Finally, in the proposed scientist–practitioner–advocate model, professional activities, particularly research, must reflect policy and advocacy implications more clearly and directly. Doing so requires abandoning the illusion of scientific detachment and objectivity that is a legacy from the positivist model of science and acceptance that all professional activities (research, teaching, training, consultation, supervision) are political acts that have social consequences. Even professionals without advocacy agendas who believe that their work is irrelevant to social issues are implicitly advancing a political position (i.e., maintaining an oppressive status quo), because their work does not attempt to challenge a society built on unequal access to power and privilege. Thus, in the proposed model of training, professionals have an important ethical responsibility to consider the potential advocacy implications of every activity in which they might engage. This approach can strengthen the science on which interventions are built, because researchers will have to determine what kinds of data-gathering efforts are credible to those outside the field, and such considerations will make research more comprehensible to the lay public (including policy makers). At the very least, researchers will not be caught off guard when their work is put to policy uses that may never have been intended. Although the notion of research as a sociopolitical act can (and should) be taught in graduate training programs, journal policies should be developed to incorporate this perspective, so that published work has been scrutinized carefully for its potential in advocacy efforts. As Harmon and Meara (1994) wisely noted, efforts to influence policy and practice in the area of women and work will not prevail without science to validate those efforts.

Harmon and Meara (1994) pointed out the gap between the publicly espoused beliefs of vocational psychologists and career counselors regarding equity and equality between women and men in the workplace and the emotional difficulty in accepting successful women or radically altering the status quo. Harmon and Meara suggested that we, as vocational psychologists and career counselors, may be just as afraid of change as those we seek to help and that this affective block needs to be addressed in our work—not only in ourselves but also in our colleagues, students, clients, and others we seek to influence. One advantage to instituting a scientist–practitioner–advocate model of professionalism is that we can rely on professional and ethical mandates when our individual courage inevitably fails us. So let us gather our collective courage and work together to create a world in which all women (including Alena, Tamara, and Kathleen) and men can live healthy, happy, productive lives.

References

Anselmi, D. L., & Law, A. L. (1998). *Questions of gender: Perspectives and paradoxes.* Boston: McGraw-Hill.

Betz, N. E. (1994). Basic issues and concepts in career counseling for women. In W. B. Walsh & S. H. Osipow (Eds.), *Career counseling for women* (pp. 1–42). Hillsdale, NJ: Lawrence Erlbaum.

Betz, N. E., & Fitzgerald, L. F. (1987). *The career psychology of women.* New York: Academic Press.

Betz, N. E., & Fitzgerald, L. F. (1993). Individuality and diversity: Theory and research in counseling psychology. *Annual Review of Psychology, 44,* 343–381.

Bingham, R. P., & Ward, C. M. (1994). Career counseling with ethnic minority women. In W. B. Walsh & S. H. Osipow (Eds.), *Career counseling for women* (pp. 165–196). Hillsdale, NJ: Lawrence Erlbaum.

Bond, J. T., Galinsky, E., & Swanberg, J. (1998). *The 1997 national study of the changing workforce.* New York: Families and Work Institute.

Brennan, M. B. (1998). Reshaping affirmative action. *Chemical & Engineering News, 76*, 17–31.

Brooks, L., & Forrest, L. (1994). Feminism and career counseling. In W. B. Walsh & S. H. Osipow (Eds.), *Career counseling for women* (pp. 87–134). Hillsdale, NJ: Lawrence Erlbaum.

Carr, P. L., Ash, A. S., Friedman, R. H., Scaramucci, A., Barnett, R. C., Szalcha, L., Palepu, A., & Moskowitz, M. A. (1998). Relation of family responsibilities and gender to the productivity and career satisfaction of medical faculty. *Annals of Internal Medicine, 129*, 532–538.

Chickering, A. W., & Reisser, L. (1993). *Education and identity* (2nd ed.). San Francisco: Jossey-Bass.

Division 17 Committee on Women, American Psychological Association. (1979). Principles concerning the counseling and therapy of women. *The Counseling Psychologist, 8*, 21.

Fassinger, R. E. (1996). Notes from the margins: Integrating lesbian experience into the vocational psychology of women. *Journal of Vocational Behavior, 48*, 160–175.

Fassinger, R. E. (1998, August). *Gender as a contextual factor in career services delivery: A modest proposal*. Paper presented at the annual meeting of the American Psychological Association, San Francisco.

Fassinger, R. E. (in press). Hitting the ceiling: Gendered barriers to occupational entry, advancement, and achievement. In L. Diamant & J. Lee (Eds.), *The psychology of sex, gender, and jobs: Issues and solutions*. Westport, CT: Greenwood Press.

Fitzgerald, L. F. (1993). *The last great open secret: The sexual harassment of women in academia and the workplace*. Washington, DC: Federation of Behavioral, Psychological, and Cognitive Sciences.

Fitzgerald, L. F., & Betz, N. E. (1994). Career development in cultural context: The role of gender, race, class, and sexual orientation. In M. L. Savickas & R. W. Lent (Eds.), *Convergence in theories of career choice and development*. (pp. 103–118) Palo Alto, CA: Consulting Psychologists Press.

Fitzgerald, L. F., Fassinger, R. E., & Betz, N. E. (1995). Theoretical advances in the study of women's career development. In W. B. Walsh & S. H. Osipow (Eds.), *Handbook of vocational psychology* (2nd ed., pp. 67–109). Hillsdale, NJ: Lawrence Erlbaum.

Fitzgerald, L. F., & Weitzman, L. M. (1992). Women's career development: Theory and practice from a feminist perspective. In Z. Leibowitz & D. Lea (Eds.), *Adult career development*, 2nd ed. (pp. 124–160). Alexandria, VA: National Career Development Association.

Harmon, L. W., & Meara, N. M. (1994). Contemporary developments in women's career counseling: Themes of the past, puzzles for the future. In W. B. Walsh & S. H. Osipow (Eds.), *Career counseling for women* (pp. 355–368). Hillsdale, NJ: Lawrence Erlbaum.

McCracken, R. S., & Weitzman, L. M. (1997). Relationship of personal agency, problem-solving appraisal, and traditionality of career choice to women's attitudes toward multiple role planning. *Journal of Counseling Psychology, 44*, 149–159.

Mintz, L. B., Rideout, C. A., & Bartels, K. M. (1994). A national survey of interns' perceptions of their preparation for counseling women and of the atmosphere of their graduate education. *Professional Psychology: Research and Practice, 25*, 221–227.

O'Brien, K. M., Friedman, S. C., Tipton, L. C., & Linn, S. G. (in press). Attachment and women's vocational development: A longitudinal analysis. *Journal of Counseling Psychology*.

Phillips, S. D., & Imhoff, A. R. (1997). Women and career development: A decade of research. *Annual Review of Psychology, 48*, 31–59.

Richie, B. S., Fassinger, R. E., Linn, S. G., Johnson, J., Prosser, J., & Robinson, S. (1997). Persistence, connection, and passion: A qualitative study of the career development of high achieving African American-Black and White women. *Journal of Counseling Psychology, 44*, 133–148.

Super, D. E. (1990). A life-span, life-space approach to career development. In D. Brown, L. Brooks, & Assoc. (Eds.), *Career choice and development: Applying contemporary theories to practice* (2nd ed., pp. 197–261). San Francisco: Jossey-Bass.

Unger, R. & Crawford, M. (1996). *Women and gender: A feminist psychology* (2nd ed.). New York: McGraw-Hill.

15

Responsible Career Counseling With Lesbian and Gay Students

Mark S. Pope, Jeffrey P. Prince, and Kathleen Mitchell

Addressing the career development needs of lesbian and gay students is critical to the delivery of any comprehensive college or university career service. Lesbian and gay students compose a significant proportion of the student body on all campuses but are, for the most part, invisible. As a result, campus career professionals often fail to design services that are both welcoming and specific to their needs (Fassinger, 1991; Taylor, Borland, & Vaughters, 1998).

Lesbian and gay students comprise a widely diverse population that varies with respect to gender, age, race, ethnicity, disability status, and socioeconomic status. They also vary in their level of comfort with their sexual orientation and in their awareness of its impact on their career development and behavior. As a socially oppressed minority group, however, lesbian and gay students typically share a number of unique career development challenges, such as employment discrimination, limited role models, and stereotyping. Traditional career interventions without such considerations, therefore, are rarely sufficient. Career services professionals often need to go beyond traditional methods of practice and attend to those issues commonly faced by students who do not share a heterosexual orientation.

Unfortunately, no substantive body of scholarly work focuses specifically on the career development needs of lesbian and gay students. Designing career interventions for this population generally requires extrapolation from vocational research that has addressed a broad range of lesbian and gay nonstudent populations. Although the literature also is limited, it has nearly tripled in size over the past 10 years. In a comprehensive literature review, Pope (1995a, 1995b) found only 31 articles focused on lesbian or gay career development, and only 15 that specifically addressed career practitioners. Pope also found that a limited number of those articles had been empirical, with the following notable exceptions: Bieschke and Matthews (1996); Chung and Harmon (1994); Etringer, Hillerbrand, and Hetherington (1990); Griffin (1992); Mobley and Slaney (1996); and Schneider (1987). Nevertheless, the recent spark of scholarly attention to the career concerns of lesbian and gay people has resulted in a valuable body of work that offers a range of expertise to campus career professionals.

This chapter draws from the general literature relevant to lesbian and gay career concerns and proposes strategies that practitioners can use to meet the career exploration and planning needs of lesbian and gay college students more effectively. Typically, campus services include bisexual and transgender students along with lesbian and gay students when designing, advertising, and delivering programs. This chapter, however, does not address the specific needs of bisexual and transgender students. Although their career concerns may be similar in many ways to those of lesbian and gay students, bisexual and transgender students also face separate and unique career issues and challenges. Unfortunately, the career literature has virtually ignored bisexual and transgender populations, so counselors have no scholarly work from which to draw when designing and delivering career services to these students. Important differences between lesbian and gay students exist, and this chapter will highlight the differences reported in the literature.

This chapter is organized into five sections: (a) historical context of gay and lesbian issues on campus, (b) assessing counselor and student attitudes, (c) creating affirmative work environments, (d) fostering a positive career identity, and (e) improving campus climate. Each section highlights a critical dimension of responsible career practice with lesbian and gay students.

Historical Context of Gay and Lesbian Issues on Campus

Every day, college and university career counseling centers face the career development needs of a changing and diverse clientele that includes substantial numbers of openly gay and lesbian students. In only three decades (1969–1999), as a direct and indirect result of a variety of societal forces, a major personal, political, and social revolution has occurred in how issues of sexual orientation are handled in the United States. Many times these changes have had their genesis on college campuses. While nonstudents were reading about the sexual revolution and the gay and lesbian rights movement, gay and lesbian college students' expectations were growing. They expected that they would be treated just like any other college student, that there would be student organizations that would meet their social needs, that they could have their own dances and even dance openly at general college functions, that they would be protected from harm and victimization, that they could be honest and open about their sexual orientation, that they could speak openly about—as Oscar Wilde stated—the "love that dared not speak its name," and that the college campus would be a safe place for them to explore their sexual orientation and to be themselves.

Assessing Counselor and Student Attitudes

Professional career counselors recognize the importance of providing students a safe and welcoming environment in which to explore career interests. Because lesbian and gay students may not have had access to unbiased career information, it is essential that career services for college students include a comprehensive program that assists counselors and students with assessing their attitudes about career options for gay men and lesbians (Gelberg & Chojnacki, 1995; Worthington, McCrary, & Howard, 1998).

How career options are discussed with students can affect a student's motivation. Some gay and lesbian students may be reluctant to consider certain career options because of concerns about discrimination or negative stereotyping. Exploring gay or lesbian students' beliefs about career options can help them address and manage limiting self-stereotyping or internalized homophobia (Chung & Harmon, 1994; Hetherington, & Orzek, 1989; Morgan & Brown, 1991; Pope, Rodriguez, & Chang, 1992).

Likewise, societal stereotyping of gay and lesbian career options may have influenced career counselors. A comprehensive program of career services might include staff development opportunities for career counselors to discuss ways to use more inclusive language, both written and spoken, that broadens career options for gay and lesbian students (Belz, 1993; Brown, 1975; Chung & Harmon, 1994; Hetherington, Hillerbrand, & Etringer, 1989; Hetherington & Orzek, 1989; Morgan & Brown, 1991; Pope, 1995c).

Occasionally, a career counselor may believe that a gay or lesbian student would benefit from referral to a colleague who is more familiar with the developmental issues of gay and lesbian students. A useful staff development resource might be a list of career counselors who are particularly knowledgeable about and sensitive to gay and lesbian identity development stages (i.e. stages in coming out to self) and how they affect the career concerns of gay and lesbian students (Hetherington & Orzek, 1989; Morgan & Brown, 1991; Orzek, 1992). Such colleagues may be more experienced with career counseling interventions that are appropriate to the gay or lesbian student's identity development stage (Fassinger, 1995; Prince, 1995).

Use of Testing

Formal career assessment tools are standard components of career counseling with college students; in fact, many of the instruments widely used by career counselors were developed and normed on this population. The use of these instruments with members of socially oppressed groups, however, has come under increased scrutiny, both ethically and psychometrically (Betz & Fitzgerald, 1995; Walsh & Betz, 1995). Both the validity and the reliability of various instruments have been questioned when used with lesbians and gay men (Buhrke & Douce, 1991; Chernin,

Holden, & Chandler, 1997; Fassinger, 1995; Hartung et al., 1998; Pope, 1992; Prince, 1997a, 1997b). In addition, psychological testing in general has been used as a tool to oppress and diagnose lesbians and gay men as mentally ill for much of this century (Pope, 1992; Prince, 1997a, 1997b). Consequently, many lesbian and gay students, as well as their counselors, may mistrust the use of formal assessment tools. Students may approach career assessment with guardedness, skepticism, or even fear of being exposed as lesbian or gay, particularly if the assessment is related to graduate school admission or job selection. For example, a student may not respond honestly to an interest inventory for fear that admitting to gender-atypical interests might draw attention to questions of her or his sexual orientation.

Only a few research efforts have investigated the use of career assessments with lesbians and gay men. Pope (1992), for example, reviewed the use and misuse of specific subscales on five major psychological inventories used in career counseling and personnel selection: the Strong Interest Inventory (Harmon, Hansen, Borgen, & Hammer, 1994), the Myers–Briggs Type Indicator (MBTI; Myers & McCaulley, 1985), the Edwards Personal Preference Schedule (Edwards, 1959), the California Psychological Inventory (Gough, 1987), and the Minnesota Multiphasic Personality Inventory (Hathaway et al., 1989). Using a case study methodology, Pope wove technical and psychometric data into the cases to illustrate how the five inventories may be misused with gay and lesbian clients. Similarly, Pope and Jelly (1991) discussed the use of the MBTI with gay and lesbian clients. They reported preliminary data suggesting that not "coming out" (i.e., revealing one's homosexuality) for a gay man or a lesbian woman may be a source of distortion on self-report inventories like the MBTI. They suggested that changes in scores may occur as a person's comfort in sexual identity develops.

Chung and Harmon (1994) evaluated the Self-Directed Search (SDS; Holland, Fritzsche, & Powell, 1994) for use with gay men, comparing the scores of gay men and heterosexual men. After matching for age, socioeconomic background, ethnicity, student status, and education, they found that gay men scored higher on the artistic and social scales and lower on the realistic and investigative scales. They did not find the SDS to be an inappropriate tool for gay men and interpreted their findings to indicate that gay men's career interests were less traditional than those of heterosexual men in their sample. In addition, they found that the two groups did not differ in their status aspirations.

These few investigations have provided some evidence for exercising caution in the use of career assessments with lesbians and gay men. Nevertheless, professional guidelines have been silent on this issue. The *Standards for Educational and Psychological Testing* (American Educational Research Association, American Psychological Association [APA], & National Council on Measurement in Education, 1985), and the *Code of Fair Testing Practices in Education* (APA, 1988) have addressed issues relating to ethnic and racial groups. They have not yet provided, however, any guidance for the use of testing with lesbians or gay men.

Prince (1997b) argued that three considerations appear critical in ensuring fair testing practice with lesbians and gay men: (a) the potential role of assessor bias, (b) the possibility of bias in the assessment instruments themselves, and (c) bias that might occur during the use and interpretation of inventories. Prince described in detail each possible source and offered strategies that can mitigate their effects. Generally, effective career testing with lesbians and gay men requires a critical evaluation and occasional transformation of traditional assessment inventories. In addition, Prince called for career professionals not only to work to eliminate harmful and biased assessment but also to create affirmative approaches.

Each instrument needs to be examined for inappropriate or offensive content, language, scales, and constructs. This step is necessary primarily because virtually all career assessment instruments have been developed from a majority, or heterosexual, perspective: Everyone is assumed to be heterosexual, and the experiences of lesbians and gay men are neglected or devalued, whether deliberately or not. Rarely do career instruments include content relating to the life events and concerns specific to lesbians and gay men. For example, Chung (1995) pointed out that several measures of career decision making are inadequate because they do not incorporate concerns that are unique to lesbians and gay men, such as conflicts arising from homophobic and oppressive work environments. Similarly, scales measuring knowledge of occupational information do not address content areas such as antidiscrimination policies or domestic partner benefits, which are particularly important to lesbian and gay students entering the job market. Assessments of career values or roles typically use exclusionary language, such as "spouse" or "marriage," and ignore more inclusive options, such as "domestic partner." Belz (1993) suggested countering such assessment bias by using creatively redesigned card sorts that include items addressing issues specific to lesbians and gay men, such as being out on the job.

Often test administrators have no idea that they are working with a lesbian or gay student because sexual orientation so often is invisible. Consequently, they may inadvertently use assessment tools designed for heterosexual clients, which measure heterosexually relevant constructs. This is particularly a risk in the career assessment of younger students and those questioning their sexual orientation, who may not be willing or able to identify themselves to a counselor as lesbian or gay. One proactive solution is to proceed with selecting and interpreting career assessments with the assumption that all clients may be either lesbian or gay. This circumvents the need to identify which students might be lesbian or gay and dictates the judicious use of all instruments with heterosexually exclusive content.

Prince (1997b) outlined the following three affirmative assessment strategies that could be adopted by college career professionals:

1. *Gather demographic information.* Many career assessment tools and questionnaires ask students to complete basic demographic

information such as age, ethnicity, and gender. Commonly used instruments could be expanded to include questions relating to sexual orientation. Although some students might feel uncomfortable answering the item honestly, the simple presence of the item helps reduce the invisibility of nonheterosexual orientations.

2. *Expand history taking and assessment interviews.* Once a student self-identifies as lesbian or gay, a number of relevant questions that go beyond the typical academic and career history can be included to gather important information specific to the student's sexual identity development. Has the student disclosed her or his sexual orientation to family members? What is the degree of the student's lesbian or gay community connections? Has the student experienced discrimination in school or on the job? Answers to these and other questions might assist in understanding the complex dynamics influencing the student's career behavior. Answers to such questions also may provide an informed context for the interpretation of assessment scores.

3. *Provide homework assignments.* Some students may not understand the connection between their career development and their sexual orientation; others may be uncomfortable discussing such issues with a career counselor they have just met. A homework assignment that allows students to reflect on these issues and write down their thoughts can provide valuable information for career assessment. For example, following the interpretation of an assessment tool, students could be given a homework assignment of describing how they think their sexual orientation relates to their assessment results.

Although the literature relating to the use of career assessments with lesbians and gay men is still in its infancy, enough information is available to provide some direction. College professionals engaging in career assessment can do much to minimize bias, to provide inclusive services, to deliver accurate interpretations, and to develop affirmative interventions.

Assessing Cultural Identity Development

Cultural identity here refers to the level of identification the person has with the gay and lesbian community, which is a minority culture within the dominant majority culture (Pope, 1995c). The stronger the identity, the more the recommendations made here are likely to be appropriate. Assessment of cultural identity can help the career counselor more accurately develop a treatment plan oriented to the person within his or her environment.

Students need to perceive that career counselors are sensitive to their needs. It is therefore imperative that career counselors learn and apply models of gay and lesbian identity development in their work with this population (Boatwright, Gilbert, Forrest, & Ketzenberger, 1996; Driscoll,

Kelley, & Fassinger, 1996; Dunkle, 1996; Fassinger, 1995, 1996; Hetherington & Orzek, 1989; Morgan & Brown, 1991; Prince, 1995). Morgan and Brown (1991), in reanalyzing data from two previously gathered large samples of lesbians, specifically addressed how the lesbian career development process seemed both similar to and different from earlier minority-group models of career development. They identified the process of identity development as critical in the lives of lesbians. To plan and provide effective career counseling with lesbian women, career counselors need to be aware of the particular stage of development as well as the age of their lesbian clients.

Dunkle (1996) integrated Super's (1990) career development stages model with Cass's (1979) sexual orientation identity development stages model and stated that, for gay men and lesbian women, the progression through the career development stages may be complicated by difficulties in integrating their gay or lesbian identity into their self-concept. Prince (1995) reviewed the literature on identity development (i.e., coming out) and career development for gay men and recommended that specific interventions be developed for use at each identity development stage, potentially corresponding to each career development stage.

Obear and Reynolds (1986) reported that the normal developmental process of coming out to self and developing a secure gay or lesbian identity has its own unique chronology and can take place over several years (see Table 15.1). Note that a 16-year gap, on average, exists between awareness of same-sex feelings and development of a positive gay or lesbian identity, 8 to 10 years between first awareness of same-sex feelings and self-labeling as gay or lesbian, and 18 years from first awareness of one's orientation to coming out professionally.

The career needs of people vary at different ages (Super, 1990), and some additional complications exist for lesbians and gay men. Because the coming-out process can begin at any age, not just adolescence, the stress and emotional energy associated with that process can have different effects, depending on when it occurs. In conjunction with the career devel-

Table 15.1.   Mean Age of Accomplishing the Coming-Out Task

Task	Age of lesbians	Age of gay men
Awareness of homosexual feelings	13.8	12.8
Understood what homosexual was	15.6	17.2
Had the first same-sex sexual experience	19.9	14.9
Had first homosexual relationship	22.8	21.9
Considered self homosexual	23.2	21.1
Acquired positive gay identity	29.7	28.5
Disclosed identity to spouse	26.7	33.3
Disclosed identity to friends	28.2	28.0
Disclosed identity to parents	30.2	28.0
Disclosed identity professionally	32.4	31.2

opment tasks, the tasks of self-concept reformation during the coming-out process can be overwhelming. Furthermore, according to Elliott (1993),

> the forces acting on a college student who has been out for four years in the late 80s and early 90s are vastly different than those experienced by someone who has been out since the mid-1950s. The trauma of changing jobs and facing the possibility of self-disclosure to a whole new cadre of co-workers can be very stressful for the middle aged lesbian or gay person who was raised in a much more restrictive age. (p. 17)

Creating an Affirming Work Environment

Coming Out

Coming out has been discussed previously as an individual developmental task that involves self-acceptance of the person's own sexual orientation; it might be better termed "coming out to self." At the same time, coming out has been described as the process of disclosing the completion of that developmental task to others. Such disclosure might be verbal or written, private or public statements to other people informing them of a person's sexual orientation. This type of coming out might be better termed "coming out to others."

Research has shown that coming out to oneself is an important developmental process to accomplish successfully and that coming out to self and others is an important reflection of psychological health (Freedman, 1971). It also suggests that well-adjusted gay men and lesbians reject the idea that homosexuality is an illness, have close and supportive associations with other lesbians and gay men, and are not interested in changing their homosexuality (Weinberg, 1971). The acceptance of who one is and the integration of one's sexuality into that identity enhances self-esteem and healthy psychological functioning (Freedman, 1971; Weinberg, 1971).

Providing assistance in coming out is the most powerful and important service career counselors can provide, according to gay and lesbian college students (D'Augelli, 1993). From the "how-tos" (i.e. how to come out; Croteau & Hedstrom, 1993; Pope & Schecter, 1992) to the "whys" (i.e. why come out; Brown, 1975; Driscoll et al., 1996; Hetherington C. et al., 1989), this issue has been part of both the professional and popular literature. Relevant interventions for college career counselors include:

- helping the student consider the advantages and disadvantages of coming out in the workplace (Belz, 1993; Brown, 1975; Croteau & Hedstrom, 1993; Elliott, 1993; Hetherington C. et al., 1989; Morgan & Brown, 1991; Pope, 1992; Pope et al., 1992; Pope & Schecter, 1992)
- giving information on how to go about coming out (Croteau & Hedstrom, 1993; Elliott, 1993; Pope & Schecter, 1992)

- publishing a list of "out" gay men or lesbians who would be available for informational interviews with clients (Belz, 1993; Croteau & Hedstrom, 1993; Hetherington C. et al., 1989);
- training clients in asking and responding to informational interview and job interview questions (Hetherington & Orzek, 1989)
- offering special programming to meet the career development needs of lesbians and gay men, including special programming on résumé writing (Elliott, 1993; Hetherington C., et al., 1989; Pope et al., 1992), interviewing (Hetherington C., et al., 1989; Pope et al., 1992), job fairs (Elliott, 1993; Hetherington et al., 1989), and support groups (Croteau & Hedstrom, 1993; Hetherington C., et al., 1989).

The Heterosexism Environmental Assessment

Learning how to construct affirming work environments is an important skill for any college student, but it is critical for gay and lesbian students who are seeking work for the first time, who want to change careers, or who have just come out to themselves and are now seeking answers to such questions (i.e., should I come out at work or how to come out at work) for the first time. The first part of such a skill is conducting an accurate "heterosexism environmental assessment" (Pope & Schecter, 1992).

In conducting a heterosexism environmental assessment, Pope and Schecter (1992) reported that the environment must be objectively observed and analyzed for actual clues to the general organizational climate (e.g., the corporate antidiscrimination statement; a gay and lesbian employees group; inclusive or exclusionary language—are only "wives and husbands" invited to events?), and the individual department's and other employees' attitudes toward sexual orientation issues (e.g., types of jokes that are told and tolerated, newspaper articles on the bulletin boards). The findings of this assessment can help the gay or lesbian student determine the degree of safety in the workplace.

As part of the heterosexism environmental assessment, it is important to discuss reasons for and against coming out with gay and lesbian college students who are seeking career counseling. Reasons to disclose one's sexual orientation to coworkers and the company include

- individual mental health reasons, because the most important reason (discussed earlier in Freedman, 1971) is the full integration of identity with behavior
- personal reasons, such as honesty, integration of sexuality into every aspect of life, recognition of who one is as a person, and support from peers
- professional, political, and societal reasons, such as providing a role model for other gay men and lesbians, desensitizing their coworkers and themselves about the issue, and eliminating any fear of blackmail

- practical reasons, such as domestic partnership benefits, being able to attend events with one's partner, and preventing the need for self-censorship and embarrassment in everyday conversation with coworkers.

Important reasons not to come out at work include

- the fear of harassment (either physical, or emotional)
- fear of the effect this disclosure may have on hiring, personnel, and advancement decisions (glass ceiling)
- fear of alienation, isolation, and rejection
- fear of being perceived as different from the majority culture or of being perceived as the same as every member of the minority culture
- fear of the invasion of privacy.

Most important, in conducting an accurate heterosexism environmental assessment, it is critical to determine if a student's fears are based on reality, on previous experiences, or on the person's own internalized homophobia. Fears, wherever they originate, must be faced, because they seem bigger if they are not confronted and discussed.

Fostering a Positive Career Identity

The purpose for the following suggestions and interventions is to prompt a discussion between the client and career counselor about factors that might block career interests from developing (Brown, 1975; Hetherington & Orzek, 1989). As with most students, career choices by gay men and lesbian women often are influenced by family and relationships. The gay or lesbian student, however, may bring to the career counselor examples of unique pressures or concerns. Family members may have rejected the gay or lesbian student and, consequently, also any chance to guide the student's career development. A career counselor often may be the first interested, positive, and encouraging role model for the student's career development.

Partners may play a significant role in the career decisions of gay or lesbian students. Especially complex may be situations in which one partner is out while the other remains "closeted." This situation may present conflicts about self-identity, privacy, and choice of career options. Referring gay or lesbian clients for couples' counseling may enhance interpersonal support for the client and his or her partner (Belz, 1993; Elliott, 1993; Eldridge, 1987; Hetherington et al., 1989; Morgan & Brown, 1991; Orzek, 1992). Additionally, couples' counseling may assist the gay or lesbian client to prepare for such questions as how to introduce one's partner to friends, colleagues, family, and employer and how to anticipate social situations as a couple (Hetherington et al., 1989). The issue of benefits for one's partner may be an important consideration for a gay or lesbian student anticipating a job offer. The career counselor can be help the client form relevant questions about domestic partnership benefits.

In some cases, a career counselor may want to explore with a gay or lesbian client why the client has chosen a career that appears to be stereotyped as safe for gay men and lesbians (Pope, 1995a). When a gay or lesbian student has been without a career role model, the career counselor can play a crucial role by referring the client to people who will speak to the student about such topics as career choice and being out in the workplace (Chung & Harmon, 1994; Elliott, 1993; Hetherington et al., 1989; Morgan & Brown, 1991; Pope & Schecter, 1992).

Career counselors can increase access to resources and role models for gay and lesbian students by offering special programs, such as discussion panels hosted by lesbian or gay professionals (Croteau & Hedstrom, 1993; Hetherington et al., 1989). Other useful interventions to familiarize gay and lesbian clients with career options include arranging career-shadowing opportunities with gay and lesbian professionals (Belz, 1993), facilitating externships or cooperative education placements in gay- and lesbian-owned or -operated businesses (Hetherington et al., 1989), and establishing mentoring programs (Elliott, 1993).

Improving Campus Climate

Sue, Arredondo, and McDavis (1992), as a component of multiculturally competent practice, advocated social action on behalf of clients that are underserved, underrepresented, and underpowered. Clearly, this call to action is paramount in creating more affirmative and inclusive academic environments for lesbian and gay students. Campus career professionals are in a unique and powerful position to create campus change and to advocate for the educational and career needs of lesbian and gay students. In fact, such advocacy and visibility on the part of campus career professionals is necessary to gain the trust of lesbian and gay clients.

Improving the campus climate for lesbian and gay students can take many forms and can range from small interventions, such as using inclusive language in advertisements of career services, to larger, campuswide efforts, such as initiating a campus committee aimed at revising a university's discriminatory policies in housing, employment, or benefits. Career services professionals often are the campus experts on issues that affect students' career development and academic progress. They are familiar with the literature related to the detrimental effects on career development and self-esteem of factors such as lack of role models, employment discrimination, and inadequate support structures. They also hear personal stories of lesbian and gay clients whose academic and career progress has been impaired through encounters with homophobic messages and interactions on campus.

The ways in which campus career development specialists can exert social change and improve the campus climate for lesbian and gay students are limited only by imagination and energy. For example, the focus can be on creating a visibly affirmative career service, or it can be on serving as consultant to the campus administrators. Whatever the emphasis, any efforts toward decreasing the invisibility and isolation of lesbian and gay students will help counteract even subtle discrimination. The following suggestions are provided as a stimulus to career counselors who are developing such efforts:

- Assist the campus in identifying lesbian and gay alumni who could provide mentorship and networking opportunities for lesbian and gay students.
- Create a campus network of student affairs professionals who are lesbian or gay, or who consider themselves allies, to facilitate referrals and provide needed support for lesbian and gay students.
- Advocate for campus domestic partner benefits and inclusive family housing, so that students receive affirming messages from campus administration.
- Provide and widely advertise career workshops and special career events specifically designed for lesbian and gay students' career and job-search concerns.
- Highlight lesbian- and gay-affirmative employers in career fairs.
- Demonstrate lesbian- and gay-friendly services by using inclusive language in all brochures, advertisements, and information-gathering forms.
- Offer panels of lesbians and gay men in the work force who can discuss their own career development strategies for dealing with job interviews, résumés, and work environments.
- Collaborate with faculty in lesbian and gay studies programs, gender studies programs, and other departments by offering in-class lectures related to the career concerns of lesbian and gay students.
- Assist in creating a gay, lesbian, bisexual, and transgender alumni association and faculty and staff association.
- Develop occupational information and employment collections relevant to the career concerns of lesbians and gay men.
- Do not assume that all students using your services are heterosexual.

Summary and Recommendations

College career counseling centers can offer a number of programs and services to promote advocacy, career success, and safety of the gay and lesbian student population. Important components of a comprehensive career counseling program include staff training in the areas of gay and lesbian developmental concerns, prevention of internal and external homophobia, and an understanding of the diversity within the gay and lesbian culture (Pope, 1995c; Worthington et al., 1998).

Professional career counselors can advocate for the cautious use of psychological tests with gay and lesbian students. Career counselors can modify career counseling tools to include topics relevant to gay and lesbian students, such as redesigning card sorts to include items addressing issues specific to lesbians and gay men (e.g., being out on the job; Belz, 1993).

Encouraging gay and lesbian students to attend stress management workshops or workshops where complex relationship issues affecting career choice can be discussed is another important role of the career counselor. Furthermore, career counselors can make available to students names of gay and lesbian professionals who are willing to discuss career issues unique to the gay and lesbian experience.

College career services centers can provide information on employment antidiscrimination laws and policies that protect gay and lesbian workers. Lists of gay and lesbian resources and community agencies are useful to students who need referrals (see Appendix 15-A).

Finally and most urgently, career counselors must accelerate efforts to provide a safe and welcoming environment on college campuses for gay and lesbian students. The recent tragic and violent murder in 1998 of Matthew Shepard, a gay college student in Wyoming, attests to the work yet to be done to ensure safety for every gay and lesbian college student and protection for exploring and finding their career path.

References

American Educational Research Association, American Psychological Association, & National Council on Measurement in Education. (1985). *Standards for educational and psychological testing* (3rd ed.). Washington, DC: American Psychological Association.

American Psychological Association, Joint Committee on Testing Practices. (1988). *Code of fair testing practices in education*. Washington, DC: Author.

Belz, J. R. (1993). Sexual orientation as a factor in career development. *Career Development Quarterly, 41*, 197–200.

Betz, N. E., & Fitzgerald, L. F. (1995). Career assessment and interventions with racial and ethnic minorities. In F. T. L. Leong (Ed.), *Career development and vocational behavior of racial and ethnic minorities* (pp. 263–279). Mahwah, NJ: Erlbaum.

Bieschke, K. J., & Matthews, C. (1996). Career counselor attitudes and behaviors toward gay, lesbian, and bisexual clients. *Journal of Vocational Behavior, 48*(2), 243–255.

Boatwright, K. J., Gilbert, M. S., Forrest, L., & Ketzenberger, K. (1996). Impact of identity development upon career trajectory: Listening to the voices of lesbian women. *Journal of Vocational Behavior, 48*(2), 210–228.

Brown, D. A. (1975). Career counseling for the homosexual. In R. D. Burack & R. C. Reardon (Eds.), *Facilitating career development* (pp. 234–247). Springfield, IL: Charles C. Thomas.

Buhrke, R. A., & Douce, L. A. (1991). Training issues for counseling psychologists in working with lesbians and gay men. *The Counseling Psychologist, 19*, 216–234.

Cass, V. C. (1979). Homosexual identity formation: A theoretical model. *Journal of Homosexuality, 7*, 219–235.

Chernin, J., Holden, J. M., & Chandler, C. (1997). Bias in psychological assessment: Heterosexism. *Measurement and Evaluation in Counseling and Development, 30*, 68–76.

Chung, Y. B. (1995). Career decision making of lesbian, gay, and bisexual individuals. *Career Development Quarterly, 44*, 178–190.

Chung, Y. B., & Harmon, L. W. (1994). The career interests and aspirations of gay men: How sex-role orientation is related. *Journal of Vocational Behavior, 45*, 223–239.

Croteau, J. M., & Hedstrom, S. M. (1993). Integrating commonality and difference: The key to career counseling with lesbian women and gay men. *Career Development Quarterly, 41*, 201–209.

D'Augelli, A. R. (1993). Preventing mental health problems among lesbian and gay college students. *Journal of Primary Prevention, 13*, 245–261.

Driscoll, J. M., Kelley, F. A., & Fassinger, R. E. (1996). Lesbian identity and disclosure in the workplace: Relation to occupational stress and satisfaction. *Journal of Vocational Behavior, 48*, 229–242.

Dunkle, J. H. (1996). Toward an integration of gay and lesbian identity development and Super's life-span approach. *Journal of Vocational Behavior, 48*, 149–159.

Edwards, A. L. (1959). *Edwards Personal Preference Schedule manual.* New York: The Psychological Corporation.

Eldridge, N. S. (1987). *Correlates of relation satisfaction and role conflict in dual-career lesbian couples.* Unpublished doctoral dissertation, University of Texas, Austin.

Elliott, J. E. (1993). Career development with lesbian and gay clients. *Career Development Quarterly, 41*, 210–226.

Etringer, B. D., Hillerbrand, E., & Hetherington, C. (1990). The influence of sexual orientation on career decision-making: A research note. *Journal of Homosexuality, 19*, 103–111.

Fassinger, R. E. (1991). The hidden minority: Issues and challenges in working with lesbian women and gay men. *The Counseling Psychologist, 19*, 157–176.

Fassinger, R. E. (1995). From invisibility to integration: Lesbian identity in the workplace. *Career Development Quarterly, 44*, 148–167.

Fassinger, R. E. (1996). Notes from the margins: Integrating lesbian experience into the vocational psychology of women. *Journal of Vocational Behavior, 48*, 160–175.

Freedman, M. (1971). *Homosexuality and psychological functioning.* Belmont, CA: Brooks/Cole.

Gelberg, S., & Chojnacki, J. T. (1995). Developmental transitions of gay/lesbian/bisexual-affirmative, heterosexual career counselors. *Career Development Quarterly, 43*, 267–273.

Gough, H. G. (1987). *California Psychological Inventory: Administrator's guide.* Palo Alto, CA: Consulting Psychologists Press.

Griffin, P. (1992). From hiding out to coming out: Empowering lesbian and gay educators. In K. M. Harbeck (Ed.), *Coming out of the classroom closet.* (pp. 167–196). Binghamton, NY: Harrington Park Press.

Harmon, L. W., Hansen, J.-I. C., Borgen, F. H., & Hammer, A. L. (1994). *Strong Interest Inventory application and technical guide.* Palo Alto, CA: Consulting Psychologists Press.

Hartung, P. J., Vandiver, B. J., Leong, F. T. L., Pope, M., Niles, S. G., & Farrow, B. (1998). Appraising cultural identity in career-development assessment and counseling. *Career Development Quarterly, 46*, 276–293.

Hathaway, S. R., McKinley, J. C., Butcher, J. N., Dahlstrom, W. W., Graham, J. R., Tellegen, A., & Kaemmer, B. (1989). *Manual for the restandardized Minnesota Multiphasic Personality Inventory: MMPI-2. An administrative and interpretive guide.* Minneapolis: University of Minnesota Press.

Hetherington, C., Hillerbrand, E., & Etringer, B. D. (1989). Career counseling with gay men: Issues and recommendations for research. *Journal of Counseling and Development, 67*, 452–454.

Hetherington, D., & Orzek, A. M. (1989). Career counseling and life planning with lesbian women. *Journal of Counseling and Development, 68*, 52–57.

Holland, J. L., Fritzsche, B. A., & Powell, A. B. (1994). *The Self-Directed Search professional user's guide.* Odessa, FL: Psychological Assessment Resources.

Mobley, M., & Slaney, R. B. (1996). Holland's theory: Its relevance for lesbian women and gay men. *Journal of Vocational Behavior, 48*, 125–135.

Morgan, K. S., & Brown, L. S. (1991). Lesbian career development, work behavior, and vocational counseling. *Counseling Psychologist, 19*, 273–291.

Myers, I. B., & McCaulley, M. H. (1985). *Manual: A guide to the development and use of the Myers-Briggs Type Indicator.* Palo Alto, CA: Consulting Psychologists Press.

Obear, K., & Reynolds, A. L. (1986). *Opening doors to acceptance and understanding: A facilitator's guide to presenting workshops on lesbian and gay issues.* Paper presented at the annual convention of the American College Personnel Association, San Francisco, CA.

Orzek, A. M. (1992). Career counseling for the gay and lesbian community. In S. Dworkin and F. Gutierrez (Eds.), *Counseling gay men and lesbians: Journey to the end of the rainbow* (pp. 23–34). Alexandria, VA: American Counseling Association.

Pope, M. (1992). Bias in the interpretation of psychological tests. In S. Dworkin and F. Gutierrez (Eds.), *Counseling gay men and lesbians: Journey to the end of the rainbow* (pp. 277–292). Alexandria, VA: American Counseling Association.

Pope, M. (1995a). Career interventions for gay and lesbian clients: A synopsis of practice knowledge and research needs. *Career Development Quarterly, 44*, 191–203.

Pope, M. (1995b). Gay and lesbian career development: Introduction to the special section. *Career Development Quarterly, 44*, 146–147.

Pope, M. (1995c). The "salad bowl" is big enough for us all: An argument for the inclusion of lesbians and gays in any definition of multiculturalism. *Journal of Counseling & Development, 73*, 301–304.

Pope, M., & Jelly, J. (1991). MBTI, sexual orientation, and career development [Summary]. *Proceedings of the 9th International Biennial Conference of the Association for Psychological Type, 9*, 231–238.

Pope, M., Rodriguez, S., & Chang, A. P. C. (1992, September). *Special issues in career development and planning for gay men.* Presented at the meeting of International Pacific Friends Societies, International Friendship Weekend 1992, San Francisco.

Pope, M., & Schecter, E. (1992, October). *Career strategies: Career suicide or career success.* Paper presented at the 2nd Annual Lesbian and Gay Workplace Issues Conference, Stanford University, Stanford, California.

Prince, J. P. (1995). Influences on the career development of gay men. *Career Development Quarterly, 44*, 168–177.

Prince, J. P. (1997a). Assessment bias affecting lesbian, gay male and bisexual individuals. *Measurement and Evaluation in Counseling and Development, 30*, 82–87.

Prince, J. P. (1997b). Career assessment with lesbian, gay and bisexual individuals. *Journal of Career Assessment, 5*, 225–238.

Schneider, B. E. (1987). Coming out at work: Bridging the private/public gap. *Work and Occupations, 13*, 463–487.

Sue, D. W., Arredondo, P., & McDavis, R. J. (1992). Multicultural counseling competencies and standards: A call to the profession. *Journal of Counseling & Development, 70*, 477–486.

Super, D. E. (1990). Career and life development. In D. Brown, L. Brooks, & Assoc. (Eds.), *Career choice and development* (2nd ed., pp. 192–234). San Francisco: Jossey-Bass.

Taylor, S. H., Borland, K. M., & Vaughters, S. D. (1998). Addressing the career needs of lesbian, gay, bisexual, and transgender college students. In R. Sanlo (Ed.), *Working with lesbian, gay, bisexual, and transgender college students: A handbook for faculty and administrators* (pp. 123–133). Westport, CT: Greenwood Press.

Walsh, W. B., & Betz, N. E. (1995). *Tests and assessment* (3rd ed.). Englewood Cliffs, NJ: Prentice-Hall.

Weinberg, G. H. (1971). *Society and the healthy homosexual.* New York: St. Martin's Press.

Worthington, R. L., McCrary, S. I., & Howard, K. A. (1998). Becoming an LGBT affirmative career adviser: Guidelines for faculty, staff, and administrators. In R. Sanlo (Ed.), *Working with lesbian, gay, bisexual, and transgender college students: A handbook for faculty and administrators* (pp. 135–143). Westport, CT: Greenwood Press.

Appendix 15-A: Gay and Lesbian Resources for Career Services Center

Baker, D., & Strub, S. (1993). *Cracking the corporate closet*. New York: Harper Collins.

Blount, J. M. (1996). Manly men and womanly women: Deviance, gender role polarization, and the shift in women's school employment, 1900–1976. *Harvard Educational Review, 66*, 318–338.

Croteau, J. M., & Bieschke, K. J. (Eds.). (1996). Beyond pioneering: An introduction to the special issue on the vocational issues of lesbian women and gay men [Special Issue]. *Journal of Vocational Behavior, 48*, 119–124.

Diamant, L. (Ed.). (1993). *Homosexual issues in the workplace*. Washington, DC: Taylor & Francis.

Friskopp, A., & Silverstein, S. (1995). *Straight jobs, gay lives: Gay and lesbian professionals, the Harvard Business School, and the American workplace*. New York: Scribner.

Harbeck, K. M. (Ed.). (1992). *Coming out of the classroom closet: Gay and lesbian students, teachers and curricula*. Harrington Park, MD: Harrington Park Press.

McNaught, B. (1993). *Gay issues in the workplace*. New York: St. Martin's Press.

Mickens, E. (1994). *The 100 best companies for gay men and lesbians*. New York: Simon & Schuster.

Pope, M. (Ed.). (1995). Gay and lesbian career development: Introduction to the special section [Special section]. *Career Development Quarterly 44*, 146–147.

Rasi, R. A., & Rodriguez-Nogues, L. (Eds.). (1995). *Out in the workplace*. Los Angeles: Alyson Publications.

Sanlo, R. (Ed.). (1998). *Working with lesbian, gay, bisexual, and transgender college students: A handbook for faculty and administrators*. Westport, CT: Greenwood Press.

Woods, J. D., & Lucas, J. H. (1993). *The corporate closet: The professional lives of gay men in America*. New York: Free Press.

Part IV

Professional Issues and Future Directions

16

Toward the Development of Systematic Career Guidance

Edward Anthony Colozzi

How can career services providers cost-effectively address the career development needs of students pursuing postsecondary education? What are the components of a systematic career guidance program that are supported by theory and practice? How can career services providers better justify their programs, even their own positions, in the context of frequent scrutiny for increased accountability and impending budget reductions? Are there implications for an "emergent role" in the way that these providers will need to approach their responsibilities? This chapter seeks to answer these questions by presenting a "blueprint in formation" for a theory-based, systematic career guidance approach for use in college and university settings. It is the intention of this chapter not to present an evaluation of a current program but rather to draw on the observations of past experiences and research to inform this working blueprint. The chapter includes a discussion of the theory behind this approach as well as National Occupational Information Coordinating Committee (NOICC)-based guidelines that support systematic career guidance. A formula to determine the base cost per contact hour of staff and technology interventions is described to assist career services providers in their planning efforts to establish such a model and for use with budget justification of career services to college and university administrators.

The Problem

Improving school-to-work transitions has become a priority for society. Career development has emerged as a vital connecting activity as stakeholders strive to build successful models to facilitate the transition into employment for millions of high school, college, and university students (Elmhirst et al., 1994; Hoyt & Lester, 1995). Career development must involve realistic and deliberate goal setting in the context of current and projected economic environments (Bloch, 1996; Herr, 1996). Student pop-

I would like to thank JoAnn Bowlsbey for her encouragement and early suggestions for this chapter.

ulations in colleges and universities are dramatically changing, and career deciders are entering higher education institutions already engaged in a variety of life roles (Levine & Cureton, 1998). These deciders often require assistance with the career development process.

Many secondary school counselors spend much of their time counseling students with critical personal problems, reducing the time available for dealing with career development issues (Conger, Hiebert, & Hong-Farrell, 1994; Hoyt & Hughey, 1995). These unmet career development needs of high school students carry over to the college environment. Considerable amounts of refocusing or refinement of career thinking is occurring throughout the college years (Pascarella & Terenzini, 1991). Adult learners returning to higher education also have a multitude of career and life needs, including easy access to labor market information and assistance with career decision-making (Hoyt & Lester, 1995). College counseling and career service centers increasingly acknowledge responsibility for responding to all students on campus. However, budget reductions are making personnel increases unlikely, and the demand for services can overwhelm staff who strive to do preventative, developmental work in addition to dealing with the increased focus on retention, outcome assessment, and an increasingly diverse population (Dean & Meadows, 1995).

With so many students requiring assistance, it is appropriate and responsible to examine what career services are provided, how they are delivered, and how they contribute to student learning, personal development, student success, the academic mission of institutions, and societal expectations concerning "human capital" needs (Helfgot & Culp, 1995; Upcraft & Schuh, 1996). Being clear about program goals, strategies for creating optimal learning environments that promote intentional career development, and the important role of outcomes assessment can facilitate the justification of career services to administrators who make budget decisions (Schroeder & Hurst, 1996).

A Possible Solution

A number of career interventions have been described throughout this book. Individual counseling has been viewed as the most efficient career intervention in terms of "amount of gain per hour of effort" (Spokane, 1991) and described as "the most effective" treatment modality on the basis of a recent meta-analyses (Sexton, Whiston, Bleuer, & Walz, 1997). Because of its reliance on a therapeutic alliance, individual counseling also has been characterized as a "superior" career intervention that should be available in comprehensive career centers (Rayman, 1996). Yet, career services providers must balance students' needs for certain types of career services with the reality of the need for cost-effective interventions. A possible solution is to consider combining approaches to create a theory-based design that is both cost-effective and meets the needs of many students (Sexton et al., 1997). Integrating a variety of strategies into a multimode, systematic approach that balances 21st-century technology with group and self-paced work and provides individual counseling when appropriate may assist overburdened centers and staff (Super, Bowlsbey, & Colozzi, 1985).

This approach—*systematic career guidance* (SCG)—combines, organizes, and integrates a variety of delivery modes to allow for individual differences and preferences and is designed to serve many students cost-effectively while meeting their individual needs. The metaphor of a college campus dining facility helps describe the SCG approach. If a college attempted to feed its many students by having them all wait in line for an appointment to meet with one or perhaps several short-order chefs, who would take individual orders, prepare them, and serve the meals directly to each student, the efficiency of the operation would be questioned. Instead, organizing a variety of food stations in a central location would facilitate individual preferences of students and allow more students to eat during the high-demand eating hours. Additionally, the entire operation could be carefully designed to provide self-service areas, special short-order stations for items requiring some preparation from attendants who are not chefs, and even a specialty-food section with a sous chef to provide individual, customized service. Ideally, a sufficient variety of fresh foods and beverages would be available, along with a means of allowing students to explore alternatives, purchase what they need, and exit in a way that efficiently and quickly assessed each student's selection, charged them accordingly, and moved them forward into the dining area, where they could eat at their leisure and even return for more food or dessert if they desired (i.e., "minicycle"; Super, Savickas, & Super, 1996). This design would efficiently satisfy students' nourishment needs and also help support an institutional educational mission that may relate to facilitating the learning and socialization activities that take place during lunch and dinner.

Likewise, meeting the career development needs of many college students can be addressed through SCG, a creative, cost-effective, systematic approach that combines, organizes, and integrates a variety of delivery modes and allows for individual differences and student preferences. This approach would include structured group sessions with professionals; independent, self-paced activities; and contact with peer paraprofessionals as well as sufficient opportunity for individual counseling where appropriate. The roots of SCG are influenced by the author's experiences with "group delivery" of career counseling during 1977 and 1978, his development of career exploration programs for college women in transition, and his role in the development of a statewide computerized career information system as coordinator of Leeward Community College's Career Development Center (Colozzi, 1981).

During the first year of the pilot period of the computerized career information system, nearly 700 students accessed the system. Early on, the use of paraprofessionals and small-group work had been introduced to help meet the large student demand for career counseling. Although individual career counseling was still provided for most students, the need for creative group interventions was apparent. Individual students and small groups were provided with "off-line" interventions to prepare them for their interaction with the career information system, and a variety of career guidance activities were successfully integrated with regular classroom instruction, at-risk and special-needs students, and entering freshmen (Colozzi & Haehnlen, 1982). However, SCG, as presented in this chapter, had not yet fully evolved and is only now being articulated as an approach that may alleviate the high counselor–student ratios that exist on many campuses. SGC is based on conceptual linkages among select theories of career development and the NOICC's *National Career Development Guidelines* (1989; Brown, 1995; Holland, 1973; Lent, Brown, & Hackett, 1996; Mitchell & Krumboltz, 1996; Super, 1957; Super et al., 1996).

Systematic Career Guidance

A suggested student activity flow (Figure 16.1) describes student, counselor, and paraprofessional interface activities, including the use of computer-assisted career guidance systems (CACGSs) and select self-paced resources. Following this discussion, a formula is presented to illustrate the cost-effectiveness of an SCG approach and a cost analysis of the various steps (Figure 16.2). This formula facilitates institutional assessment of the cost-effectiveness of local career guidance interventions and can help justify career services programs. Referring to both figures throughout this discussion will help readers gain a sense of the student flow and the various interventions described.

Serving Students Differently

Designing an SCG approach can provide a cost-effective way to meet the varied learning styles of today's diverse college populations. All students with career-related needs are encouraged by the college to go through a coordinated process and assume an active and personal involvement with the career development process, such as attending group orientations about the career development process, learning about the World-of-Work map (ACT, 1996; see Figure 16.1, Step 1), participating and sharing in a group exercise to determine one's Holland-type personality code (Holland, 1973), and discussing personal difficulties and stresses associated with procrastination and decision making (see Figure 16.1, Steps 3 and 7). The intention is to encourage student investment of the time and energy necessary to bring about the desired learning and development. Consequently, SCG focuses on the behavioral mechanisms or processes that facilitate student development—the *how* of student development (Astin, 1984)—and emphasizes the active participation of students in their own learning processes.

The activities of the SCG approach can be varied to accommodate learning styles and provide many opportunities for peer interaction, es-

SYSTEMATIC CAREER GUIDANCE (SCG)
(A Seven Step Process)

START AT STEP 1.

STEP 1: INTAKE SESSION with GROUP and PROFESSIONAL STAFF

Meet with your counselor to discuss your goals, interests, and experiences. Participate in your introduction to an enjoyable and guided career/life exploration and planning process that is self-paced and designed to fit your personal class schedule.

STEP 2: SELF-PACED EXPLORATION

Learn more about the career development process. Try out some easy exercises and take some inventories that will help you understand your personality type and where you fit in the world of work. Ask your peer counselors for assistance as needed, and remember to go at your own pace!

STEP 3: REVIEW with GROUP and PROFESSIONAL STAFF

Meet again with your counselor and group to learn how your personality type matches certain occupations in the world of work. Discover how your interests relate to the courses or a major you are taking now or may want to take next semester.

STEP 4: EXPLORING with SUPPORT STAFF

Browse through our Occupational Summaries to discover what matches your personality type and select your favorite choices for more exploration. Your peer counselors are available to assist you throughout this process.

STEP 5: DETAILED EXPLORATION with SUPPORT STAFF

Explore and use the many resources available, including our computer guidance system, to help you discover more detailed and useful information about your favorite choices including salary, educational or training requirements, and job outlook. Use these resources alone or with staff assistance as needed.

STEP 6: SELF REVIEW and SUMMARY

Use your Career/Life Summary Plan to record and summarize the information you have learned about yourself and the world of work. Bring this to *STEP 7* and save it for future reference. Visit with your peer counselors for assistance as you prepare your Summary Plan, and return to any *STEPS* as needed.

STEP 7: FINAL GROUP REVIEW and PLANNING with PROFESSIONAL

Share your Career/Life Summary Plan with your counselor. Now that you are more focused, you can start planning your next steps, including the best courses for next semester. Continue to "mini-cycle" back to the *STEPS* and use our services as needed!

Exploration Mini-cycles

(Individual Counseling by Referral)

Note: Edward Anthony Colozzi © 1985, rev. 1995, 1996, 1998, 1999

Figure 16.1.   Systematic career guidance.

STEP 1: Intake Session With Professional Staff

P (1 hour Group/2 hours Preparation); STS (1 hour)
Intake Interview–Career Development Overview; initiation of self-assessment process and setting of career/life counseling goals.
COST = $10 ABC (group of 6)

STEP 2: Self-Paced Career/Life Exploration

STS (3–4 hours)
Self-paced career exploration materials/interest inventories/other assessment.
COST = $0 ABC (self-paced)

STEP 3: Review With Professional Staff

P (1 hour Group/2 hours Preparation); STS (1 hour)
Review and discussion of self-paced materials.
COST = $10 ABC (group of 6)

ABC = Actual Base Cost per contact hour

To compute the ABC cost, divide the hourly costs (including fringe benefits) of professional and support staff, plus appropriate preparation time, plus the hourly cost of technology used, by the average number of clients serviced per hour.

STEP 7: Final Review and Planning With Professional Staff

P (1 hour Group/2 hours Preparation); STS (1 hour)
Counselor and students meet for summary session.
COST = $10 ABC (group of 6)

STEP 6: Self-Review and Summary

STS (3–4 hours)
Students do homework and integrate occupational/educational information into self-paced materials.
COST = $0 ABC (self-paced)

STEP 5: Detailed Exploration With Support Staff

S (10–15 minutes); T (1 hour); STS (2–3 hours)
Students obtain detailed occupational/educational information using staff and available technology.
COST = (S) $1.50 + (T) $.75 or $2.25 ABC

STEP 4: Browsing With Support Staff

S (10–15 minutes); STS (1–2 hours)
Students (groups of 4–6) browse self-paced occupational information.
COST = $1.50 ABC

KEY:

P = Professional   ($20.00 hourly cost includes fringe benefits)
S = Support Staff   ($7.00 hourly cost for paraprofessionals)
T = Technology   ($1.50 hourly cost after first year)
STS = Students

Note: Edward Anthony Colozzi © 1985, rev. 1995, 1996, 1998, 1999

Figure 16.2. Cost analysis of systematic career guidance.

pecially with peer paraprofessionals (see Figure 16.1, Steps 4 and 5). This type of peer-group interaction is especially effective because it has the capacity to involve the student more intensely in the educational experience. Longitudinal research shows that peer-group involvement is the strongest source of influence on cognitive and affective student development (Astin, 1996). Because most peer groups operate primarily outside formal classroom settings, co-curricular career exploration activities in an SCG context provide a natural setting that encourages significant peer group involvement. Individual career counseling can supplement SCG, but it is not relied on as a primary intervention. It is available for students at any time on a referral basis (see Figure 16.1).

Evidence shows that undecided students can be divided into multiple subtypes, each responding to different career interventions (Larson, Heppner, Ham, & Dugan, 1988). Consequently, more thorough examination of subtypes may be necessary before any real progress can be made in developing treatment interventions. The various interventions proposed in Larson et al.'s study as suitable for the subtypes ranged from more structured and extensive learning situations combined with personal counseling to self-directed interventions, such as resource libraries, self-scored interest assessments, computerized programs, and brief workshops. An SCG intervention could accommodate multiple subtypes by using multidimensional scales capable of distinguishing among the subtypes (Savickas, 1995) and referring students to the most suitable intervention activities before the intake session (see Figure 16.1). At any time during this exploration-rich environment, a student may "minicycle" back to any previous step (see Figure 16.1), including receiving individual counseling when appropriate. This approach encourages *involved exploration* and is adaptive to students' needs throughout the process.

A critical component of SCG is the use of the intake session (see Figure 16.1, Step 1) to elicit a student's career concerns, collect important demographic measures, and provide an engaging overview of the career exploration and planning process. The overview can be accomplished through a brief (7- to 10-minute) video presentation and supplemented with appropriate attributional retraining concepts for students who exhibit, for example, an external career locus of control (Luzzo, Funk, & Strang, 1996). Large-group intake sessions (40–50 students) easily are managed with a minimum of two paraprofessional staff and usually take approximately 90 minutes.

Ideally, measures of different dimensions of students' career development can be completed before the intake session (Osborne, Brown, Niles, & Miner, 1997), such as during a college orientation activity. Student assessment occurs throughout the SCG process, and the use of self-paced resources, inventories, tests, guided imagery, CACGSs, and various multimedia technologies helps students develop and accept an integrated picture of themselves and their life roles. SCG is a task-focused approach that is preferred by students (Galassi et al., 1992 as cited in Sexton et al., 1997).

Learning and Learning Environments

At the core of SCG is the creation of an optimal learning environment characterized by specific conditions aimed at enhancing student learning and personal development. The opportunity for students to sit together in small peer groups with a professional counselor (Figure 16.1, Steps 1, 3, and 7) and discuss various topics, sharing with and listening to each other as they experience the journey together, helps foster the conditions that are key to student learning. These conditions are reinforced when students return to the career center for self-paced browsing or access to a CACGS with assistance from paraprofessionals (Figure 16.1, Steps 4, 5, and 6). Students' active engagement in challenging activities in the context of a support structure that provides prompt, concrete, and detailed feedback focused on modifiable behavior results in learning that can be integrated with curricular and co-curricular experiences (Blocher, 1978 as cited in Schroeder & Hurst, 1996). Interventions that encourage such interactions may provide a suitable environment for acquiring and modifying career self-efficacy beliefs (Lent & Hackett, 1987) and promoting values clarification (Colozzi & Haehnlen, 1982).

Outcomes Assessment

The important role of outcomes assessment in career center operations helps connect what career services providers do with how they contribute to the academic enterprise (Upcraft & Schuh, 1996). Determining the effectiveness of an intervention such as SCG is an important task that can be accomplished using an appropriate outcomes assessment process (Terenzini & Upcraft, 1996). The design of the assessment process depends on the intended goal of the career intervention (Sexton et al., 1997). Is the goal of the intervention to help a client choose a career or become more certain about his or her career choice? Or are the intended goals to reduce the anxiety of students as they deal with career exploration *and* promote and support student learning and success in the classroom? At a basic level, students' use of services can be tracked, or a college can assess student needs to determine the match between needs assessment results and available services.

The Program in Action

The following SCG scenario and discussion illustrates the benefits associated with an SCG approach.

Patrika, Rosaria, Dumar, and Marc are new students at Somewhere University and have been there for 3 weeks. Patrika is 19 and Rosaria is 45. Both are immigrants from different countries and have become friends since they met standing in the registration line. Patrika is unemployed, lives with her single-parent mother, and is the oldest of three sisters and one infant brother. She helps her mother with raising the family and homemaking chores. She is enrolled in four classes. Rosaria is a married mother of three children, the youngest of which is a high school sophomore. She works part-time and is enrolled in three classes, including one evening class. Dumar is 34 and unmarried, works full-time, and lives alone in a small apartment. He is enrolled in two classes. Marc is 23, works part-time, lives with his parents, and is enrolled in four classes. All are undecided about a college major, lack career goals, and need career counseling. All are focused on their courses and view college as a means of increasing their career mobility and obtaining a better job; none sought career services as entering students.

Ideally, if the four students were enrolled at a college that did not have an SCG program but that provided effective individual career counseling and sufficient outreach activities to attract the attention of students needing career services, some of them would most likely experience several sessions of individual career counseling and testing, combined with self-paced browsing of various resources, including a CACGS. There would be time for follow-up discussions, and some of the students would enroll in a career exploration course or participate in a small-group workshop.

What is more likely is that as the career services staff experiences an increase in student demand for services as the semester progresses, the waiting period for new students desiring to obtain these services will increase, as will the delay between appointment times for returning students. Some students might lose interest and terminate their counseling; others will become discouraged by the campus gossip regarding perceived difficulties associated with obtaining services and will never seek career counseling. In short, only some of the students will have their career counseling needs met.

Likewise, the same four students seeking services at a college that does not have an SCG program and does not provide effective individual career counseling and outreach activities will most likely experience frustration and disappointment. Some will graduate and be unaware of the services they never experienced until later, as they encounter career transitions and reflect on their past decision-making processes. Chapter 4 provides some reflections by clients who did not receive career counseling when they needed it as students.

In this context, it may be helpful to refer to Figure 16.1 and imagine how these four students might interact with a college career center that does have an SCG program. During new-student orientation, all four students would be exposed to an entertaining and engaging brief video that introduced career services staff and described career services at the university. They would have the opportunity to indicate their lack of career goals in a safe environment and would have an understanding early in their college experience of how to use career services to explore alternatives and narrow options. They would learn about SCG through this video and receive directions on how to initially sign up for an intake session before leaving the new student orientation.

Patrika, Rosaria, and Dumar might decide to sign up for the intake designed for students wanting a multicultural orientation. Rosaria and

Dumar could sign up for the intake geared to adults in transition, during which the counselor would tailor the intake agenda to match the content and examples to the actual concerns of older students (Arthur, 1998). Patrika and Marc might run into each other in a similar group of younger deciders. All the students would move onto the second step, "self-paced exploration," and have the opportunity to interact with peer counselors when assistance is needed. Even if Patrika and Rosaria had selected different intake sessions on the basis of their ages, they could meet at the career services center (Steps 2, 4, 5, and 6), where they could share their experiences and renew their friendship and support for each other as they participate in the process.

If Dumar and Rosaria miss Step 3 because of their work schedules, a sufficient ongoing series of Step 1, 3, and 7 groups will be taking place to meet student demand, making it relatively easy to minicycle throughout the process. All of the students can experience Steps 4, 5, and 6 at their convenience, visiting with support staff as needed to accomplish their exploration activities. All the students may meet at Step 7 to share their insights and begin academic advising. They may complete the process at different times; some may even choose to minicycle back to a previous step that facilitates their exploration. If needed, individual counseling is available and facilitated by referral from paraprofessional staff. Even if Rosaria left school for a semester because of work and family demands, her records would be available when she returned and she could start at whatever step most facilitated her career exploration, including Step 1.

Because an SCG approach does not rely on individual career counseling as the primary intervention, career services staff focus on small groups, as indicated in Figure 16.1. Through small-group interaction, students can discuss and reflect on their career journey, deal effectively with feelings (e.g., anxiety, helplessness, or confusion), and receive feedback and encouragement from professionals and peers. Considering the major effect of peer influence on cognitive and affective development (Astin, 1996), such structured group interactions are important and may contribute to the modification of career self-efficacy beliefs (Lent & Brown, 1996). The SCG model also provides a cost-effective approach to the delivery of career services, which is critical to the justification of career services programs.

Reaching More Students Cost-Effectively

To facilitate institutional assessment of the cost-effectiveness of the various interventions used in an SCG approach, a fairly simple and logical formula (Equation 16.1) was developed to determine the base cost per contact hour of interventions. Termed *actual base cost* per contact hour (ABC), the institution's ABC is the hourly cost of professional (P) and support (S) staff, including the estimated percentage of their fringe benefits (f) package ($Pf + Sf$) plus the hourly cost of technology (T) used in the intervention process (excluding any start-up costs), plus the hourly cost of appropriate professional staff preparation time [pt] divided by the average number of clients serviced per hour (C):

$$ABC = \frac{Pf + Sf + T + pt}{C} \qquad (16.1)$$

To calculate an estimated median ABC rate as a way of demonstrating the cost-effectiveness of the SCG approach, the estimated median hourly rate of counselors is used here. To calculate this rate, the national median annual earnings for professional counselors was obtained from the *Occupational Outlook Handbook* (U.S. Department of Labor, 1998, p. 172). The reported median annual earnings (*Mdn* = $35,800) was then divided by 52 (weeks per year) and by 40 (hours per week) to arrive at the $17.20 per hour rate. To this figure was added $2.92 (or 17%), representing a modest fringe benefits package available at most colleges and university settings, thus totaling $20.12 and rounded to $20 as the estimated national median hourly earnings for counselors. (To calculate the actual cost for personnel at a local institution, merely substitute the actual annual salary and benefits package percentage in lieu of the national median annual earnings and fringe benefits used here.)

The *ABC* of a counselor working with a student for 1 hour in a traditional individual-based approach (including 1 hour of preparation time before or following the counseling session) without support staff or a CACGS is estimated to be $40 ($20/hr × 2 hours). Because individual counseling is the most effective treatment modality, and because "career counseling will be more effective if it is longer and involves more sessions" (Sexton et al., 1997, p. 107), if one counselor sees a client for the minimum recommended 10 hour-long sessions, it costs the institution approximately $400 to serve that student ($40/hour [including preparation time] × 10 hours = $400). Traditional individual-based career counseling approaches are costly to an institution and less able to meet the demands of the large numbers of students.

For approximately $360, a savings of $40 that can be applied to paraprofessional and technology costs, that same professional counselor providing career counseling in an SCG approach (see Figure 16.2, Steps 1, 3, and 7), can service up to 12 students (two group cycles of 6 students). This calculation assumes that the counselor spends a total of 3 hours with each group (1 hour each at Steps 1, 3, and 7), and has 2 additional preparation hours for each of the contact hours with students in the two groups. This effort adds up to 6 contact hours for the time spent with the two groups plus the additional 12 hours of preparation time multiplied by $20, or 18 hours × $20/hr totaling $360. In the SCG environment, the individual counselor works with two groups of 6 students, or 12 students, not 1 individual student. This translates into a 1,200% increase in the institution's ability to cost-effectively provide services to the large number of students who may require career counseling interventions and who, with a traditional individual-based approach, might not be adequately served. Put another way, using counseling staff in the context of SCG reduces the $40 *ABC* (in a traditional approach) by 75% to a $10 *ABC* (in an SCG approach) and potentially increases the number of students cost-effectively served 12-fold.

Technology and Support Staff Costs

Additional minimal costs of approximately $25 (see Figure 16.2, Steps 4 and 5) include support staff (paraprofessionals or career assistants) and CACGS costs (excluding computer start-up costs). The hourly rate of pay for support peer paraprofessional staff was calculated to be approximately $7/hour, an amount that was based on prevailing rates of pay offered by most institutions using federal financial aid guidelines. To calculate an approximate average cost per hour of technology used in the intervention process, an analysis of costs of 12 CACGs revealed the mean cost to be $1,390 (Sampson et al., 1994). Assuming 6 uses per day for 200 days to-taling a minimum of 1,200 uses in 1 year (Bowlsbey, n.d.), the *ABC* for technology would be $1.16. An analysis of comparison costs of the five most expensive systems revealed the mean cost to be $1,822. Assuming 1,200 annual uses, the *ABC* for the most expensive systems would be approxi-mately $1.50 and would drop to $0.75 with 2,400 annual uses.

A higher rate of use of technology occurs in an SCG approach, which facilitates increased student access to detailed occupational and educa-tional information (see Figure 16.2, Step 5) without the student actually having to spend time online, unlike the traditional practice of full student interaction with a CACGS. Career assistants or paraprofessionals can quickly provide students requesting specific occupational and educational information with the necessary computer printouts without taking up val-uable time of either the student or the CACGS. Once the information is obtained from the CACGS, it can be placed in a designated file or other appropriate area in the career center from which students can easily re-trieve the requested information. This practice frees the sophisticated technology for students who may require full interaction with the system. This cost-effective use of proven cost-effective technology provides addi-tional efficiency to the CACGS, enhancing optimal use of resources. The role of paraprofessionals is crucial in an SCG approach, and regularly scheduled training and dialogue with professional staff can ensure the highest quality of service to all students.

Implementation Issues

Possible obstacles that could hinder the implementation of SCG include ignorance or fear-based resistance from members of the general college community or the counseling staff, who may not comprehend the overall mission and goals of career services and therefore not perceive the rele-vance for a systematic approach to reaching more students. Counselors who wish to implement SCG may have to deal with teaching faculty, ad-ministrative and support staff, the college president, members of the board of trustees, fellow counselors, and even the dean of students. A limited vision regarding the institutional and student benefits of a proactive and responsive career services program may result in an incorrect perception of an "aggressive" career staff intending simply to increase its budget allocation and resources at the expense of other departments. Informed dialogue to impart accurate information can serve as an effective public relations vehicle to win over skeptics. Some may have the attitude of "Why fix it if it's not broken?" and may require additional needs assessment data, clearly presented in user-friendly formats, to more fully understand students' needs for career services and the need for a cost-effective approach.

The Counselor–Coordinator Role

Some career counselors may be concerned that an SCG approach will reduce their individual counseling appointments and change their job tasks in ways that would involve more group presentations, causing them some discomfort. This is an accurate concern, because the amount of time dedicated to individual career counseling will decrease in an SCG approach, whereas time for structured group presentations will increase. A main goal of SCG is to do things differently to cost-effectively increase needed services. Counselors will need to adapt from thinking in terms of individual career counseling to thinking in terms of institutional needs; they also will need to ensure that the services they provide will promote student learning in the classroom and overall student success. In this way, they will take on the role of counselor–coordinator.

Counselor–coordinators will need to learn how to creatively collaborate with other staff and departments and manage, coordinate, and interface their career services programs throughout the college environment. Staff development activities, resources, budgets, outcomes assessment, and student usage must be justified to the general college community— more specifically, to the chief student affairs officers, who will have to defend requested budgets at upper-level staff meetings. In short, an SCG approach calls for resolve among diverse players within the college community to provide needed services more cost-effectively.

Problems Inherent in Meeting Critical Needs

Student Involvement

Getting students' attention can be a major hurdle. Motivating them to engage in career planning work is critical, particularly for students engaged in multiple roles, such as those who are employed part-time or full-time, parents of young children, or caregivers for elderly parents. The availability of career programs and services is no guarantee that those most in need will seek them out. The NCDA [National Career Development Association] Gallup Survey (Hoyt & Lester, 1995) indicated that only 17% of adults reported using a career information center in a community college or in a four-year college or university. An even more surprising result is that fewer than 7% reported ever using a computerized career information system in any setting to obtain career or job information. It is important to identify students with unmet needs and aggressively solicit their participation in career planning, exploring, and decision-making activities, especially those who may be unlikely to seek assistance without external support and encouragement (Hess & Winston, 1995). Unfocused advertising of programs does not appear to attract students with the most need. The challenge is to involve students when they are ready to be engaged and to continually develop ways to generate a sense of urgency in other students by creating conditions in which students become willing participants ready to self-engage.

Changing Student Population

Schroeder (1996) noted how higher education is in the midst of a major transformation involving shifting demographics, changing economic agendas, eroding public confidence, demands for accountability, and increasingly diverse student populations. In an extensive review of American higher education, Levine and Cureton (1998) described how the largest recent change in higher education is in who the students are: Fewer than one in six of current undergraduates fit the traditional stereotype of the American college student (i.e., ages 18–22, enrolled full-time, and living on campus). Their investigation helps illuminate the reality that for many undergraduates, college is not the most important of the numerous activities that take up their time and energy. Indeed, students increasingly are bringing to colleges and universities exactly the same consumer expectations for quality, service, and cost that they have for other commercial enterprises. Research findings indicate that students are less well prepared for college academically: In the past decade, the proportion of students requiring remedial or developmental education at two-year (81%) and four-year (64%) colleges has grown (Levine & Cureton, 1998). Amid all the change, students' career needs must be met.

A Call for Change

Colleges and Career Development

Secondary school students' needs for career guidance remain largely unmet (Herr & Cramer, 1996), and they bring their needs to the college environment. Half of all undergraduates in colleges and universities are estimated to need some form of career assistance. Colleges have long been seen as one of the most important single agents of career development (Super, 1957) and are challenged to get on track and prepare undergraduates for the realities of life and the world in which they will live (Levine & Cureton, 1998). Fiscal constraints and limitations in U.S. colleges and universities today are perhaps only too familiar as institutions attempt to provide career interventions to large numbers of deciders. As Super (1957) noted more than 40 years ago, career development needs are not going to be properly met with the handicap of a limited philosophy or limited staff and resources.

Encouraging Committed Career Exploration

Practitioners and researchers have been encouraged to examine the efficacy of combined approaches that may be both cost-effective and highly productive (Sexton et al., 1997). The reality is that career services providers have their hands full. Many colleges offer career planning courses and provide workshops to reach the many students with career planning needs, yet the prevailing treatment modality remains "career counseling by appointment," a familiar, comfortable, and proven intervention. Some of the many deciders in colleges and universities may enroll for a career planning class; some may attend a workshop, visit the career center, browse occupational information, or even use a CACGS; and some may even take time to make an appointment for career counseling. Yet most deciders will probably experience their college years without spending sufficient time and energy in "committed" career exploration activities. Committed career exploration activities consist of all activities, whether spontaneous or planned, that have as their prime objective thorough and honest self-exploration and reflection, especially with regard to work, life roles, and education or training. The goal is to discover one's calling (see chapter 4 of this book), or at least specific avenues of work that most satisfactorily match one's interests, values, and abilities. Committed career exploration activities include the development of a realistic action plan that moves one closer to specific career and life goals (with timelines and contingency plans for adapting to inevitable changes), with a clear understanding of the relevance of one's present and planned educational curriculum to achieving those goals.

This definition reflects an attitude and set of behaviors that can be learned, modeled, and encouraged in a variety of ways (e.g., through new-student orientation sessions, workshops, short videos, a personal welcome letter from the dean of students, or even a spontaneous discussion between a counselor or faculty member and a student). The challenge is to create conditions in which most students not involved in committed career exploration activities will choose to become eager participants, active learners and navigators in their own journeys. Considering the major effects of peer influence on cognitive and affective development (Astin, 1996), especially in the context of discussions about sources of efficacy information, such as vicarious learning and social persuasion (Hackett & Byars, 1996; Lent et al., 1996), the wisdom of relying primarily on individual career interventions at colleges and universities experiencing large student demand needs to be carefully examined.

The realities of an increasingly diverse student body, especially in the context of increased accountability and budget restrictions, contribute to the need for a thorough understanding of what works best, produces the most gain, and helps the largest number of students. Although career services providers face the challenge of assessing current programs and delivering more cost-effective services, the outcome does not necessarily mean doing less with less. Rather, the challenge is to do things differently and cost-effectively—to create new ways of thinking while thinking about new ways of creating.

Supporting Theory and NOICC Guidelines

Supporting Theory

If fundamental career counseling goals are to help students (a) develop and accept an integrated and adequate picture of themselves and the life roles that they experience (i.e., self-concept), (b) test that self-concept against reality, and (c) implement the self-concept in ways that are personally satisfying and beneficial to society (Super, 1957), interventions need to be designed as flexible, continual, and sometimes cyclical activities that serve diverse students who are experiencing changes and making choices about their lives. The cyclical use of nondirective and directive counseling methods described by Super (1957) can be creatively applied throughout the SCG process facilitating

1. nondirective problem exploration and self-concept portrayal;
2. directive topic setting, for further exploration;
3. nondirective reflection and clarification of feeling for self-acceptance and insight;
4. directive exploration of factual data from tests, occupational pamphlets, extracurricular experiences, grades, etc., for reality testing;
5. nondirective exploration and working through of attitudes and feelings aroused by reality testing; and
6. nondirective consideration of possible lines of action, for help in decision making. (Super, 1957, p. 308)

These counseling methods can be integrated within an SCG approach (see Figure 16.1) through structured group discussions; self-paced, independent activities facilitated by peer paraprofessionals; and discussions with counselors or visiting faculty members who may participate in select group presentations and discussions. Encouraging the frequent participation of classroom faculty in the structured group settings could be a highly productive activity, because frequent participation with faculty has been found to be more strongly related to satisfaction with college than any other type of student involvement (Astin, 1984).

Attention to both life space and life span concepts should be integrated into orientation activities or overviews of the career planning process during intake. Dealing with these concepts early on gives counselors the opportunity to assess the importance of the work and student roles and initiate discussion regarding career stages. Many traditional-aged college students are in the life stage of exploration; returning-adult students in the establishment or maintenance stage (see chapter 4, this volume) may be dealing with concerns related to the roles they are playing at those stages as well as the need to recycle through the exploration stage as they reevaluate themselves and their options (Super et al., 1996) in search of an optimal solution (Peterson, Sampson, Reardon, & Lenz, 1996).

Life space–life span discussions, including discussions of coping with the stresses of transitions, provides an important, context-rich forum for dealing with issues facing many students (Blustein, 1997). In an SCG approach, it may be helpful to organize homogeneous groups of adult deciders, such as women and men in transition, and provide an opportunity for them to experience the process together (see Figure 16.1, Steps 1, 3, and 7). This type of group approach allows counselors to tailor agendas to meet the developmental concerns of students in each group so that content and examples can be matched to the real-life concerns of students in different age groups (Arthur, 1998). Similar groups of younger deciders also can be organized. Homogeneous groups enable participants to discover and experience life space and life span concerns in an empathy-loaded environment, in which the honest sharing of successes, hopes, anxieties, fears, and other feelings and issues are freely shared with like-minded people. Structured group interactions may contribute to the modification of career self-efficacy beliefs (Lent & Brown, 1996). Through small-group interaction, students can discuss their career journey's obstacles and accomplishments and experience appropriate modeling interventions from counselors and their peers. This type of setting also permits students to deal effectively with feelings and receive feedback and encouragement from professionals and peers.

As Hackett and Byars (1996) noted in their discussion of the career development of African American women, encouragement alone from counselors and others is inadequate. The interactive effects of social persuasion with other learning experiences, including acquiring career and educational information, will have the greatest positive influence when presented in ways that are relevant to the lives and experiences of African American women. Bandura's (1997) construct of collective efficacy, a group's sense of power and ability to effect change, may be relevant to the homogeneous grouping suggested in the SCG approach; such groups can provide social support, mentoring, networking, and collective action as participants move through the seven-step SCG process together.

NOICC Guidelines

One initiative sponsored by the NOICC (1989) was the development of the *National Career Development Guidelines*. The guidelines were a catalyst for the development of state and local standards nationwide that fostered excellence in career development programs for all ages, kindergarten through adult. The NOICC model for comprehensive career development emphasized three major features: program content, process, and structure. Program content is organized around three areas—self-knowledge, educational and occupational exploration, and career planning—whereas processes are the strategies that actually deliver the program content (e.g., counseling, instruction, assessment, and placement activities). The program structure is the organizational structure that facilitates successful delivery of the program processes and supports the program's activities. Examples of program structure components are the management team (or person) responsible for organizing program planning, securing resources, monitoring program delivery, and revising the program; other personnel who help serve career development needs, usually through direct involvement with deciders; facilities that ensure the delivery of career development services; and the resources required to purchase the needed material and equipment to implement a career development program. The guidelines are useful in the development, evaluation, and justification of career services programs and are the basis of a "Justification Scenario" (see Appendix 16-A).

The Challenge

It is unfair and irresponsible to assume that the professional and support staff at many counseling and career services centers can meet the career counseling needs of large numbers of students effectively through a traditional, individual-based counseling approach. Systematic career guidance may provide a cost-effective alternative. A few of the building blocks necessary to implement SCG may already be in place at many institutions, such as the use of group guidance, CACGSs, and self-paced materials. The approach is ineffective, however, if peer paraprofessionals or career assistants are not available to help students during the seven-step process in situations in which a professional counselor's expertise is not necessary. Considering the important role of computer-guidance technology, it may be equally important to teach professional and paraprofessional staff how to use it cost-effectively and efficiently.

Career services staff members need the full support of administration and faculty, including adequate budget allocations to successfully implement an SCG approach. Obtaining this support will require a common understanding and agreement regarding the important contribution of career services to student learning and the academic enterprise. Although student affairs administrators often are more opposed to the reduction of career services than are academic administrators, budget reallocation and downsizing activities in higher education are common and complex phenomena that often place student affairs and academic affairs administrators in opposition to each other for funding and staff positions (Dickman, Fuqua, Coombs, & Seals, 1996). It is important that staffing and equipment requests be in line with documented student needs; nothing less will justify support for a career services program during difficult fiscal periods. Students lacking career goals will be less motivated in classroom environments, possibly resulting in higher attrition rates (Astin, 1984).

It is inappropriate for any college that serves a minority population, older adults in transition, at-risk students, and special-needs populations to neglect their career development needs. When students drop out of college, they lose an opportunity to develop their potential to be productive and fulfilled workers and citizens and are more likely to experience unemployment (Pascarella & Terenzini, 1991). That loss to the greater community, over time, negatively affects society. Those who do secure employment often end up "floundering in the secondary labor market in positions that contribute only marginally to either worker satisfaction or societal benefits" (Hoyt & Lester, 1995, p. 92). Gardner (1999), a longtime champion of the freshman-year experience, cautioned that institutions of higher education face increasing scrutiny from a variety of sectors about the value of higher education. He recommended a special focus on and assessment of the current status of the campus career center, which must be a top priority of administration and faculty (Gardner, 1999).

It is essential for colleges to prepare students to actively participate as job-ready graduates in a high-skilled work force—people who can be self-directed and self-managed. The role of SCG is to facilitate students' progress throughout the college experience and contribute to student learning and personal development, helping them find a sense of purpose, declare a goal, and successfully achieve that goal, thereby promoting student success (Helfgot & Culp, 1995). Colleges need to assess their priorities and resources to determine the best course of action regarding the full implementation of SCG. More outcome research—ideally, longitudinal— is necessary, including the use of multiple outcome measures appropriate to students and people in the work force (Fretz, 1981; Oliver & Spokane, 1988). It is important not only to determine the cost-effectiveness of career intervention modes but also to develop a clearer understanding of how various combinations of interventions can serve students in the context of budget realities, institutional mission and, most important, promoting student learning.

Career services professionals do not pretend to know the many needs and program requests that eventually filter through the desks of deans and to college presidents, who have to make difficult decisions. They do know how to help students become clear about their career goals, relate their course work to their goals, and stay on track. They also need to know how to help their institution cost-effectively meet the career development needs of students. Doing so may involve motivating staff dealing with burnout and low morale to shift perceptions, take on new roles of leadership, and better focus on providing the best possible career guidance services. One measure of success will be the extent to which colleges and universities have created climates in which students choose to become willing, eager participants in the discovery of their own career development process—an active search for self.

Establishing an SCG Program

Suggestions to facilitate the establishment of an SCG program at a college or university setting are as follows:

1. Participate with colleagues in the Justification Scenario presented in Appendix 16-A.
2. Keep key people above you on the organizational chart aware of all that you are doing. Make sure that they receive reports and funding requests that are based on research concerning your career services program, particularly needs assessment data and outcome assessments. Those who control the budget need to understand what they are funding (and maybe even fight for on your behalf) in situations in which you will not be present to make your own case. To that end, some of the following approaches work well:
   - Conduct a needs assessment to gather information about the current status of your career services program, and present the information in a user-friendly format to appropriate faculty and administrators.
   - Use charts and graphs to highlight significant findings, and cite relevant research.
   - Keep your direct supervisor informed about the status of your program, staffing and resource needs, and innovative ideas that will more cost-effectively accomplish program goals and objectives.
   - Make sure that colleagues and administrators clearly see, understand, and appreciate the "big" picture regarding students' needs and how your career services program is a vital component that contributes to the educational mission of your institution and specifically to student learning and success.
3. Form alliances with teaching faculty and other college personnel who are in a position to advocate for an SCG program to the administration and students. Create a campuswide ad hoc advisory committee to guide the SCG program and help publicize it, assist with evaluating its effectiveness, and visibly support its operation and growth.
4. Network with colleagues from other institutions, participate at local and national conferences, share ideas, and contribute to the knowledge base of the profession by submitting articles to professional journals. Doing so will help you develop your leadership potential and raise your efficacy as a catalyst for change.
5. Most important, be willing to shift from comfortable and familiar paradigms that were useful in the past to new, more effective paradigms that may help determine what services are offered, how and when they are delivered, and who delivers them. Consider transforming from a traditional role to a counselor–coordinator role, whose top priority is creative collaboration to ensure student success.

Creating ways to serve students differently can offer career services providers additional variety and new challenges that revitalize the worker and the setting. This will require taking time to reflect on existing services and asking questions that thoroughly examine the essence of what, how, and why career services staff do what they have been used to doing. It will require more attention to meeting institutional needs and designing and implementing services that promote student learning and success. It will also require a transformation of thinking and behaving and a willingness to emerge into the role of counselor-coordinator. This new role will allow career services providers to more fully realize their potential amidst the diverse student populations that require assistance with career development needs.

References

ACT. (1996). *The world-of-work map.* Iowa City, IA: Author.

Arthur, N. (1998). The effects of stress, depression, and anxiety on postsecondary students' coping strategies. *Journal of College Student Development, 39,* 11–22.

Astin, A. W. (1984). Student involvement: A developmental theory for higher education. *Journal of College Student Development, 25,* 297–308.

Astin, A. W. (1996). Involvement in learning revisited: Lessons we have learned. *Journal of College Student Development, 37,* 123–134.

Bandura, A. (1997). *Self-efficacy: The exercise of control.* New York: W. H. Freeman.

Bloch, D. P. (1996). Career development and workforce preparation: Educational policy versus school practice. *Career Development Quarterly, 45,* 20–40.

Blustein, D. L. (1997). A context-rich perspective of career exploration across the life roles. *Career Development Quarterly, 45,* 260–274.

Bowlsbey, J. H. (n.d.). *The computer's role in enhancing career development.* Paper presented at colloquium conducted at Johns Hopkins University, Baltimore, MD.

Brown, D. (1995). A values-based approach to career transitions. *Career Development Quarterly, 44,* 4–11.

Colozzi, E. A. (1981). *The Leeward experience: A report on data localization and demonstration activities relating to Career Kokua The Hawaii Career Information System.* Unpublished manuscript, Leeward Community College, Oahu, HI.

Colozzi, E. A., & Haehnlen, F. P. (1982). The impact of a computerized career information system on a community college in an island state. *International Journal for the Advancement of Counseling, 5,* 273–282.

Conger, S. D., Hiebert, B., & Hong-Farrell, E. (1994). *Career and employment counselling in Canada. A report to the Canadian Labour Force Development Board (CLFDB) by the Canadian Guidance and Counseling Foundation.* Ottawa, Ontario: CLFDB.

Dean, J. A., & Meadows, M. E. (1995). College counseling: Union and intersection. *Journal of Counseling & Development, 74,* 139–142.

Dickman, M. M., Fuqua, D. R., Coombs, W. T., & Seals, J. M. (1996). Downsizing in higher education: Institutional budget reduction priorities and strategies. *Journal of College Student Development, 37,* 457–467.

Elmhirst, P., Riche, N., Blais, E., Gilmone, B., Irwin, W. J., Lee, E. L., Lerner, R., Reberg, B., & Stone, J. (1994). *Putting the pieces together: Toward a coherent transition system for Canada's labour force.* Report of the Task force on Transition into Employment to the Canadian Labour Force Development Board (CLFDB). Ottawa, Ontario: CLFDB.

Fretz, B. R. (1981). Evaluating the effectiveness of career interventions [Monograph]. *Journal of Counseling Psychology Monograph, 28,* 77–90.

Gardner, J. N. (1999). The senior year experience. *About CAMPUS, 4,* 5–11.

Hackett, G., & Byars, A. M. (1996). Social cognitive theory and the career development of African American women. *Career Development Quarterly, 44,* 322–340.

Helfgot, S. R., & Culp, M. M. (1995). Promoting student success in the community college. *New Directions for Student Services, 69*. San Francisco: Jossey-Bass.

Herr, E. L. (1996). Perspective on ecological context, social policy, and career guidance. *Career Development Quarterly, 45*, 5–19.

Herr, E. L., & Cramer, S. H. (1996). *Career guidance and counseling through the life span: Systematic approaches* (5th ed.). New York: HarperCollins.

Hess, D. W., & Winston, R. B., Jr. (1995). Developmental task achievement and students' intentions to participate in developmental activities. *Journal of College Student Development, 36*, 314–321.

Holland, J. L. (1973). *Making vocational choices: A theory of career*. Englewood Cliffs, NJ: Prentice-Hall.

Hoyt, K., & Hughey, J. K. (1995). *Counseling for high skills (CHS)*. Kansas State University, College of Education, Manhattan, KS.

Hoyt, K., & Lester, J. (1995). *Learning to work: The NCDA Gallup survey*. Alexandria, VA: National Career Development Association.

Larson, L. M., Heppner, P. P., Ham, T., & Dugan, K. (1988). Investigating multiple subtypes of career indecision through cluster analysis. *Journal of Counseling Psychology, 35*, 439–446.

Lent, R. W., & Brown, S. D. (1996). Social cognitive approach to career development: An overview. *Career Development Quarterly, 44*, 310–321.

Lent, R. W., Brown, S. D., & Hackett, G. (1996). Career development from a social cognitive perspective. In D. Brown, L. Brooks, & Assoc. (Eds.), *Career choice and development* (3rd ed., pp. 373–421). San Francisco: Jossey-Bass.

Lent, R. W., & Hackett, G. (1987) Career self efficacy: Empirical status and future directions [Monograph]. *Journal of Vocational Behavior, 30*, 347–382.

Levine. A. & Cureton, J. S. (1998). What we know about today's college students. *About CAMPUS, 3*, 4–9.

Luzzo, D. A., Funk, D. P., & Strang, J. (1996). Attributional retraining increases career decision-making self-efficacy. *Career Development Quarterly, 44*, 378–386.

Mitchell, L. K., & Krumboltz, J. D. (1996). Krumboltz's learning theory of career choice and counseling. In D. Brown, L. Brooks, & Assoc. (Eds.), *Career choice and development* (3rd ed., pp. 233–280). San Francisco: Jossey-Bass.

National Occupational Information Coordinating Committee. (1989). *National career development guidelines*. Washington, DC: U.S. Government Printing Office.

Oliver, L. W., & Spokane, A. R. (1988) Career-intervention outcome: What contributes to client gain? *Journal of Counseling Psychology, 35*, 447–462.

Osborne, W. L., Brown, S., Niles, S. G., & Miner, C. (1997). *Career development, assessment, and counseling*. Alexandria, VA: American Counseling Association

Pascarella, E. T., & Terenzini, P. T. (1991). *How college affects students*. San Francisco: Jossey-Bass.

Peterson, G. W., Sampson, J. P., Jr., Reardon, R. C., & Lenz, J. G. (1996). A cognitive information processing approach to career problem solving and decision making. In D. Brown, L. Brooks, & Assoc. (Eds.), *Career choice and development* (3rd ed., pp. 423–475). San Francisco: Jossey-Bass.

Rayman, J. (1996). Apples and oranges in the career center: Reaction to R. Reardon. *Journal of Counseling & Development, 74*, 286–287.

Sampson, J. P., Jr., Reardon, R. C., Norris, D. S., Wilde, C. K., Slatten, M. L., Garis, J. W., Saunders, D. E., Strausberger, S. J., Sankofa-Amammere, K. T., Peterson, G. W., & Lenz, J. G. (1994). *A differential feature-cost analysis of seventeen computer-assisted career guidance systems: Technical report number 10*. Tallahassee, FL: Center for the Study of Technology in Counseling and Career Development.

Savickas, M. L. (1995). Constructivist counseling for career indecision. *Career Development Quarterly, 43*, 363–373.

Schroeder, C. C. (1996). Focus on student learning: An imperative for student affairs. *Journal of College Student Development, 37*, 115–117.

Schroeder, C. C., & Hurst, J. C. (1996). Designing learning environments that integrate curricular and cocurricular experiences. *Journal of Collage Student Development, 37*, 174–181.

Sexton, T. L., Whiston, S. C., Bleuer, J. C., & Walz, G. R. (1997). *Integrating outcome research into counseling practice and training*. Alexandria, VA: American Counseling Association.

Spokane, A. R. (1991). *Career interventions*. Englewood Cliffs, NJ: Prentice-Hall.

Super, D. E. (1957). *The psychology of careers*. New York: Harper and Row.

Super, D. E., Bowlsbey, J. H., & Colozzi, E. A. (1985). *Creating a multi-mode, life-span approach to career guidance*. Presentation at the annual conference of the American Association of Counseling and Development, New York.

Super, D. E., Savickas, M. L., & Super, C. M. (1996). The life-span, life-space approach to careers. In D. Brown, L. Brooks, & Assoc. (Eds.), *Career choice and development* (3rd ed., pp. 121–178). San Francisco: Jossey-Bass.

Terenzini, P. T., & Upcraft, L. M. (1996). Assessing program and service outcomes. In M. L. Upcraft & J. H. Schuh (Eds.), *Assessment in student affairs* (pp. 217–239). San Francisco: Jossey-Bass.

Upcraft, M. L., & Schuh, J. H. (Eds.). (1996). *Assessment in student affairs*. San Francisco: Jossey-Bass.

U.S. Department of Labor, Bureau of Labor Statistics. (1998). *Occupational outlook handbook, 1998–99 edition*. Washington, DC: U.S. Government Printing Office.

Appendix 16-A: Justification Scenario

The following scenario can stimulate an initial dialogue among career services providers who may need to provide budget justification for their programs. Four or more people can participate in the exercise, which uses small-group discussions and role playing.

One or two people should be in the role of having to "justify" a career services program. They should read the scenario and be given sufficient time to prepare their responses. The other participants then should gather in a small group and use the justification evaluation (see below) to monitor and rate the efforts of the group responsible for providing program justification.

The responses on the justification evaluation are presented only as a guide and may be modified to more closely match a local college or university setting. Once the scenario is used, it may be appropriate to have multiple follow-up discussions among staff members, even over several weeks, and then use it again as a way of preparing for an impending program justification.

Scenario

New organizational leadership at your institution has mandated a restructuring initiative, which will result in downsizing and budget reductions for most of the departments and possible reorganization or elimination of several. An independent agency has been contracted to conduct program reviews and make recommendations regarding the justification of departments. Two or more agency representatives will be meeting with you to review your program and hear your justification. You will be asked to discuss the following three areas concerning your career services program:

1. *Program content*—what your program is based on.
2. *Program processes*—the strategies that are used to deliver the program content.
3. *Program structure*—the framework that supports successful delivery of the program, including leadership, staffing, facilities, management of day-to-day operations, and budget.

Your program justification will be evaluated and recommendations will be forwarded to the new organizational leadership for their consideration and final action.

Justification Evaluation

Rating Scale

A = Warrants *additional funding* because responses match more than 80% of suggested responses *and* justification was based on a cost-effective delivery of services.

B = Warrants *level funding* because responses match approximately 70% to 80% of suggested responses *and* justification was based on a cost-effective delivery of services.

C = Warrants *downsizing and severe budget cuts* because responses match fewer than 70% of suggested responses *and* justification was not based on a cost-effective delivery of services.

D = Warrants *possible elimination of department* and consolidation of activities and personnel into other departments because responses match fewer than 50% of suggested answers *and* justification was not based on a cost-effective delivery of services.

Suggested Discussion Questions (Q) and Responses (R)

1. **Program Content** (what the program is based on)
Q   Discuss what your program is based on.
R   Be sure to look for evidence of the following:
   - Staff uses theory-based approaches in developing the program.
   - Program is based on NOICC's *National Career Development Guidelines*.
   - Program is competency based and organized around self-knowledge, educational and occupational exploration, and career planning.
2. **Program Processes** (the strategies that deliver the program content)
Q   Discuss the various processes at your organization that deliver the program content.
R   Be sure to look for evidence that the program
   - provides outreach to inform potential students about career development
   - offers group and individual counseling and uses group work effectively (and therefore is more cost-effective by not relying primarily on individual counseling)
   - provides assessment
   - provides classroom instruction and workshops
   - uses multimedia delivery, including CACGSs and written and audiovisual materials
   - provides work experience, if applicable (e.g., cooperative education opportunities)
   - provides placement activities, if applicable.
3. **Program Structure** (the framework that supports successful delivery of the program processes, including leadership, staffing, facilities, management of day-to-day operations and budget)
Q   Discuss how the leadership at your organization implements the program in accordance with its goals and objectives.
R   Be sure to look for evidence that the top administrator
   - sees the big picture
   - supports needs assessment
   - has a clear purpose or mission statement
   - is providing leadership for a competency-based program

- initiates periodic evaluations of program
- develops clear budget requests
- coordinates program activities with others in organization
- initiates staff meetings that encourage dialogue and staff development.

Q Briefly describe the qualifications and characteristics of your staff that support the achievement of the goals of the program.

R Be sure to look for evidence that the staff is knowledgeable about the following and has a *justified need* for any increase in professional, paraprofessional or clerical staff. Look for evidence that staff members

- use theory-based approaches, including the NOICC *Guidelines*
- use group work effectively and do not rely primarily on individual counseling
- are familiar with educational, occupational, and employment resources
- are able to work with groups having special needs and with people from different ethnic backgrounds
- work well with guidance-related computer technology.

Q Describe how your facility supports the program goals and objectives.

R Look for evidence of clearly *justified* need (not merely a request for more of something) related to the need for equipment or other resources.

Q Briefly summarize how your program activities are marketed, meet student needs, are evaluated, and support the mission statement and goals of the program.

R Look for evidence of the following:

- periodic needs assessment and program evaluation
- effective outreach within the organization and to the community to market services *and* coordinate or articulate program activities (e.g., orientation for entering students, infusion activities in classes, and outreach to groups with special needs and diverse populations)
- ongoing staff development and evidence of a *justified need* for additional activities, such as special conferences related to counseling techniques and new technology.

Q Justify your program in light of the impending restructuring initiative.

R Look for evidence of cost-effective delivery of services.

17

The Identification of a Career Development Research and Practice Agenda for the 21st Century

Sarah M. Toman

A crystal ball certainly would have been useful when I took on the task of predicting and identifying the direction of 21st-century research and practice in the career development of college students. Given that crystal-ball gazing, tarot cards, I Ching, or an appointment with a psychic might be frowned on by more scientifically minded readers, I have chosen, instead, to follow my academic training and turn to the literature for predictions.

As Spokane (1991) stated, "Attempts to fortify the theories with practical implications are more common now than they have been in many years, and more people are now both theorists and practitioners than was once the case" (p. xii). It is my hope that this chapter will inspire career counseling professionals to continue the trend of merging theory and practice. With the latest technological advances in communications, collaboration between practitioners and researchers is possible almost anywhere in the world. In a circular fashion, research can add to the efficacy of interventions, and practitioners can influence the directions of future research in the career development literature.

The literature sources for this chapter consisted of journal articles published from 1996 through 1998. The process was simple. By collecting all the sentences typically found toward the end of each article (e.g., "Future research should . . ."), I began to see patterns, trends, or directions. Gaps in the proposed research became apparent as well. This chapter describes the data collection process for and the content of my collection of future-research sentences. Bronfenbrenner (1993) described the sentiments of undertaking a project like this when he wrote,

> Whether the effort brings us closer to heaven or hell remains to be seen. Perhaps the best I can hope for is to be left in limbo; by which I mean that the reader will reserve judgment, pending further developments. (p. 3)

Method

The process of collecting future-research sentences involved making a series of decisions governing the rules for data collection. The first decision, selection of the journals, was the most difficult because of the quantity of materials. I chose to narrow the field to journals from the career counseling and vocational psychology literature, eliminating articles from the business or organizational development literature and popular media. Included in the process were the *Career Development Quarterly,* the *Journal of Career Assessment,* the *Journal of Career Development,* the *Journal of College Student Development,* the *Journal of Counseling Psychology*, and the *Journal of Vocational Behavior.*

The next decision involved selecting the articles. The first rule was to include only articles that had a career focus. Selection of the *Journal of Counseling Psychology* and the *Journal of College Student Development* made this rule necessary, because both publications have a broad scope. The next rule, to include only articles related to college students, was established to fulfill the purpose of this book. Eliminated articles included studies with children, adolescents in high school, non-college-bound youth, employees, retirees, and career counselor trainees. Theoretical articles were eliminated if the subject matter was not pertinent to the career development concerns of a college population. Adhering to the two rules involved some subjectivity, and other authors may have made different selections. However, differences in the selection process probably would not have significantly altered the outcomes.

Many articles met the criteria for the above rules but nevertheless were eliminated from further analyses: My final rule specified that the article must have an explicit section on future research or a sentence on the subject. "Current Career Literature" columns, book reviews, case studies and responses, pieces for special issues, and commentaries not containing explicit future-research sentences were not considered. Annual reviews were not tallied in the results, but they are addressed in the Discussion section of this chapter as a source for comparison. Table 17-1 depicts the results of applying the selection rules to the identified publications.

In summary, 696 articles from six journals were previewed. Of those, 167 (24%) met all criteria and were further analyzed for the content of the future-research statements. The analysis process consisted of first reading the abstract and discussion sections of each article to locate the statements. If the author did not include future-research statements there, the remainder of the article was read in its entirety. Future-research statements were extracted and grouped into like categories.

Results

Analyzing the content of future-research statements from the selected journal articles published between 1996 and 1998 resulted in the identi-

Table 17.1. Summary of Articles From Each Selected Journal

Journal volume and issue	Number of articles	Career	Not college	College	Usable college	Not usable college
CDQ 44(3)–47(1)	89	89	50	39	32	7
JCA 4(1)–6(4)	82	82	25	57	51	6
JCD 22(3)–25(1)	59	59	45	14	10	4
JCSD 37(1)–39(5)	202	13	1	12	10	2
JCP 43(1)–45(3)	136	28	11	17	16	1
JVB 48(1)–53(1)	128	128	67	61	48	13
Totals	696	399	199	200	167	33

Note. CDQ = Career Development Quarterly, JCA = Journal of Career Assessment, JCD = Journal of Career Development, JCSD = Journal of College Student Development, JCP = Journal of Counseling Psychology, JVB = Journal of Vocational Behavior. "Current Career Literature" columns, annual reviews, and book reviews are not tallied in any columns.

fication of 5 themes, with 17 subthemes. This chapter describes each theme and subtheme and provides corresponding references. In addition, this collection of references provides a somewhat comprehensive review of recent research on the career development of college students. Table 17-2 depicts the frequency of sentences within each theme and subtheme.

Theme 1: Diversity

Under the main theme of diversity, the future-research sentences were split into the two subthemes of first gender and second, ethnicity, race, and culture.

Gender. Of the 71 sentences addressing issues of diversity, 25 authors called for more research regarding diverse influences of gender. Hackett (1997) and Farmer (1997) asked for future research that includes special domains of women's career development, whereas Jackson and Neville (1998) wanted to see more exploration of the career development complexities of African American men. The choice of nontraditional careers was the future focus for Brown, Eisenberg, and Sawilowsky (1997); Dawson-Threat and Huba (1996); Meldahl and Muchinsky (1997); and Morrow, Gore, and Campbell (1996). Dawson-Threat and Huba also called for more research on comfort level with regard to androgyny and nontraditional majors. Brown, Eisenberg, et al. (1997); Lucas, Wanberg, and Zytowski (1997); and Morrow et al. (1996) called for more research on gender differences in self-efficacy.

Other gender-related topics included gender differences in career decision making (Luzzo & Jenkins-Smith, 1998), gender roles (Jome & Tokar, 1998), role salience (Nevill & Calvert, 1996), representation and development of career interests (Anderson, Tracey, & Rounds, 1997; Tracey & Rounds, 1996a), adjustment and satisfaction (Raskin, Kummel, & Bannister, 1998), achievement motivation (Farmer, 1997), content of adult career concerns (Cairo, Kritis, & Myers, 1996), impact of sexual orientation (Jome & Tokar, 1998; Lonborg & Phillips, 1996), and factors that inhibit women's

Table 17.2. Summary of Themes from Future-Research Sentences

Theme	Subtheme	Subtotal	Total
Diversity			71
	Gender	25	
	Ethnicity, race, and culture	46	
Methodology			101
	Design	45	
	Validity and reliability	24	
	Measurement	32	
Theory			36
	Holland's typology	11	
	Social–cognitive theory	12	
	Social learning theory	1	
	Developmental theory	7	
	Roe's constructs	3	
	Work adjustment theory	2	
Intervention			37
Other			66
	Career decision	14	
	Barriers	5	
	Parents and family	18	
	Political	8	
	Technology	4	
	"Hmm"	21	
Total			311

ambitions (Antony, 1998). Also of interest to the college population was future research regarding gender differences in content and style of on-campus interviews (DeBell & Dinger, 1997), gender differences in pay expectations (Gasser, Oliver, & Tan, 1998), and the disclosure of sexual orientation in work versus other contexts (Lonborg & Phillips, 1996).

Ethnicity, Race, and Culture. An example of the ethnicity, race, and culture subtheme is Leong's (1997) call for future research that views the meaning of career interests from individualistic and collectivist cultures, distinguishing between cultural comparison (etic view) and the examination of one culture (emic view). Others (Blustein, 1997a; Lent, 1996; McWhirter, Torres, & Rasheed, 1998; Stead & Watson, 1998) also pointed to the importance of studying career diversity in context. Another frequently cited future-research topic was the impact of cultural and racial identity (Bauman & Gerstein, 1998; Hartung et al., 1998; Lonborg & Phillips, 1996). Other research recommendations included a call to examine differences in the career decision-making process (Luzzo & Jenkins-Smith, 1998), career decision-making self-efficacy (Peterson & del Mas, 1998), career decision-making attribution style (Luzzo, James, & Luna, 1996; Luzzo & Jenkins-Smith, 1998), career aspirations (Chung, Loeb, & Gonzo, 1996), factors affecting career development (Bauman & Gerstein, 1998; Nevill & Calvert, 1996; Rounds & Tracey, 1996; Schmitt-Rodermund & Silbereisen, 1998), retention (Patterson-Stewart, Ritchie, & Saunders, 1997), cross-cultural research of the data–ideas dimension (Tracey, Watanabe, & Schneider, 1997), choice restrictions (Jackson & Neville, 1998), effects of multiple status (Eby & Russell, 1998), international influences (Leong, Hesketh, & Savickas, 1998), and the impact of immigration (Sagy & Liberman, 1997). One future-research sentence, by Leong and Hartung (1997), addressed the need for a cross-cultural counseling model.

Related to the diversity theme was the endorsement by many authors for using more diverse participant samples. Future-research statements calling for diversity sampling were suggested in 19 published articles (e.g., Betsworth & Fouad, 1997; Bowman, 1998; Chung et al., 1996; Croteau & Bieschke, 1996; Hitchings, Luzzo, Retish, Horvath, & Ristow, 1998; Ketterson & Blustein, 1997; Lent, Lopez, Brown, & Gore, 1996; Luzzo, McWhirter, & Hutcheson, 1997; Meir, Tziner, & Glazner, 1997; Niles, Erford, Hunt, & Watts, 1997; Niles, Lewis, & Hartung, 1997; Swanson, Daniels, & Tokar, 1996). In addition, two sentences addressed the unique career development experiences of those with physical disabilities (Friehe, Aune, & Leuenberger, 1996; Ohler, Levinson, & Barker, 1996).

Recommendations. In all, 46 future-research recommendations in the ethnicity–race–culture subtheme and 25 in the gender subtheme were endorsed in the selected career development articles. Clearly, diversity will continue to be one of the hot research and practice topics of the 21st century. Career counselors in urban universities and colleges could make a substantial contribution to the career development literature by researching and describing career issues and interventions with their diverse student populations.

Theme 2: Methodology

The methodology main theme included the subthemes of design, validity and reliability, and measurement. From the selected publications, 12 articles recommended using longitudinal research designs (Betz & Luzzo, 1996; Farmer, Rotella, Anderson, & Wardrop, 1998; Lonborg & Phillips, 1996; Lucas, 1997; Luzzo, Funk, & Strang, 1996; Mau, Calvert, & Gregory, 1997; Meir, Rubin, Temple, & Osipow, 1997; Mobley & Slaney, 1996; Munson & Widmer, 1997; Peterson & del Mas, 1998; Russell & Burgess, 1998; Schaefers, Epperson, & Nauta, 1997). Nine articles contained recommendations for use of qualitative research methods (Bikos, Krieshok, & O'Brien, 1998; Blustein, 1997b; Fassinger, 1996; Lucas, 1997; Jackson & Neville, 1998; Jones, 1998; Subich, 1998; Sweeney & Schill, 1998; Whiston, 1996), whereas 6 others (Lent, Brown, Gover, & Nijer, 1996; Lonborg & Phillips, 1996; Mobley & Slaney, 1996; Morrow et al., 1996; Russell & Burgess, 1998; Stead & Watson, 1998) suggested using multiple methods.

Design. This subtheme contained 45 design recommendations for future research. Peterson (1998) suggested using card sorts as a research methodology, Subich (1998) suggested interviews, Lunneborg (1997) and Sagy (1997) called for more use of case studies, and Damarin (1998) recommended additional research in lab settings. Brown, Lum, and Voyle (1997) and Lonborg and Phillips (1996) both suggested using structural equation modeling; Saks, Wiesner, and Summers (1996) asked for the development of new experimental manipulations; Meir and colleagues (1997) recommended time-series designs; and Lent and colleagues (1996) suggested multivariate causal models. Lonborg and Phillips (1996) also offered several design recommendations: path analysis, use of the critical-incident technique, and measurement of within-group differences.

As in the diversity theme, the issue of sampling surfaced in the design subtheme. Authors would like to see additional older American samples (Osipow & Gati, 1998), "real" clients (Leong & Chervinko, 1996; Moore & Neimeyer, 1997), larger samples (Wade & Kinicki, 1997), and samples that are more "systematically selected" (Hartung, Speight, & Lewis, 1996). Jackson and Neville (1998) further recommended using race as a "psychological variable" instead of a demographic variable.

Validity and Reliability. In the validity and reliability subtheme, most future-research statements called for validation studies of specific career assessment instruments. Donnay and Borgen (1996) recommended predictive validation of the latest version of the Strong Interest Inventory (Harmon, Hansen, Borgen, & Hammer, 1994); Luzzo and Jenkins-Smith (1998) made validity recommendations regarding their Assessment of Attributions for Career Decision Making; and Lucas, Wanberg, and Zytowski (1997) called for additional reliability and validity studies of their Kuder Task Self-Efficacy Scale. Other recommended validation or reliability studies included examinations of Myers and McCaulley's (1985) Myers–Briggs Type Indicator (Carson, Stalikas, & Bizot, 1997; Jackson, Parker, & Dipboye, 1996); Super, Thompson, Lindeman, Jordaan, and Myers's (1981) Career Development Inventory (Savickas & Hartung, 1996); Super, Thompson, and Lindeman's (1988) Adult Career Concerns Inventory (Cairo et al., 1996); Crites's (1978) Career Maturity Inventory–1995 Revision (Crites & Savickas, 1996); and Chartrand, Robbins, Morrill, and Boggs's (1990) Career Factors Inventory (Chartrand & Nutter, 1996).

Additional statements included Knapp-Lee's (1996) call for further validation of the Career Orientation Placement and Evaluation Survey (COPES; Knapp, Knapp-Lee, & Knapp, 1995), Osipow and Temple's (1996) suggestion for further evaluation of the Task-Specific Occupational Self-Efficacy Scale (Osipow & Rooney, 1989), and Weitzman and Fitzgerald's (1996) suggestion that the Attitudes Toward Multiple Role Planning scale (Weitzman, 1992) be studied further. Jaros (1998) called for further validation research for the Affective Commitment Scale (Meyer & Allen, 1984); Stockdale and Hope (1998), for the Sexual Experiences Questionnaire

(Fitzgerald et al., 1988); and Meir, Rubin, and colleagues (1997), for the RAMACK and Courses Interest Inventory (Meir, 1995).

Some authors made recommendations for validation studies that did not pertain to specific tests or inventories but to types of career assessment. Future assessment validation studies could include card sorts (Bikos et al., 1998), the use of Holland's (1985) model with international students (Farh, Leong, & Law, 1998), the development and validation of indigenous assessments (Tan, 1998), the validity of a given occupational interest scale as the score increases (Prediger, 1998), the spherical structure of interests (Tracey & Rounds, 1996a), the "psychometrics of instruments" with diverse groups (Kerr & Fisher, 1997), and the construct "reptest" based on Kelly's (1955) repertory grid (Russ-Eisenschenk & Neimeyer, 1996). Finally, Osipow (1997) suggested that validity studies of new concepts be conducted rather than of old.

Measurement. Some recommendations in the measurement subtheme were for specific measures, and some were for concepts. The conceptual recommendations were for measuring career needs of international students (Spencer-Rodgers & Cortijo, 1998); career barriers (Luzzo, 1996); diverse populations (Eby & Russell, 1998; Glidden-Tracey & Parraga, 1996); unbiased assessment and interpretation for lesbian, gay, and bisexual clients (Prince, 1997); and stage of gay identity development across expressed or inventoried career choices (Mobley & Slaney, 1996). Authors also recommended measuring effects of feedback (Hall, Kelly, Hansen, & Gutwein, 1996), spatial ability of engineer majors (Schaefers et al., 1997), physiological qualities (Hallett & Gilbert, 1997), identity development (Lucas, 1997), developing indigenous test items (Farh et al., 1998), and multidimensional and multivariate interest measurement (Donnay, 1997). Career maturity with special populations (Jackson & Healy, 1996), prestige in interest-item assessment (Tracey & Rounds, 1996a), dual-career conflicts and coping strategies (Hallett & Gilbert, 1997), career exploration (Hamer & Bruch, 1997), need frustration in parent–child relationship (Brown & Voyle, 1997), and pre- and post-career decision-making difficulties (Osipow & Gati, 1998) also were suggested topics.

Many researchers noted the need for measurement research using specific instruments with diverse populations. Future-research sentences referenced the Career Thoughts Inventory (Sampson, Peterson, Lenz, Reardon, & Saunders, 1998), the Decisional Process Inventory (Hartung & Marco, 1998), Super's (1983) Career-Development Assessment and Counseling measures (Hartung et al., 1998), and the Career Decision-Making Difficulties Questionnaire (Osipow & Gati, 1998).

Additional sentences asked for studies involving the relationship of a specific construct to an assessment. These sentences included comparing the construct of self-rated and measured abilities in relation to the Skills Confidence Inventory (Parsons & Betz, 1998), and the constructs of IQ, grade point average, and interests to the Career Factors Inventory (Sweeney & Schill, 1998); an identification of Career Decisions Difficulties

Questionnaire items that are associated with career decision-making self-efficacy (Gati, Krausz, & Osipow, 1996); and the relationship between the Minnesota Importance Questionnaire (Gay, Weiss, Dawis, & Lofquist, 1971) and Maslow's needs hierarchy (Brown, Lum, et al., 1997).

Future research regarding treatment application was suggested for Holland and Gottfredson's (1994) Career Attitudes and Strategies Inventory (Gottfredson, 1996); Betz, Borgen, and Harmon's (1996) Skills Confidence Inventory (Harmon et al., 1996); and Super and colleagues (1988) Adult Career Concerns Inventory, Form B (Niles, Lewis, et al., 1997). Additionally, Donnay and Borgen (1996) would like future work to "better explicate" the dimensions of the Strong Interest Inventory Basic Interest Scales (Harmon et al., 1994), and Glidden-Tracy and Greenwood (1997) have called for a new Spanish translation of Holland's (1970) Self-Directed Search. Related to all the recommendations in this category is that of Hitchings and colleagues (1998) to use measurements other than self-report when assessing the career development of college students.

Recommendations. College student career counselors are encouraged to consider implementing future research addressing the recommendations included in the methodology theme. College counselors are in an ideal situation for evaluating the efficacy of career assessments and interventions and for applying qualitative, quantitative, case study, and longitudinal designs when doing so.

Theme 3: Theory

The main theme of theory was represented by subthemes that were calls for future research on Holland's (1985) typology; Roe's constructs (Roe & Klos, 1972); and social–cognitive, developmental, social learning, and work adjustment theories.

Holland's typology. The need for research on person–environment fit or Holland typology was noted by Betz, Harmon, and Borgen (1996); Farmer and colleagues (1998); Gati, Fassa, and Mayer (1998); Gati, Garty, and Fassa (1996); Lowman (1997); Meir, Tziner, and colleague (1997); Mobley and Slaney (1996); Osipow and Temple (1996); Smart (1997); Tracey and colleagues (1997); and Zacher and Leong (1997).

Social learning theory. In comparison to 11 calls for continued research on Holland's theory, only 1 article mentioned future research needs of social learning theory (Barnes & Herr, 1998).

Work adjustment theory. Constructs from the work adjustment theory (Dawis & Lofquist, 1984) were mentioned for future research by two authors: Knapp-Lee (1996) and Dawis (1997).

Developmental theory. Research on constructs of developmental career theories was mentioned by Bowman and Gerstein (1998); Cairo et al. (1996); Dunkle (1996); Niles and Goodnough (1996); Smallman and Sowa (1996); and Toman and Savickas (1997). Savickas (1997) called for research replacing the developmental construct of career maturity with career adaptability.

Roe's constructs. Articles also addressed the work of Roe. Brown and Voyle (1997) recommended research merging Roe's constructs with those of work adjustment theory (Dawis & Lofquist, 1984) and Maslow's needs hierarchy. Lunneborg (1997) asked for studies that place Roe's needs structure into a contemporary perspective, whereas Russell and Adams (1997) suggested future research using Roe's framework to predict career change over the life span.

Social–cognitive theory. One of the more recently introduced career theories, Lent, Brown, and Hackett's (1994) social–cognitive career theory (SCCT), received 12 recommendations for future research. The need for more research on SCCT constructs was addressed by Betsworth and Fouad (1997); Hackett and Byars (1996); Lent, Lopez, and colleagues (1996); Luzzo and colleagues (1997); and McWhirter and colleagues (1998). Future research on the more specific construct of career self-efficacy was recommended by Betz and Luzzo (1996); Gianakos (1996); Lent, Brown, and Gore (1997); Lent, Brown, and colleagues (1996); Lucas and colleagues (1997); Peterson and del Mas (1998); and Solberg (1998).

Recommendations. Theorists certainly have not exhausted the possible explanations of career development phenomena. Future researchers and practitioners not only have recommendations to follow from past researchers, but also opportunities to develop new theories or merge existing ones.

Theme 4: Interventions

The emerging interest in SCCT and self-efficacy applications to career surfaced in 9 future-research sentences (Betz, Harmon, et al., 1996; Betz & Klein, 1996; Betz, Klein, & Taylor, 1996; Betz & Luzzo, 1996; Brown, S. D., & Lent, 1996; Lent et al., 1997; Lent, Lopez et al., 1996; Luzzo & Jenkins-Smith, 1998; Solberg, 1998). Future research on career decision interventions was recommended in 6 articles (Gati et al., 1996; Gordon, 1998; Leong & Chervinko, 1996; Luzzo & Jenkins-Smith, 1998; Moore & Neimeyer, 1997; Peterson & del Mas, 1998).

An additional 14 sentences called for future intervention research that relates to structured versus unstructured treatment (Barnes & Herr, 1998), perceived barriers (Swanson & Woitke, 1997), work and family interactions (Harmon, 1997), career choice readiness (Toman & Savickas,

1997), gifted clients (Kerr & Fisher, 1997), career beliefs (Walsh, Thompson, & Kapes, 1997), relationship of personality and aptitudes (Carson et al., 1997), effects of attributional retraining (Luzzo et al., 1996), and multiple role planning (McCracken & Weitzman, 1997). The sentences involving intervention research also included time perspective (Marko & Savickas, 1998), appropriateness to sexual orientation (Lonberg & Phillips, 1996; Morrow et al., 1996), the spherical structure of interests (Harmon, 1996), and career transitions (Lent, 1996).

The interventions theme ends with a call for research on career counseling utilization (Leong & Hartung, 1997; Mobley & Slaney, 1996) and the evaluation of career plans or programs (Brown & Bohac, 1997; Farmer et al., 1998; Osipow & Winer, 1996; Solberg et al., 1998). Jackson and Neville (1998) asked for more research to understand the relationship between issues and interventions. In addition, Ketterson and Blustein (1997) wanted more empirical support for interventions that do not create an artificial distinction between career and other types of counseling.

Recommendations. The identification of only 37 of 311 articles that can be categorized as promoting future interventions research highlights a huge gap in the literature. Savickas (1994) wrote, "It seems to me that we have lost track of the intimate relationship between theory and practice, a relationship of personal shaping" (p. 239). Identification of this gap, I hope, will help inspire researchers and clinicians to reconsider further study of the relationships between theory and practice, shaping not only future research but also the practice of career counseling with college students.

Theme 5: Other

The theme of other contains six subthemes: career decisions, perceived barriers, parents and family, political, technology, and "Hmm."

Career Decisions. Fourteen future-research sentences related to career decisions, including the role of college student employment (Luzzo et al., 1997), perceived controllability (Brown & Crace, 1996), influence of values and interests (Brown & Crace, 1996), developmental stage (Phillips, 1997), student characteristics and environmental influences (Gordon, 1998), cognitive complexity (Gati, 1998), the role of outcome expectancies (Fassinger, 1996), attributional retraining (Luzzo et al., 1996), self-efficacy across the life span (Gianakos, 1996), introversion and extroversion (Leong & Chervinko, 1996), and perceived barriers (Luzzo, 1996). Lonborg and Phillips (1996) wondered how the career decision-making process might be different for gay and lesbian clients versus heterosexual clients. Gati, Krausz, and Osipow (1996) believed that future research could be the development of a work-indecision taxonomy. Krieshok (1998) called for discovering new influences in career decision-making theory and intervention.

Perceived Barriers. Luzzo (1996); Morrow et al. (1996); Russell and Burgess (1998); and Swanson and Woitke (1997) all noted the influence of perceived barriers. Swanson, Daniels, and Tokar (1996) called for research that crosses gender and ethnic diversity with perceptions of barriers.

Parents and Family. The subtheme of parents and family contained 18 future-research sentences. Research on parental and child-rearing influences on career was suggested by Dunkle (1996); Brown, Lum, and colleague (1997); Brown and Voyle (1997); Hall and colleagues (1996); Lent, Lopez, and colleagues (1996); Lunneborg (1997); and Trusty and Watts (1996). Family variables for future studies were noted by Bowman and Gerstein (1998); Fassinger (1996); Harmon (1997); Mobley and Slaney (1996); Ryan, Solberg, and Brown (1996); Solberg (1998); and Whiston (1996). The final four sentences pertained to fostering ambition of male children (Antony, 1998), success of women (Russell & Burgess, 1998), perceived barriers (Swanson et al., 1996), and influence of attachment (Ketterson & Blustein, 1997).

Political. Eight future-research sentences seemed political in nature. Research that accounts for political and societal context was recommended by Betsworth and Fouad (1997), Bowman and Gerstein (1998), Meara (1997), and Santos and Ferreira (1998). Labor market changes (Blustein, 1997b), economic realities (Stead & Watson, 1998), and government policies affecting gay and lesbian clients (Lonborg & Phillips, 1996) also were noted for future topics. Tracey and Rounds (1996b) recommended studying how changes in the world may affect the usefulness of current career models.

Technology. Only four future-research statements (Carson, 1998; Hartung, 1996; Donnay, 1997; Watts, 1996) related to the subtheme of technology. Before analyzing the sentences from the articles cited in this chapter, I would have predicted technology to be a major theme in future-research recommendations. The extreme between my prediction and the identification of only 4 articles may mean that I need a new crystal ball. However, it also could indicate another large gap in the literature.

"Hmm." The final subtheme is titled "Hmm" because I had difficulty grouping this collection of future-research sentences and linking them to the others. Two sentences pertained to information. Shivy, Phillips, and Koehly (1996) were interested in occupational representations, and Hartung (1996) suggested further research on the impact of visual career images. Two studies called for future research on job selection interviews (Saks et al., 1996; Wade & Kinicki, 1997) and 1 (Turbin,

Forret, & Hendrickson, 1998) called for perceptions of recruiters' behaviors.

Other future research topics in this category were positive and negative self-esteem (Borgen, Amundson, & Tench, 1996), internal and external influences on career satisfaction (Brown & Crace, 1996), tolerance and complaint of sexual harassment (Summers, 1996), dual careers of lesbian partners (Fassinger, 1996), effects of shyness (Hamer & Bruch, 1997), work ethic (Blau & Ryan, 1997), leisure activity (Munson & Widmer, 1997), unemployment (Hesketh, Watson-Brown, & Whiteley, 1998), change constructs (Hesketh, 1998), the role of formal education (Stead & Watson, 1998), and differences between persisting and nonpersisting engineer majors (Schaefers, Epperson, & Nauta, 1997). In addition, several researchers proposed further examination of a spherical representation of interests (Tracey & Rounds, 1996a; Harmon, 1996; Gonzalez, 1996). Finally, 2 sentences (Blustein, 1997a; Niles, Anderson, & Goodnough, 1998) called for including more variables in the study of career exploration.

Recommendations. The identification of 65 future-research sentences in an other category may, in itself, be a topic for future research. Further content analysis could reveal that there truly is a pattern or theme between the 6 other subthemes, or that some topics may fit within the themes of Diversity, Methodology, Theory, or Intervention. I leave that decision up to the reader.

Discussion and Conclusion

This chapter places 311 future-research statements into the categories of diversity, methodology, theory, intervention, or other. If we believe that those who publish in the professional career counseling literature are in a good position to know the directions for future career development research and practice, then we can predict that the early 21st century will include more of a focus than in the past on the career decision needs of diverse students, will expand the current use of methodology and measurement, will advance theory and practice, and will continue to identify additional variables of meaning to the field.

Future-research sentences from the annual reviews of the *Career Development Quarterly (CDQ)* and the *Journal of Career Assessment (JCA)* confirmed the categories extracted from the journal articles. In the 1994 *CDQ* review by Walsh and Srsic (1995), the themes of diversity, method, and theory were apparent in the authors' statement of "a need for theoretical, conceptual, and empirical work with Native Americans and other minority groups" (p. 124). Stoltz-Loike's (1996) *CDQ* review included recommendations that mostly focused on large systems rather than on individuals or small groups. Her suggestions fit best with the political subtheme in the Other category. Recommendations from Oliver, Lent, and Zack's (1998) *JCA* review centered on the methodology theme, with challenges to incorporate more literature from outside the career field.

In his *CDQ* Annual Review, Niles (1997) wrote that "one of the most urgent areas where more research is needed is in the use of technology in the delivery of career services" (p. 135). The analysis conducted for this chapter located only four future research statements that addressed technology, supporting Niles's (1997) statement. Technology may be leaps and bounds ahead of us, but technology and the career literature appear to be miles apart.

Another outcome of the analysis of future-research statements was the identification of themes and subthemes that lean in the direction of postmodernism. Popkewitz (1997) wrote "issues of inclusion/exclusion relate to how the playing field can be leveled so all actors can be equally represented" (p. 24). Savickas (1993) wrote that "as a society, we seem to be moving from an 'us versus them' singular perspective toward a multiple perspective discourse" (p. 208). The 71 calls for diversity in future research endorsed this multiple view of career development research and practice. Practitioners who work with a diverse population of clientele would be a valued addition to future-research designs with multiple perspectives.

The 12 recommendations for longitudinal research and the 9 suggestions for qualitative research methods coincided with Contas's (1998) identification of "an interest in narrative methodology" (p. 27) in the postmodern era. We can give different voices to the issues and hear things from another perspective by continuing to develop the way we listen to data.

As practitioners, teachers, mentors, researchers, and students of career development and counseling, we have countless opportunities to contribute to the current literature on career counseling with college students. The 311 future-research sentences referenced in this chapter alone can provide endless combinations of research topics, designs, and methodologies. The collected sentences illustrate how additional research is needed on the details of isolated variables and topics (e.g., validation studies of specific assessment instruments and interventions) as well as the more global topics of government policies, labor market influences, and social context. Opportunities abound in this field for novices and experts alike. It is time to merge the views of researchers and clinicians to provide a more complete picture of the meaning and usefulness of our findings.

It is my hope that the 21st century will bring a more postmodern or contextual research sensitivity. I would recommend further development of case study, longitudinal, narrative, and qualitative approaches to complement our already highly developed use of quantitative designs. Such dialogue-based data collections may appeal to those practicing in the field who enjoy collecting stories of clients' careers.

Furthermore, at least two large gaps in the literature need to be filled. The first is the embarrassingly low percentage of calls for intervention research. Researching the practice of career counseling lends itself well to the case study and qualitative designs just noted. The identified technology gap also could be filled with an intervention focus. For example, do we understand the efficacy of online career counseling and the validity of results for people who complete career assessments on the Internet? We need to consider the ethical concerns of technology and client welfare.

The 21st century may open with a continuation of traditional relationship and correlational studies and sophisticated quantitative analyses. However, we have an opportunity and obligation to listen to our clients and their counselors. I hope that the 21st century also will include innovations that help personalize our understanding of the career development of college students.

To return to the opening 1993 statement by Bronfenbrenner, the process of conducting this analysis was not exactly heaven, nor was it hell. My own recommendation for future research of this nature would be to use one of the computer programs available for analyzing qualitative data. Finally, we need to reserve our judgments about the accuracy of the future-research and future-practice topics identified through this analysis by awaiting the creative efforts of researchers and clinicians in the years to come.

References

Anderson, M. Z., Tracey, T. J. G., & Rounds, J. (1997). Examining the invariance of Holland's vocational interest model across gender. *Journal of Vocational Behavior, 50*, 349–364.

Antony, J. S. (1998). Exploring the factors that influence men and women to form medical career aspirations. *Journal of College Student Development, 39*, 417–426.

Barnes, J. A., & Herr, E. L. (1998). The effects of interventions on career progress. *Journal of Career Development, 24*, 179–193.

Bauman, S. L., & Gerstein, L. H. (1998). Demographics, causality, work salience, and career maturity of African American students: A causal model. *Journal of Vocational Behavior, 53*, 15–27.

Betsworth, D. G., & Fouad, N. A. (1997). Vocational interests: A look at the past 70 years and a glance at the future. *Career Development Quarterly, 46*, 23–47.

Betz, N. E., Borgen, F. H., & Harmon, L. W. (1996). *Skills Confidence Inventory applications and technical guide*. Palo Alto, CA: Consulting Psychologists Press.

Betz, N. E., Harmon, L. W., & Borgen, F. H. (1996). The relationships of self-efficacy for the Holland themes to gender, occupational group membership, and vocational interests. *Journal of Counseling Psychology, 43*, 90–98.

Betz, N. E., & Klein, K. L. (1996). Relationships among measures of career self-efficacy, generalized self-efficacy, and global self-esteem. *Journal of Career Assessment, 4*, 285–298.

Betz, N. E., Klein, K. L., & Taylor, K. M. (1996). Evaluation of a short form of the Career Decision-Making Self-Efficacy Scale. *Journal of Career Assessment, 4*, 47–57.

Betz, N. E., & Luzzo, D. A. (1996). Career assessment and the Career Decision-Making Self-Efficacy Scale. *Journal of Career Assessment, 4*, 413–428.

Bikos, L. H., Krieshok, T. S., & O'Brien, K. M. (1998). Evaluating the psychometric properties of the Missouri Occupational Card Sort. *Journal of Vocational Behavior, 52*, 135–155.

Blau, G., & Ryan, J. (1997). On measuring work ethic: A neglected work commitment facet. *Journal of Vocational Behavior, 51*, 435–448.

Blustein, D. L. (1997a). A context-rich perspective of career exploration across the life roles. *Career Development Quarterly, 45*, 260–274.

Blustein, D. L. (1997b). The role of work in adolescent development. *Career Development Quarterly, 45*, 381–389.

Borgen, W. A., Amundson, N. E., & Tench, E. (1996). Psychological well-being throughout the transition from adolescence to adulthood. *Career Development Quarterly, 45*, 189–199.

Bowman, S. L. (1998). Minority women and career adjustment. *Journal of Career Assessment, 6,* 417–431.

Bowman, S. L., & Gerstein, L. H. (1998). Demographics, causality, work salience, and career maturity of African American students: A causal model. *Journal of Vocational Behavior, 53,* 15–27.

Bronfenbrenner, U. (1993). The ecology of cognitive development: Research models and fugitive findings. In R. H. Wozniak & K. W. Fischer (Eds.), *Development in context: Acting and thinking in specific environments* (pp. 3–44). Hillsdale, NJ: Lawrence Erlbaum.

Brown, C., & Bohac, J. (1997). Beyond athletic participation: Career development interventions with student athletes. *Journal of College Student Development, 38,* 671–673.

Brown, D., & Crace, R. K. (1996). Values in life role choices and outcomes: A conceptual model. *Career Development Quarterly, 44,* 211–223.

Brown, M. T., Eisenberg, A. I., & Sawilowsky, S. S. (1997). Traditionality and the discriminating effects of expectations of occupational success and occupational values for women within math-oriented fields. *Journal of Vocational Behavior, 50,* 418–431.

Brown, M. T., Lum, J. L., & Voyle, K. (1997). Roe revisited: A call for the reappraisal of the theory of personality development and career choice. *Journal of Vocational Behavior, 51,* 283–294.

Brown, M. T., & Voyle, K. M. (1997). Rejoinder without Roe. *Journal of Vocational Behavior, 51,* 310–318.

Brown, S. D., & Lent, R. W. (1996). A social cognitive framework for career choice counseling. *Career Development Quarterly, 44,* 354–366.

Cairo, P. C., Kritis, K. J., & Myers, R. M. (1996). Career assessment and the Adult Career Concerns Inventory. *Journal of Career Assessment, 4,* 189–204.

Carson, A. D. (1998). Why has musical aptitude assessment fallen flat? And what can we do about it? *Journal of Career Assessment, 6,* 311–328.

Carson, A. D., Stalikas, A., & Bizot, E. B. (1997). Correlations between the Myers-Briggs Type Indicator and measures of aptitudes. *Journal of Career Assessment, 5,* 81–104.

Chartrand, J. M., & Nutter, K. J. (1996). The Career Factors Inventory: Theory and applications. *Journal of Career Assessment, 4,* 205–218.

Chartrand, J. M., Robbins, S. B., Morrill, W. H., & Boggs, K. (1990). Development and validation of the Career Factors Inventory. *Journal of Counseling Psychology, 37,* 491–501.

Chung, Y. B., Loeb, J. W., & Gonzo, S. T. (1996). Factors predicting the educational and career aspirations of Black college freshmen. *Journal of Career Development, 23,* 127–135.

Contas, M. A. (1998). The changing nature of educational research and a critique of postmodernism. *Educational Researcher, 27,* 26–33.

Crites, J. O. (1978). *The Career Maturity Inventory* (2nd ed.). Monterey, CA: CTB/McGraw-Hill.

Crites, J. O., & Savickas, M. L. (1996). Revision of the Career Maturity Inventory. *Journal of Career Assessment, 4,* 131–138.

Croteau, J. M., & Bieschke, K. J. (1996). Beyond Pioneering: An introduction to the special issue on vocational issues of lesbian women and gay men [Special issue]. *Journal of Vocational Behavior, 48,* 119–124.

Damarin, F. L. (1998). Accuracy and exaggeration in occupational stereotypes exemplified with clinical psychology. *Journal of Vocational Behavior, 53,* 1–14.

Dawis, R. V. (1997). Revisiting Roe: Comments on Brown, Lum and Voyle (1997). *Journal of Vocational Behavior, 51,* 295–300.

Dawis, R. V., & Lofquist, L. H. (1984). *A psychological theory of work adjustment.* Minneapolis: University of Minnesota Press.

Dawson-Threat, J., & Huba, M. E. (1996). Choice of major and clarity of purpose among college seniors as a function of gender. *Journal of College Student Development, 37,* 297–308.

DeBell, C., & Dinger, T. J. (1997). Campus interviews: Some challenges to conventional wisdom. *Journal of College Student Development, 38,* 553–564.

Donnay, D. A. C. (1997). E. K. Strong's legacy and beyond: 70 years of the Strong Interest Inventory. *Career Development Quarterly, 46,* 2–22.

Donnay, D. A. C., & Borgen, F. H. (1996). Validity, structure, and content of the 1994 Strong Interest Inventory. *Journal of Counseling Psychology, 43*, 275–291.

Dunkle, J. H. (1996). Toward an integration of gay and lesbian identity development and Super's life-span approach. *Journal of Vocational Behavior, 48*, 149–159.

Eby, L. T., & Russell, J. E. A. (1998). A psychometric review of career assessment tools for use with diverse individuals. *Journal of Career Assessment, 6*, 269–310.

Farh, J., Leong, F. T. L., & Law, K. S. (1998). Cross-cultural validity of Holland's model in Hong Kong. *Journal of Vocational Behavior, 42*, 425–440.

Farmer, H. S. (1997). Women's motivation related to mastery, career salience, and career aspiration: A multivariate model focusing on the effects of sex role socialization. *Journal of Career Assessment, 5*, 355–381.

Farmer, H. S., Rotella, S., Anderson, C., & Wardrop, J. (1998). Gender differences in science, math, and technology careers: Prestige level and Holland interest type. *Journal of Vocational Behavior, 53*, 73–96.

Fassinger, R. E. (1996). Notes from the margins: Integrating lesbian experience into the vocational psychology of women. *Journal of Vocational Behavior, 48*, 160–175.

Fitzgerald, L. F., Shullman, S. L., Bailey, N., Richards, M., Swecker, J., Gold, Y., Ormerod, A. J., & Weitzman, L. (1988). The incidence and dimensions of sexual harassment in academia and the workplace. *Journal of Vocational Behavior, 32*, 152–175.

Friehe, M., Aune, B., & Leuenberger, J. (1996). Career service needs of college students with disabilities. *Career Development Quarterly, 44*, 289–300.

Gasser, M. B., Oliver, J. A., & Tan, R. N. (1998). The influence of age and type of job on gender differences in pay expectancies. *Career Development Quarterly, 47*, 36–46.

Gati, I. (1998). Using career-related aspects to elicit preferences and characterize occupations for a better person-environment fit. *Journal of Vocational Behavior, 52*, 343–356.

Gati, I., Fassa, N., & Mayer, Y. (1998). An aspect-based approach to person-environment fit: A comparison between the aspect structure derived from characteristics of occupations and that derived from counselee's preferences. *Journal of Vocational Behavior, 53*, 28–43.

Gati, I., Garty, Y., & Fassa, N. (1996). Using career-related aspects to assess person-environment fit. *Journal of Counseling Psychology, 43*, 196–206.

Gati, I., Krausz, M., & Osipow, S. H. (1996). A taxonomy of difficulties in career decision making. *Journal of Counseling Psychology, 43*, 510–526.

Gay, E. G., Weiss, D. J., Dawis, R. V., & Lofquist, L. H. (1971). *Manual for the Minnesota Importance Questionnaire*. Minnesota Studies in Vocational Rehabilitation, 28.

Gianakos, I. (1996). Career development differences between adult and traditional-aged learners. *Journal of Career Development, 22*, 211–223.

Glidden-Tracey, C., & Greenwood, A. K. (1997). A validation study of the Spanish Self-Directed Search using back-translation procedures. *Journal of Career Assessment, 5*, 105–113.

Glidden-Tracey, C., & Parraga, M. I. (1996). Assessing the structure of vocational interests among Bolivian university students. *Journal of Vocational Behavior, 48*, 96–106.

Gonzalez, R. (1996). Circles and squares, spheres and cubes: What's the deal with circumplex models? *Journal of Vocational Behavior, 48*, 77–84.

Gordon, V. N. (1998). Career decidedness types: A literature review. *Career Development Quarterly, 46*, 386–403.

Gottfredson, G. D. (1996). The assessment of career status with the Career Attitudes and Strategies Inventory. *Journal of Career Assessment, 4*, 363–381.

Hackett, G. (1997). Promise and problems in theory and research on women's career development: Comment on Lucas (1997), Richie et al. (1997), McCracken and Weitzman (1997), Rainey and Borders (1997), and Schaefers, Epperson, and Nauta (1997). *Journal of Counseling Psychology, 44*, 184–188.

Hackett, G., & Byars, A. M. (1996). Social cognitive theory and the career development of African American women. *Career Development Quarterly, 44*, 322–340.

Hall, A. S., Kelly, K. R., Hansen, K., & Gutwein, A. K. (1996). Sources of self-perceptions of career-related abilities. *Journal of Career Assessment, 4*, 331–343.

Hallett, M. B., & Gilbert, L. A. (1997). Variables differentiating university women consid-ering role-sharing and conventional dual-career marriages. *Journal of Vocational Behavior, 50,* 308–322.

Hamer, R. J., & Bruch, M. A. (1997). Personality factors and inhibited career development: Testing the unique contribution of shyness. *Journal of Vocational Behavior, 50,* 382–400.

Harmon, L. W. (1996). Lost in space: A response to "The spherical representation of voca-tional interests" by Tracey and Rounds. *Journal of Vocational Behavior, 48,* 53–58.

Harmon, L. W. (1997). Do gender differences necessitate separate career development the-ories and measures? *Journal of Career Assessment, 5,* 463–470.

Harmon, L. W., Borgen, F. H., Berreth, J. M., King, J. C., Schauer, D., & Ward, C. C. (1996). The Skills Confidence Inventory: A measure of self-efficacy. *Journal of Career Assess-ment, 4,* 457–477.

Harmon, L. W., Hansen, J.-I. C., Borgen, F. H., & Hammer, A. L. (1994). *Strong Interest Inventory: Applications and technical guide.* Palo Alto, CA: Consulting Psychologists Press.

Hartung, P. J. (1996). Work illustrated: Attending to visual images in career information materials. *Career Development Quarterly, 44,* 234–241.

Hartung, P. J., Speight, J. D., & Lewis, D. M. (1996). Individualism-collectivism and the vocational behavior of majority culture college students. *Career Development Quarterly, 45,* 87–96.

Hartung, P. J., Vandiver, B. J., Leong, F. T. L., Pope, M., Niles, S. G., & Farrow, B. (1998). Appraising cultural identity in career-development assessment and counseling. *Career Development Quarterly, 46,* 276–293.

Hesketh, B. L. (1998). Career advice and tertiary decision-making "downunder" in Australia. *Journal of Vocational Behavior, 52,* 396–408.

Hesketh, B. L., Watson-Brown, C., & Whiteley, S. (1998). Time-related discounting of value and decision-making about job options. *Journal of Vocational Behavior, 52,* 89–105.

Hitchings, W. E., Luzzo, D. A., Retish, P., Horvath, M., & Ristow, R. S. (1998). Identifying the career development needs of college students with disabilities. *Journal of College Student Development, 39,* 23–32.

Holland, J. L. (1970). *Self-Directed Search.* Palo Alto, CA: Consulting Psychologists Press.

Holland, J. L. (1985). *Making vocational choices: A theory of vocational personalities and work environments* (2nd ed.). Englewood Cliffs, NJ: Prentice-Hall.

Holland, J. L., & Gottfredson, G. D. (1994). *Career Attitudes and Strategies Inventory: An inventory for understanding adult careers.* Odessa, FL: Psychological Assessment Re-sources.

Jackson, C. C., & Neville, H. A. (1998). Influence of racial identity attitudes on African American college students' vocational identity and hope. *Journal of Vocational Behavior, 53,* 97–113.

Jackson, G. C., & Healy, C. C. (1996). Career development profiles and interventions for underrepresented college students. *Career Development Quarterly, 44,* 258–269.

Jaros, S. J. (1998). An assessment of Meyer and Allen's (1991) three-component model of organizational commitment and turnover intentions. *Journal of Vocational Behavior, 51,* 319–337.

Jome, L. M., & Tokar, D. M. (1998). Dimensions of masculinity and major choice tradition-ality. *Journal of Vocational Behavior, 52,* 120–134.

Jones, L. K. (1998). The Career Decision Profile: Using a measure of career decision status in counseling. *Journal of Career Assessment, 6,* 209–230.

Kelly, G. A. (1955). *The psychology of personal constructs.* New York: Norton.

Kerr, B., & Fisher, T. (1997). Career assessment with gifted and talented students. *Journal of Career Assessment, 5,* 239–251.

Ketterson, T. U., & Blustein, D. L. (1997). Attachment relationships and the career explo-ration process. *Career Development Quarterly, 46,* 167–178.

Knapp, L., Knapp-Lee, L., & Knapp, R. (1995). *Career Orientation Placement and Evalua-tion Survey.* San Diego, CA: EdITS.

Knapp-Lee, L. J. (1996). Use of the COPES, a measure of work values, in career assessment. *Journal of Career Assessment, 4,* 429–443.

Krieshok, T. S. (1998). An anti-introspectivist view of career decision. *Career Development Quarterly, 46*, 210–229.

Lent, R. W. (1996). Career counseling, science, and policy: Revitalizing our paradigms and roles. *Career Development Quarterly, 45*, 58–64.

Lent, R. W., Brown S. D., & Gore, P. A., Jr. (1997). Discriminant and predictive validity of academic self-concept, academic self-efficacy, and mathematics-specific self-efficacy. *Journal of Counseling Psychology, 44*, 307–315.

Lent, R. W., Brown, S. D., Gover, M. R., & Nijer, S. K. (1996). Cognitive assessment of the sources of mathematics self-efficacy: A though-listing analysis. *Journal of Career Assessment, 4*, 33–46.

Lent, R. W., Brown S. D., & Hackett, G. (1994). Toward a unifying social cognitive theory of career and academic interest, choice and performance. *Journal of Vocational Behavior, 45*, 79–122.

Lent, R. W., Lopez, F. G., Brown, S. D., & Gore, P. A., Jr. (1996). Latent structure of the sources of mathematics self-efficacy. *Journal of Vocational Behavior, 49*, 292–308.

Leong, F. T. L. (1997). Cross-cultural career psychology: Comment on Fouad, Harmon, and Borgen (1997) and Tracey, Watanabe, and Schneider (1997). *Journal of Counseling Psychology, 44*, 355–359.

Leong, F. T. L., & Chervinko, S. (1996). Construct validity of career indecision: Negative personality traits as predictors of career indecision. *Journal of Career Assessment, 4*, 315–329.

Leong, F. T. L., & Hartung, P. J. (1997). Career assessment with culturally different clients: Proposing an integrative-sequential conceptual framework for cross-cultural career counseling research and practice. *Journal of Career Assessment, 5*, 183–202.

Leong, F. T. L., Hesketh, B. L., & Savickas, M. L. (1998). Guest editors' introduction to international perspectives on vocational psychology. *Journal of Vocational Behavior, 52*, 271–274.

Lonborg, S. D., & Phillips, J. M. (1996). Investigating the career development of gay, lesbian, and bisexual people: Methodological considerations and recommendations. *Journal of Vocational Behavior, 48*, 176–194.

Lowman, R. L. (1997). Career assessment and psychological impairment: Integrating inter-domain and work dysfunctions theory. *Journal of Career Assessment, 5*, 213–224.

Lucas, M. (1997). Identity development, career development, and psychological separation from parents: Similarities and differences between men and women. *Journal of Counseling Psychology, 44*, 123–132.

Lucas, J. L., Wanberg, C. R., & Zytowski, D. G. (1997). Development of a career task self-efficacy scale: The Kuder Task Self-Efficacy Scale. *Journal of Vocational Behavior, 50*, 432–459.

Lunneborg, P. W. (1997). Putting Roe in perspective. *Journal of Vocational Behavior, 51*, 301–305.

Luzzo, D. A. (1996). Exploring the relationship between the perception of occupational barriers and career development. *Journal of Career Development, 22*, 239–248.

Luzzo, D. A., Funk, D. P., & Strang, J. (1996). Attributional retraining increases career decision-making self-efficacy. *Career Development Quarterly, 44*, 378–386.

Luzzo, D. A., James, T., & Luna, M. (1996). Effects of attributional retraining on the career beliefs and career exploration behavior of college students. *Journal of Counseling Psychology, 43*, 415–422.

Luzzo, D. A., & Jenkins-Smith, A. (1998). Development and initial validation of the assessment of attributions for career decision-making. *Journal of Vocational Behavior, 52*, 224–245.

Luzzo, D. A., McWhirter, E. H., & Hutcheson, K. G. (1997). Evaluating career decision-making factors associated with employment among first-year college students. *Journal of College Student Development, 38*, 166–171.

Marko, K. W., & Savickas, M. L. (1998). Effectiveness of a career time perspective intervention. *Journal of Vocational Behavior, 52*, 106–119.

Mau, W., Calvert, C., & Gregory, R. (1997). Effects of career interventions on vocational cognitive complexity. *Journal of Career Development, 23*, 279–293.

McCracken, R. S., & Weitzman, L. M. (1997). Relationship of personal agency, problem-solving appraisal, and traditionality of career choice to women's attitudes toward multiple role planning. *Journal of Counseling Psychology, 44*, 149–159.

McWhirter, E. H., Torres, D., & Rasheed, S. (1998). Assessing barriers to women's career adjustment. *Journal of Career Assessment, 6*, 449–479.

Meara, N. M. (1997). Changing the structure of work. *Journal of Career Assessment, 5*, 471–474.

Meir, E. I. (1995). *Manual for the RAMACK and Courses Interest Inventories*. Tel Aviv, Israel: Tel Aviv University, Department of Psychology.

Meir, E. I., Rubin, A., Temple, R., & Osipow, S. H. (1997). Examination of interest inventories based on Roe's classification. *Career Development Quarterly, 46*, 48–61.

Meir, E. I., Tziner, A., & Glazner, Y. (1997). Environmental congruence, group importance, and job satisfaction. *Journal of Career Assessment, 5*, 343–353.

Meldahl, J. M., & Muchinsky, P. M. (1997). The neurotic dimension of vocational indecision: Gender comparability? *Journal of Career Assessment, 5*, 317–331.

Meyer, J., & Allen, N. (1984). Testing the side-bet theory of organizational commitment: Some methodological considerations. *Journal of Applied Psychology, 69*, 372–378.

Mobley, M., & Slaney, R. B. (1996). Holland's theory: Its relevance for lesbian women and gay men. *Journal of Vocational Behavior, 48*, 125–135.

Moore, M. A., & Neimeyer, G. J. (1997). Personal meaning and vocational differentiation: Reversing the decrement effect. *Journal of Career Development, 24*, 83–94.

Morrow, S. L., Gore, P. A., Jr., & Campbell, B. W. (1996). The application of a socio cognitive framework to the career development of lesbian women and gay men. *Journal of Vocational Behavior, 48*, 136–148.

Munson, W. M., & Widmer, M. A. (1997). Leisure behavior and occupational identity in university students. *Career Development Quarterly, 46*, 190–198.

Myers, I. B., & McCaulley, M. H. (1985). *Manual: A guide to the development and use of the Myers-Briggs Type Indicator*. Palo Alto, CA: Consulting Psychologists Press.

Nevill, D. D., & Calvert, P. D. (1996). Career assessment and the Salience Inventory. *Journal of Career Assessment, 4*, 399–412.

Niles, S. G., Anderson, W. P., Jr., & Goodnough, G. (1998). Exploration to foster career development. *Career Development Quarterly, 46*, 262–275.

Niles, S. G., Erford, B. T., Hunt, B., & Watts, R. H., Jr. (1997). Decision-making styles and career development in college students. *Journal of College Student Development, 38*, 479–488.

Niles, S. G., & Goodnough, G. E. (1996). Life-role salience and values: A review of recent research. *Career Development Quarterly, 45*, 65–86.

Niles, S. G., Lewis, D. M., & Hartung, P. J. (1997). Using the Adult Career Concerns Inventory to measure task involvement. *Career Development Quarterly, 46*, 87–97.

Ohler, D. L., Levinson, E. M., & Barker, W. F. (1996). Career maturity in college students with learning disabilities. *Career Development Quarterly, 44*, 278–288.

Oliver, L. W., Lent, E. B., & Zack, J. S. (1998). Career and vocational assessment 1995–1996: A biennial review. *Journal of Career Assessment, 6*, 231–268.

Osipow, S. H. (1997). Roe revisited: Why? *Journal of Vocational Behavior, 51*, 306–309.

Osipow, S. H., & Gati, I. (1998). Construct and concurrent validity of the Career Decision-Making Difficulties Questionnaire. *Journal of Career Assessment, 6*, 347–364.

Osipow, S. H., & Rooney, R. A. (1989). *Task-Specific Occupational Self-Efficacy Scale*. Columbus, OH: Authors.

Osipow, S. H., & Temple, R. D. (1996). Development and use of the Task-Specific Occupational Self-Efficacy Scale. *Journal of Career Assessment, 4*, 445–456.

Osipow, S. H., & Winer, J. L. (1996). The use of the Career Decision Scale in career assessment. *Journal of Career Assessment, 4*, 117–130.

Parsons, E., & Betz, N. E. (1998). Test-retest reliability and validity studies of the Skills Confidence Inventory. *Journal of Career Assessment, 6*, 1–12.

Patterson-Stewart, K. E., Ritchie, M. H., & Saunders, E. T. W. (1997). Interpersonal dynamics of African American persistence in doctoral programs at predominantly white universities. *Journal of College Student Development, 38*, 489–498.

Peterson, G. W. (1998). Using a vocational card sort as an assessment of occupational knowledge. *Journal of Career Assessment, 6*, 49–67.

Peterson, S. L., & del Mas, R. C. (1998). The component structure of career decision-making self-efficacy for under prepared college students. *Journal of Career Development, 24*, 209–225.

Phillips, S. D. (1997). Toward an expanded definition of adaptive decision making. *Career Development Quarterly, 45*, 275–287.

Popkewitz, T. S. (1997). A changing terrain of knowledge and power: A social epistemology of educational research. *Educational Researcher, 26*, 18–29.

Prediger, D. J. (1998). Is interest profile level relevant to career counseling? *Journal of Counseling Psychology, 45*, 204–211.

Prince, J. P. (1997). Career assessment with lesbian, gay, and bisexual individuals. *Journal of Career Assessment, 5*, 225–238.

Raskin, P. M., Kummel, P., & Bannister, T. (1998). The relationship between coping styles, attachment, and career salience in partnered working women with children. *Journal of Career Assessment, 6*, 403–416.

Roe, A., & Klos, D. (1972). Classification of occupations. In J. M. Whiteley & A. Resnikoff (Eds.), *Perspectives on vocational development* (pp. 199–221). Washington, DC: American Personnel and Guidance Association.

Rounds, J., & Tracey, T. J. (1996). Cross-cultural structural equivalence of RIASEC models and measures. *Journal of Counseling Psychology, 43*, 310–329.

Russ-Eisenschenk, L., & Neimeyer, G. J. (1996). The stability of vocational differentiation, integration, and conflict: A replication and extension. *Journal of Career Assessment, 4*, 299–314.

Russell, J. E. A., & Adams, D. M. (1997). The changing nature of mentoring in organizations: An introduction to the special issue on mentoring in organizations. *Journal of Vocational Behavior, 51*, 1–14.

Russell, J. E. A., & Burgess, J. R. D. (1998). Success and women's career adjustment. *Journal of Career Assessment, 6*, 365–387.

Ryan, N. E., Solberg, V. S., & Brown, S. D. (1996). Family dysfunction, parental attachment, and career search self-efficacy among community college students. *Journal of Counseling Psychology, 43*, 84–89.

Sagy, S. (1997). Work values: Comparing Russian immigrants and Israeli students. *Journal of Career Development, 23*, 231–243.

Sagy, S., & Liberman, O. (1997). Social cultural factors influencing occupational choice: The selection of a nursing career by ex-Soviet immigrant students. *Journal of Career Development, 24*, 147–159.

Saks, A. M., Wiesner, W. H., & Summers, R. J. (1996). Effects of job previews and compensation policy on applicant attraction and job choice. *Journal of Vocational Behavior, 49*, 68–85.

Sampson, J. P., Jr., Peterson, G. W., Lenz, J. G., Reardon, R. C., & Saunders, D. E. (1998). The design and use of a measure of dysfunctional career thoughts among adults, college students, and high school students: The Career Thoughts Inventory. *Journal of Career Assessment, 6*, 115–134.

Santos, E. J., & Ferreira, J. A. (1998). Career counseling and vocational psychology in Portugal: A political perspective. *Journal of Vocational Behavior, 52*, 312–322.

Savickas, M. L. (1993). Career counseling in the postmodern era. *Journal of Cognitive Psychotherapy, 7*, 205–215.

Savickas, M. L. (1994). Convergence prompts theory renovation, research unification, and practice coherence. In M. L. Savickas & R. W. Lent (Eds.), *Convergence in career development theories*. (pp. 235–257). Palo Alto, CA: Consulting Psychologists Press.

Savickas, M. L. (1997). Career adaptability: An integrative construct for life-span, life-space theory. *Career Development Quarterly, 45*, 247–259.

Savickas, M. L., & Hartung, P. J. (1996). The Career Development Inventory in review: Psychometric and research findings. *Journal of Career Assessment, 4*, 171–188.

Schaefers, K. G., Epperson, D. L., & Nauta, M. M. (1997). Women's career development: Can theoretically derived variables predict persistence in engineering majors? *Journal of Counseling Psychology, 44*, 173–183.

Schmitt-Rodermund, E., & Silbereisen, R. K. (1998). Career maturity determinants: Individual development, social context, and historical time. *Career Development Quarterly, 47*, 16–31.

Shivy, V. A., Phillips, S. D., & Koehly, L. M. (1996). Knowledge organization as a factor in career intervention outcome: A multidimensional scaling analysis. *Journal of Counseling Psychology, 43*, 178–186.

Smallman, E., & Sowa, C. J. (1996). Career maturity levels of male intercollegiate varsity athletes. *Career Development Quarterly, 44*, 270–277.

Smart, J. C. (1997). Academic subenvironments and differential patterns of self-perceived growth during college: A test of Holland's theory. *Journal of College Student Development, 38*, 68–77.

Solberg, V. S. (1998). Assessing career search self-efficacy: Construct evidence and developmental antecedents. *Journal of Career Assessment, 6*, 181–193.

Solberg, V. S., Gusavac, N., Hamann, T., Felch, J., Johnson, J., Lamborn, S., & Torres, J. (1998). The Adaptive Success Identity Plan (ASIP): A career intervention for college students. *Career Development Quarterly, 47*, 48–95.

Spencer-Rodgers, J., & Cortijo, A. (1998). An assessment of the career development needs of international students. *Journal of College Student Development, 39*, 509–513.

Spokane, A. R. (1991). *Career intervention*. Englewood Cliffs, NJ: Prentice-Hall.

Stead, G. B., & Watson, M. B. (1998). Career research in South Africa: Challenges for the future. *Journal of Vocational Behavior, 52*, 289–299.

Stockdale, M. S., & Hope, K. G. (1998). Confirmatory factor analysis of U.S. Merit Systems Protective Board's Survey of Sexual Harassment: The fit of a three-factor model. *Journal of Vocational Behavior, 51*, 338–357.

Stoltz-Loike, M. (1996). Annual review: Practice and research in career development and counseling—1995. *Career Development Quarterly, 45*, 99–140.

Subich, L. M. (1998). Women's work and life satisfaction in relation to career adjustment. *Journal of Career Assessment, 6*, 389–402.

Summers, R. J. (1996). The effect of harasser performance status and complaint tolerance on reactions to a complaint of sexual harassment. *Journal of Vocational Behavior, 49*, 53–67.

Super, D. E., Thompson, A. S., & Lindeman, R. H. (1988). *Adult Career Concerns Inventory: Manual for research and exploratory use in counseling*. Palo Alto, CA: Consulting Psychologists Press.

Super, D. E., Thompson, A. S., Lindeman, R. H., Jordaan, J. P., & Myers, R. A. (1981). *The Career Development Inventory*. Palo Alto, CA: Consulting Psychologists Press.

Swanson, J. L., Daniels, K. K., & Tokar, D. M. (1996). Assessing the perceptions of career-related barriers: The Career Barriers Inventory. *Journal of Career Assessment, 4*, 219–244.

Swanson, J. L., & Woitke, M. B. (1997). Theory into practice in career assessment for women: Assessment and interventions regarding perceived career barriers. *Journal of Career Assessment, 5*, 443–462.

Sweeney, M. L., & Schill, T. R. (1998). The association between self-defeating personality characteristics, career indecision, and vocational identity. *Journal of Career Assessment, 6*, 69–81.

Tan, E. (1998). Research on vocational behavior: The Singapore perspective. *Journal of Vocational Behavior, 52*, 323–342.

Toman, S. M., & Savickas, M. L. (1997). Career choice readiness moderates the effects of interest inventory interpretation. *Journal of Career Assessment, 5*, 275–291.

Tracey, T. J. G., & Rounds, J. (1996a). The spherical representation of vocational interests. *Journal of Vocational Behavior, 48*, 3–41.

Tracey, T. J. G., & Rounds, J. (1996b). Contributions of the spherical representation of vocational interests. *Journal of Vocational Behavior, 48*, 85–95.

Tracey, T. J. G., Watanabe, N., & Schneider, P. L. (1997). Structural invariance of vocational interests across Japanese and American cultures. *Journal of Counseling Psychology, 44*, 346–354.

Trusty, J., & Watts, R. E. (1996). Parents' perceptions of career information resources. *Career Development Quarterly, 44*, 242–249.

Turbin, D. B., Forret, M. L., & Hendrickson, C. L. (1998). Applicant attraction to firms: Influences of organization, reputation, job and organizational attributes, and recruiter behaviors. *Journal of Vocational Behavior, 52*, 24–44.

Wade, K. J., & Kinicki, A. J. (1997). Subjective applicant qualifications and interpersonal attraction as mediators within a process model of interview selection decisions. *Journal of Vocational Behavior, 50*, 23–40.

Walsh, B. D., Thompson, B., & Kapes, J. T. (1997). The construct validity of scores on the Career Beliefs Inventory. *Journal of Career Assessment, 5*, 31–46.

Walsh, W. B., & Srsic, C. (1995). Annual review: Vocational behavior and career development—1994. *Career Development Quarterly, 44*, 98–145.

Watts, A. G. (1996). Toward a policy for lifelong career development: A transatlantic perspective. *Career Development Quarterly, 45*, 41–53.

Weitzman, L. M. (1992). *The development and validation of scales to assess realism of attitudes towards multiple role planning*. Unpublished doctoral dissertation, University of Illinois, Urbana-Champaign.

Weitzman, L. M., & Fitzgerald, L. F. (1996). The development and initial validation scales to assess attitudes toward multiple role planning. *Journal of Career Assessment, 4*, 269–284.

Whiston, S. C. (1996). The relationship among family interaction patterns and career indecision and career decision-making self-efficacy. *Journal of Career Development, 23*, 137–149.

Zacher, P., & Leong, F. T. L. (1997). General versus specific predictors of specialty choice in psychology: Holland codes and theoretical orientations. *Journal of Career Assessment, 5*, 333–341.

Author Index

An italicized page number indicates where that name is found in the references.

Subject Index

About the Editor

Darrell Anthony Luzzo received his bachelor's degree in psychology and master's and doctoral degrees in counseling from the University of California, Los Angeles (UCLA). Since graduating from UCLA in 1990, Dr. Luzzo has worked—primarily as a faculty member—at several colleges and universities, including Johnson County Community College (Overland Park, Kansas), St. Ambrose University (Davenport, Iowa), the University of North Alabama (Florence, Alabama), Texas A&M University—Corpus Christi (Corpus Christi, Texas), and Auburn University (Auburn, Alabama). He also has more than 10 years of experience as a career counselor and vocational research scientist, including 2 years of service at ACT, Inc., as the Director of Career Transitions Research. Dr. Luzzo currently serves as the Dean of Career Development Services at Mt. Hood Community College in Gresham, Oregon.

Throughout his professional career, Dr. Luzzo has engaged in research focusing on the career development of college students. His publication record includes authorship of more than 50 journal articles, book chapters, and monographs. He is the author of *Making Career Decisions That Count: A Practical Guide,* a career exploration and planning workbook for college students. Dr. Luzzo's editorial experience includes current service on the editorial boards of several professional journals, including the *Journal of Counseling and Development,* the *Career Development Quarterly,* the *Journal of Career Assessment,* and the *Journal of Career Development.*

In addition to his writing and editorial activities, Dr. Luzzo is an active member of several professional associations, including the American Counseling Association, the American Psychological Association, the American College Personnel Association, and the National Career Development Association. His current research interests focus on the career decision-making attributional style of college students and the evaluation of career counseling interventions.

Dr. Luzzo lives in Oregon City, Oregon, with his wife, Denise, and their five children.